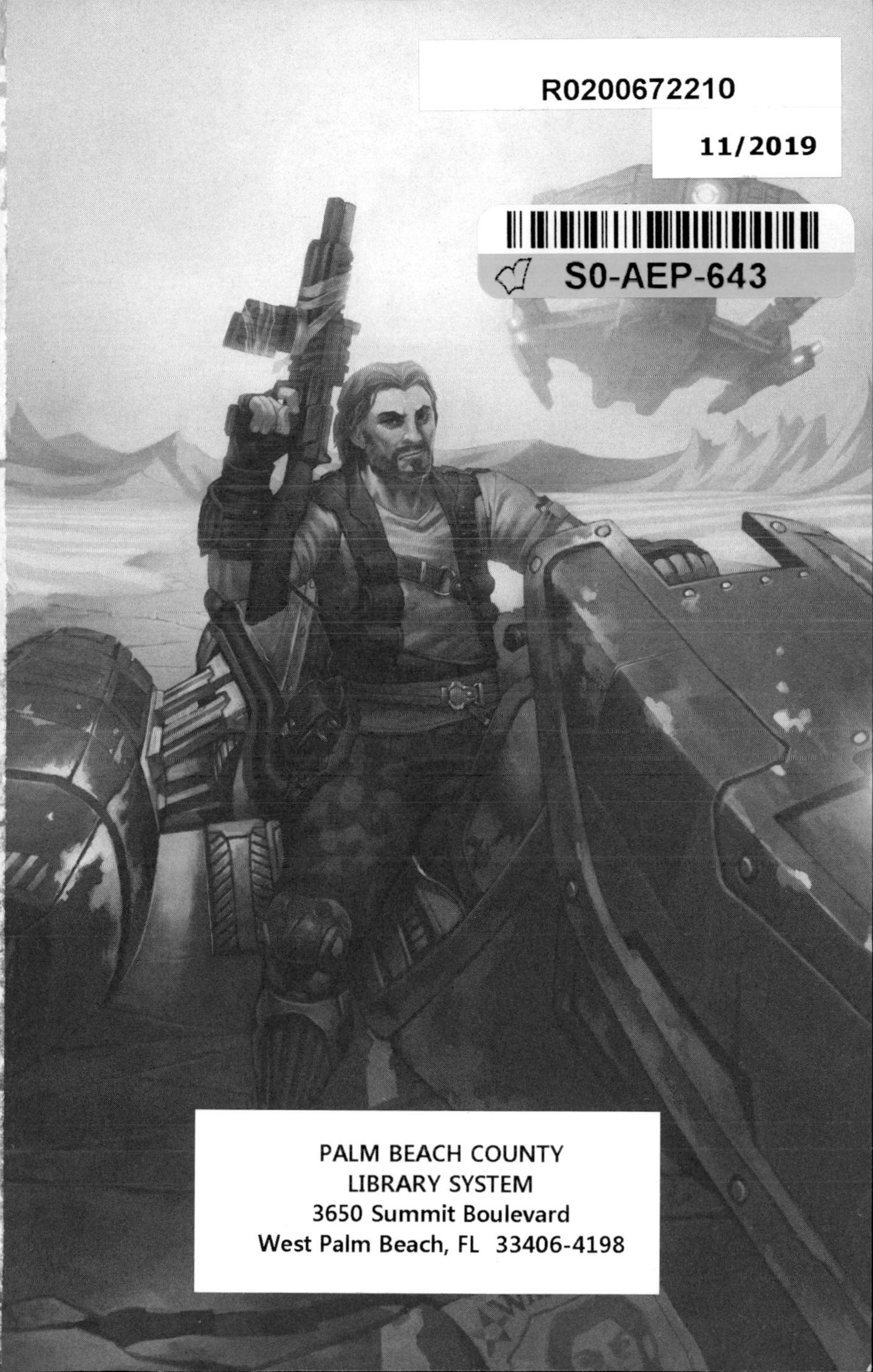

StarCraft: Frontline Vol. 4

Contributing Editor - Troy Lewter
Layout, Lettering and Retouch Artist - Michael Paolilli
Creative Consultant - Michael Paolilli
Graphic Designer - Louis Csontos
Cover Artist - UDON with Saejin Oh

Editor - Hope Donovan
Print Production Manager - Lucas Rivera
Managing Editor - Vy Nguyen
Senior Designer - Louis Csontos
Director of Sales and Manufacturing - Allyson De Simone
Associate Publisher - Marco F. Pavia
President and C.O.O. - John Parker
C.E.O. and Chief Creative Officer - Stu Levy

BLIZZARD ENTERTAINMENT

Senior Vice President,
Story and Franchise Development - Lydia Bottegoni
Director, Creative Development - Ralph Sanchez
Lead Editor, Publishing - Paul Morrissey
Senior Editor - Cate Gary
Copy Editor - Allison Irons
Producer - Brianne M Loftis
Vice President, Global Consumer Products - Matt Beecher
Senior Manager, Global Licensing - Byron Parnell
Special Thanks - Sean Copeland, Evelyn Fredericksen, Phillip Hillenbrand, Christi Kugler, Alix Nicholaeff, Justin Parker

BLIZZARD ENTERTAINMENT

gear.blizzard.com

This book contains material originally published by TOKYOPOP Inc.

First Blizzard Entertainment printing: April 2019

ISBN: 978-1-9456835-0-3

10 9 8 7 6 5 4 3 2 1

Printed in the USA

StarCraft®

Frontline™

Volume 4

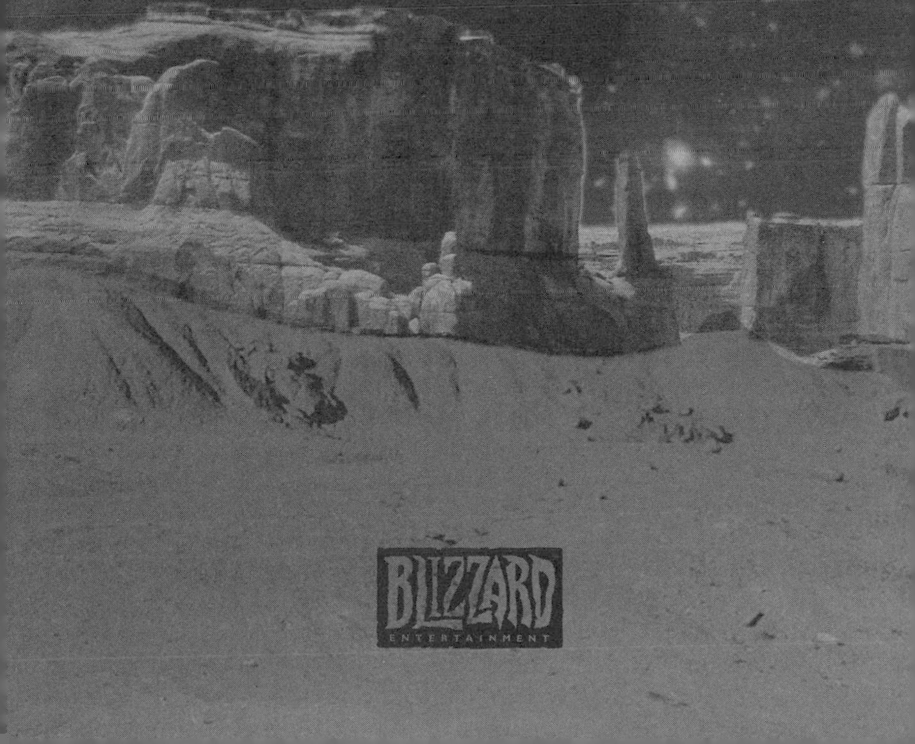

Blizzard Entertainment

STARCRAFT
FRONTLINE
VOLUME 4

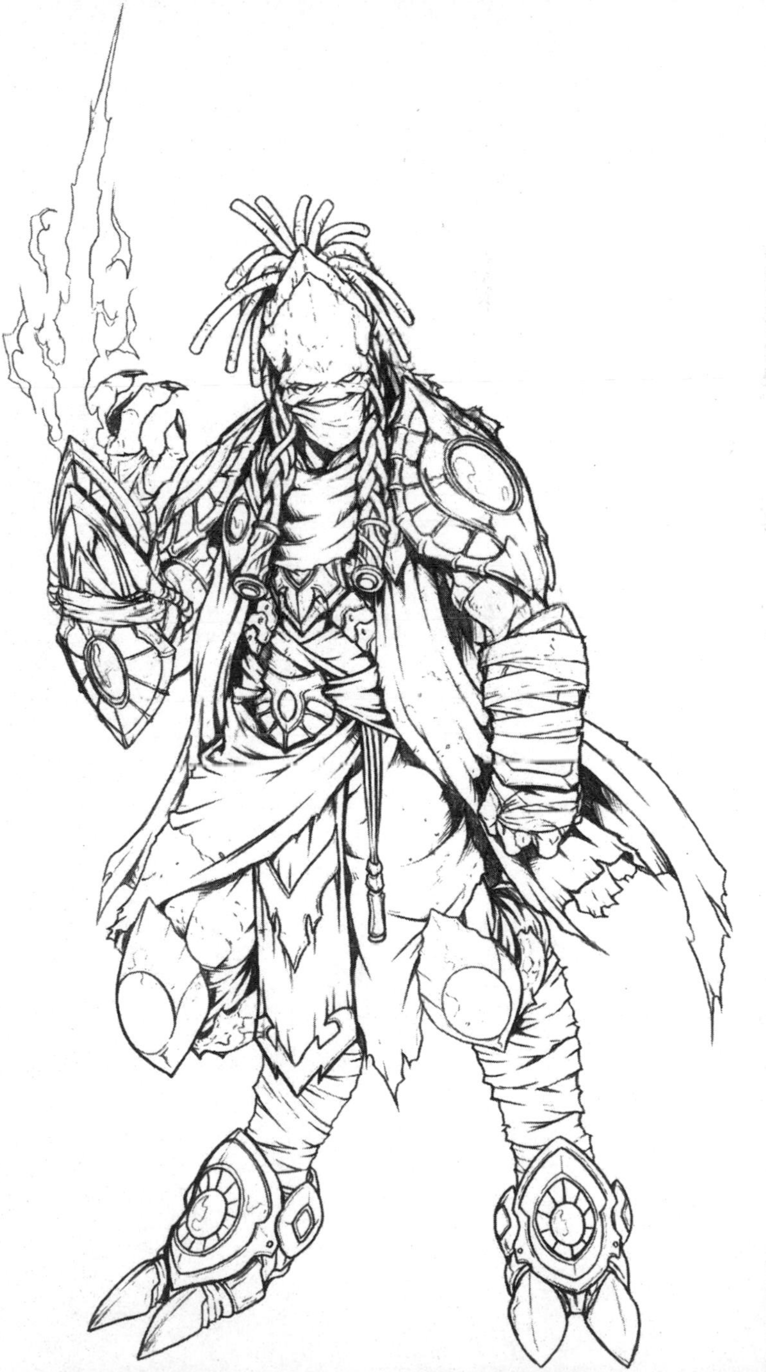

StarCraft

Frontline

Volume 4

Homecoming

Written by Chris Metzen

Art by Hector Sevilla

Letterer: Michael Paolilli

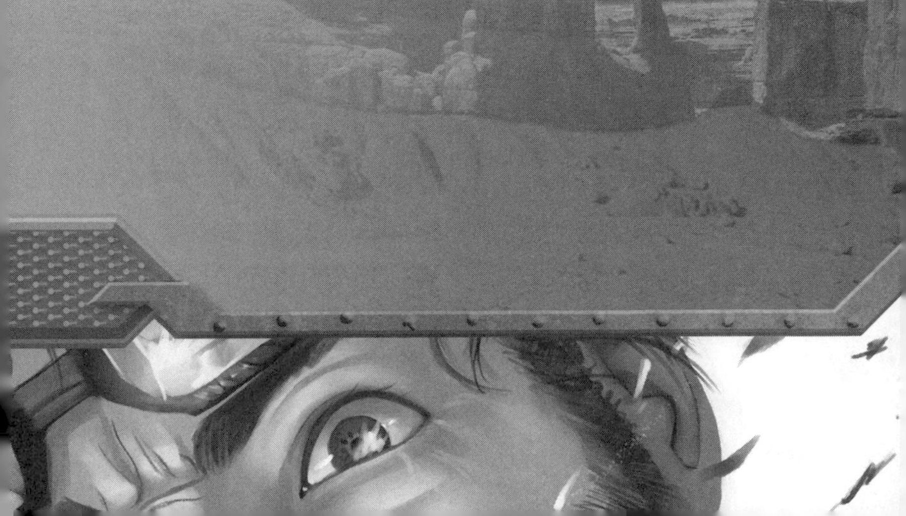

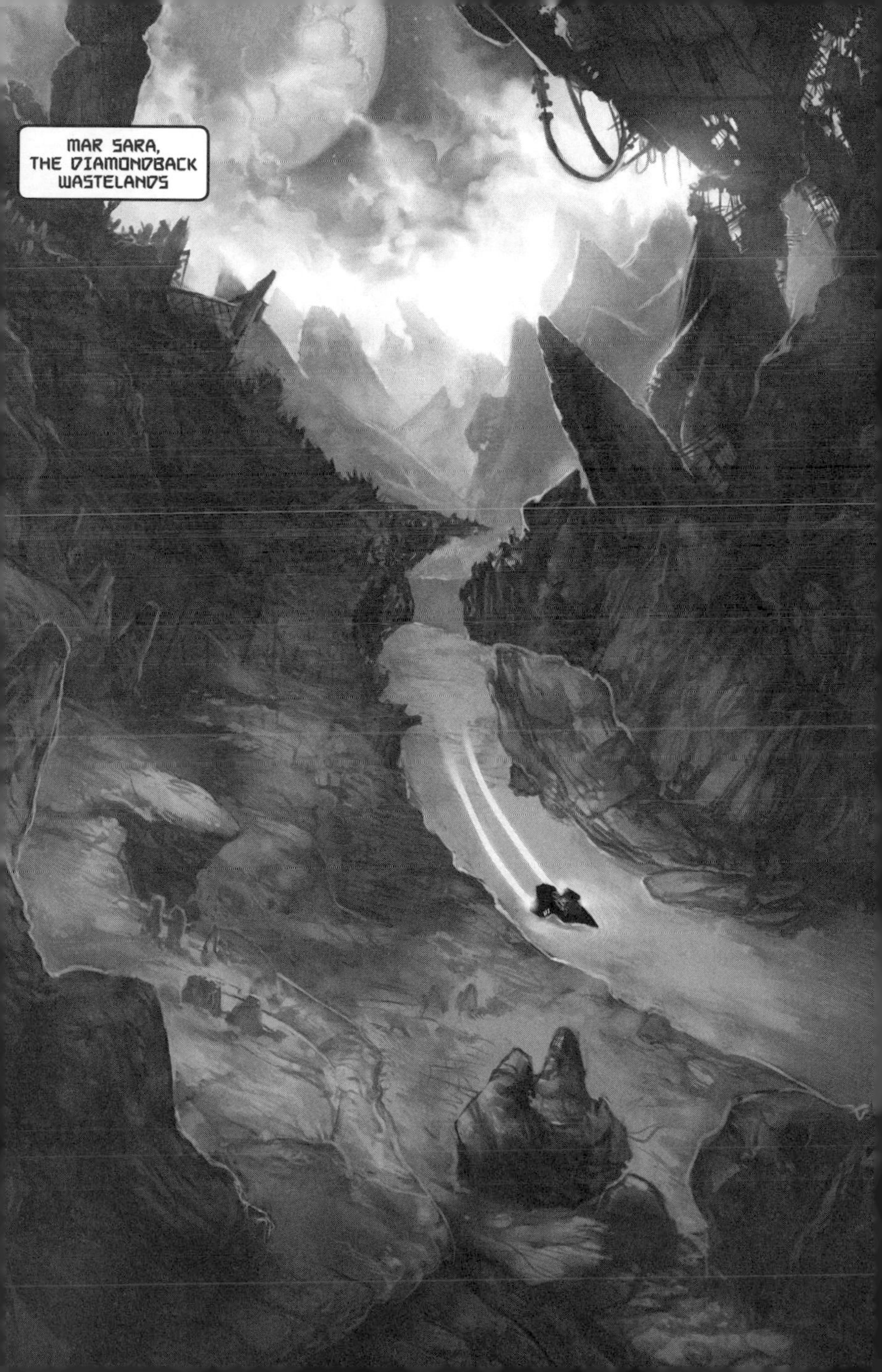
MAR SARA,
THE DIAMONDBACK
WASTELANDS

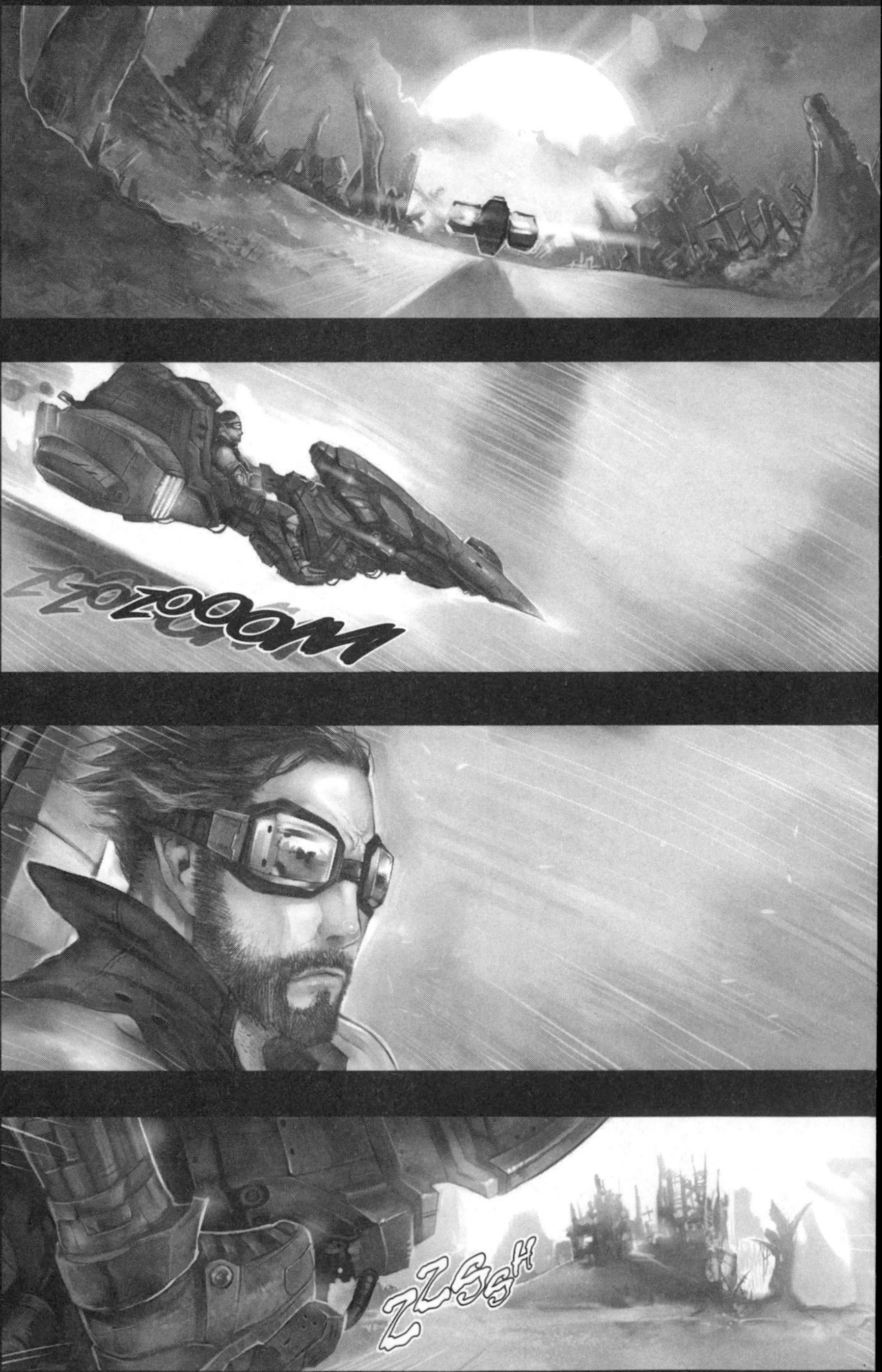
ZZOOOOM
ZZSSH

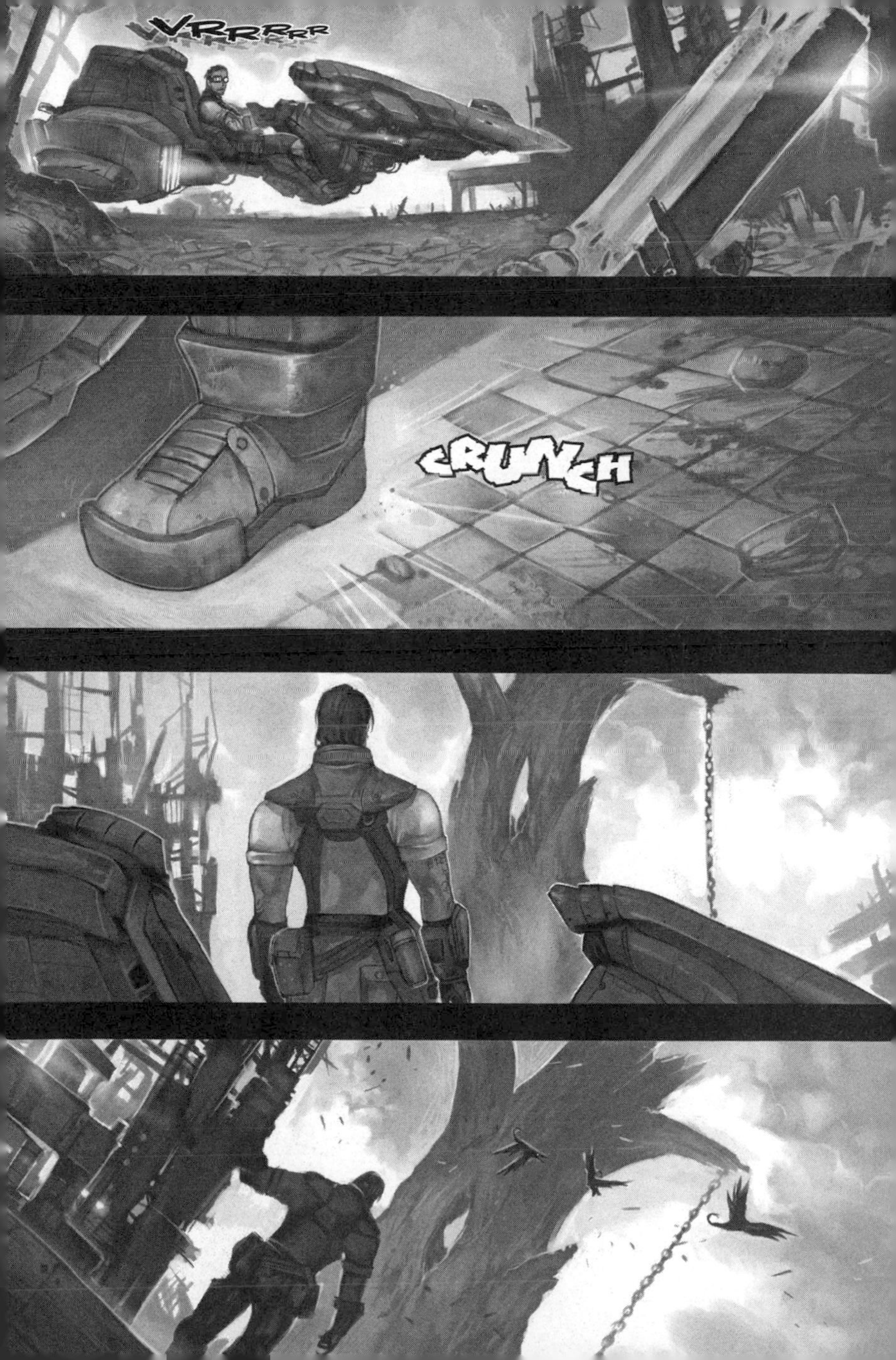
VRRRRRR
CRUNCH

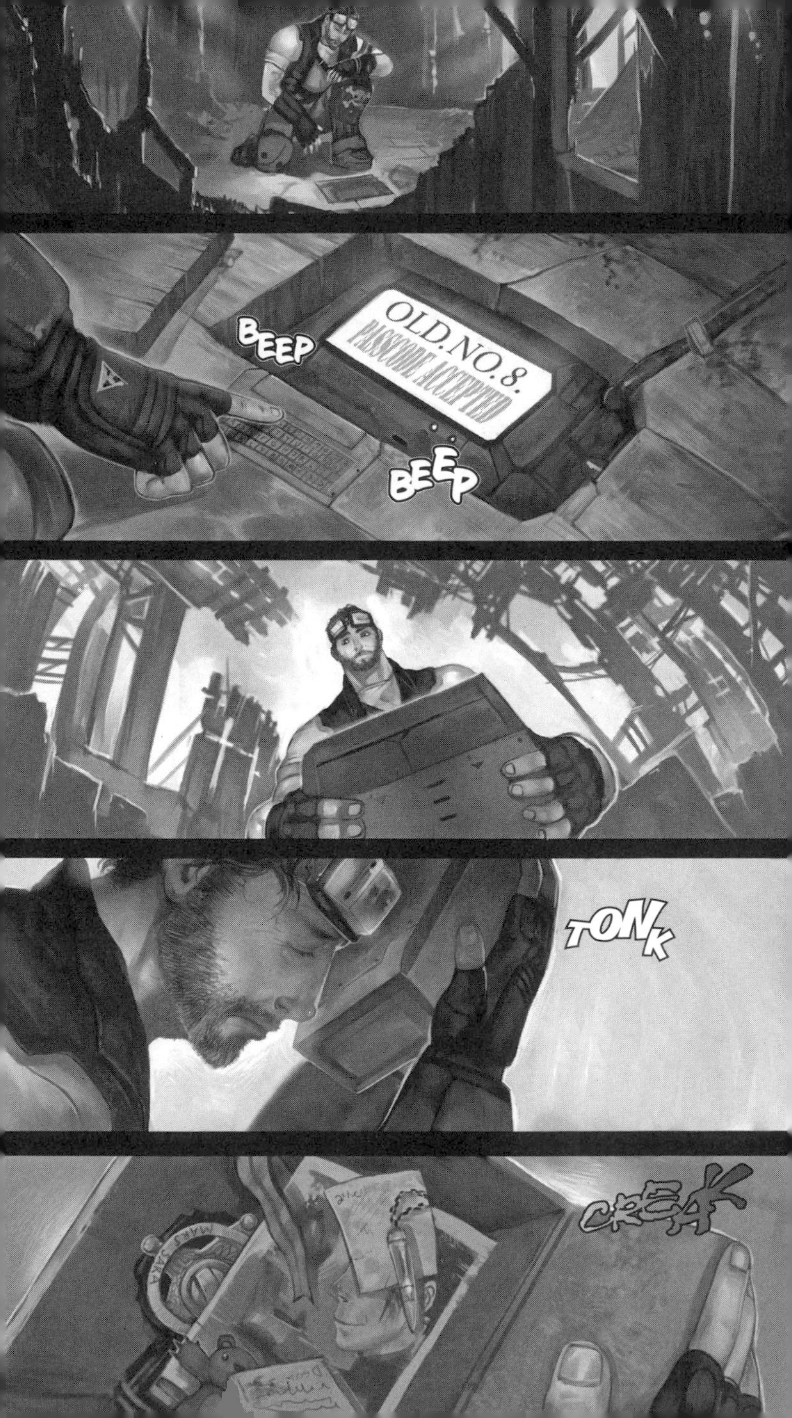
BEEP
OLD.NO.8.
PASSCODE ACCEPTED
BEEP
TONK
CREAK

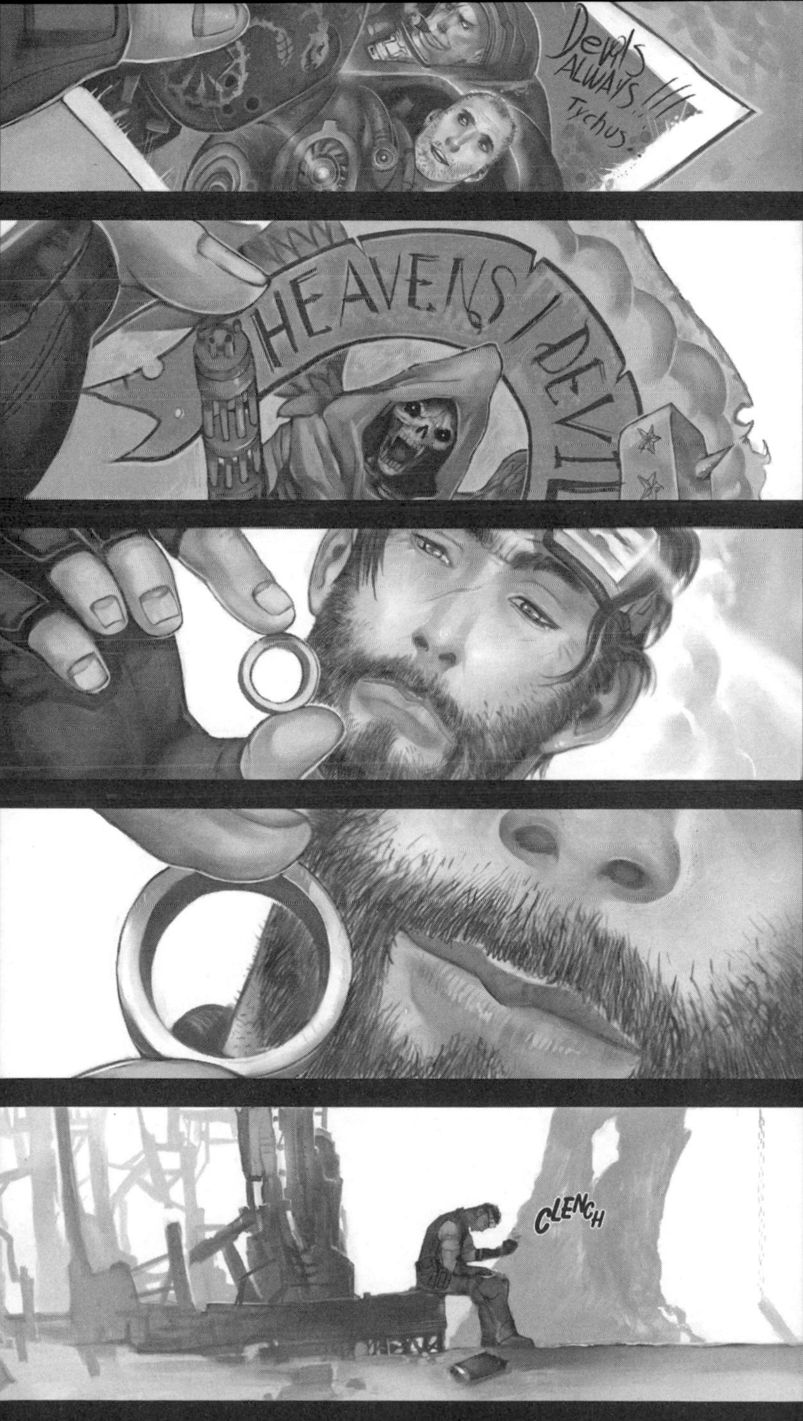
Devils ALWAYS!!!
Tychus
HEAVENS DEVIL
CLENCH

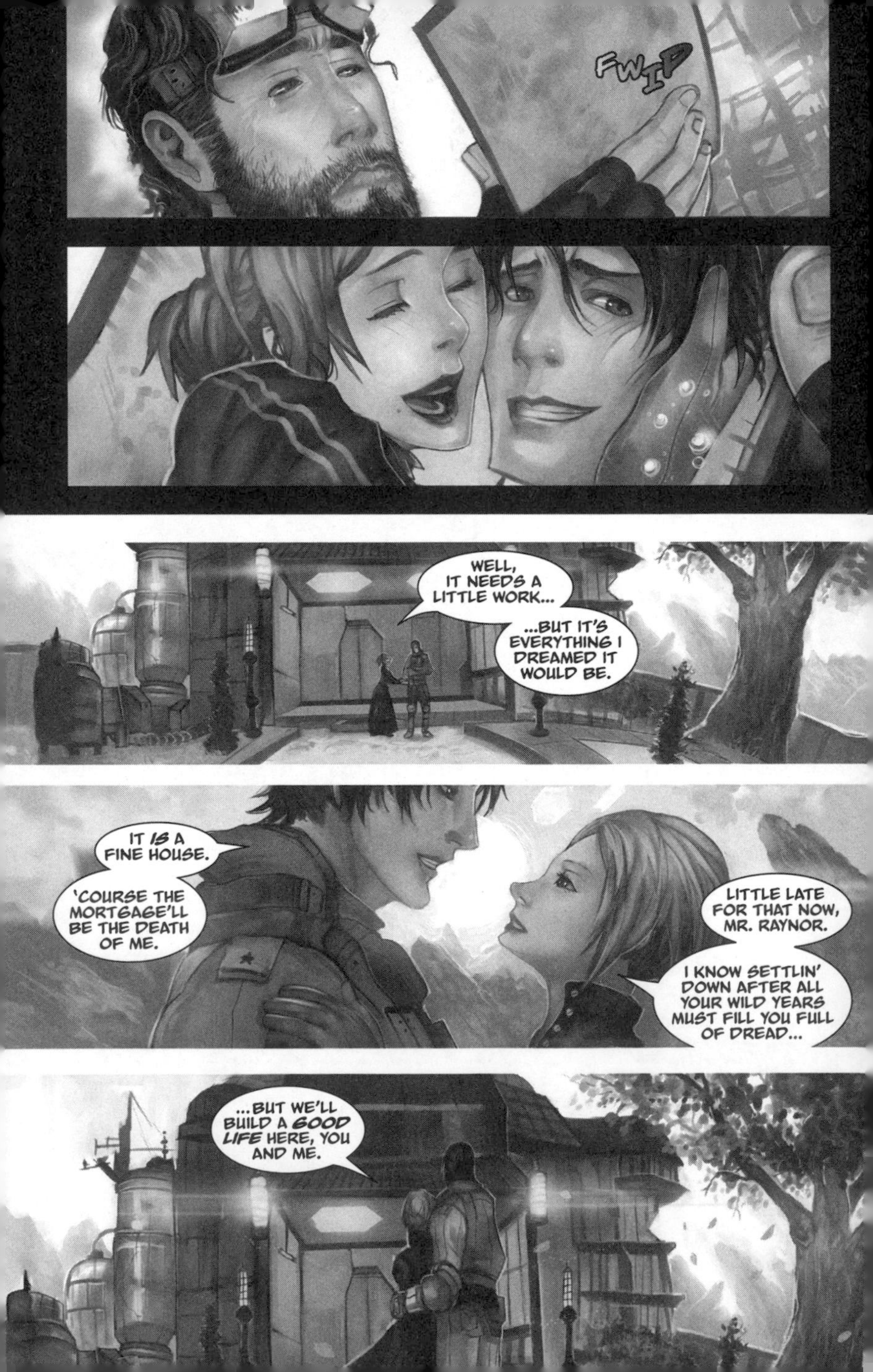
FWIP
WELL, IT NEEDS A LITTLE WORK...
...BUT IT'S EVERYTHING I DREAMED IT WOULD BE.
IT *IS* A FINE HOUSE.
'COURSE THE MORTGAGE'LL BE THE DEATH OF ME.
LITTLE LATE FOR THAT NOW, MR. RAYNOR.
I KNOW SETTLIN' DOWN AFTER ALL YOUR WILD YEARS MUST FILL YOU FULL OF DREAD...
...BUT WE'LL BUILD A *GOOD LIFE* HERE, YOU AND ME.

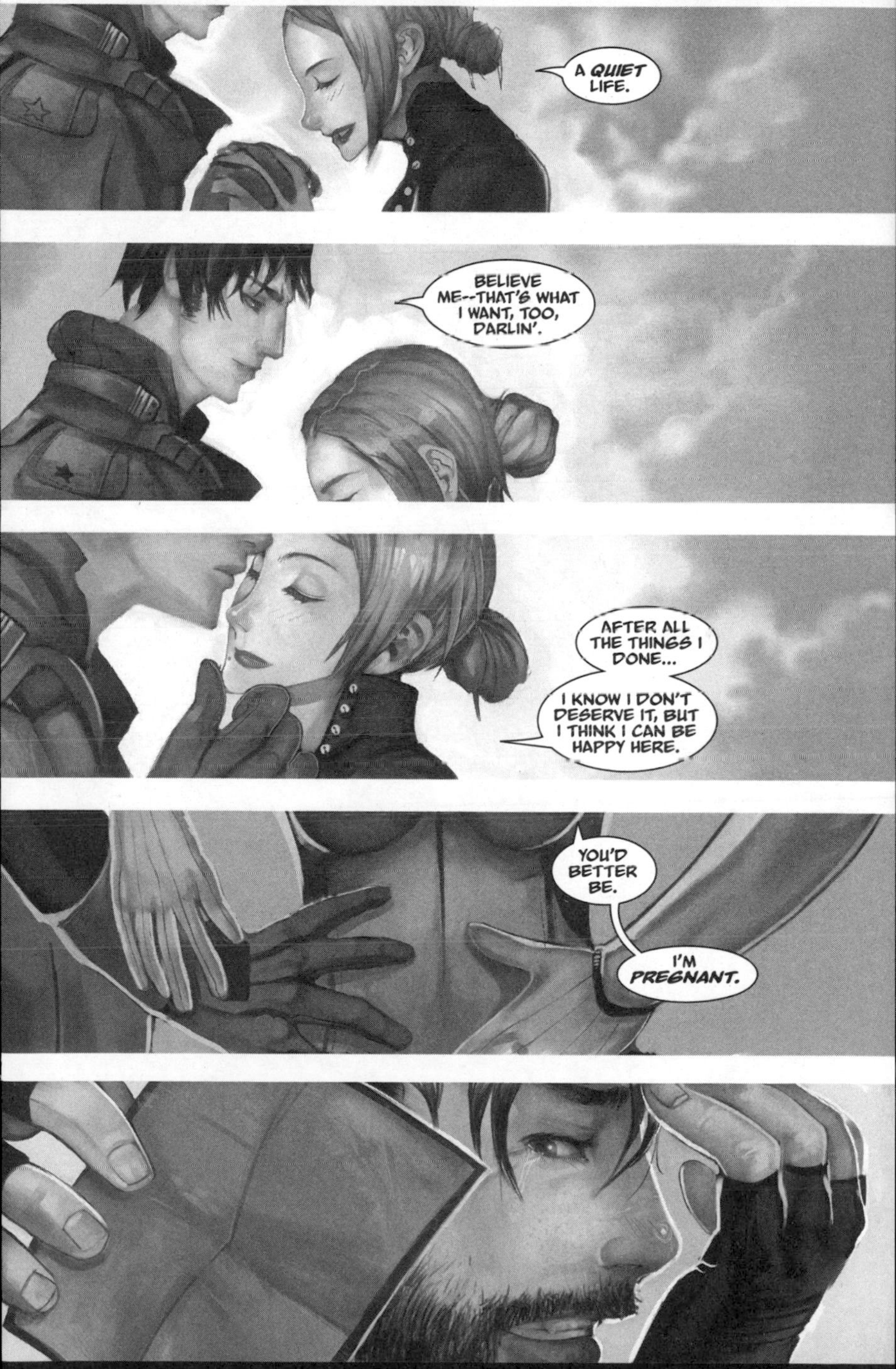
A QUIET LIFE.
BELIEVE ME--THAT'S WHAT I WANT, TOO, DARLIN'.
AFTER ALL THE THINGS I DONE...
I KNOW I DON'T DESERVE IT, BUT I THINK I CAN BE HAPPY HERE.
YOU'D BETTER BE.
I'M PREGNANT.

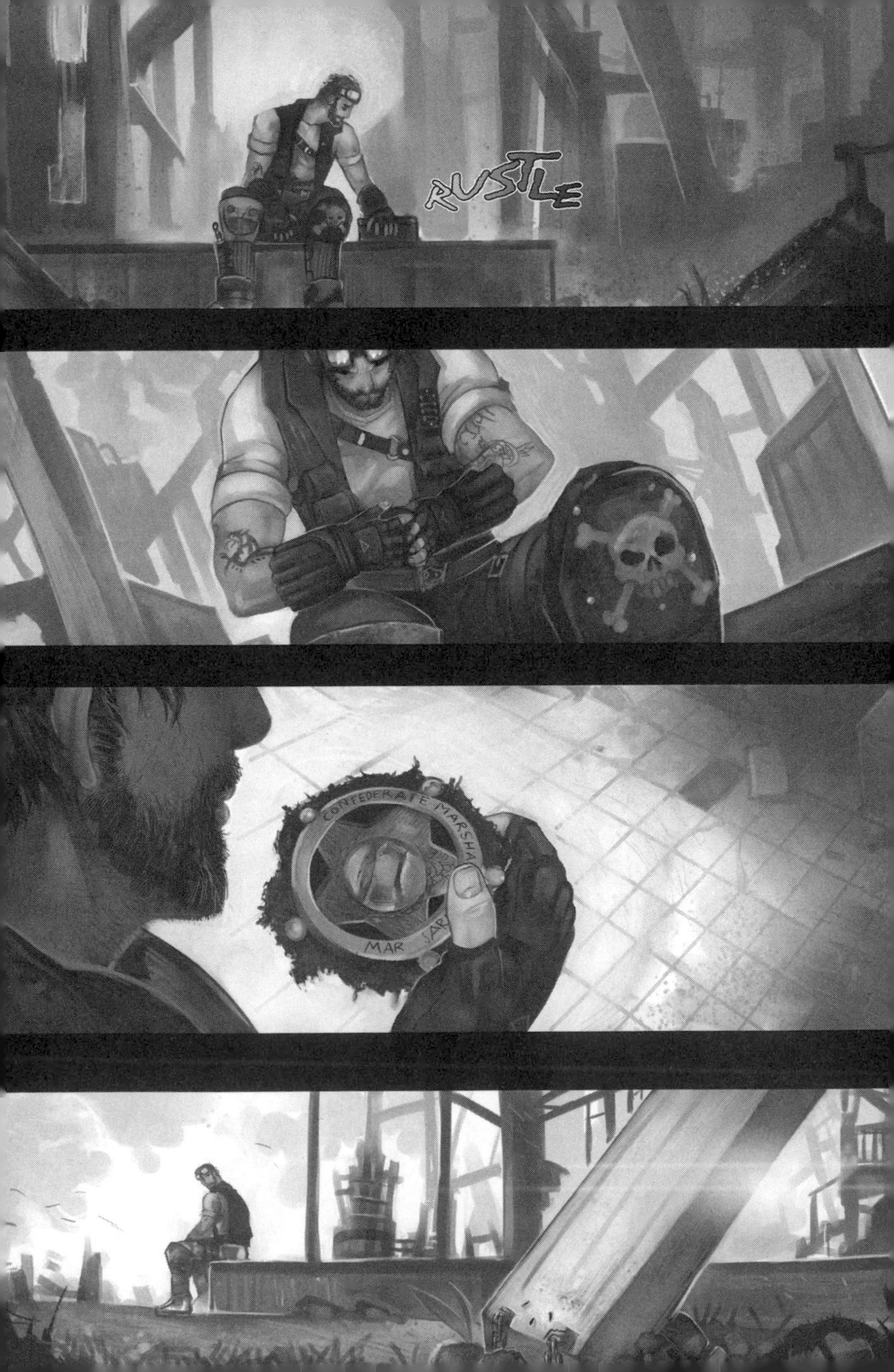
RUSTLE
CONFEDERATE MARSHA
MAR SAR

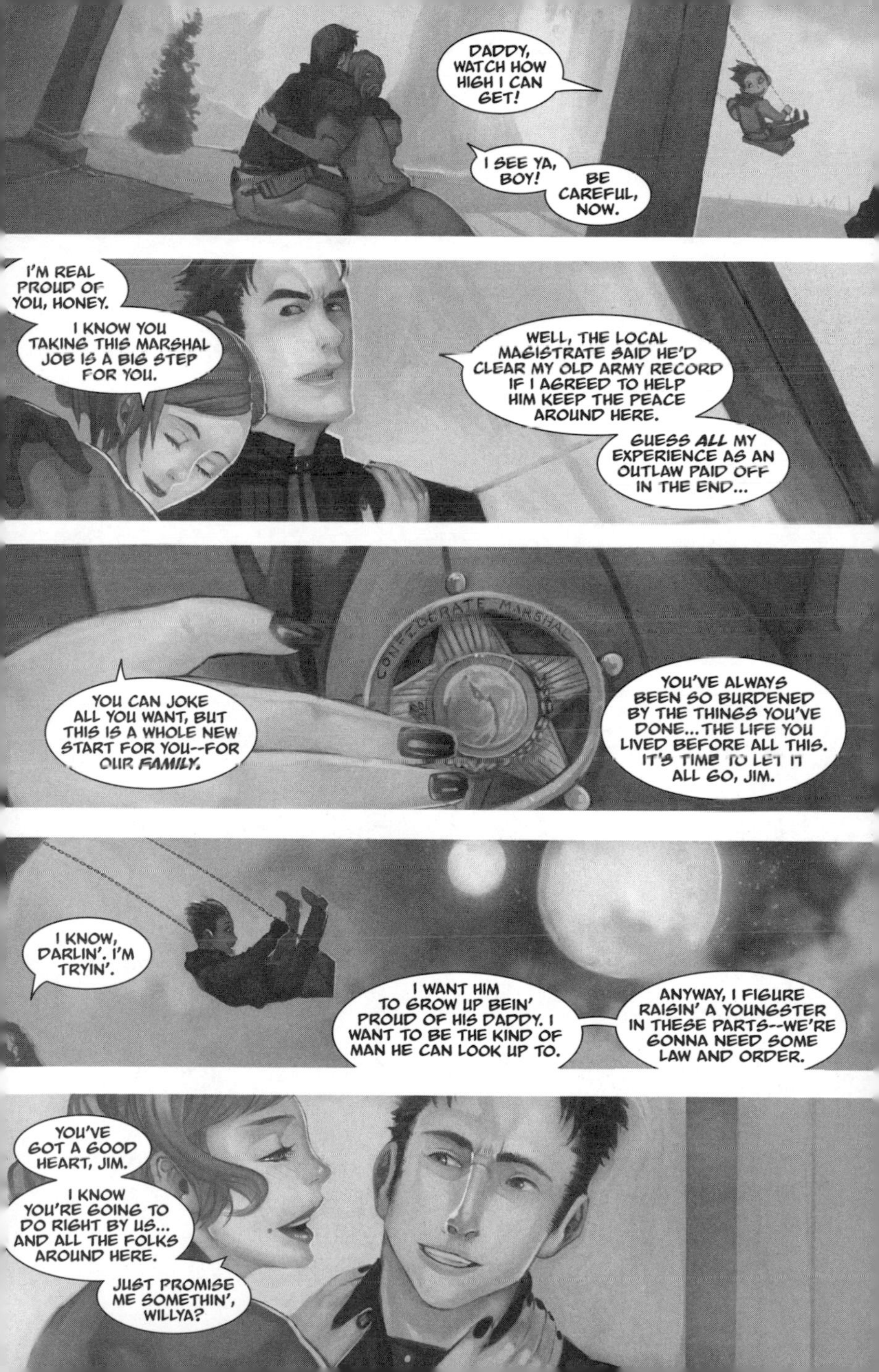
DADDY, WATCH HOW HIGH I CAN GET!
I SEE YA, BOY!
BE CAREFUL, NOW.
I'M REAL PROUD OF YOU, HONEY.
I KNOW YOU TAKING THIS MARSHAL JOB IS A BIG STEP FOR YOU.
WELL, THE LOCAL MAGISTRATE SAID HE'D CLEAR MY OLD ARMY RECORD IF I AGREED TO HELP HIM KEEP THE PEACE AROUND HERE.
GUESS ALL MY EXPERIENCE AS AN OUTLAW PAID OFF IN THE END...
CONFEDERATE MARSHAL
YOU CAN JOKE ALL YOU WANT, BUT THIS IS A WHOLE NEW START FOR YOU--FOR OUR FAMILY.
YOU'VE ALWAYS BEEN SO BURDENED BY THE THINGS YOU'VE DONE...THE LIFE YOU LIVED BEFORE ALL THIS. IT'S TIME TO LET IT ALL GO, JIM.
I KNOW, DARLIN'. I'M TRYIN'.
ANYWAY, I FIGURE RAISIN' A YOUNGSTER IN THESE PARTS--WE'RE GONNA NEED SOME LAW AND ORDER.
I WANT HIM TO GROW UP BEIN' PROUD OF HIS DADDY. I WANT TO BE THE KIND OF MAN HE CAN LOOK UP TO.
YOU'VE GOT A GOOD HEART, JIM.
I KNOW YOU'RE GOING TO DO RIGHT BY US... AND ALL THE FOLKS AROUND HERE.
JUST PROMISE ME SOMETHIN', WILLYA?

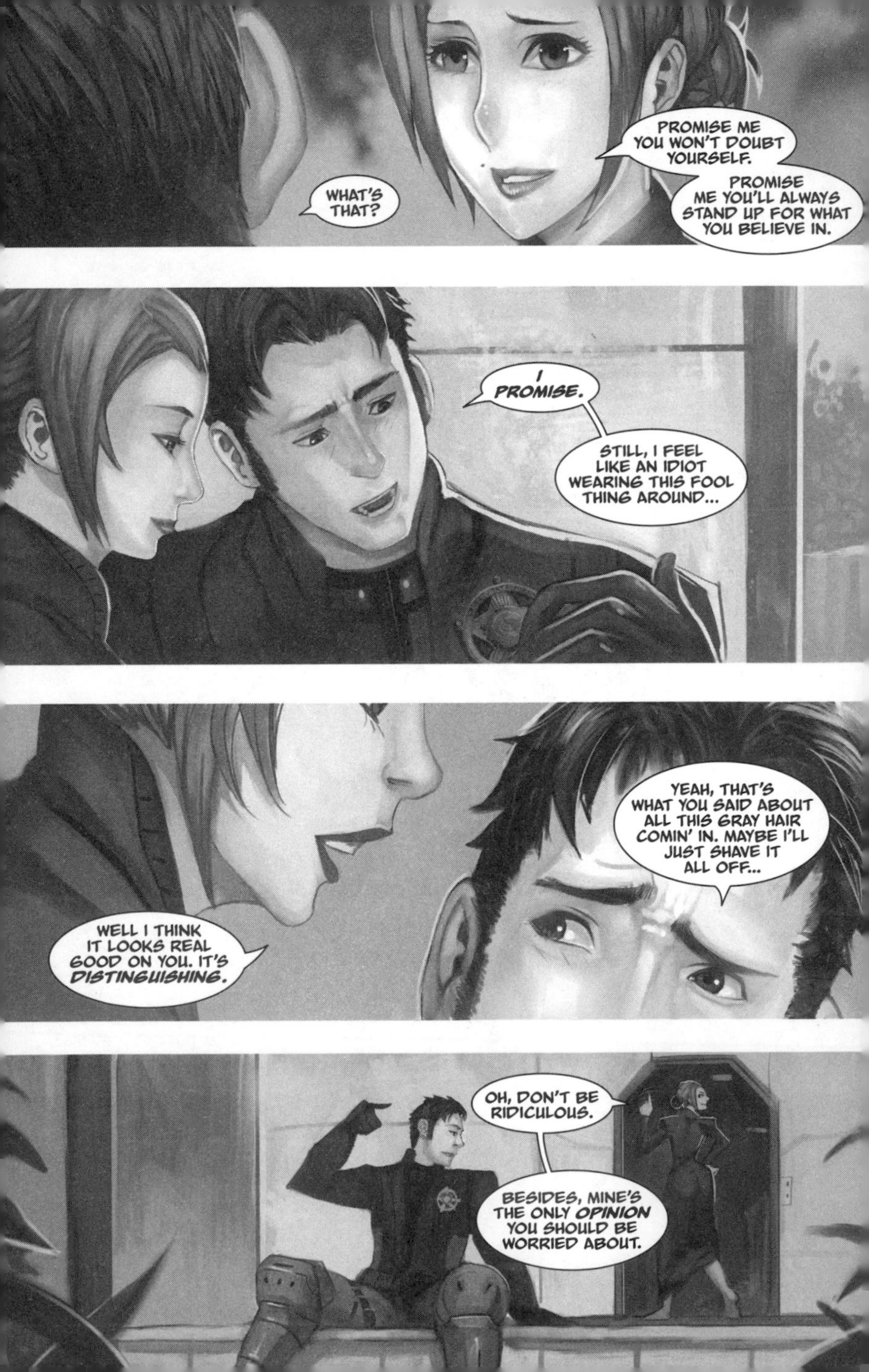
PROMISE ME YOU WON'T DOUBT YOURSELF.
PROMISE ME YOU'LL ALWAYS STAND UP FOR WHAT YOU BELIEVE IN.
WHAT'S THAT?
I *PROMISE.*
STILL, I FEEL LIKE AN IDIOT WEARING THIS FOOL THING AROUND...
WELL I THINK IT LOOKS REAL GOOD ON YOU. IT'S *DISTINGUISHING.*
YEAH, THAT'S WHAT YOU SAID ABOUT ALL THIS GRAY HAIR COMIN' IN. MAYBE I'LL JUST SHAVE IT ALL OFF...
OH, DON'T BE RIDICULOUS.
BESIDES, MINE'S THE ONLY *OPINION* YOU SHOULD BE WORRIED ABOUT.

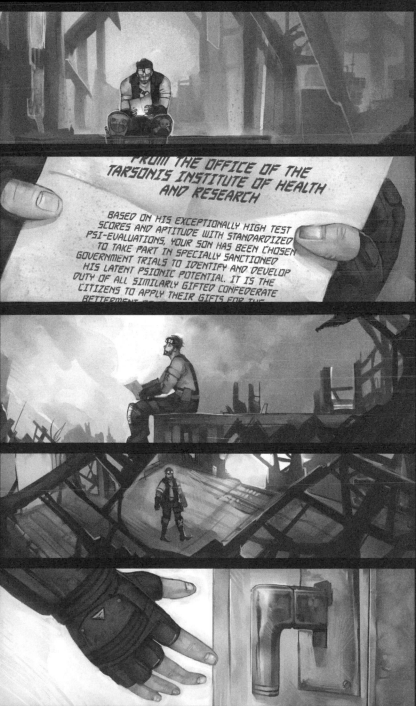

FROM THE OFFICE OF THE
TARSONIS INSTITUTE OF HEALTH
AND RESEARCH

BASED ON HIS EXCEPTIONALLY HIGH TEST
SCORES AND APTITUDE WITH STANDARDIZED
PSI-EVALUATIONS, YOUR SON HAS BEEN CHOSEN
TO TAKE PART IN SPECIALLY SANCTIONED
GOVERNMENT TRIALS TO IDENTIFY AND DEVELOP
HIS LATENT PSIONIC POTENTIAL. IT IS THE
DUTY OF ALL SIMILARLY GIFTED CONFEDERATE
CITIZENS TO APPLY THEIR GIFTS FOR THE
BETTERMENT

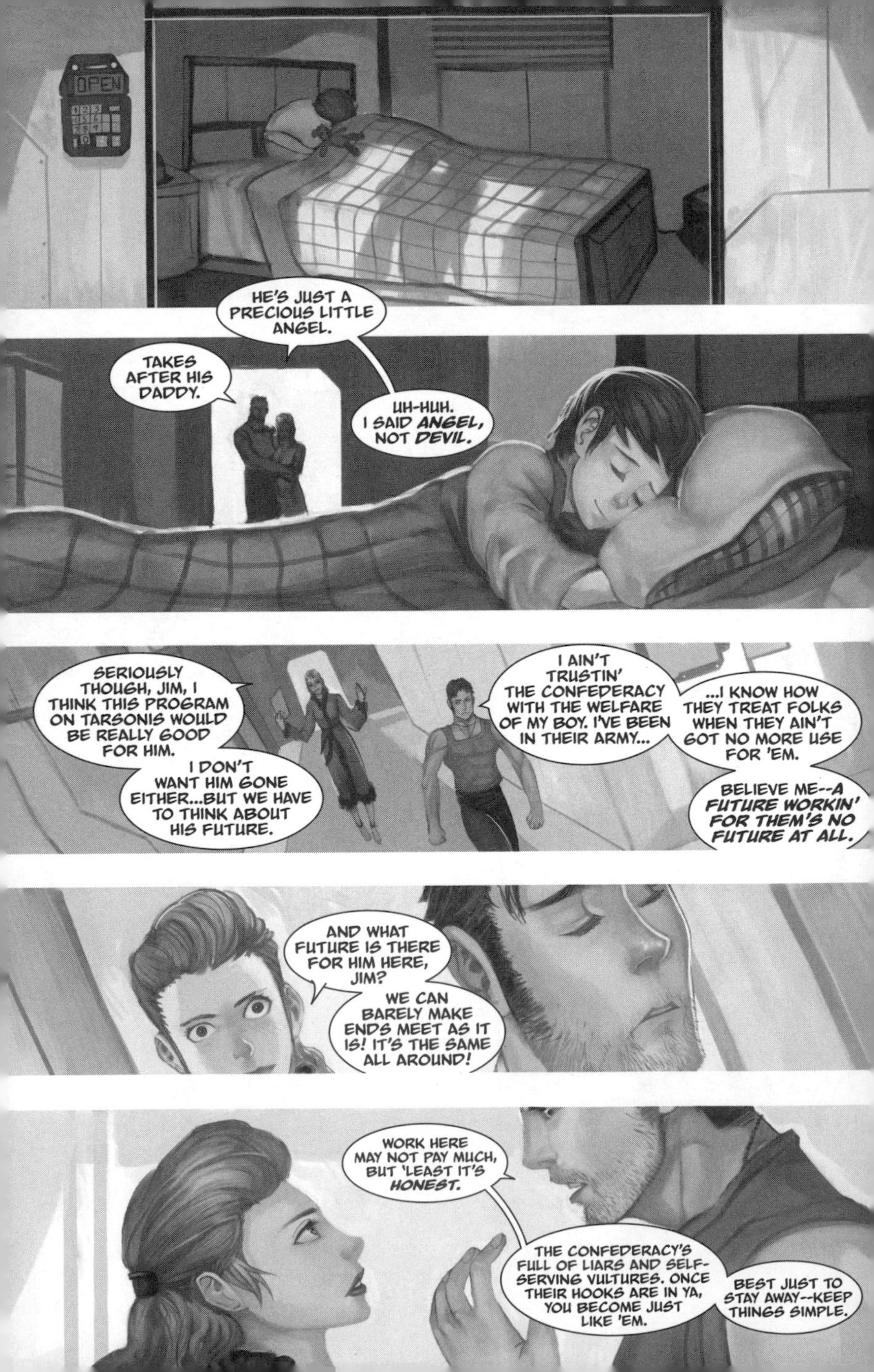
OPEN
HE'S JUST A PRECIOUS LITTLE ANGEL.
TAKES AFTER HIS DADDY.
UH-HUH. I SAID ANGEL, NOT DEVIL.
SERIOUSLY THOUGH, JIM, I THINK THIS PROGRAM ON TARSONIS WOULD BE REALLY GOOD FOR HIM.
I DON'T WANT HIM GONE EITHER...BUT WE HAVE TO THINK ABOUT HIS FUTURE.
I AIN'T TRUSTIN' THE CONFEDERACY WITH THE WELFARE OF MY BOY. I'VE BEEN IN THEIR ARMY...
...I KNOW HOW THEY TREAT FOLKS WHEN THEY AIN'T GOT NO MORE USE FOR 'EM.
BELIEVE ME--A FUTURE WORKIN' FOR THEM'S NO FUTURE AT ALL.
AND WHAT FUTURE IS THERE FOR HIM HERE, JIM?
WE CAN BARELY MAKE ENDS MEET AS IT IS! IT'S THE SAME ALL AROUND!
WORK HERE MAY NOT PAY MUCH, BUT 'LEAST IT'S HONEST.
THE CONFEDERACY'S FULL OF LIARS AND SELF-SERVING VULTURES. ONCE THEIR HOOKS ARE IN YA, YOU BECOME JUST LIKE 'EM.
BEST JUST TO STAY AWAY--KEEP THINGS SIMPLE.

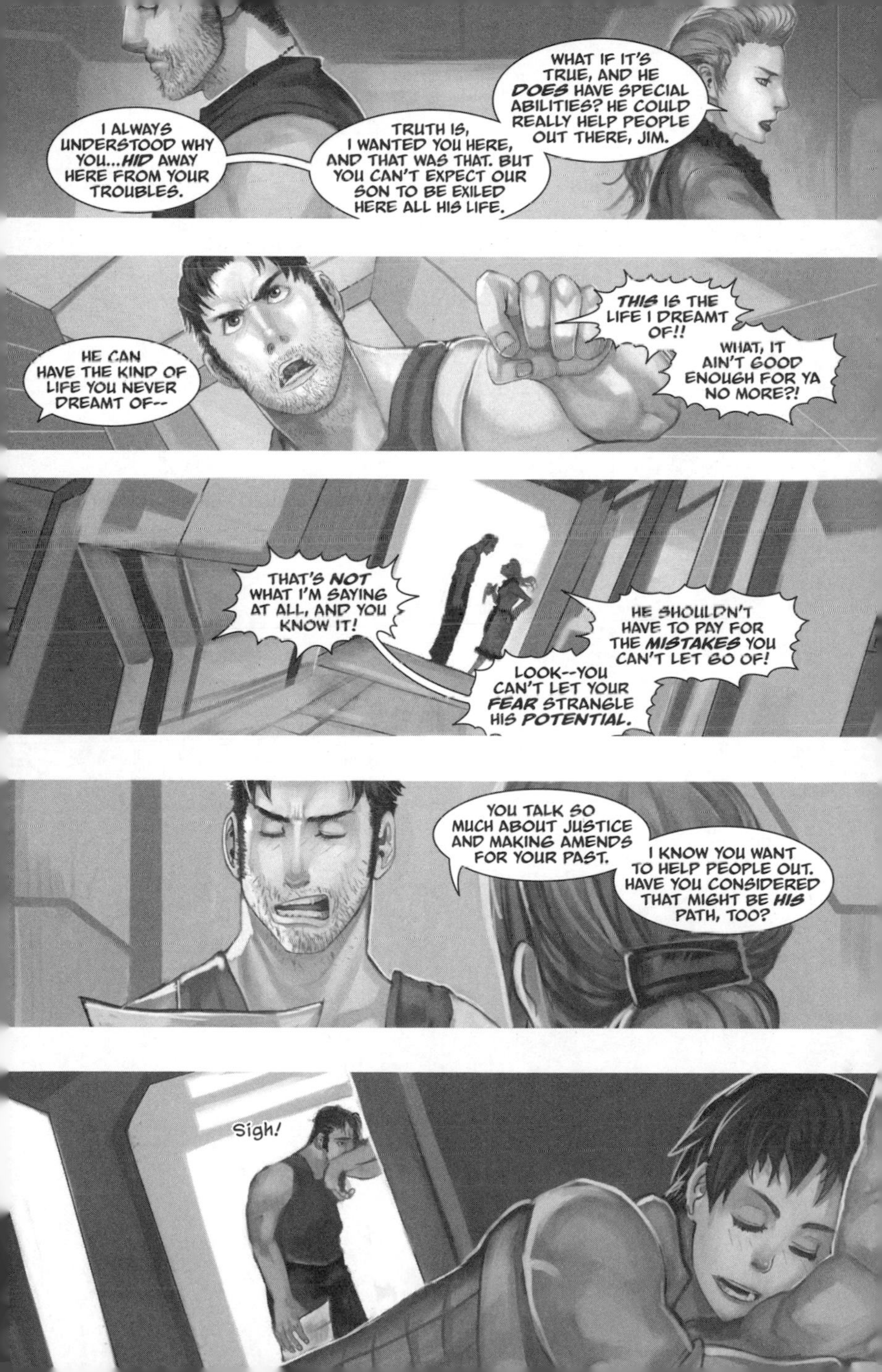
I ALWAYS UNDERSTOOD WHY YOU...*HID* AWAY HERE FROM YOUR TROUBLES.
TRUTH IS, I WANTED YOU HERE, AND THAT WAS THAT. BUT YOU CAN'T EXPECT OUR SON TO BE EXILED HERE ALL HIS LIFE.
WHAT IF IT'S TRUE, AND HE *DOES* HAVE SPECIAL ABILITIES? HE COULD REALLY HELP PEOPLE OUT THERE, JIM.
HE CAN HAVE THE KIND OF LIFE YOU NEVER DREAMT OF--
THIS IS THE LIFE I DREAMT OF!!
WHAT, IT AIN'T GOOD ENOUGH FOR YA NO MORE?!
THAT'S *NOT* WHAT I'M SAYING AT ALL, AND YOU KNOW IT!
HE SHOULDN'T HAVE TO PAY FOR THE *MISTAKES* YOU CAN'T LET GO OF!
LOOK--YOU CAN'T LET YOUR *FEAR* STRANGLE HIS *POTENTIAL*.
YOU TALK SO MUCH ABOUT JUSTICE AND MAKING AMENDS FOR YOUR PAST.
I KNOW YOU WANT TO HELP PEOPLE OUT. HAVE YOU CONSIDERED THAT MIGHT BE *HIS* PATH, TOO?
Sigh!

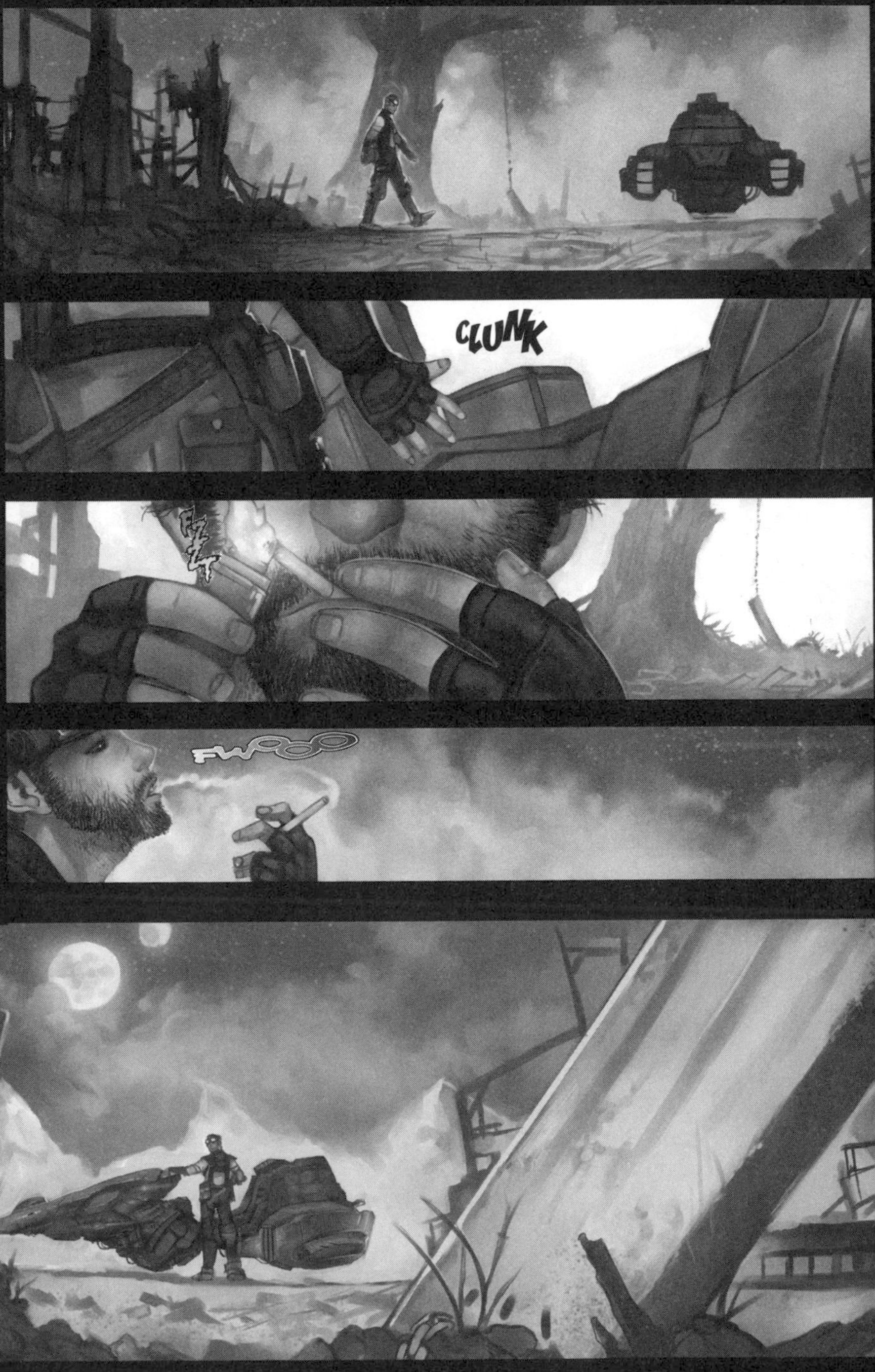
CLUNK
FWOOO

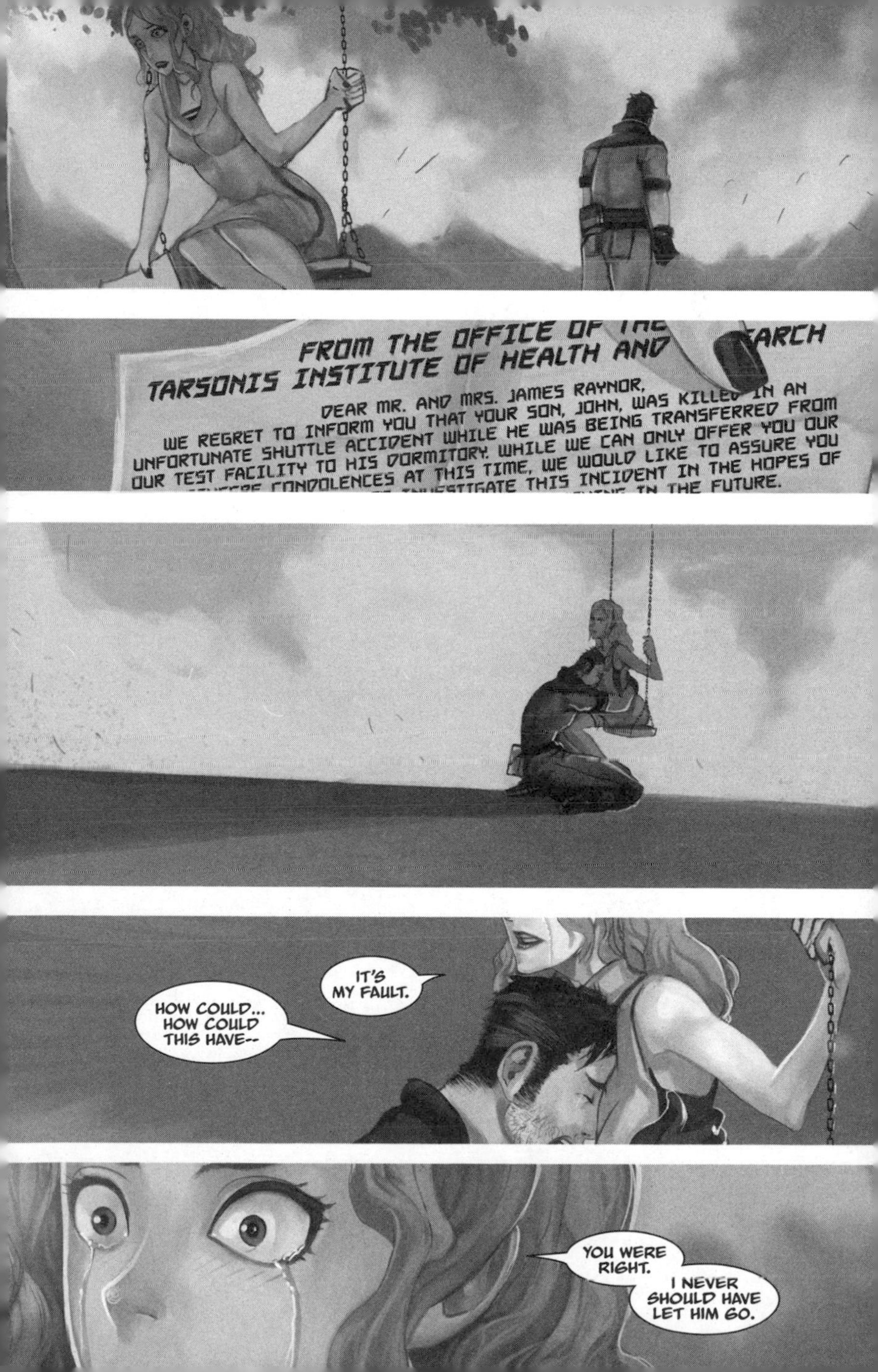
FROM THE OFFICE OF THE
TARSONIS INSTITUTE OF HEALTH AND
DEAR MR. AND MRS. JAMES RAYNOR,
WE REGRET TO INFORM YOU THAT YOUR SON, JOHN, WAS KILLED IN AN
UNFORTUNATE SHUTTLE ACCIDENT WHILE HE WAS BEING TRANSFERRED FROM
OUR TEST FACILITY TO HIS DORMITORY. WHILE WE CAN ONLY OFFER YOU OUR
CONDOLENCES AT THIS TIME, WE WOULD LIKE TO ASSURE YOU
INVESTIGATE THIS INCIDENT IN THE HOPES OF
IN THE FUTURE.
HOW COULD... HOW COULD THIS HAVE--
IT'S MY FAULT.
YOU WERE RIGHT.
I NEVER SHOULD HAVE LET HIM GO.

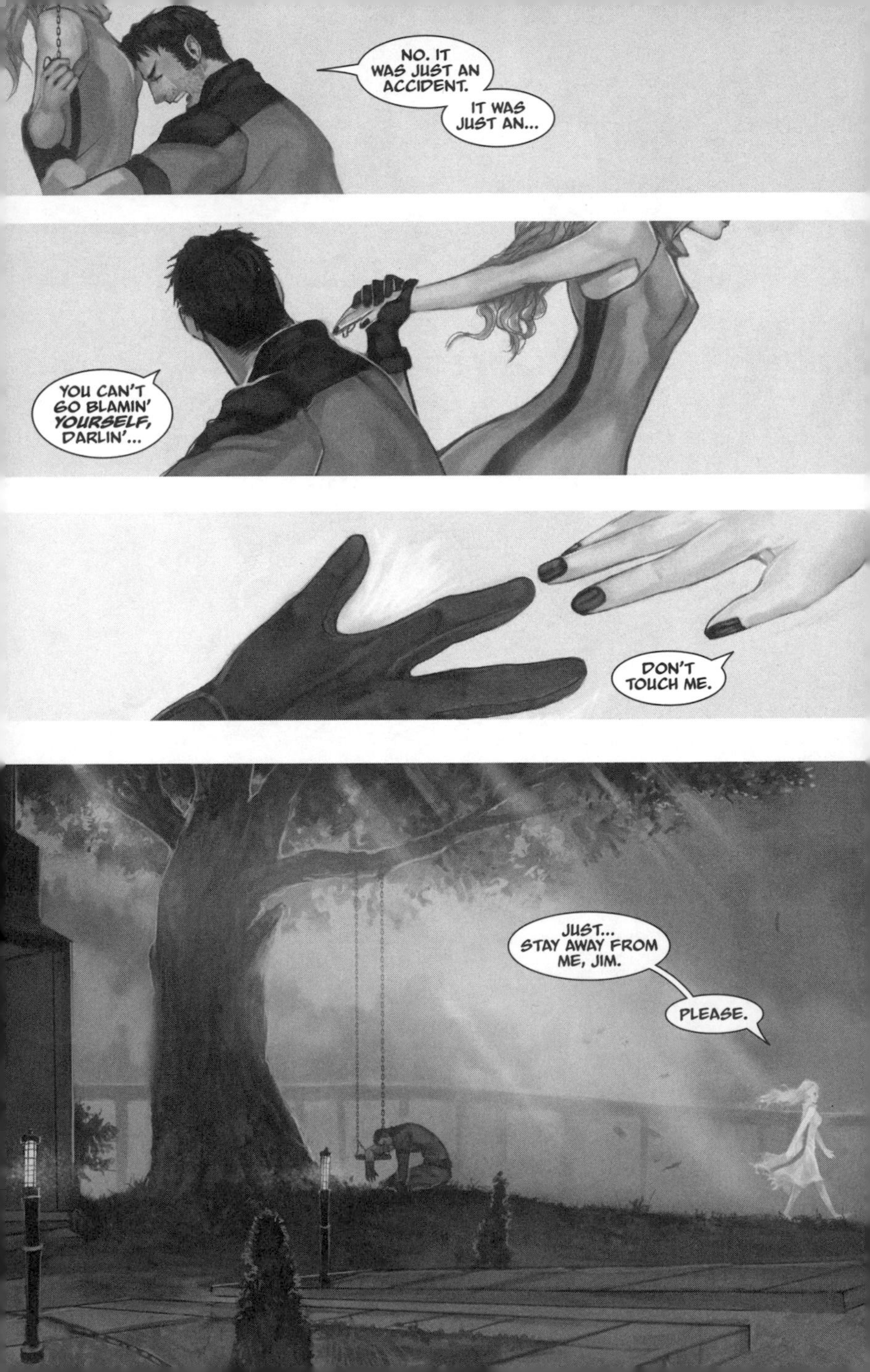
NO. IT WAS JUST AN ACCIDENT.
IT WAS JUST AN...
YOU CAN'T GO BLAMIN' *YOURSELF*, DARLIN'...
DON'T TOUCH ME.
JUST... STAY AWAY FROM ME, JIM.
PLEASE.

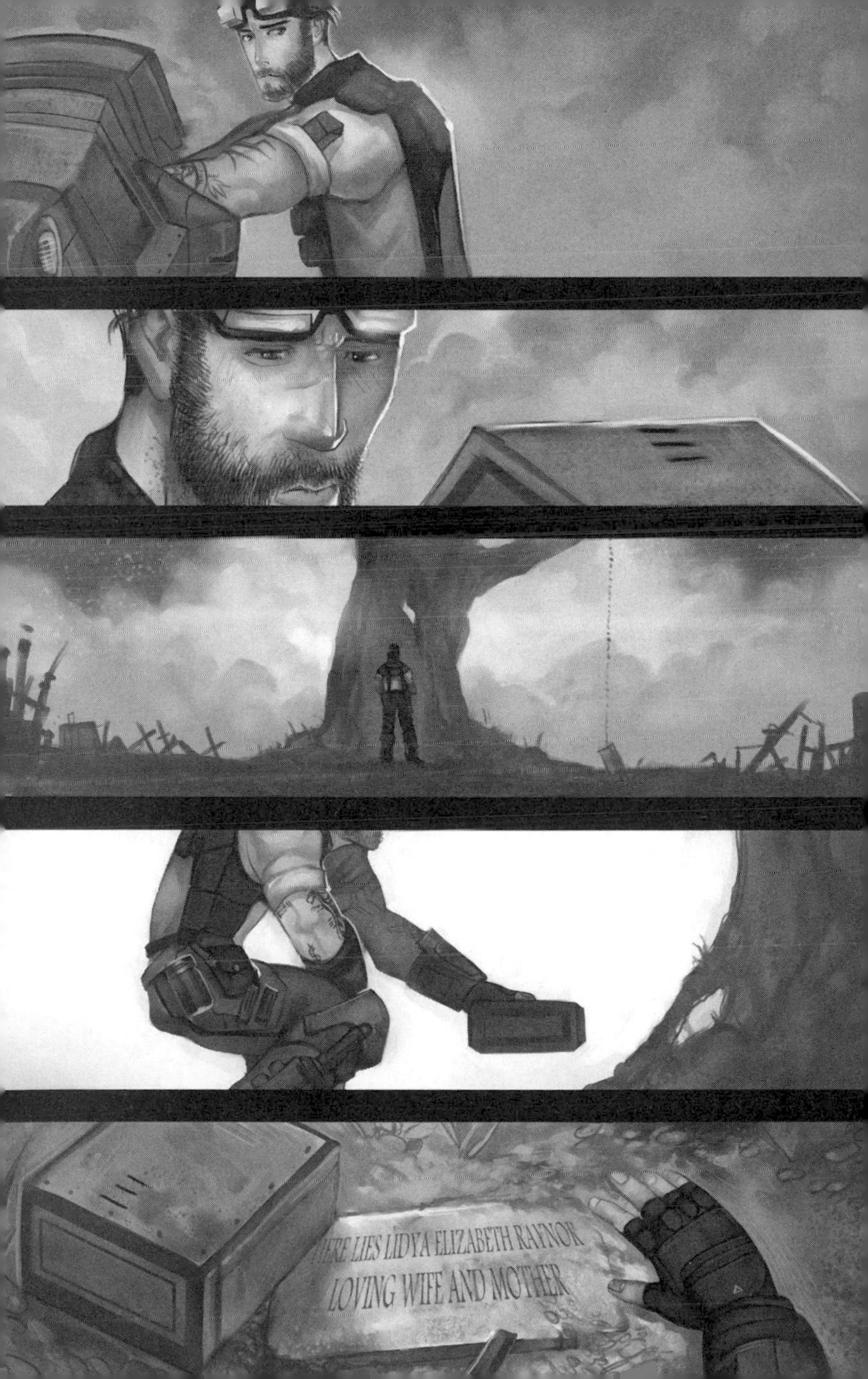
HERE LIES LIDYA ELIZABETH RAYNOR
LOVING WIFE AND MOTHER

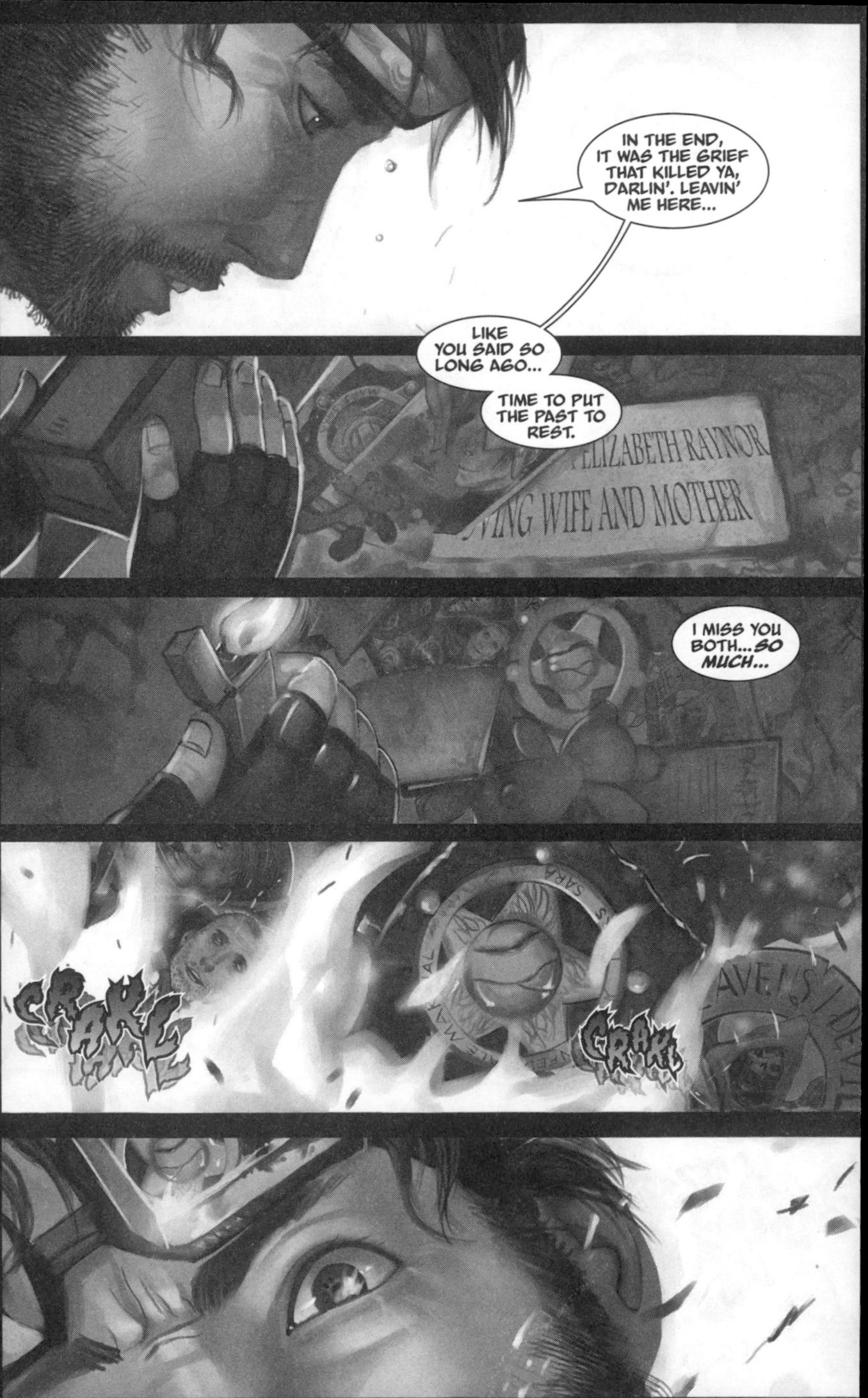
IN THE END, IT WAS THE GRIEF THAT KILLED YA, DARLIN'. LEAVIN' ME HERE...
LIKE YOU SAID SO LONG AGO...
TIME TO PUT THE PAST TO REST.
ELIZABETH RAYNOR
VING WIFE AND MOTHER
I MISS YOU BOTH...SO MUCH...
CRAKL
CRAKL

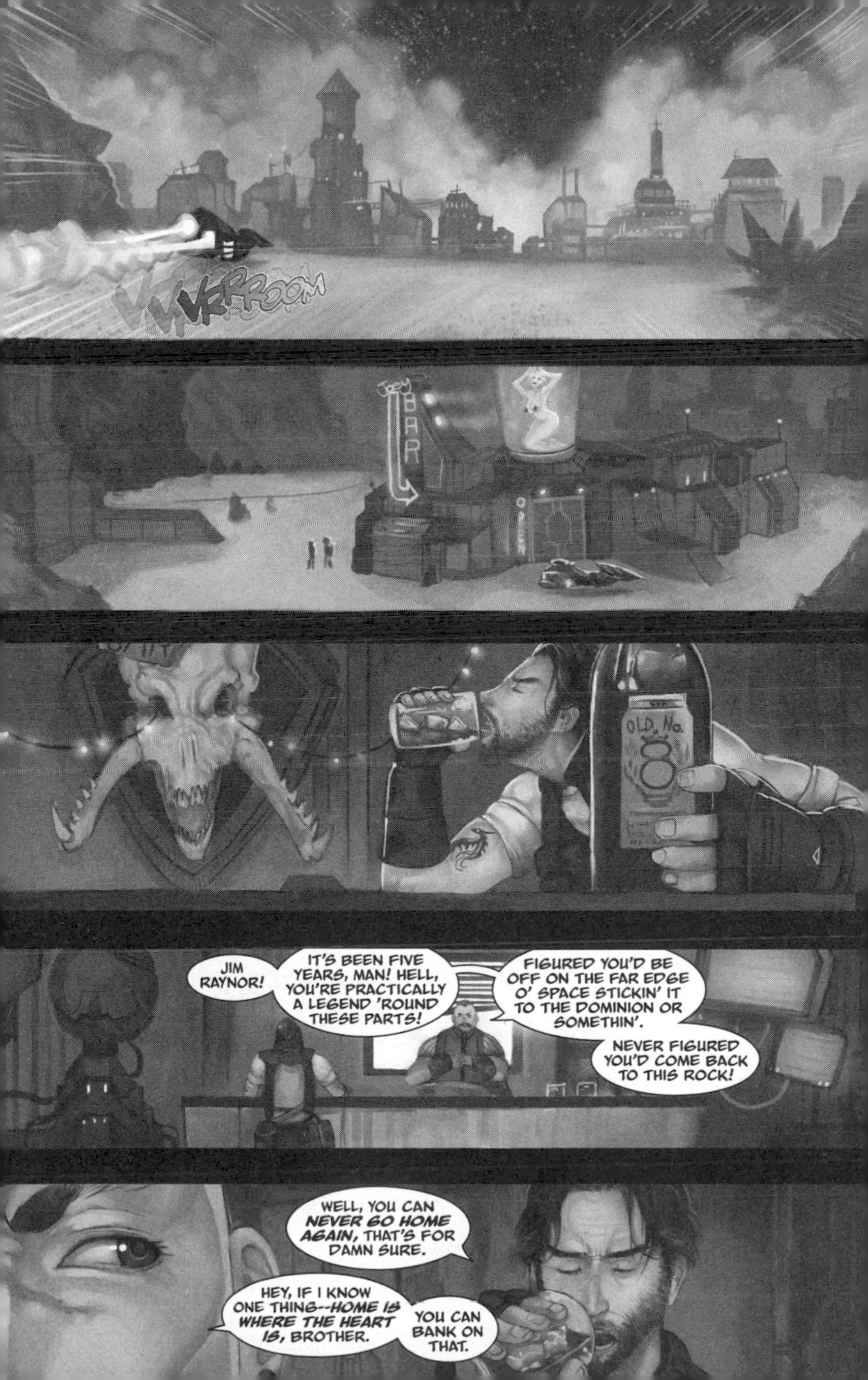
VVVRROOM
Joey BAR
OLD. No. 8
JIM RAYNOR!
IT'S BEEN FIVE YEARS, MAN! HELL, YOU'RE PRACTICALLY A LEGEND 'ROUND THESE PARTS!
FIGURED YOU'D BE OFF ON THE FAR EDGE O' SPACE STICKIN' IT TO THE DOMINION OR SOMETHIN'.
NEVER FIGURED YOU'D COME BACK TO THIS ROCK!
WELL, YOU CAN *NEVER GO HOME AGAIN*, THAT'S FOR DAMN SURE.
HEY, IF I KNOW ONE THING--*HOME IS WHERE THE HEART IS*, BROTHER.
YOU CAN BANK ON THAT.

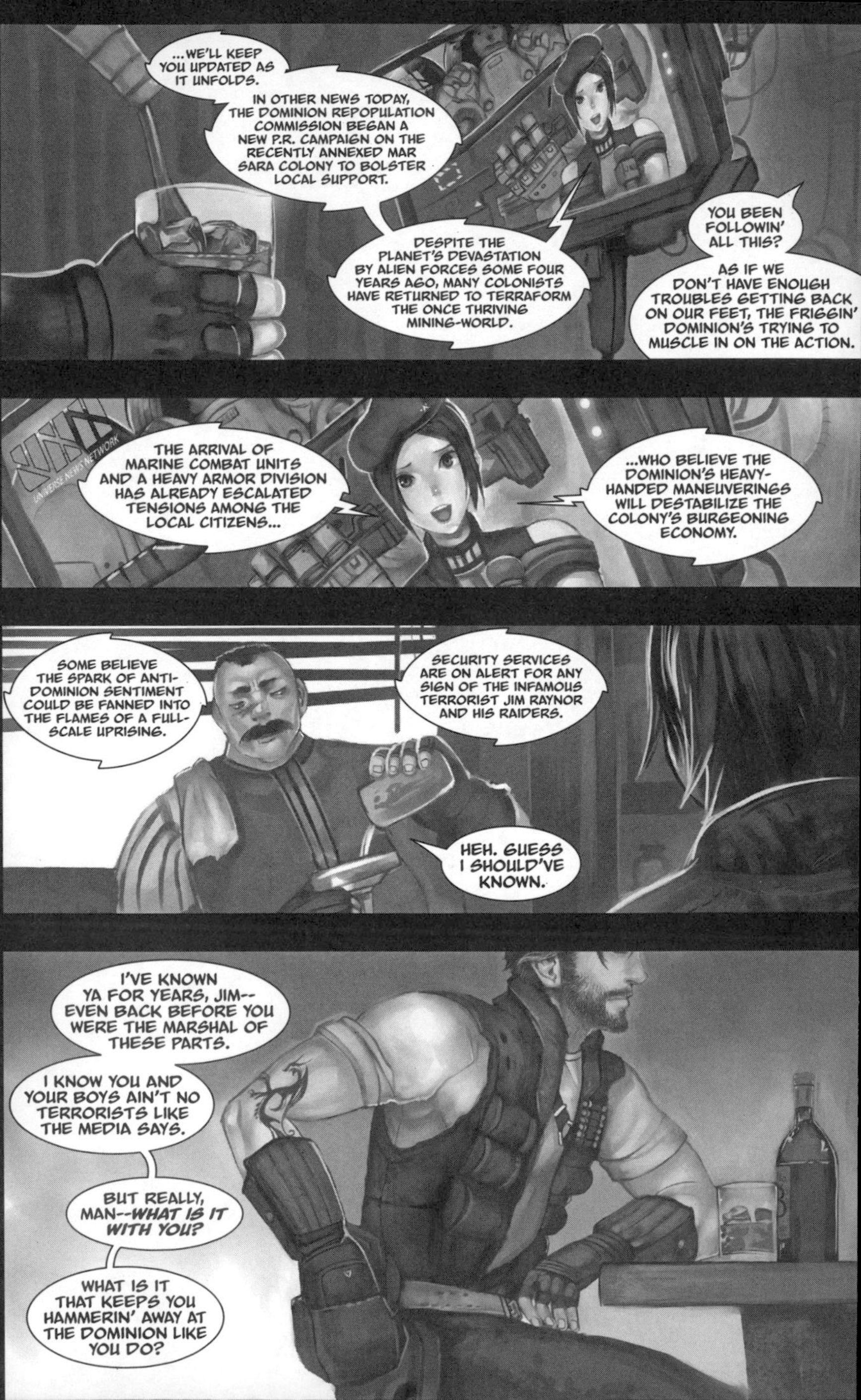
...WE'LL KEEP YOU UPDATED AS IT UNFOLDS.
IN OTHER NEWS TODAY, THE DOMINION REPOPULATION COMMISSION BEGAN A NEW P.R. CAMPAIGN ON THE RECENTLY ANNEXED MAR SARA COLONY TO BOLSTER LOCAL SUPPORT.
DESPITE THE PLANET'S DEVASTATION BY ALIEN FORCES SOME FOUR YEARS AGO, MANY COLONISTS HAVE RETURNED TO TERRAFORM THE ONCE THRIVING MINING-WORLD.
YOU BEEN FOLLOWIN' ALL THIS?
AS IF WE DON'T HAVE ENOUGH TROUBLES GETTING BACK ON OUR FEET, THE FRIGGIN' DOMINION'S TRYING TO MUSCLE IN ON THE ACTION.
UNIVERSE NEWS NETWORK
THE ARRIVAL OF MARINE COMBAT UNITS AND A HEAVY ARMOR DIVISION HAS ALREADY ESCALATED TENSIONS AMONG THE LOCAL CITIZENS...
...WHO BELIEVE THE DOMINION'S HEAVY-HANDED MANEUVERINGS WILL DESTABILIZE THE COLONY'S BURGEONING ECONOMY.
SOME BELIEVE THE SPARK OF ANTI-DOMINION SENTIMENT COULD BE FANNED INTO THE FLAMES OF A FULL-SCALE UPRISING.
SECURITY SERVICES ARE ON ALERT FOR ANY SIGN OF THE INFAMOUS TERRORIST JIM RAYNOR AND HIS RAIDERS.
HEH. GUESS I SHOULD'VE KNOWN.
I'VE KNOWN YA FOR YEARS, JIM-- EVEN BACK BEFORE YOU WERE THE MARSHAL OF THESE PARTS.
I KNOW YOU AND YOUR BOYS AIN'T NO TERRORISTS LIKE THE MEDIA SAYS.
BUT REALLY, MAN--*WHAT IS IT WITH YOU?*
WHAT IS IT THAT KEEPS YOU HAMMERIN' AWAY AT THE DOMINION LIKE YOU DO?

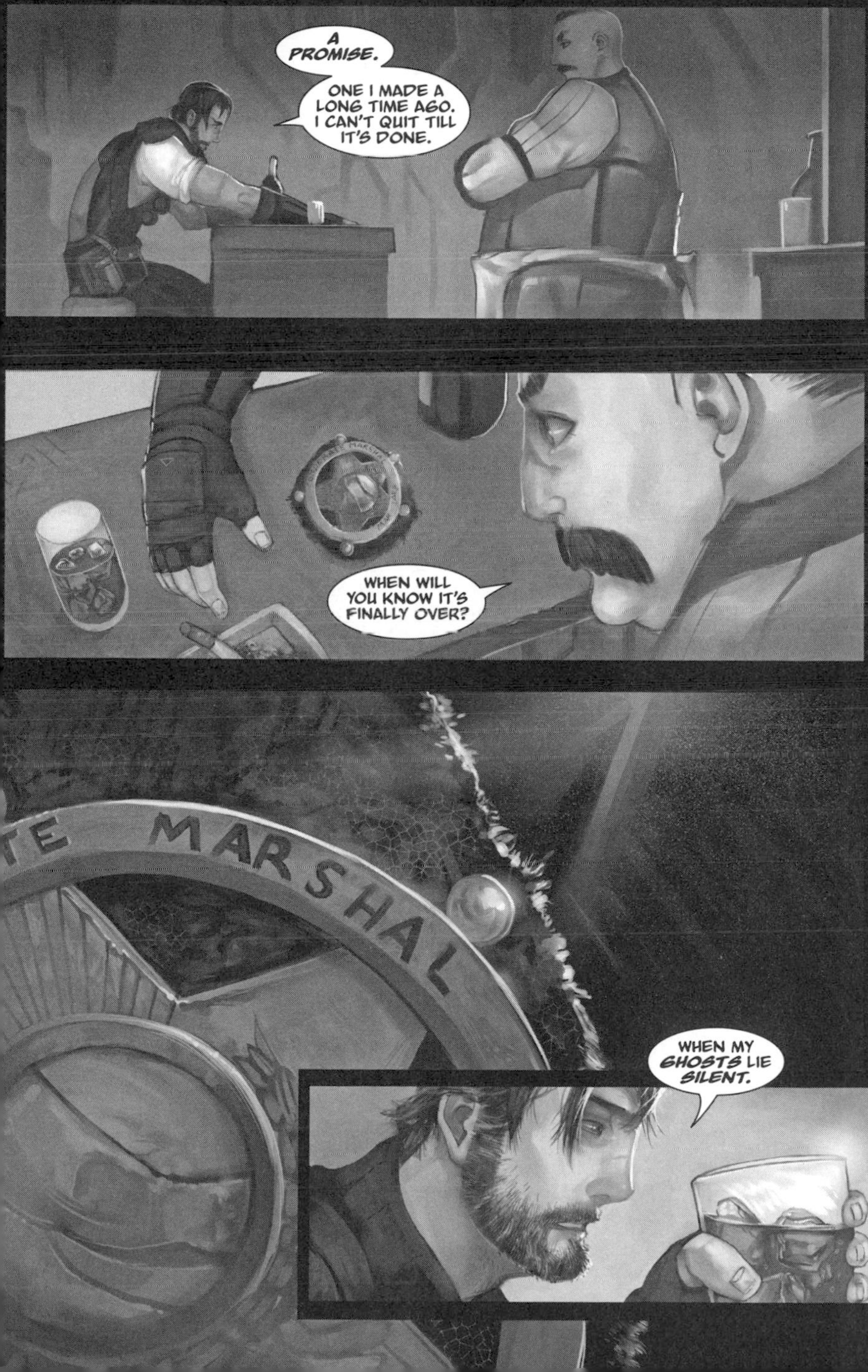
A PROMISE.
ONE I MADE A LONG TIME AGO. I CAN'T QUIT TILL IT'S DONE.
WHEN WILL YOU KNOW IT'S FINALLY OVER?
MARSHAL
WHEN MY *GHOSTS* LIE *SILENT.*

StarCraft

Frontline

Volume 4

Fear the Reaper

Written by David Gerrold

Pencils by Ruben de Vela

Inks by Dan Borgonos

Tones by Gonzalo Duarte

Letterer: Michael Paolilli

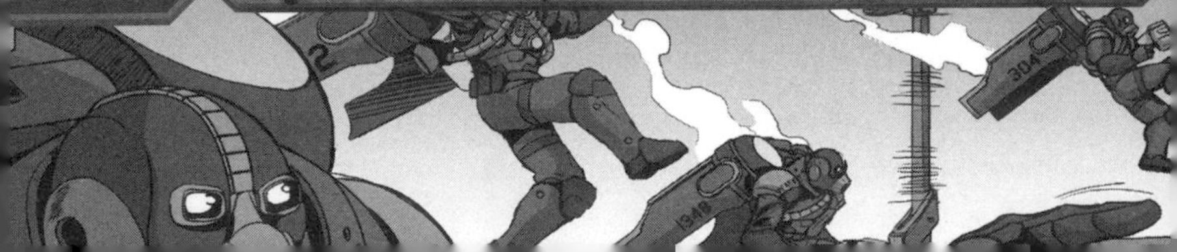

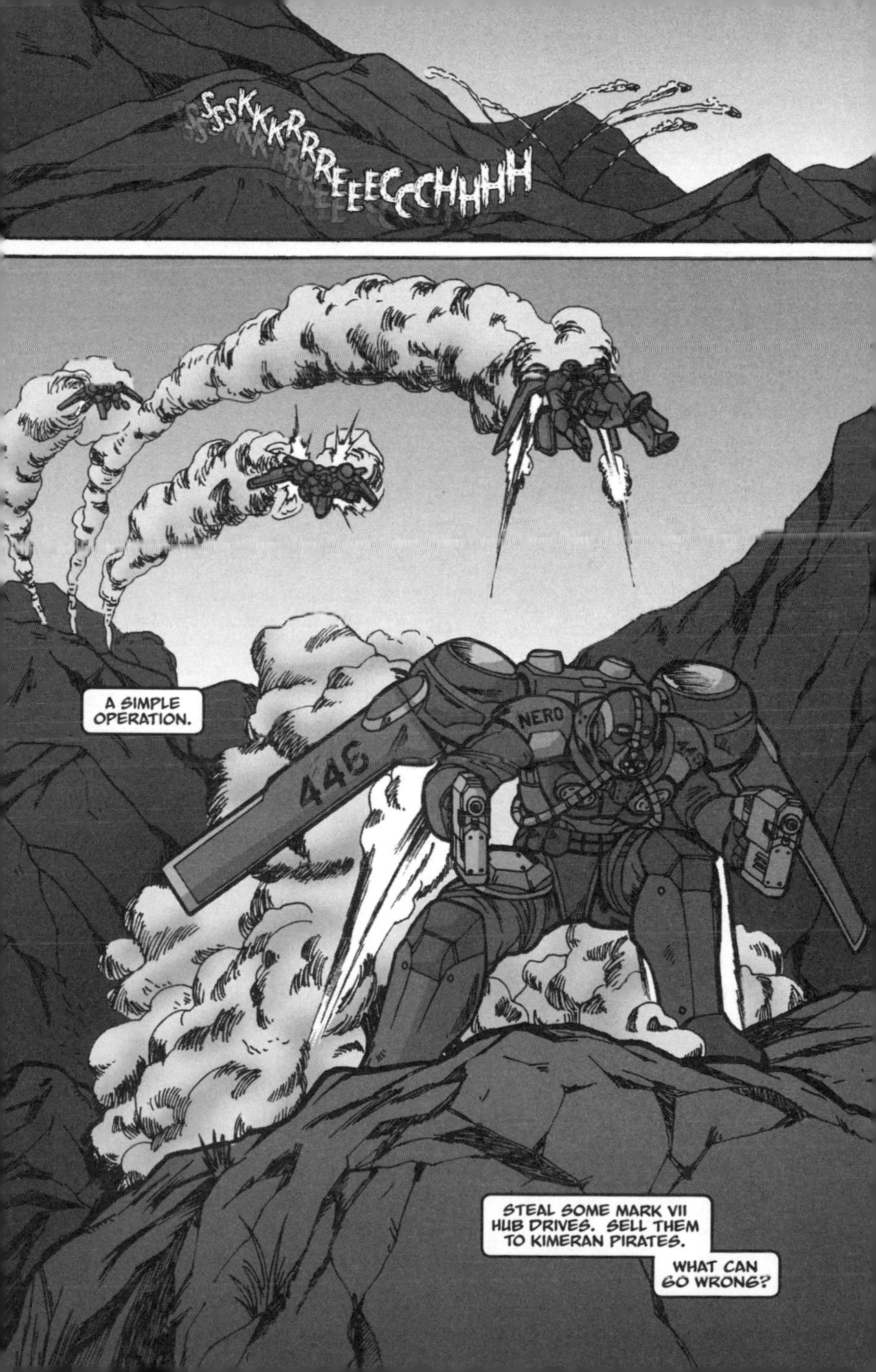
SSSKKKRRREEECCCHHHH
A SIMPLE OPERATION.
NERO
446
STEAL SOME MARK VII HUB DRIVES. SELL THEM TO KIMERAN PIRATES.
WHAT CAN GO WRONG?

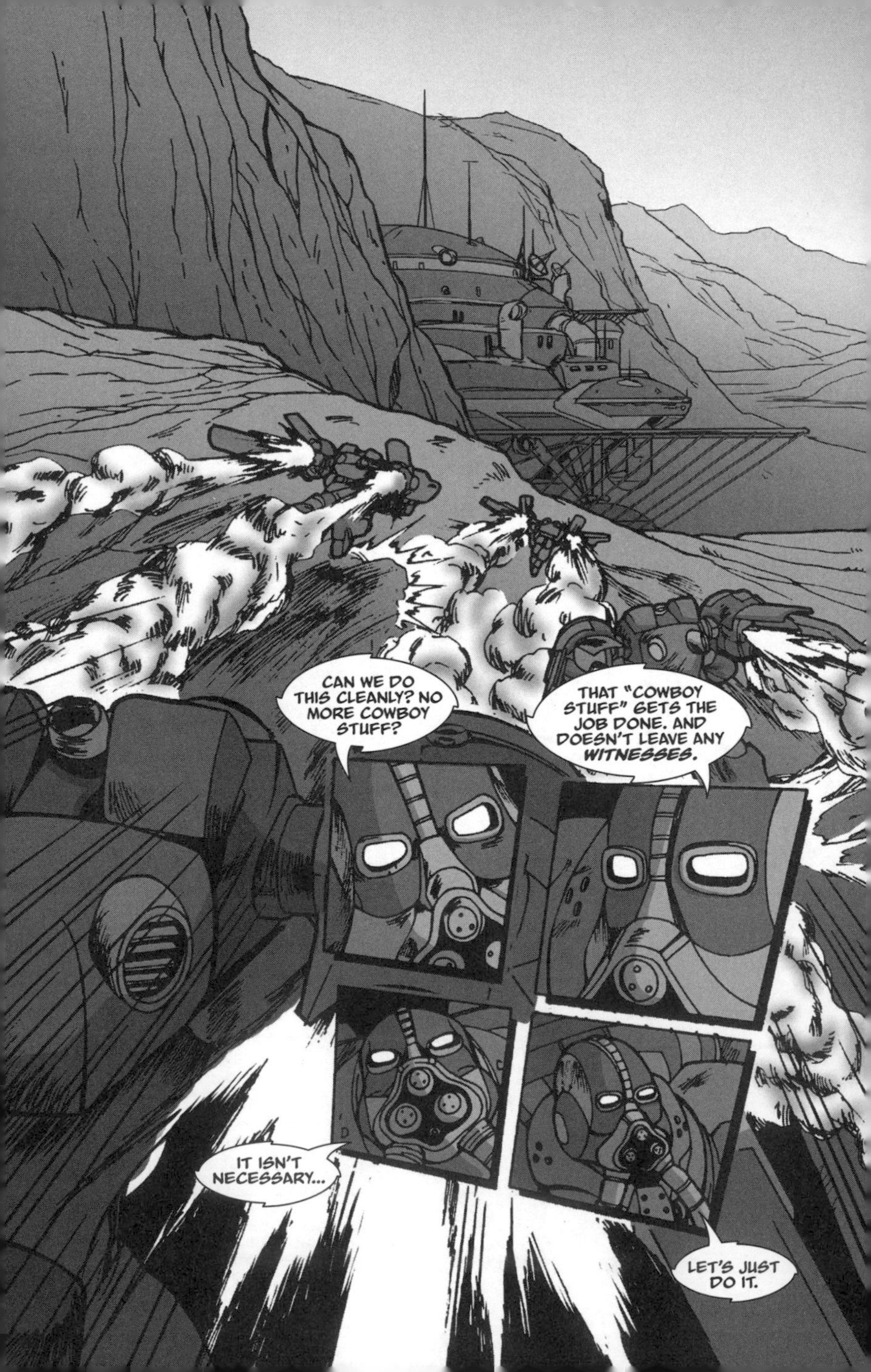
CAN WE DO THIS CLEANLY? NO MORE COWBOY STUFF?
THAT "COWBOY STUFF" GETS THE JOB DONE. AND DOESN'T LEAVE ANY WITNESSES.
IT ISN'T NECESSARY...
LET'S JUST DO IT.

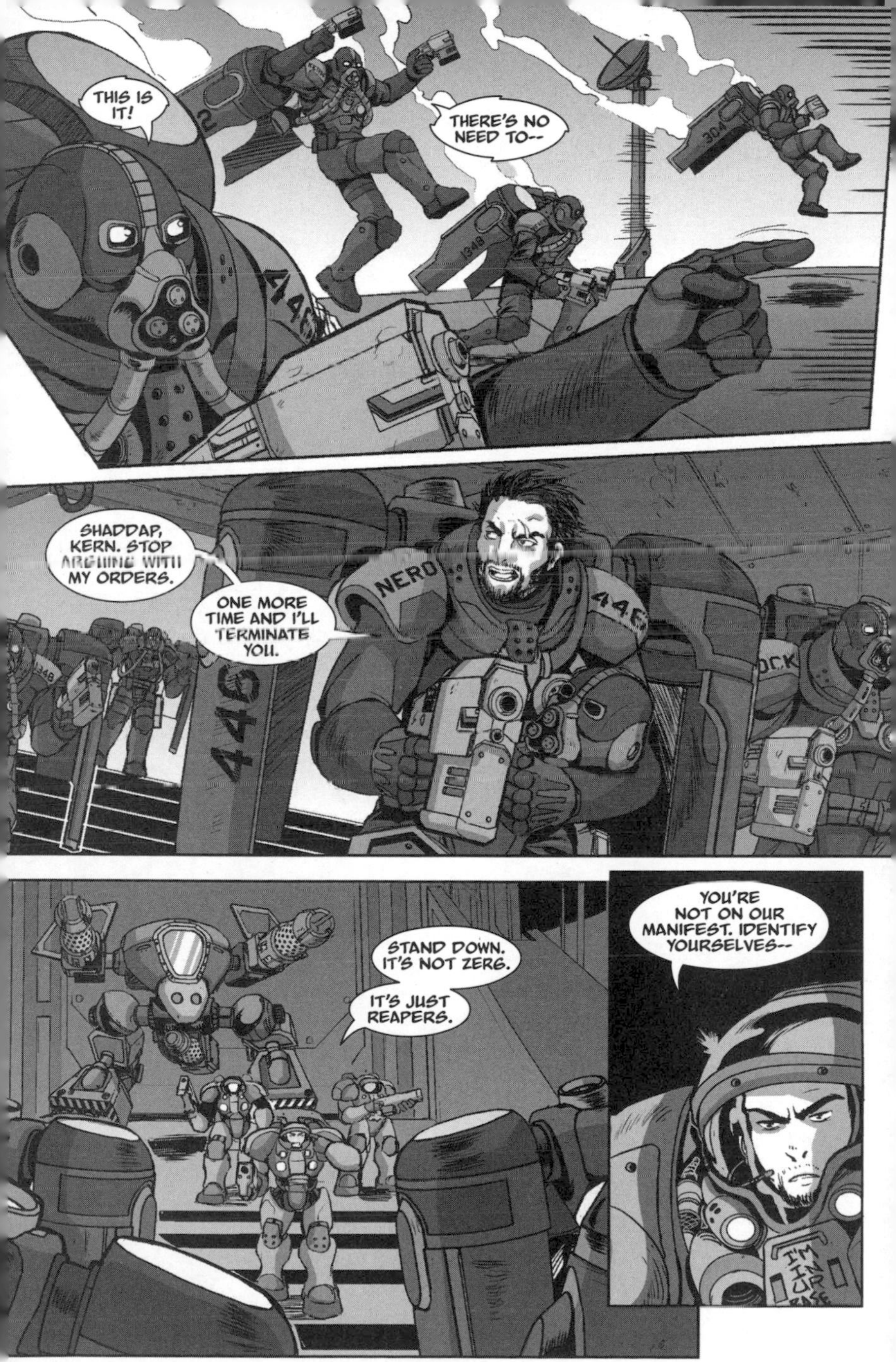
THIS IS IT!
THERE'S NO NEED TO--
SHADDAP, KERN. STOP ARGUING WITH MY ORDERS.
ONE MORE TIME AND I'LL TERMINATE YOU.
STAND DOWN. IT'S NOT ZERG.
IT'S JUST REAPERS.
YOU'RE NOT ON OUR MANIFEST. IDENTIFY YOURSELVES--

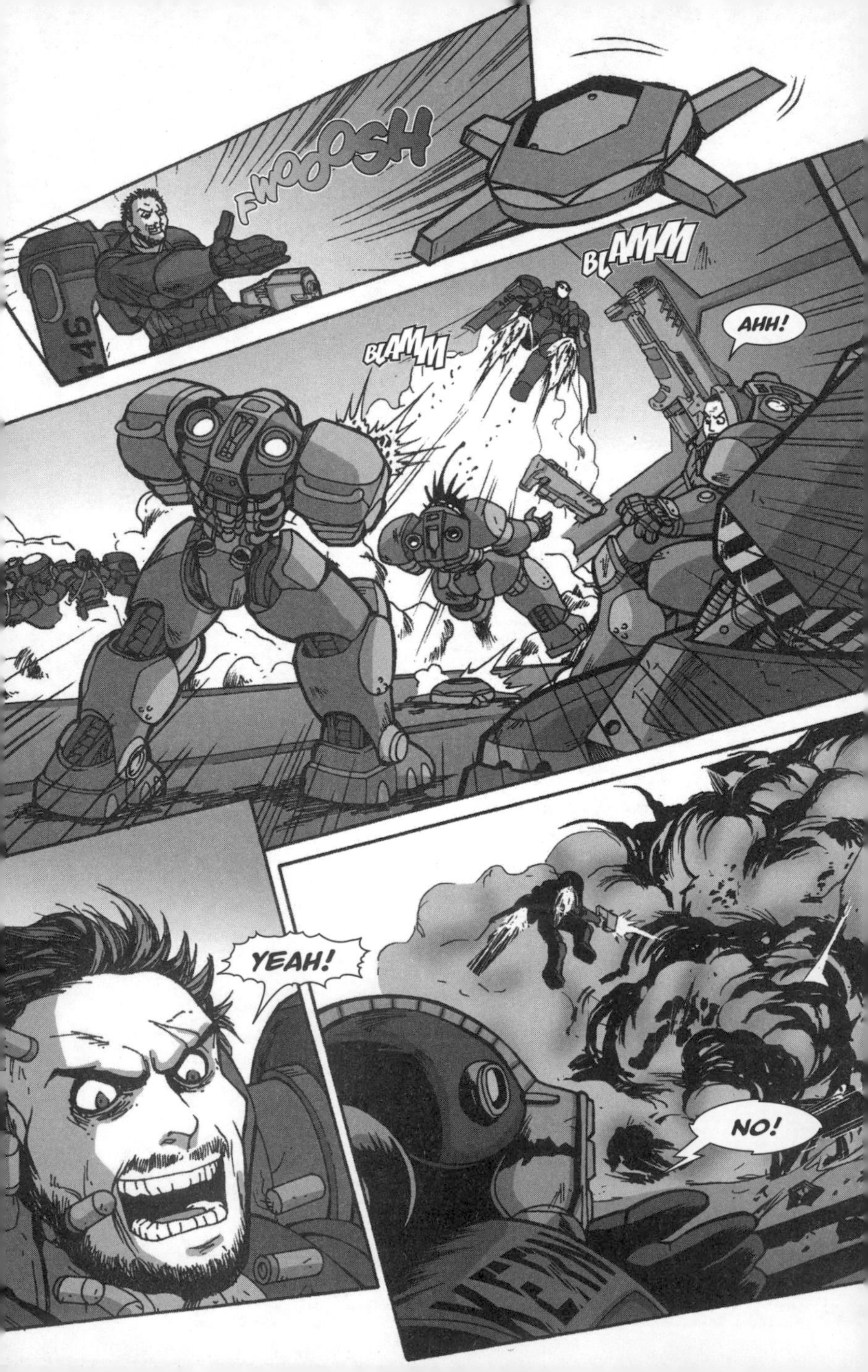
FWOOOSH
BLAMM
BLAMM
AHH!
YEAH!
NO!

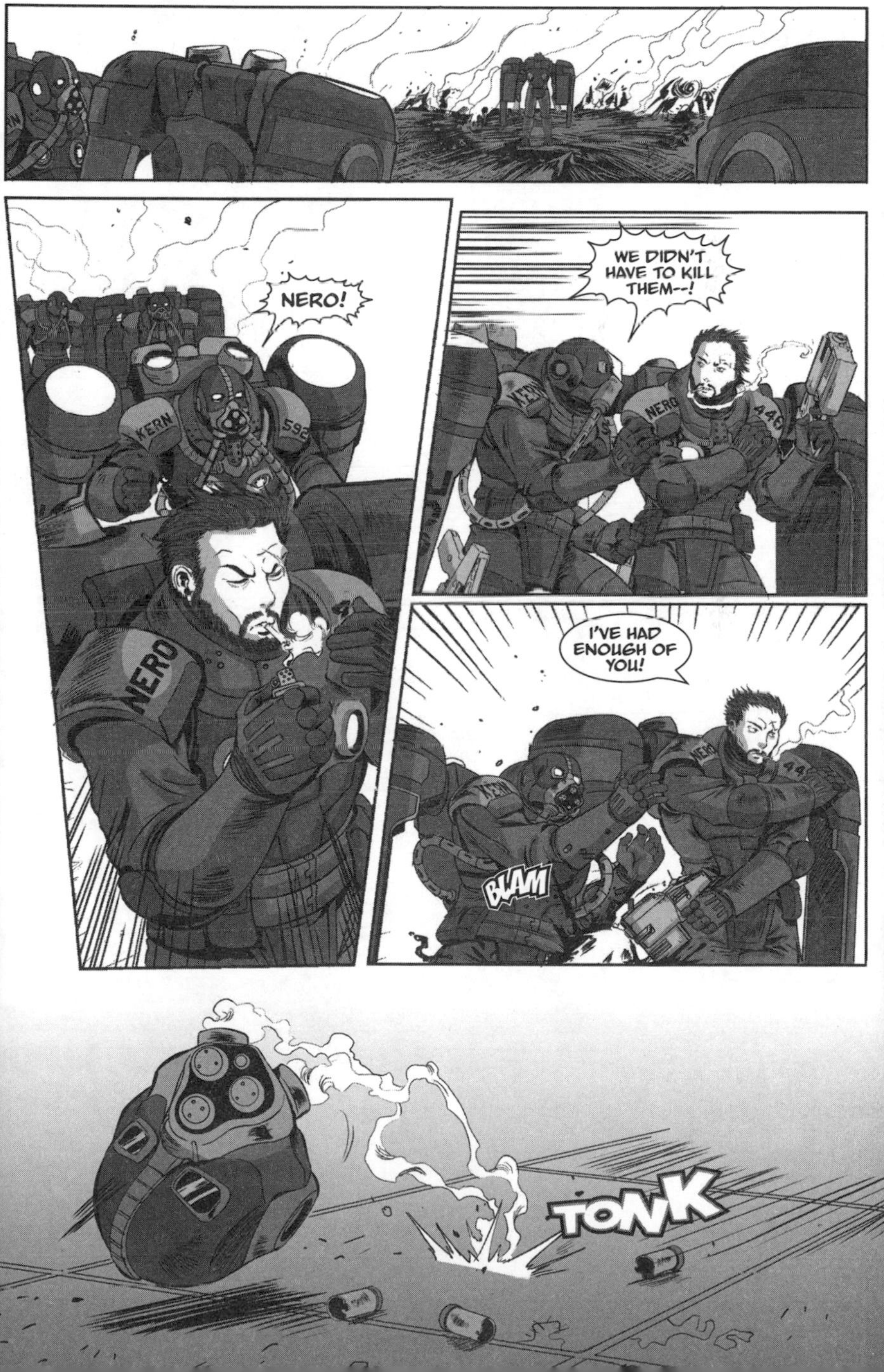

NERO!
WE DIDN'T HAVE TO KILL THEM--!
I'VE HAD ENOUGH OF YOU!
BLAM
TONK

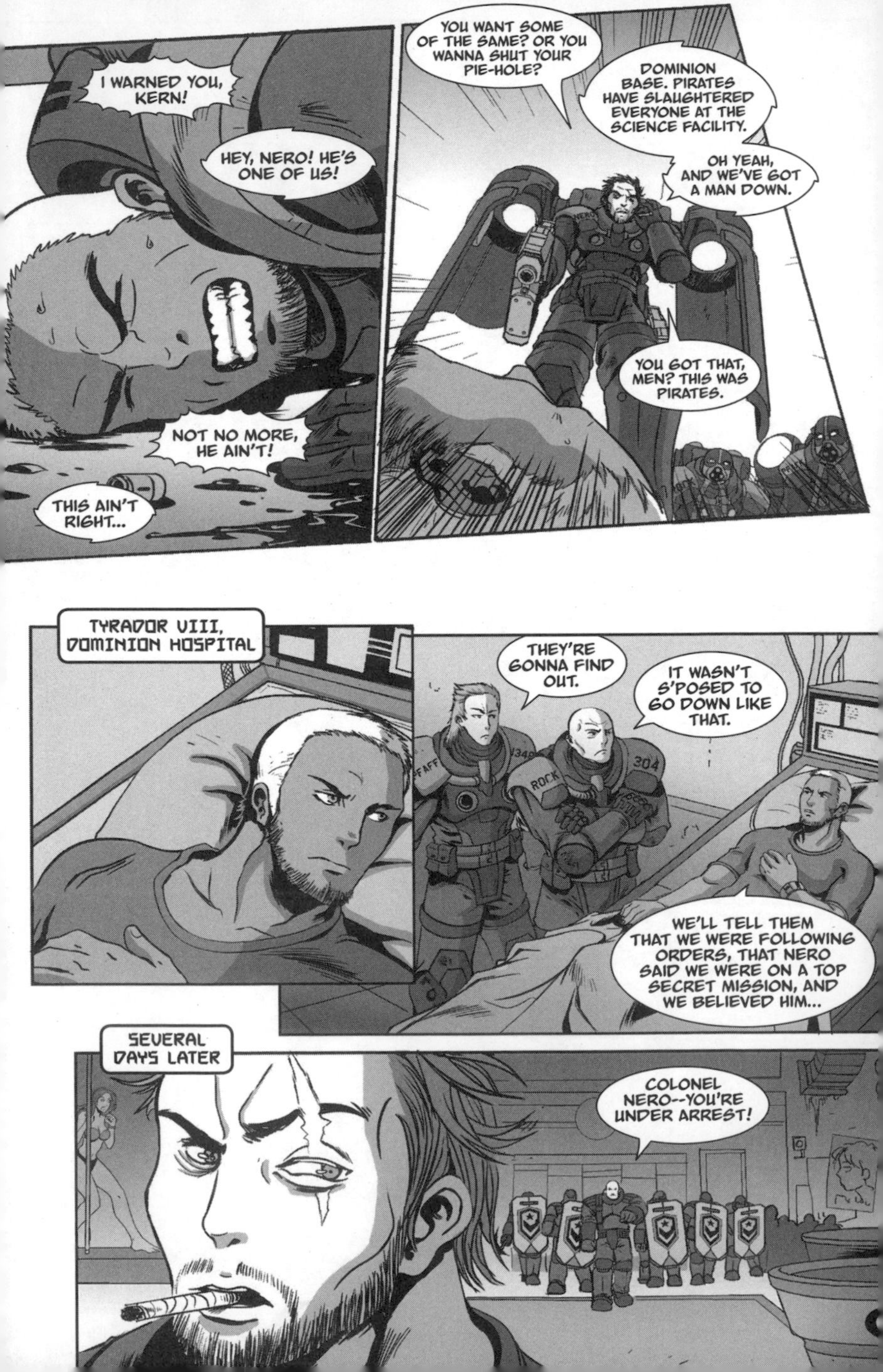
I WARNED YOU, KERN!
HEY, NERO! HE'S ONE OF US!
NOT NO MORE, HE AIN'T!
THIS AIN'T RIGHT...
YOU WANT SOME OF THE SAME? OR YOU WANNA SHUT YOUR PIE-HOLE?
DOMINION BASE. PIRATES HAVE SLAUGHTERED EVERYONE AT THE SCIENCE FACILITY.
OH YEAH, AND WE'VE GOT A MAN DOWN.
YOU GOT THAT, MEN? THIS WAS PIRATES.
TYRADOR VIII, DOMINION HOSPITAL
THEY'RE GONNA FIND OUT.
IT WASN'T S'POSED TO GO DOWN LIKE THAT.
WE'LL TELL THEM THAT WE WERE FOLLOWING ORDERS, THAT NERO SAID WE WERE ON A TOP SECRET MISSION, AND WE BELIEVED HIM...
SEVERAL DAYS LATER
COLONEL NERO--YOU'RE UNDER ARREST!

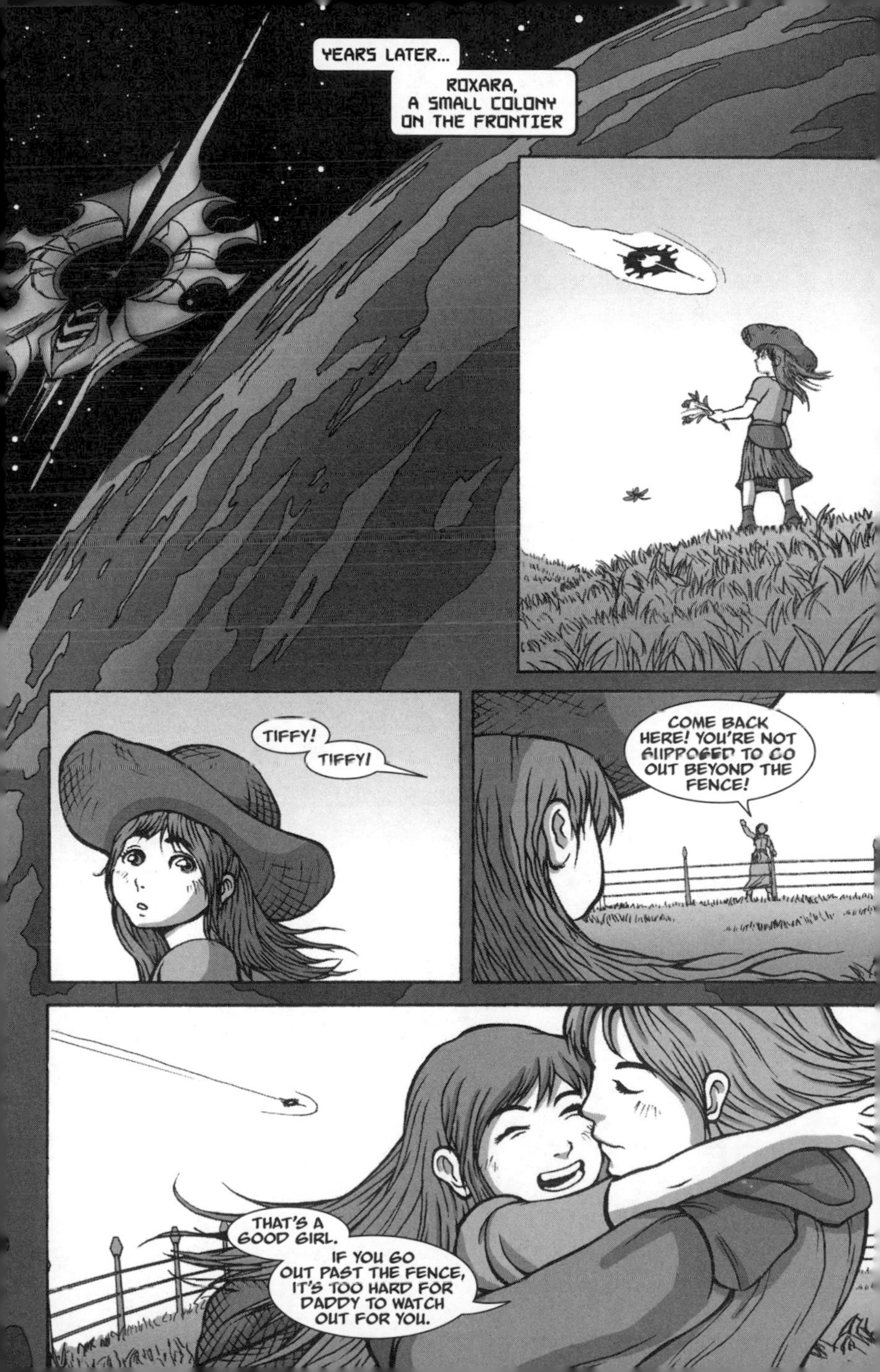
YEARS LATER...
ROXARA, A SMALL COLONY ON THE FRONTIER
TIFFY!
TIFFY!
COME BACK HERE! YOU'RE NOT SUPPOSED TO GO OUT BEYOND THE FENCE!
THAT'S A GOOD GIRL.
IF YOU GO OUT PAST THE FENCE, IT'S TOO HARD FOR DADDY TO WATCH OUT FOR YOU.

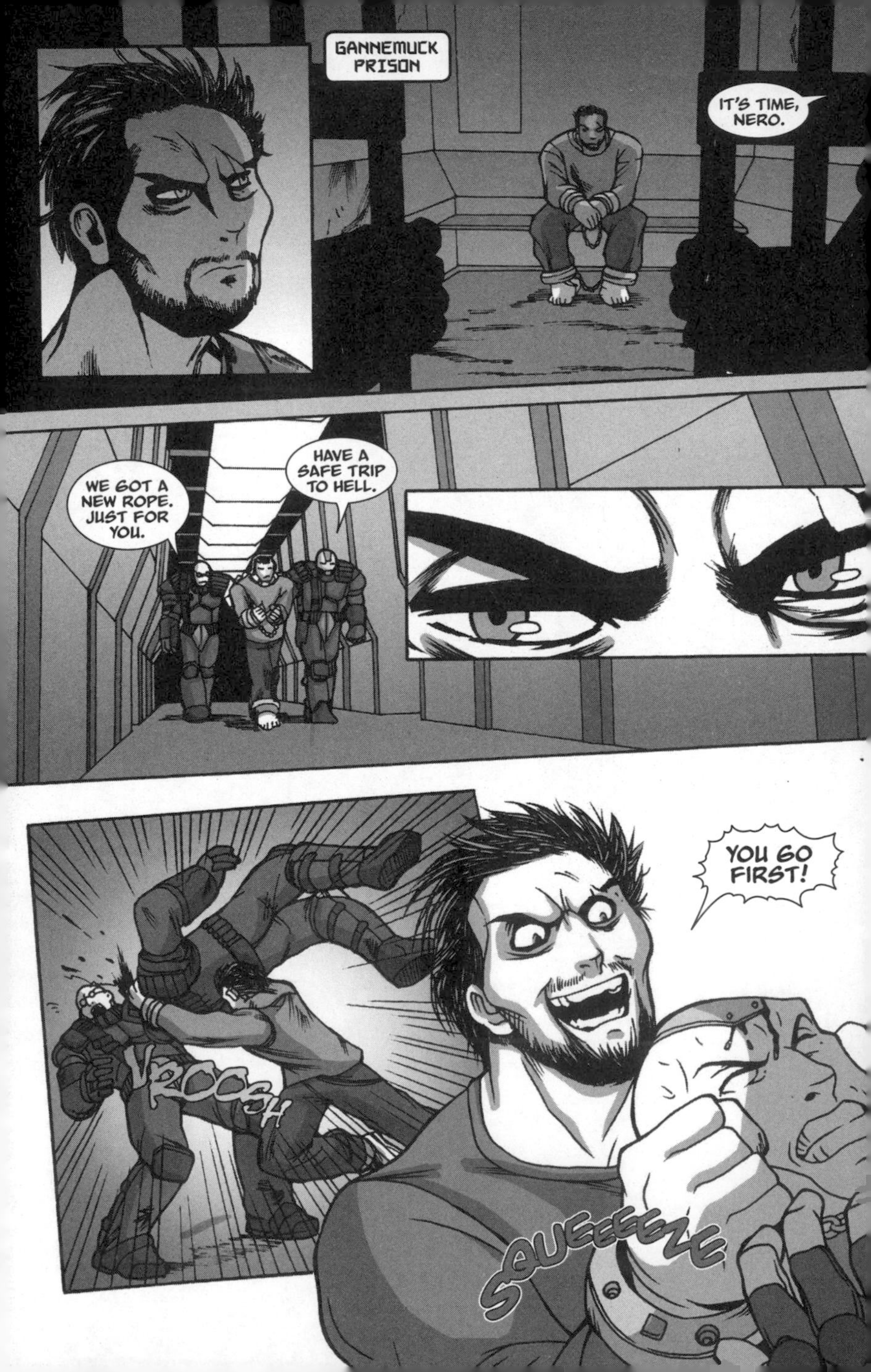
GANNEMUCK PRISON
IT'S TIME, NERO.
WE GOT A NEW ROPE. JUST FOR YOU.
HAVE A SAFE TRIP TO HELL.
YOU GO FIRST!
VROOSH
SQUEEEEEZE

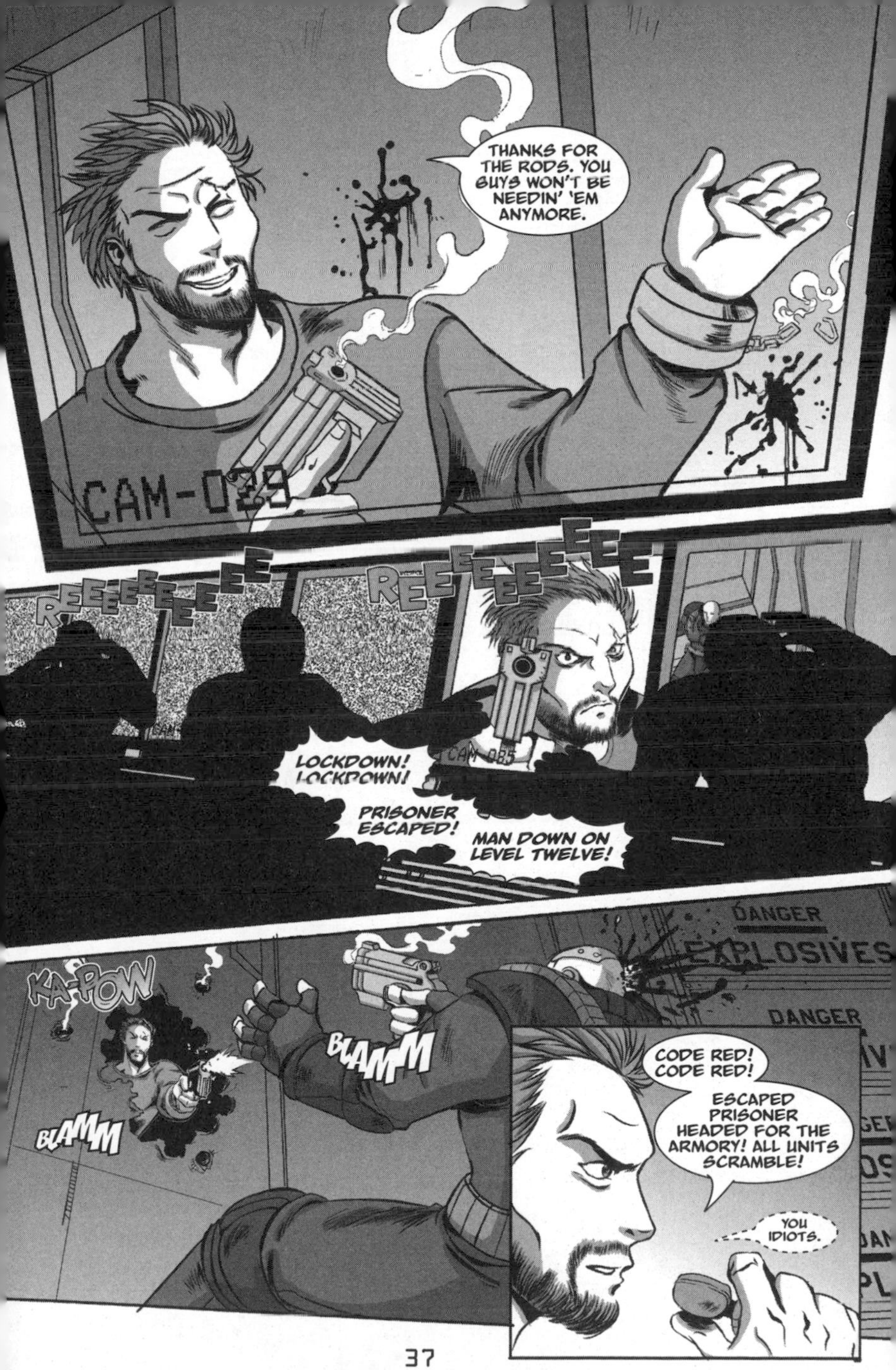
THANKS FOR THE RODS. YOU GUYS WON'T BE NEEDIN' 'EM ANYMORE.
CAM-028
REEEEEEEEEE
REEEEEEEEEEEE
LOCKDOWN! LOCKDOWN!
PRISONER ESCAPED!
MAN DOWN ON LEVEL TWELVE!
DANGER
EXPLOSIVES
DANGER
KA-POW
BLAMMM
BLAMMM
CODE RED! CODE RED!
ESCAPED PRISONER HEADED FOR THE ARMORY! ALL UNITS SCRAMBLE!
YOU IDIOTS.

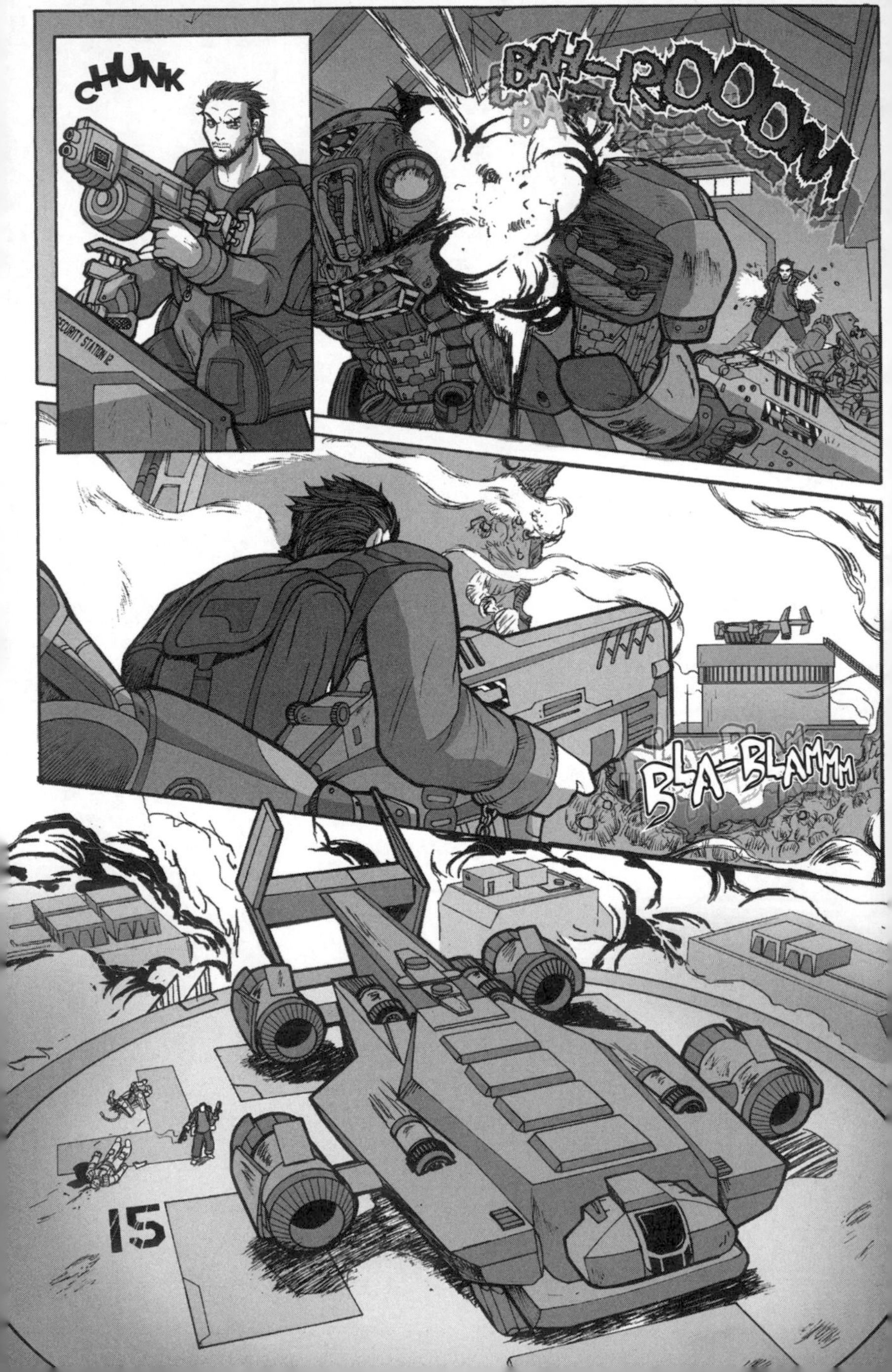
CHUNK
SECURITY STATION 12
BAH-ROOOM
BLA-BLAMMM
15

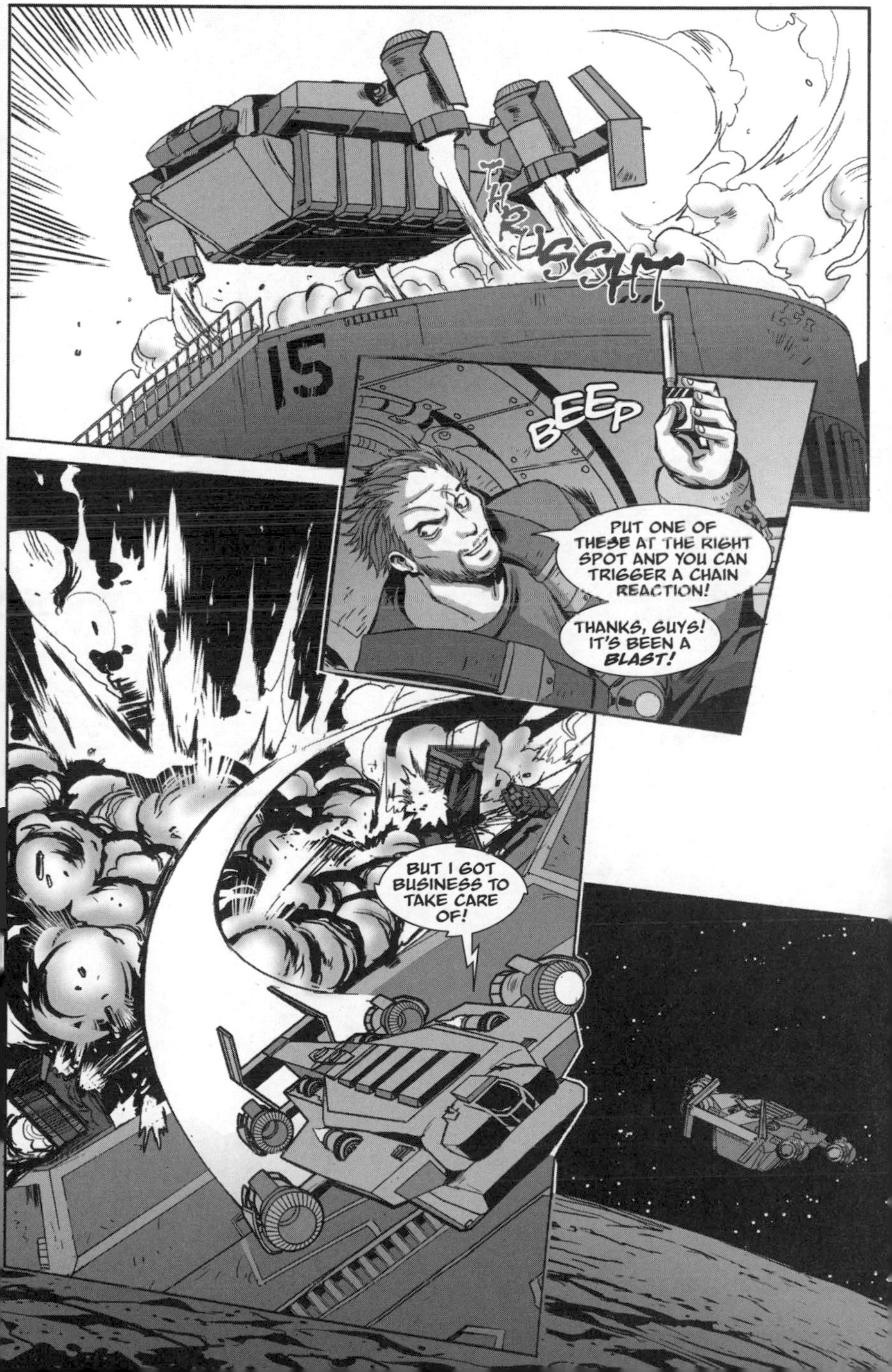
THRUSSHT
BEEP
PUT ONE OF THESE AT THE RIGHT SPOT AND YOU CAN TRIGGER A CHAIN REACTION!
THANKS, GUYS! IT'S BEEN A *BLAST*!
BUT I GOT BUSINESS TO TAKE CARE OF!

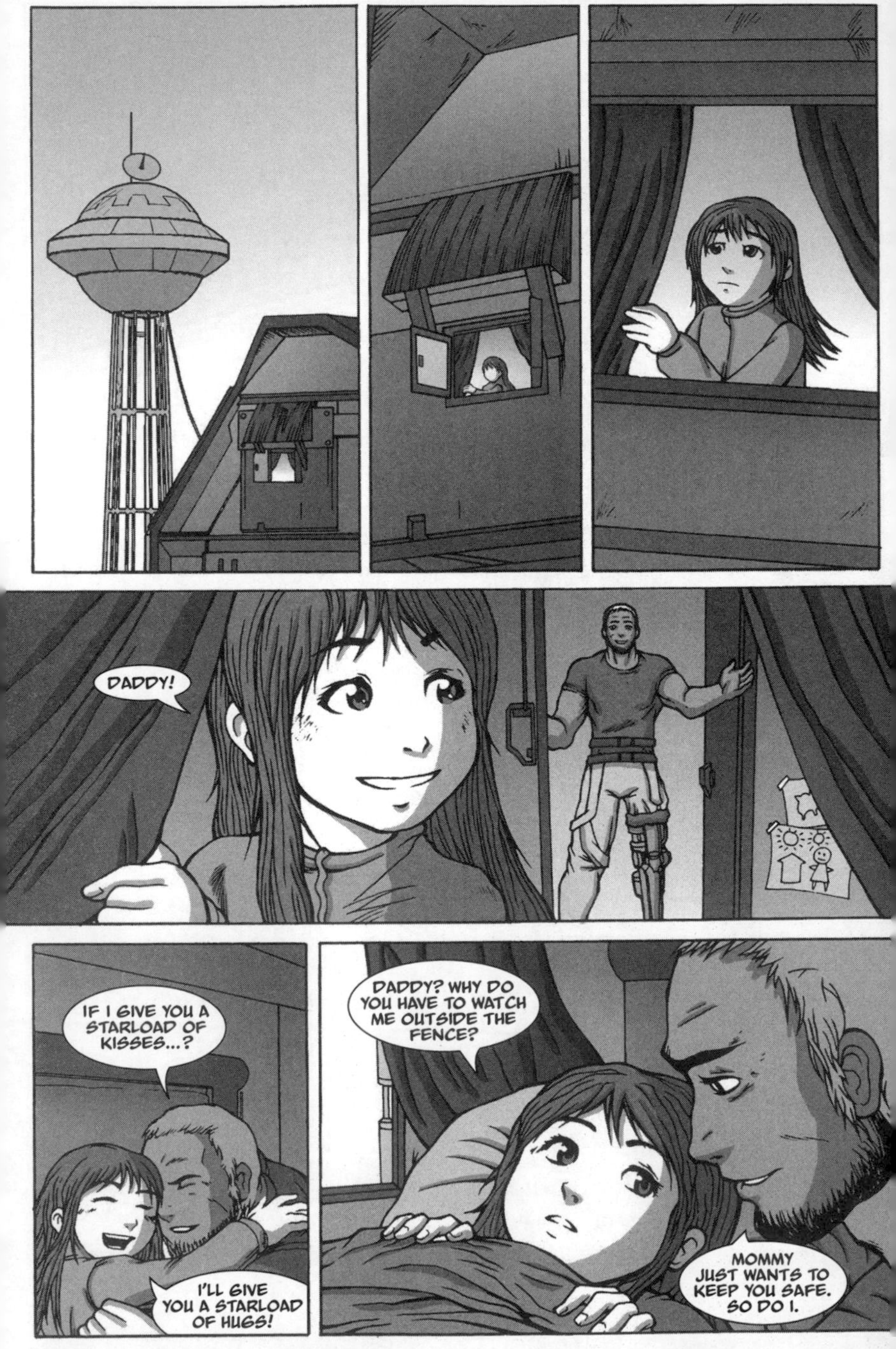
DADDY!
IF I GIVE YOU A STARLOAD OF KISSES...?
I'LL GIVE YOU A STARLOAD OF HUGS!
DADDY? WHY DO YOU HAVE TO WATCH ME OUTSIDE THE FENCE?
MOMMY JUST WANTS TO KEEP YOU SAFE. SO DO I.

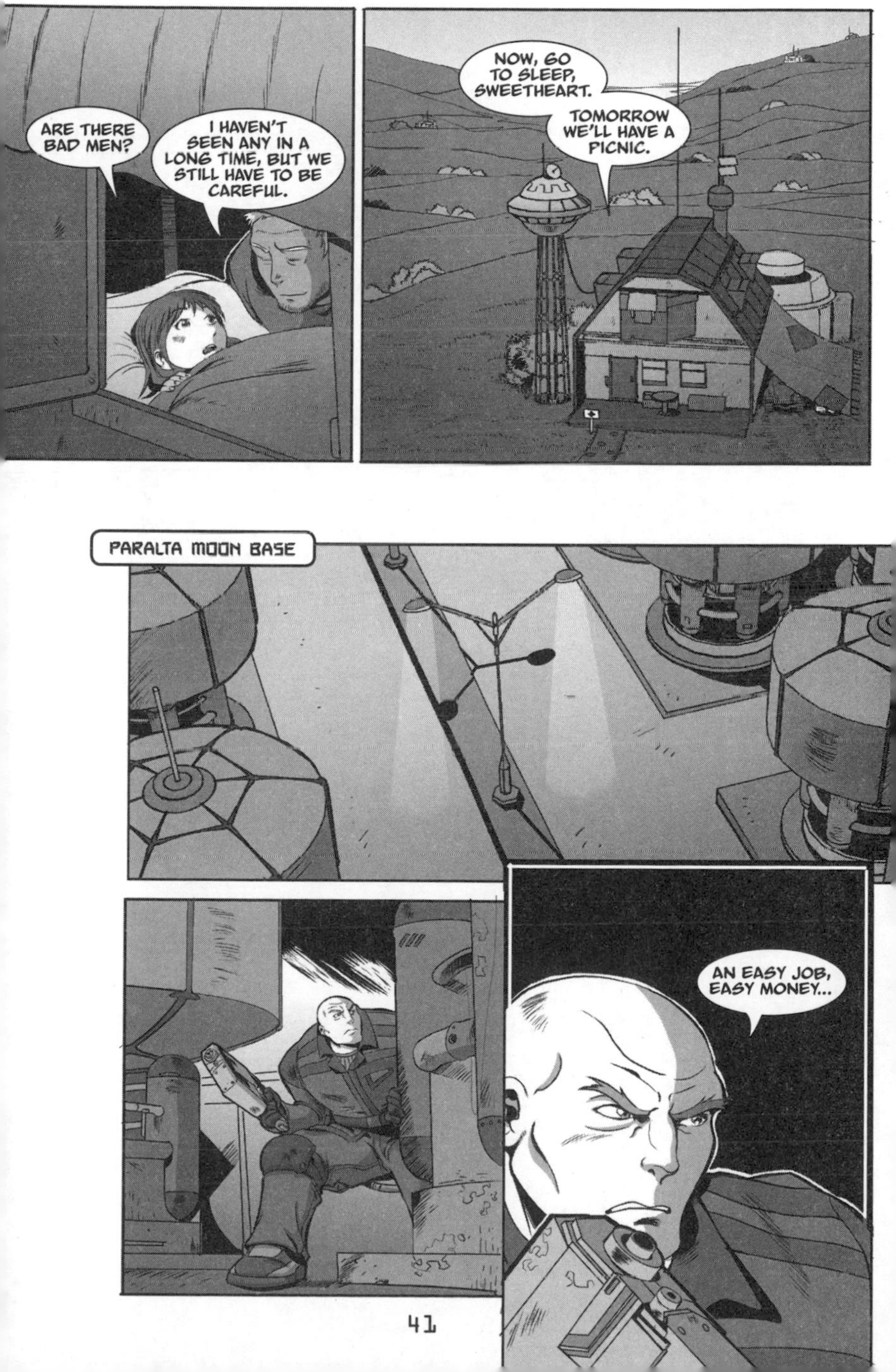
ARE THERE BAD MEN?
I HAVEN'T SEEN ANY IN A LONG TIME, BUT WE STILL HAVE TO BE CAREFUL.
NOW, GO TO SLEEP, SWEETHEART.
TOMORROW WE'LL HAVE A PICNIC.
PARALTA MOON BASE
AN EASY JOB, EASY MONEY...

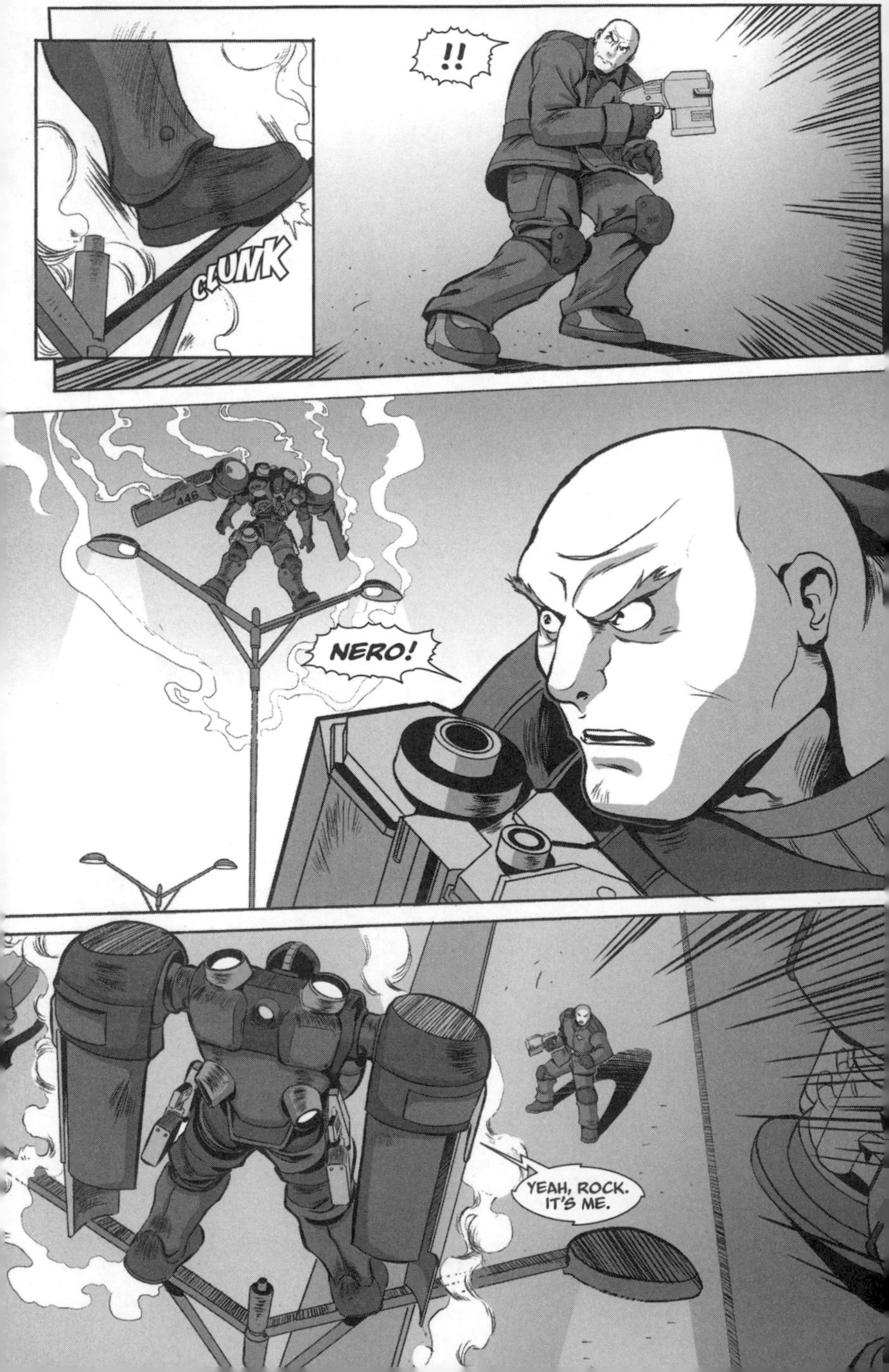

CLUNK
!!
NERO!
YEAH, ROCK. IT'S ME.

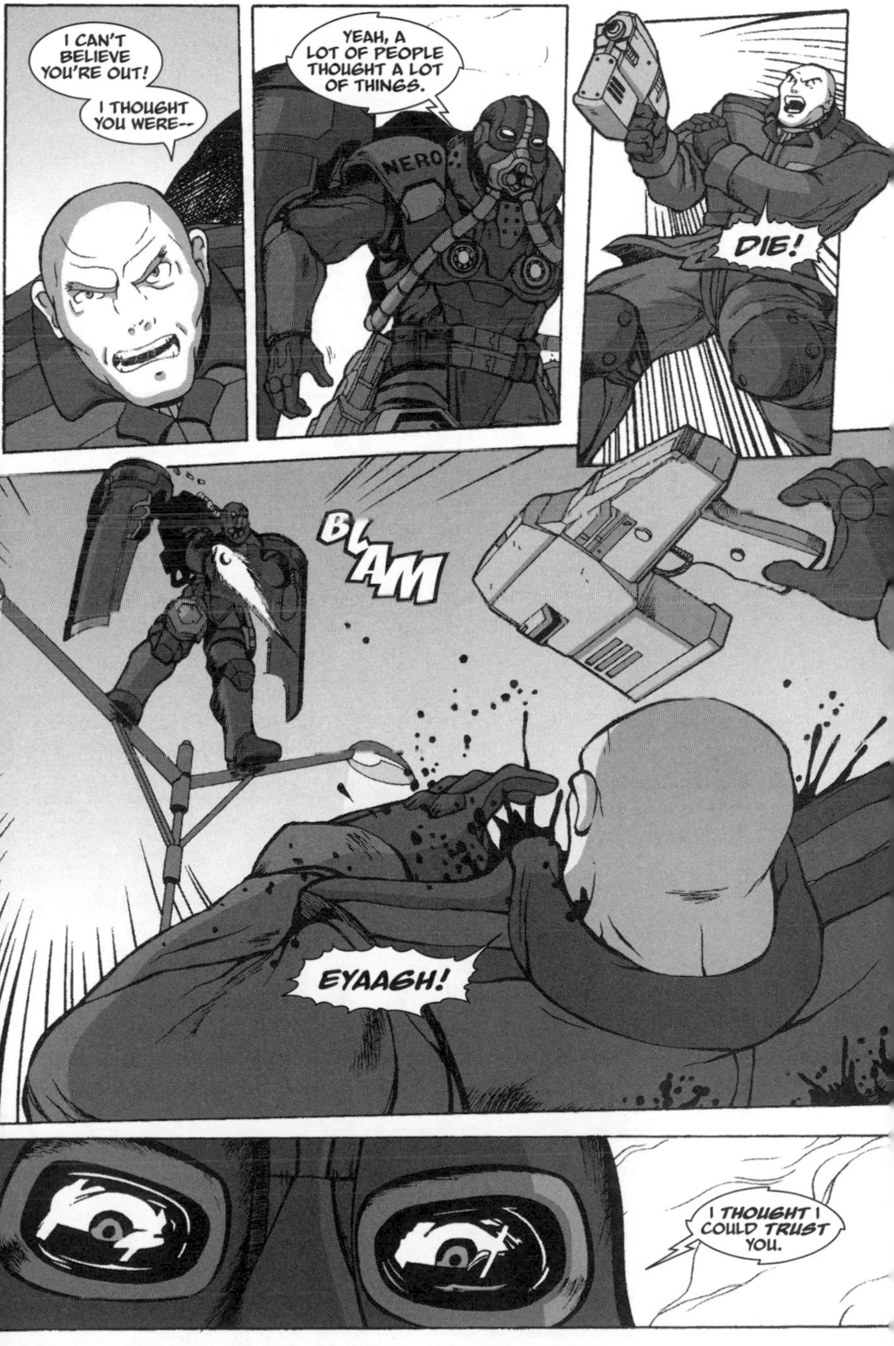
I CAN'T BELIEVE YOU'RE OUT!
I THOUGHT YOU WERE--
YEAH, A LOT OF PEOPLE THOUGHT A LOT OF THINGS.
NERO
DIE!
BLAM
EYAAGH!
I THOUGHT I COULD TRUST YOU.

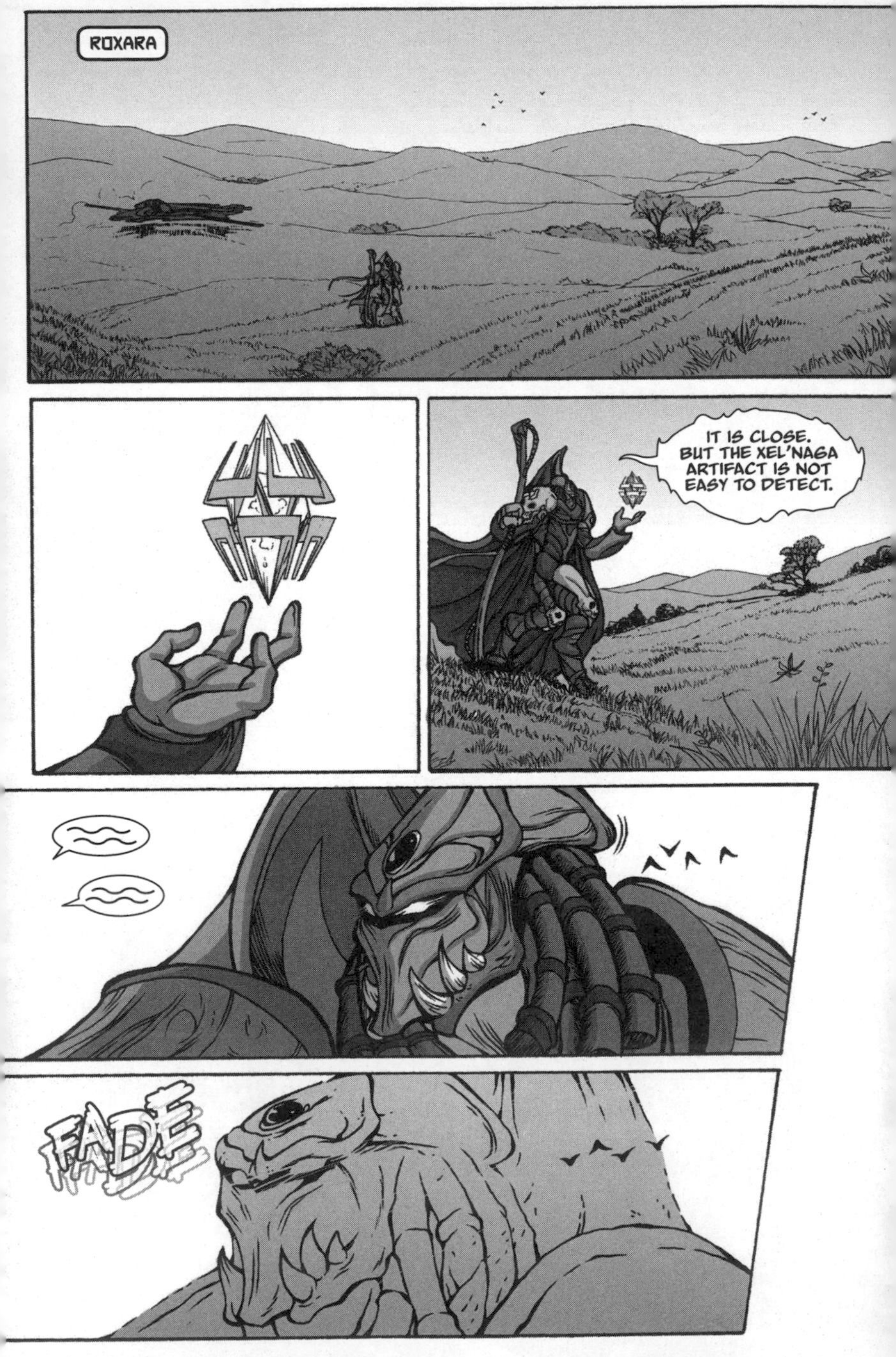
ROXARA
IT IS CLOSE. BUT THE XEL'NAGA ARTIFACT IS NOT EASY TO DETECT.
FADE

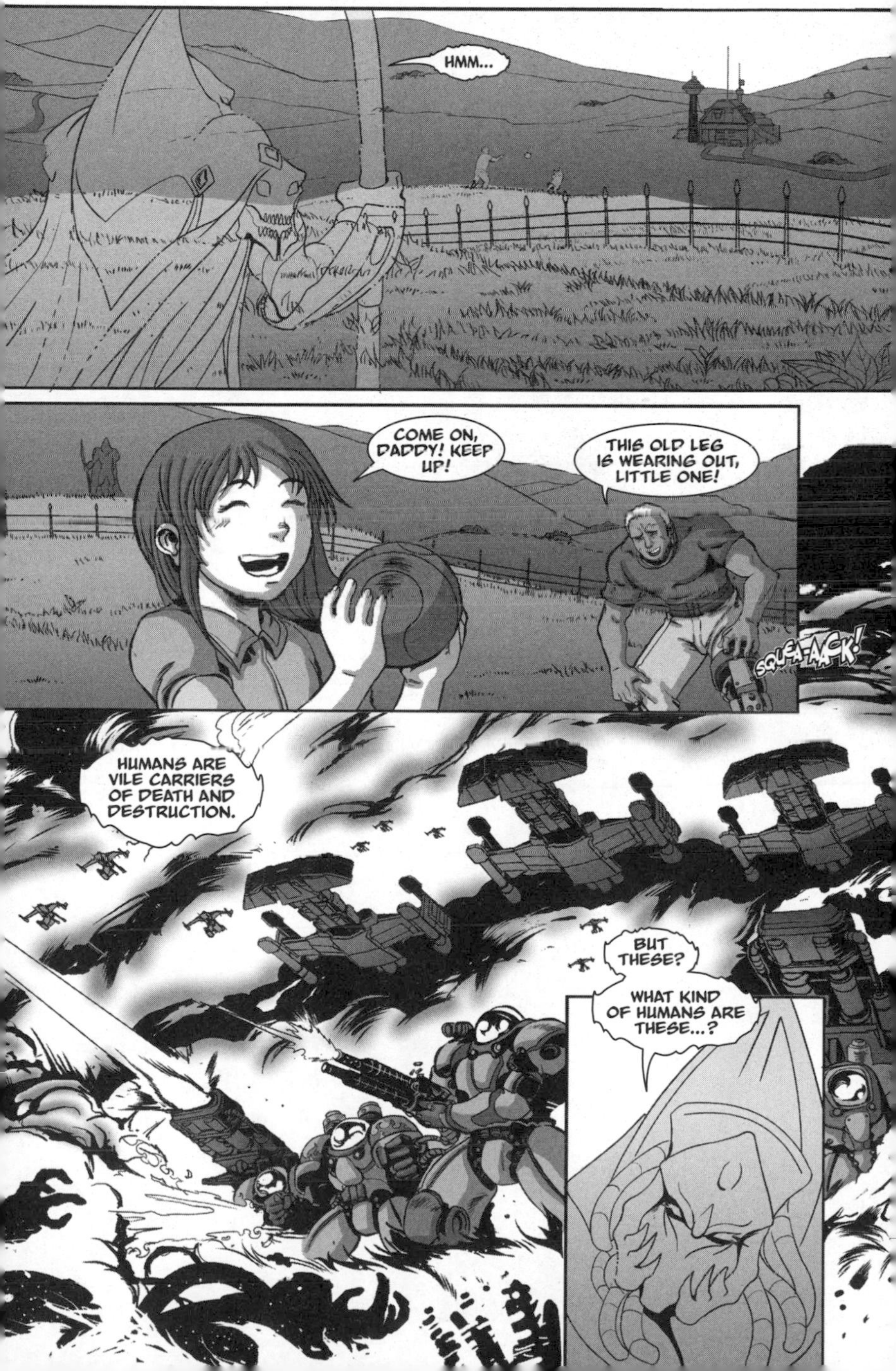
HMM...
COME ON, DADDY! KEEP UP!
THIS OLD LEG IS WEARING OUT, LITTLE ONE!
SQUEA-AACK!
HUMANS ARE VILE CARRIERS OF DEATH AND DESTRUCTION.
BUT THESE?
WHAT KIND OF HUMANS ARE THESE...?

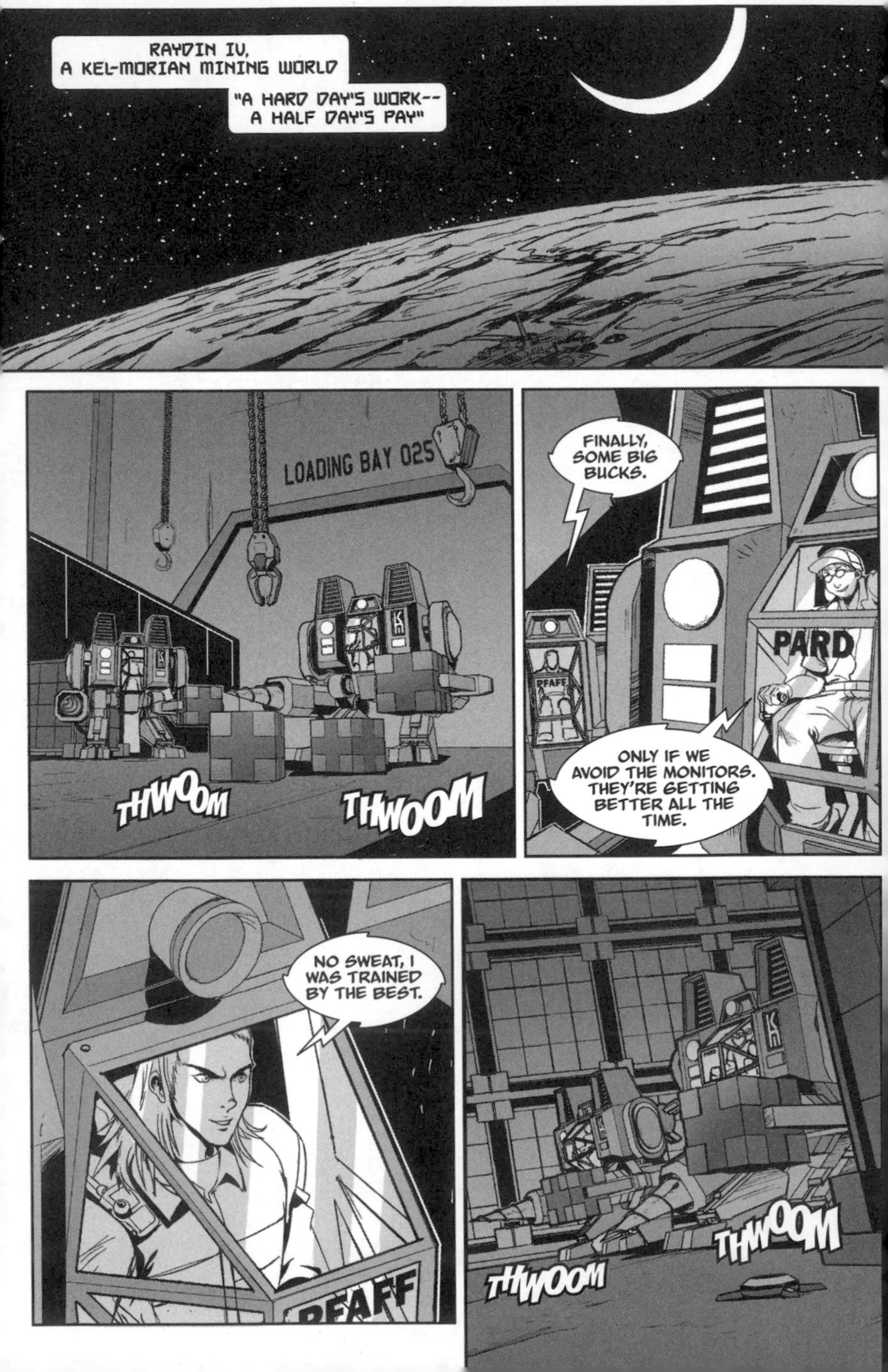
RAYDIN IV,
A KEL-MORIAN MINING WORLD
"A HARD DAY'S WORK--
A HALF DAY'S PAY"
LOADING BAY 025
THWOOM
THWOOM
FINALLY, SOME BIG BUCKS.
PARD
RFAFF
ONLY IF WE AVOID THE MONITORS. THEY'RE GETTING BETTER ALL THE TIME.
NO SWEAT, I WAS TRAINED BY THE BEST.
RFAFF
THWOOM
THWOOM

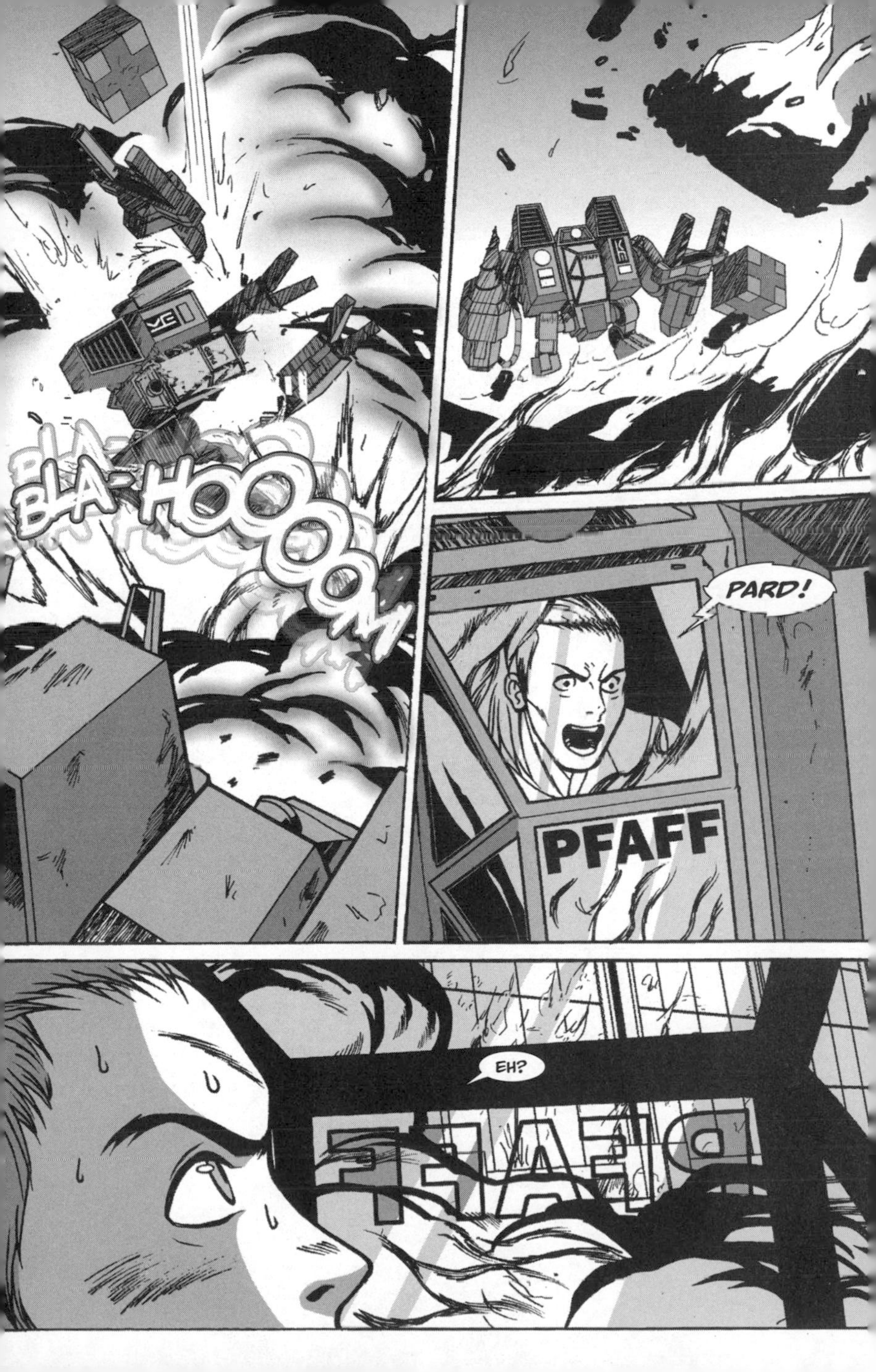
BLA-HOOOOOM
PARD!
PFAFF
EH?

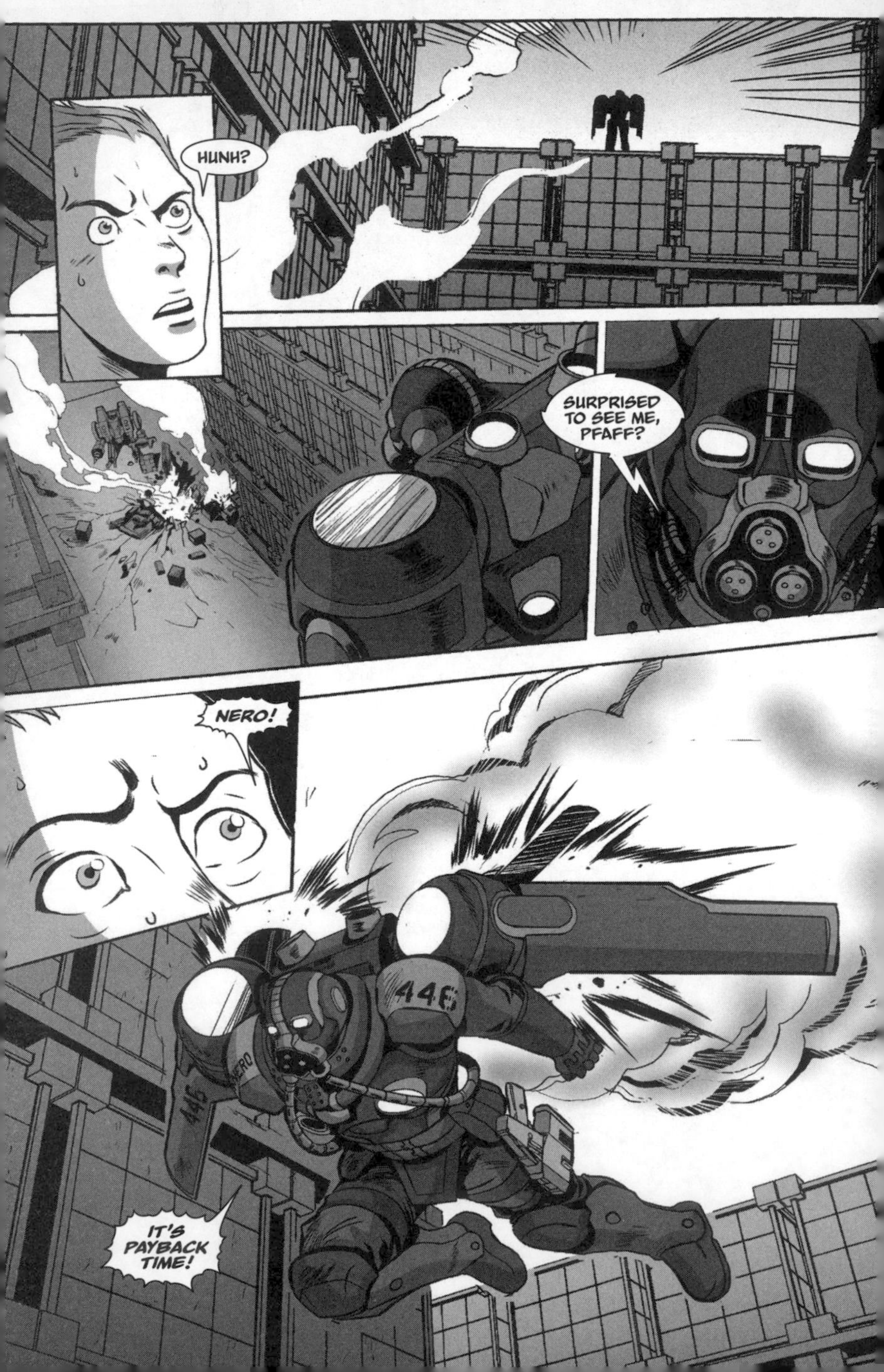
HUNH?
SURPRISED TO SEE ME, PFAFF?
NERO!
IT'S PAYBACK TIME!

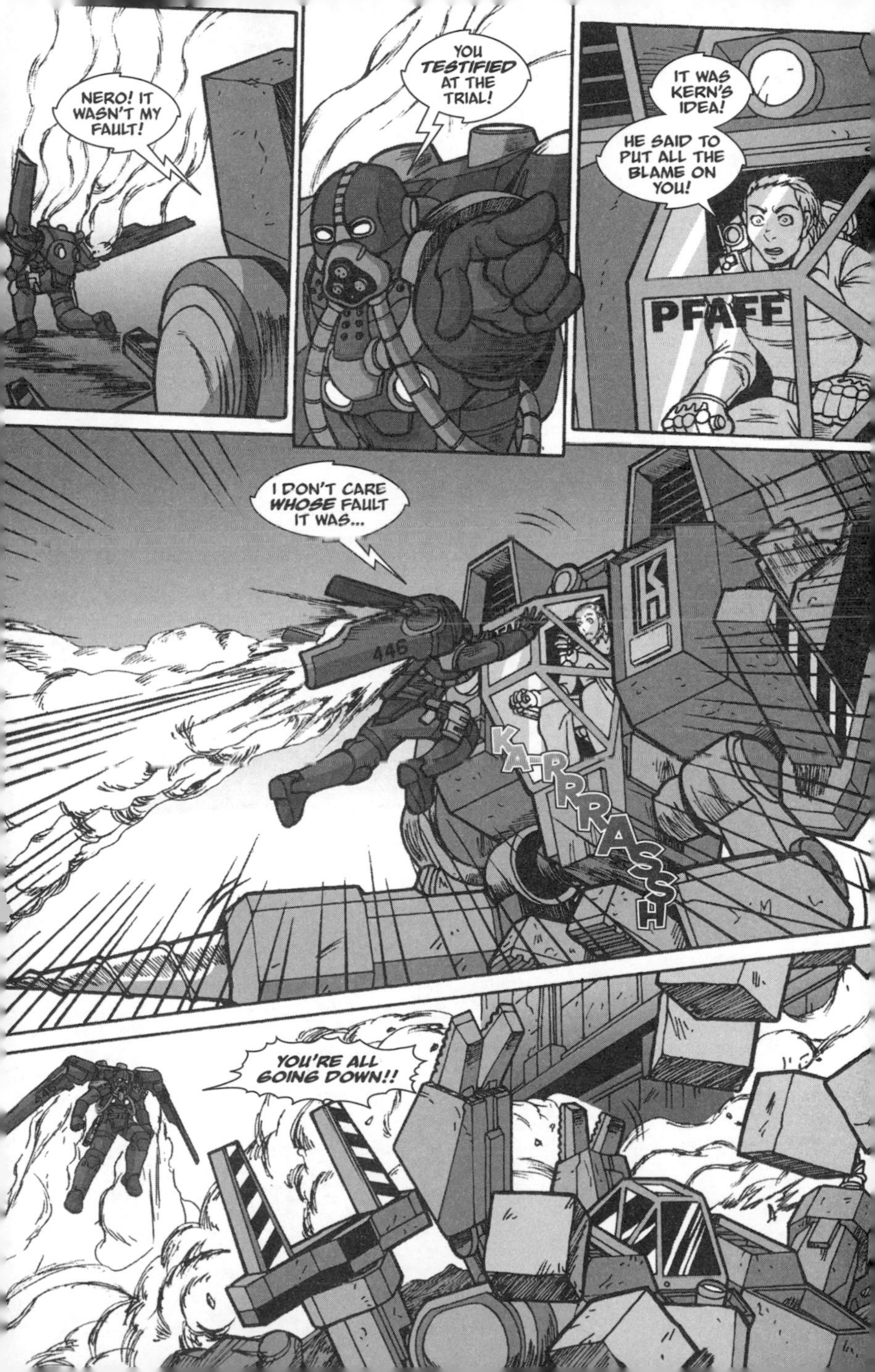
NERO! IT WASN'T MY FAULT!
YOU *TESTIFIED* AT THE TRIAL!
IT WAS KERN'S IDEA!
HE SAID TO PUT ALL THE BLAME ON YOU!
PFAFF
I DON'T CARE *WHOSE* FAULT IT WAS...
446
KA-RRRASSH
YOU'RE ALL GOING DOWN!!

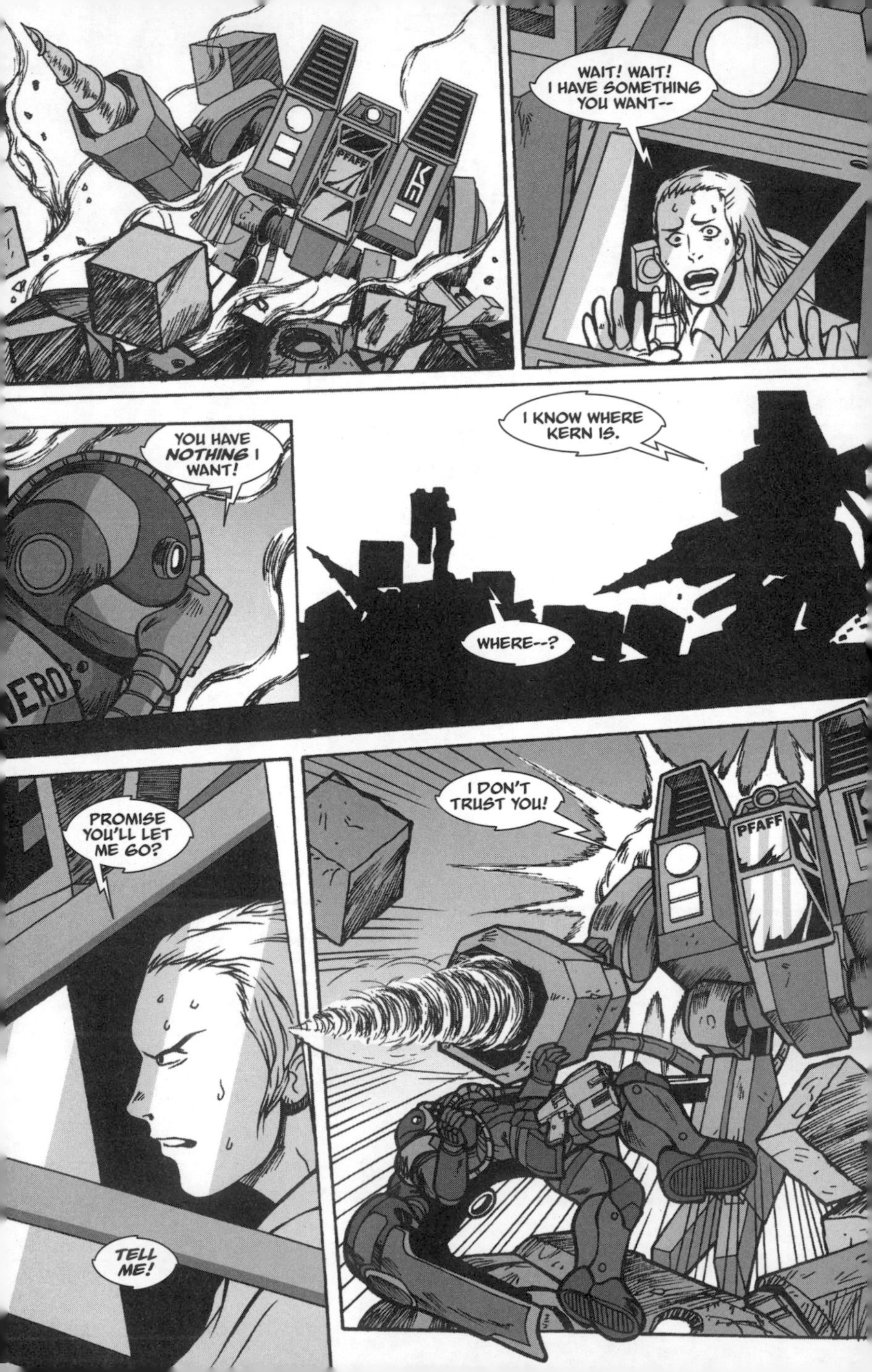
PFAFF
WAIT! WAIT! I HAVE SOMETHING YOU WANT--
YOU HAVE NOTHING I WANT!
ERO
I KNOW WHERE KERN IS.
WHERE--?
PROMISE YOU'LL LET ME GO?
TELL ME!
I DON'T TRUST YOU!
PFAFF

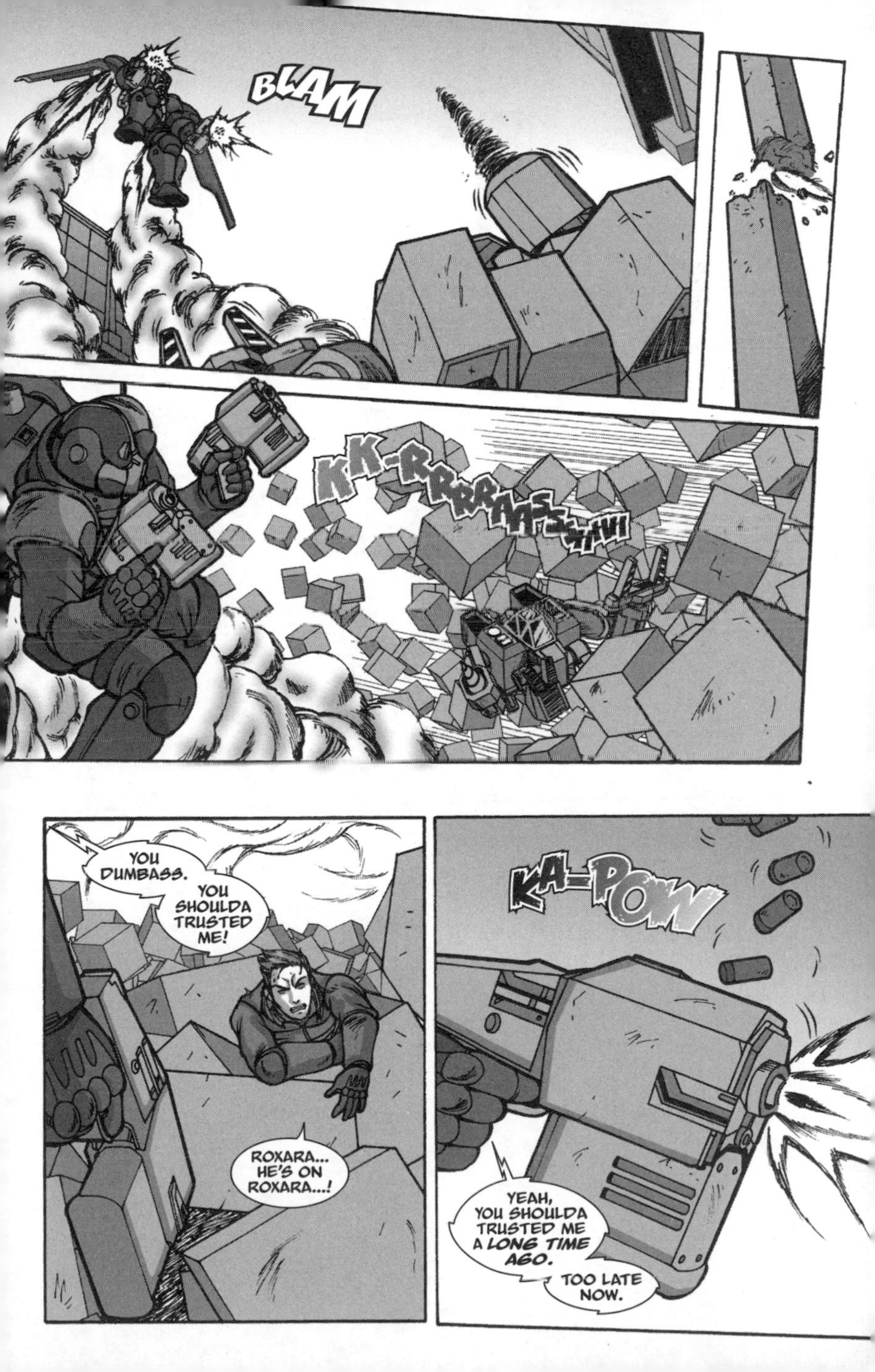
BLAM
KK-RRRRAASSHHH
YOU DUMBASS.
YOU SHOULDA TRUSTED ME!
ROXARA... HE'S ON ROXARA...!
KA-POW
YEAH, YOU SHOULDA TRUSTED ME A *LONG TIME AGO.*
TOO LATE NOW.

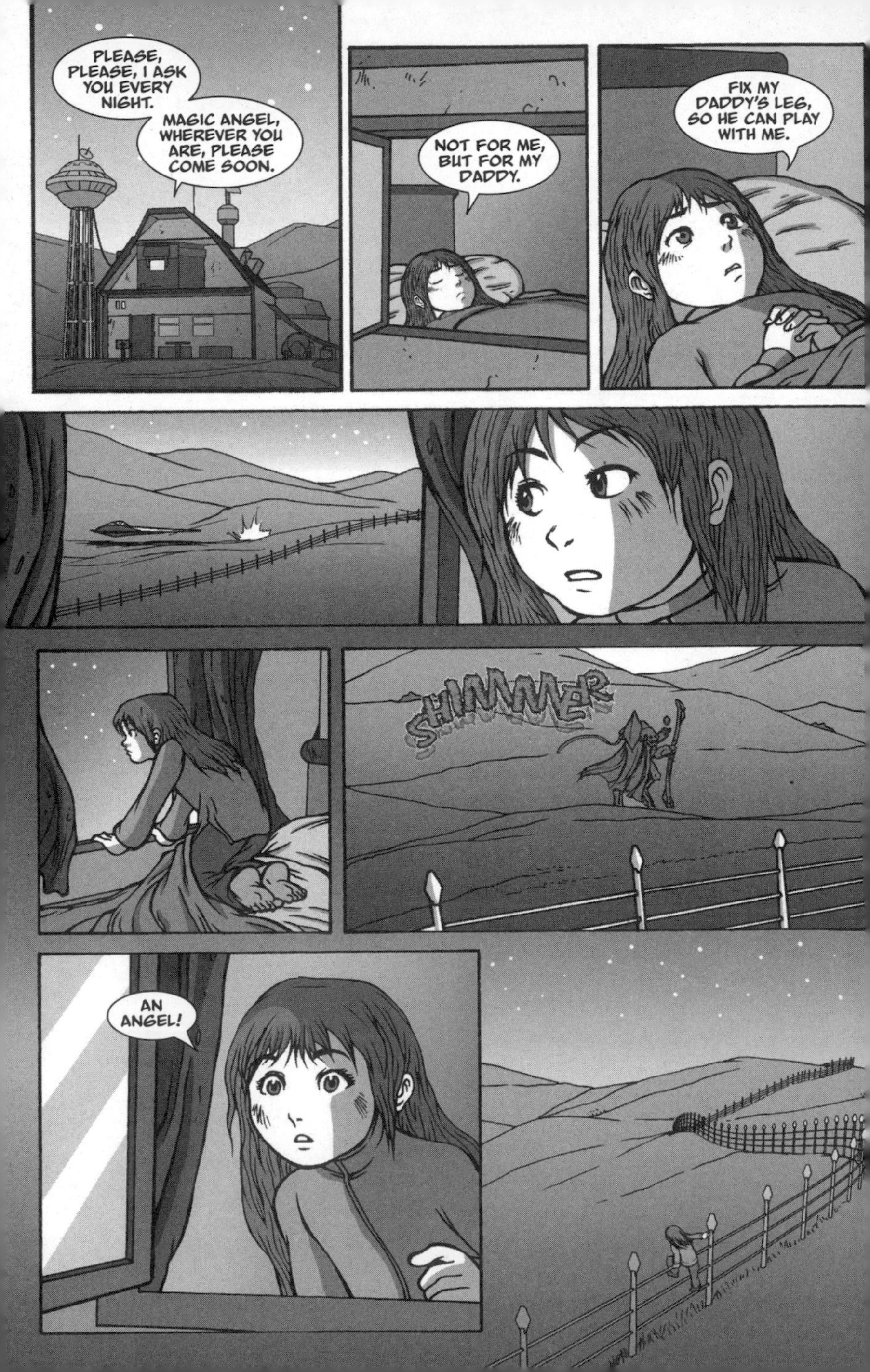
PLEASE, PLEASE, I ASK YOU EVERY NIGHT.
MAGIC ANGEL, WHEREVER YOU ARE, PLEASE COME SOON.
NOT FOR ME, BUT FOR MY DADDY.
FIX MY DADDY'S LEG, SO HE CAN PLAY WITH ME.
SHIMMER
AN ANGEL!

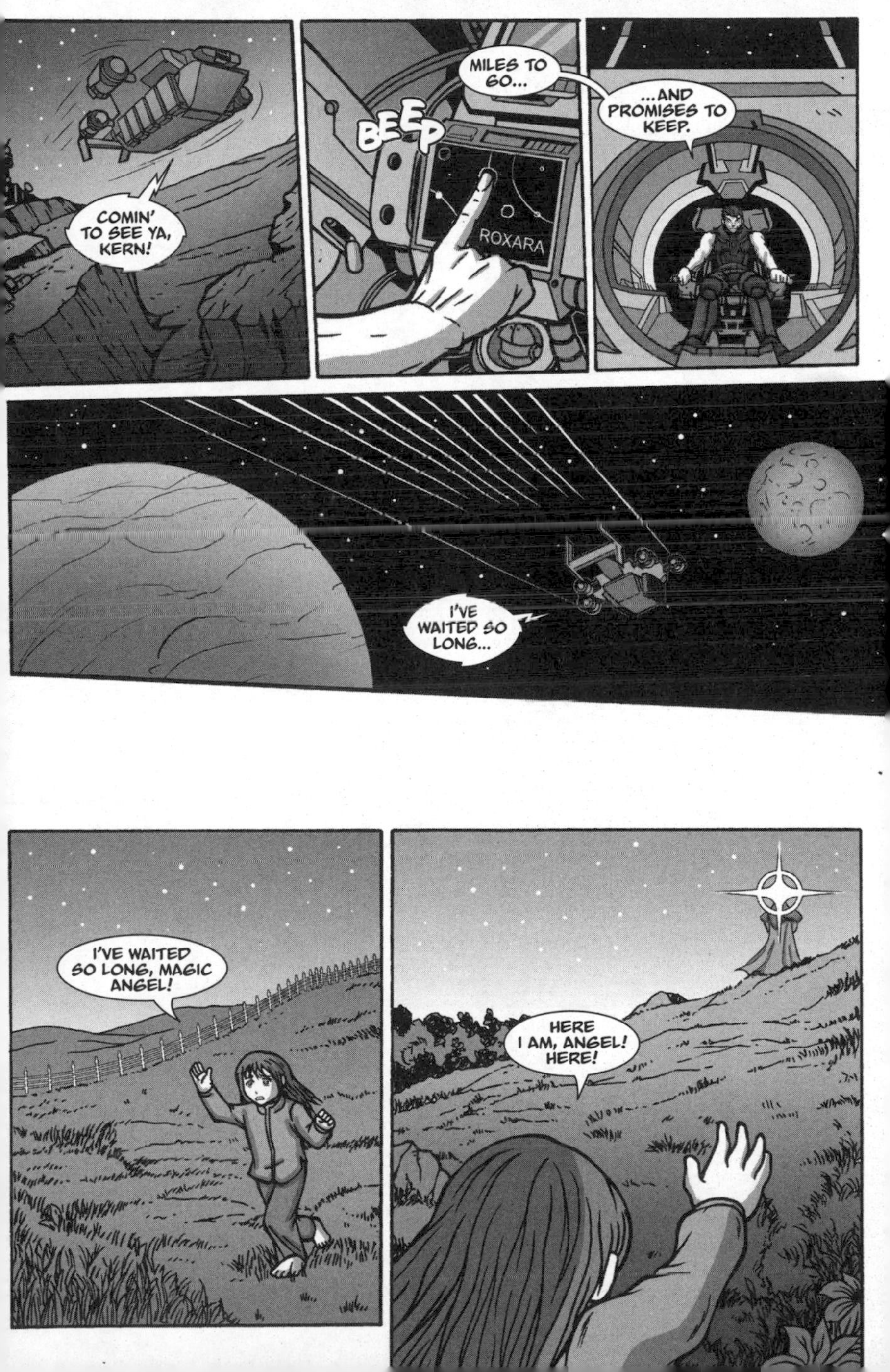
COMIN' TO SEE YA, KERN!
BEEP
ROXARA
MILES TO GO...
...AND PROMISES TO KEEP.
I'VE WAITED SO LONG...
I'VE WAITED SO LONG, MAGIC ANGEL!
HERE I AM, ANGEL! HERE!

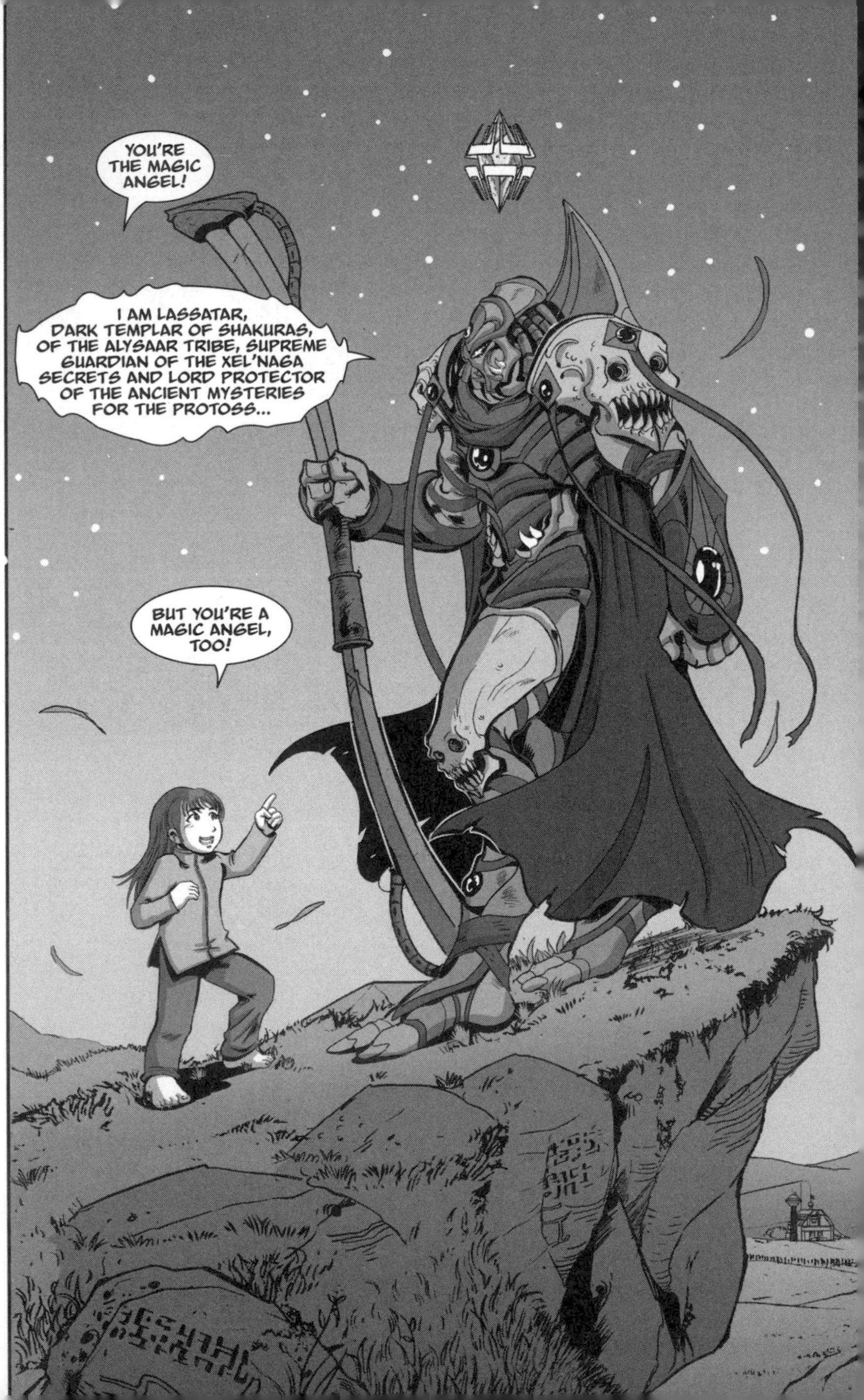
YOU'RE THE MAGIC ANGEL!
I AM LASSATAR, DARK TEMPLAR OF SHAKURAS, OF THE ALYSAAR TRIBE, SUPREME GUARDIAN OF THE XEL'NAGA SECRETS AND LORD PROTECTOR OF THE ANCIENT MYSTERIES FOR THE PROTOSS...
BUT YOU'RE A MAGIC ANGEL, TOO!

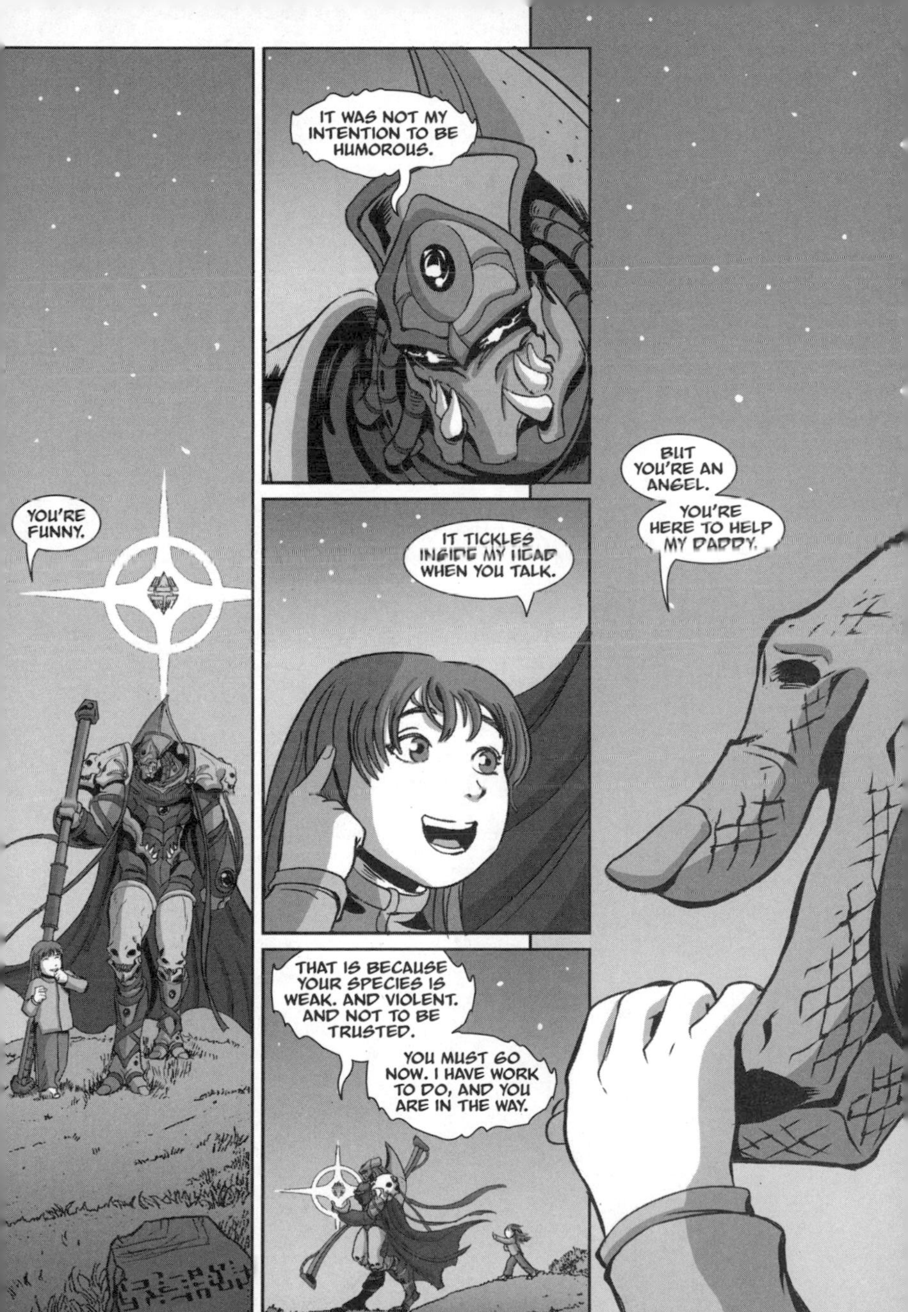
YOU'RE FUNNY.
IT WAS NOT MY INTENTION TO BE HUMOROUS.
IT TICKLES INSIDE MY HEAD WHEN YOU TALK.
THAT IS BECAUSE YOUR SPECIES IS WEAK. AND VIOLENT. AND NOT TO BE TRUSTED.
YOU MUST GO NOW. I HAVE WORK TO DO, AND YOU ARE IN THE WAY.
BUT YOU'RE AN ANGEL.
YOU'RE HERE TO HELP MY DADDY.

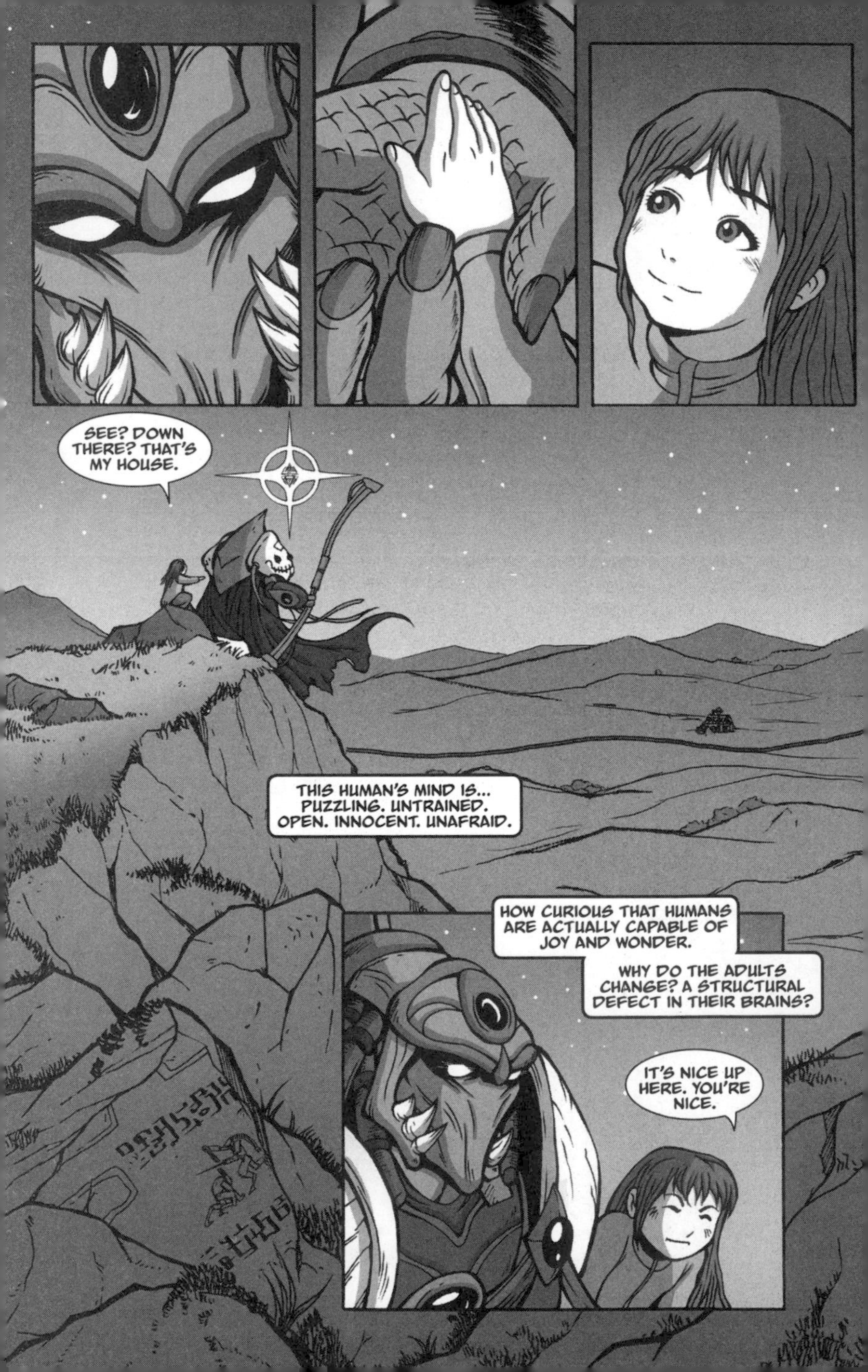
SEE? DOWN THERE? THAT'S MY HOUSE.
THIS HUMAN'S MIND IS... PUZZLING. UNTRAINED. OPEN. INNOCENT. UNAFRAID.
HOW CURIOUS THAT HUMANS ARE ACTUALLY CAPABLE OF JOY AND WONDER.
WHY DO THE ADULTS CHANGE? A STRUCTURAL DEFECT IN THEIR BRAINS?
IT'S NICE UP HERE. YOU'RE NICE.

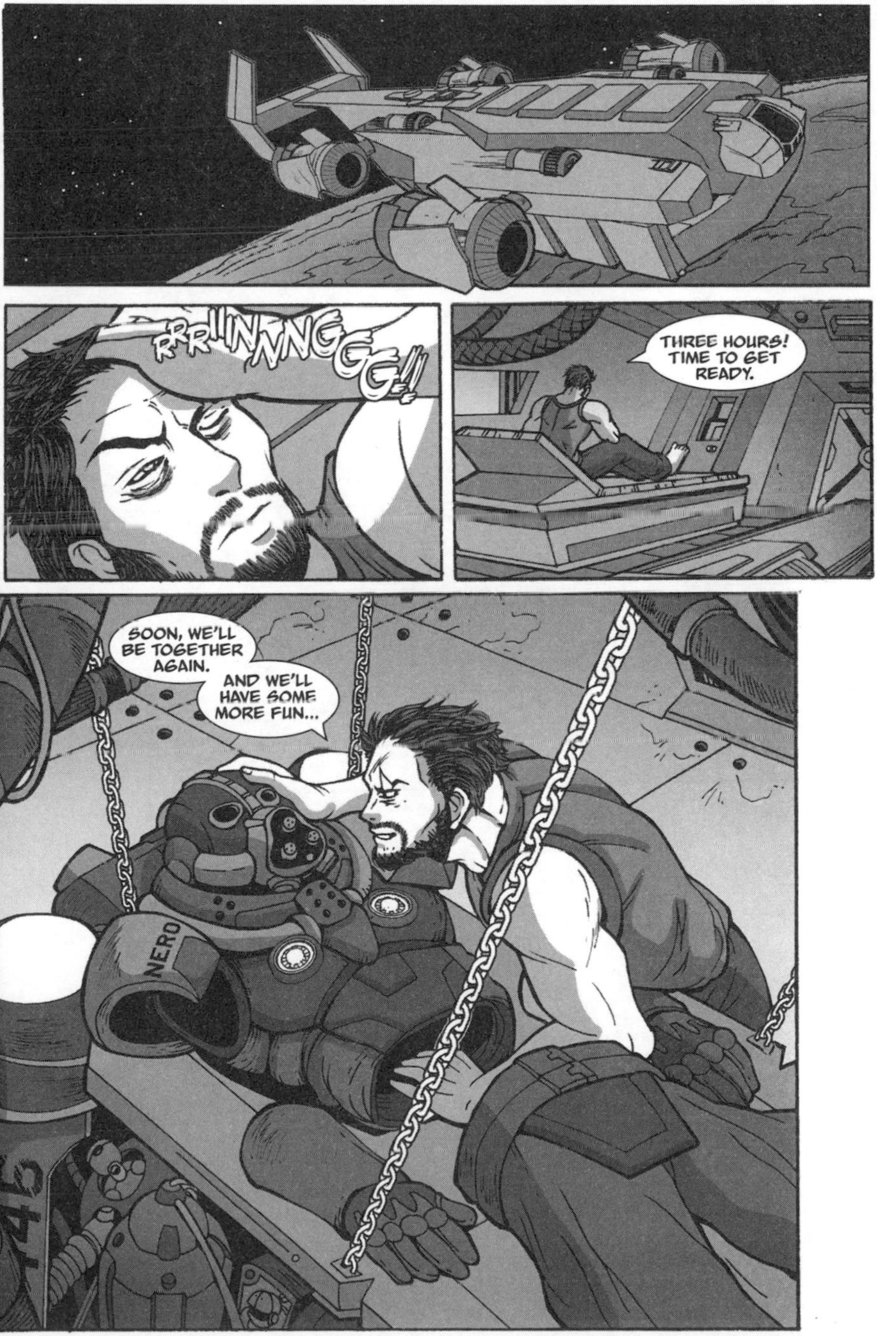
RRRIINNNNGGG!!
THREE HOURS! TIME TO GET READY.
SOON, WE'LL BE TOGETHER AGAIN.
AND WE'LL HAVE SOME MORE FUN...
NERO
446

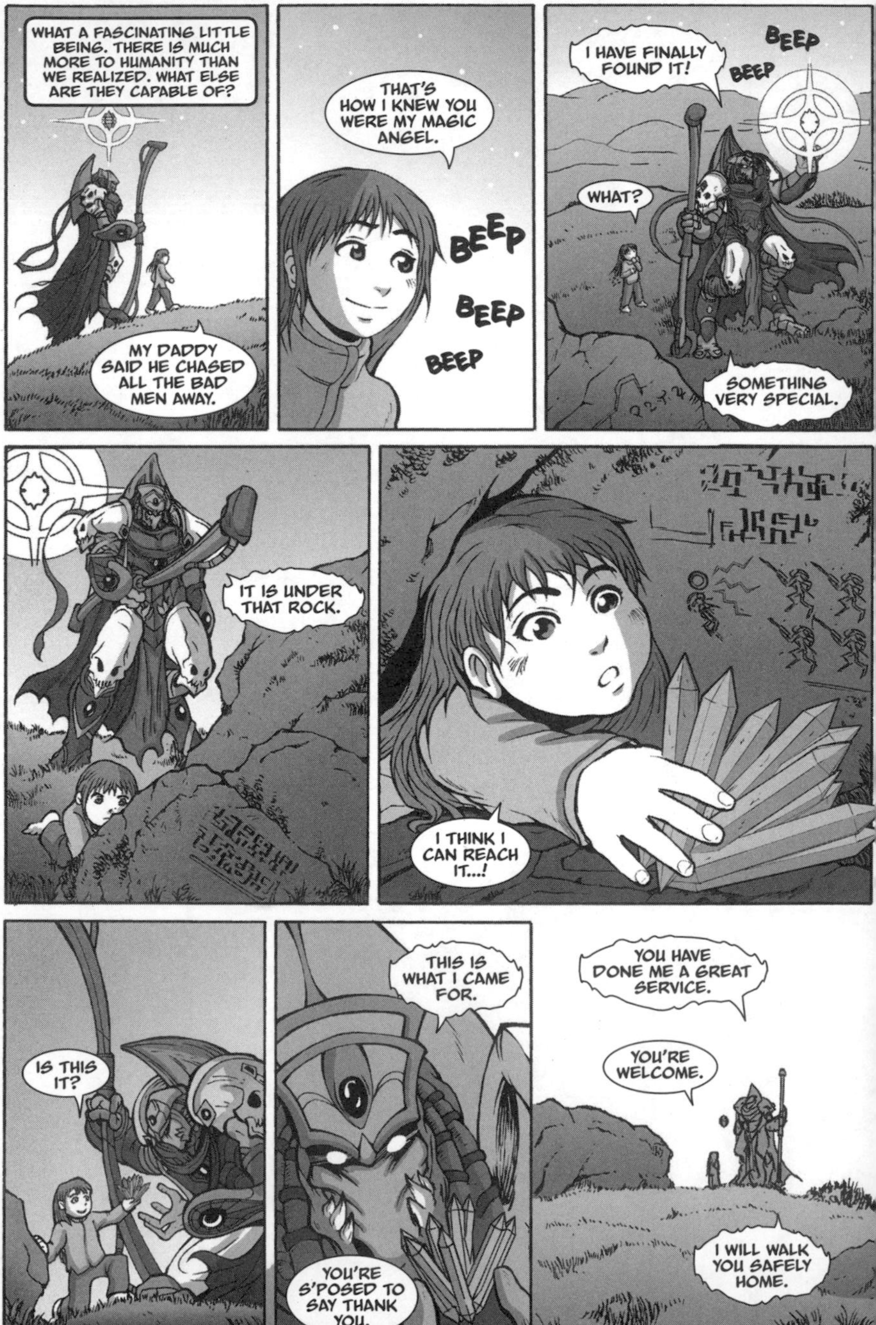
WHAT A FASCINATING LITTLE BEING. THERE IS MUCH MORE TO HUMANITY THAN WE REALIZED. WHAT ELSE ARE THEY CAPABLE OF?
MY DADDY SAID HE CHASED ALL THE BAD MEN AWAY.
THAT'S HOW I KNEW YOU WERE MY MAGIC ANGEL.
BEEP
BEEP
BEEP
I HAVE FINALLY FOUND IT!
BEEP
BEEP
WHAT?
SOMETHING VERY SPECIAL.
IT IS UNDER THAT ROCK.
I THINK I CAN REACH IT...!
IS THIS IT?
THIS IS WHAT I CAME FOR.
YOU'RE S'POSED TO SAY THANK YOU.
YOU HAVE DONE ME A GREAT SERVICE.
YOU'RE WELCOME.
I WILL WALK YOU SAFELY HOME.

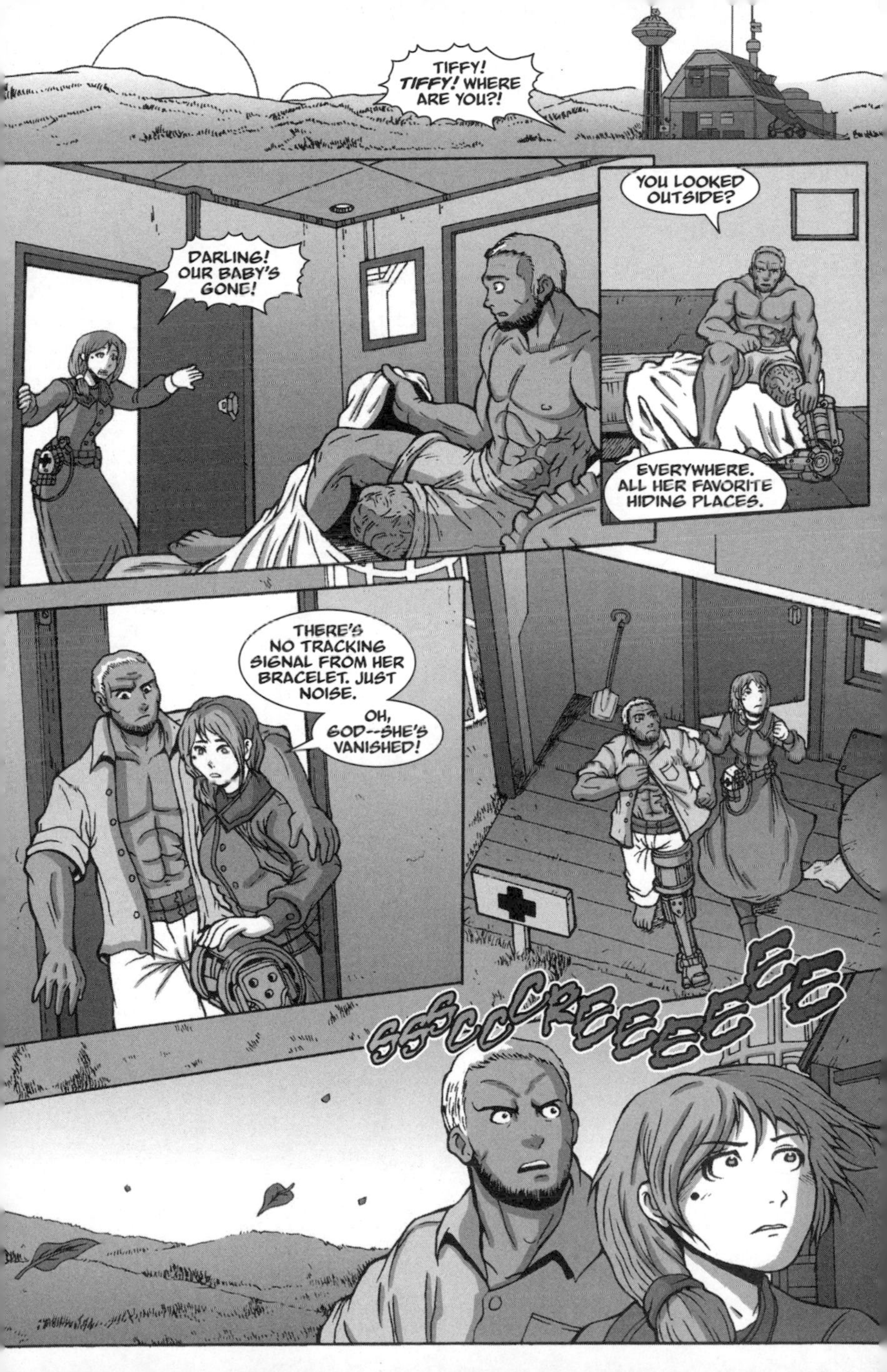
TIFFY! *TIFFY!* WHERE ARE YOU?!
DARLING! OUR BABY'S GONE!
YOU LOOKED OUTSIDE?
EVERYWHERE. ALL HER FAVORITE HIDING PLACES.
THERE'S NO TRACKING SIGNAL FROM HER BRACELET. JUST NOISE.
OH, GOD--SHE'S VANISHED!
SSSCCCREEEEEEEE

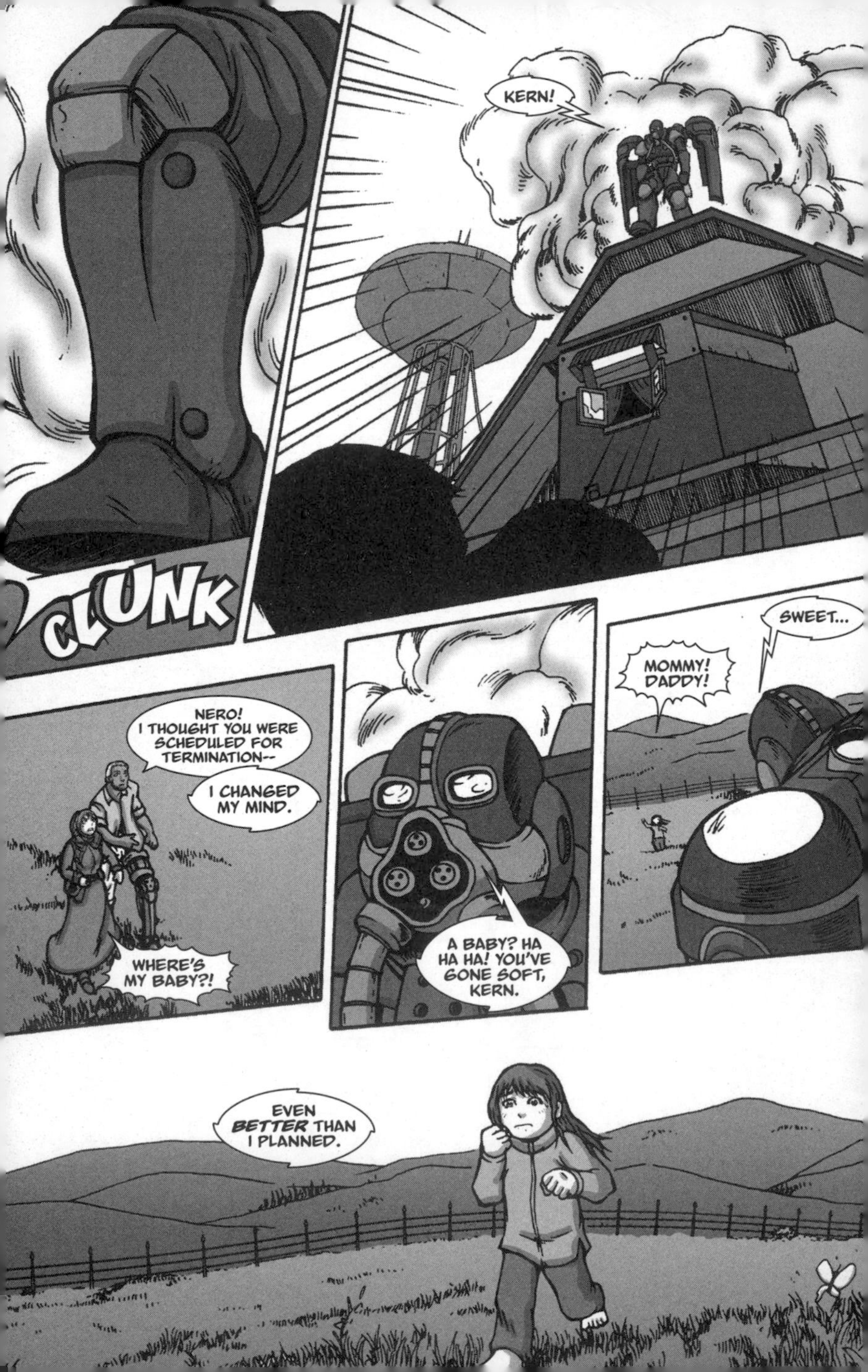
KERN!
CLUNK
NERO! I THOUGHT YOU WERE SCHEDULED FOR TERMINATION--
I CHANGED MY MIND.
WHERE'S MY BABY?!
A BABY? HA HA HA! YOU'VE GONE SOFT, KERN.
SWEET...
MOMMY! DADDY!
EVEN BETTER THAN I PLANNED.

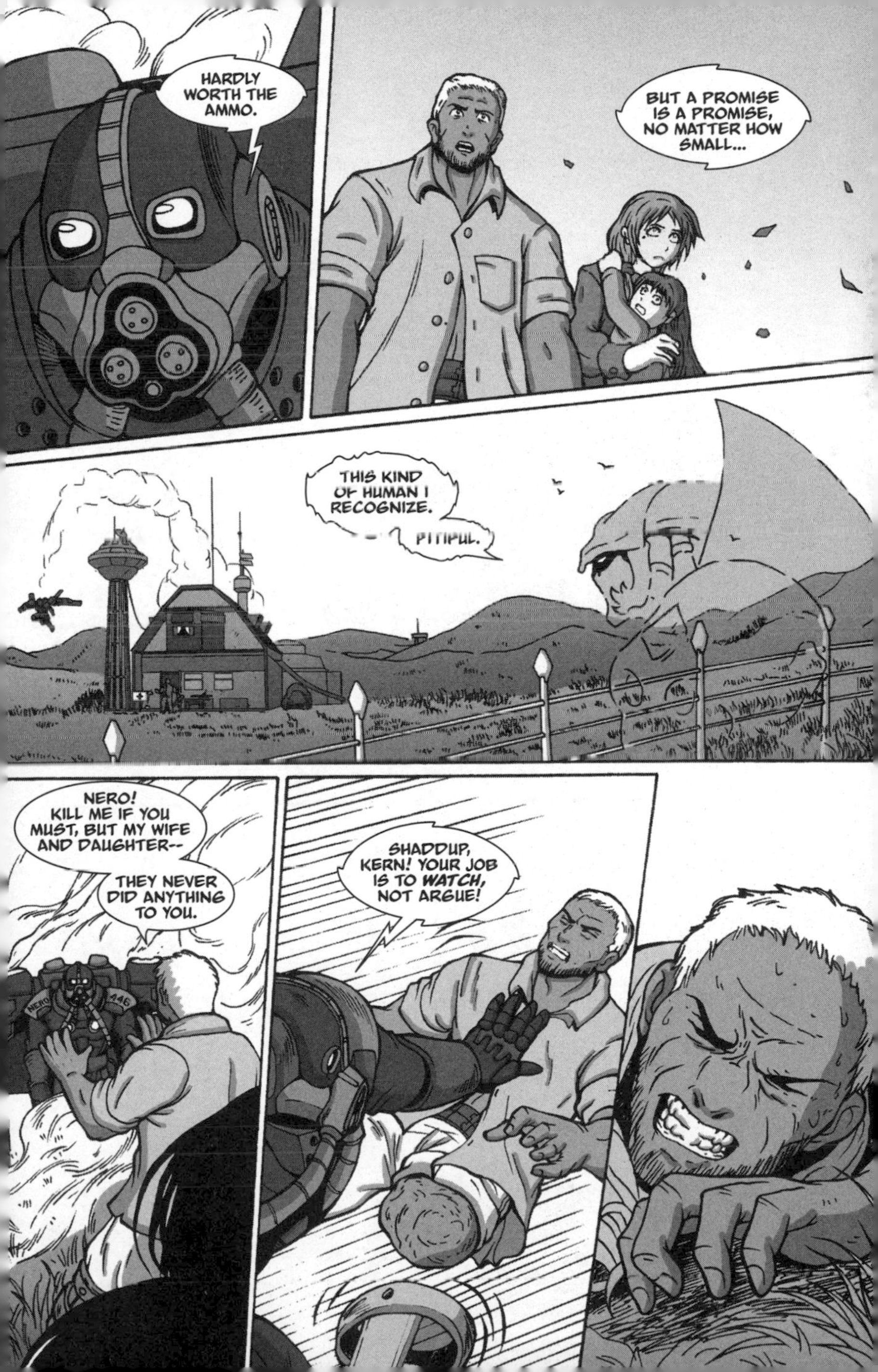
HARDLY WORTH THE AMMO.
BUT A PROMISE IS A PROMISE, NO MATTER HOW SMALL...
THIS KIND OF HUMAN I RECOGNIZE.
PITIFUL.
NERO! KILL ME IF YOU MUST, BUT MY WIFE AND DAUGHTER--
THEY NEVER DID ANYTHING TO YOU.
SHADDUP, KERN! YOUR JOB IS TO *WATCH*, NOT ARGUE!
NERO
446

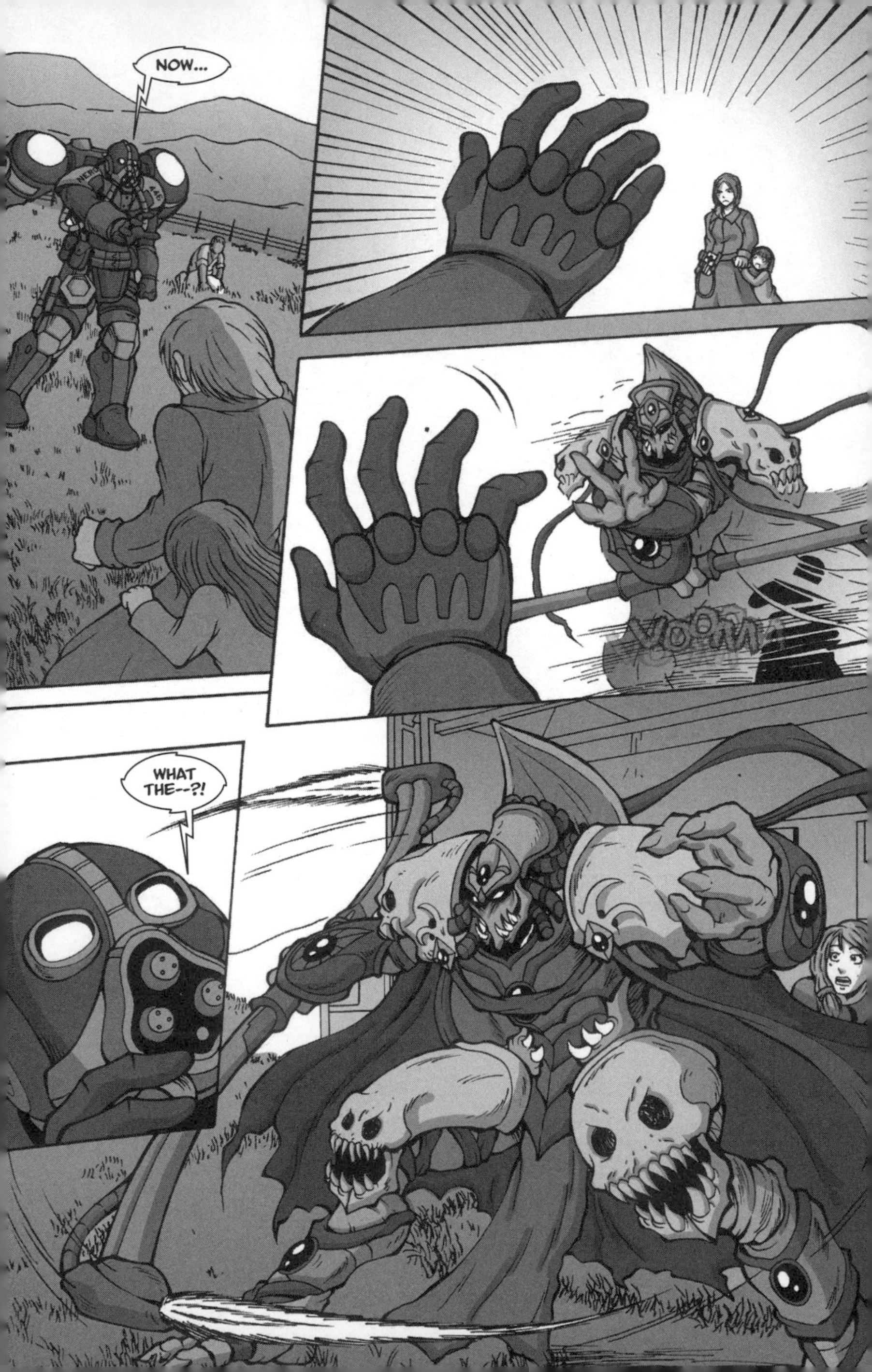
NOW...
VOOM
WHAT THE--?!

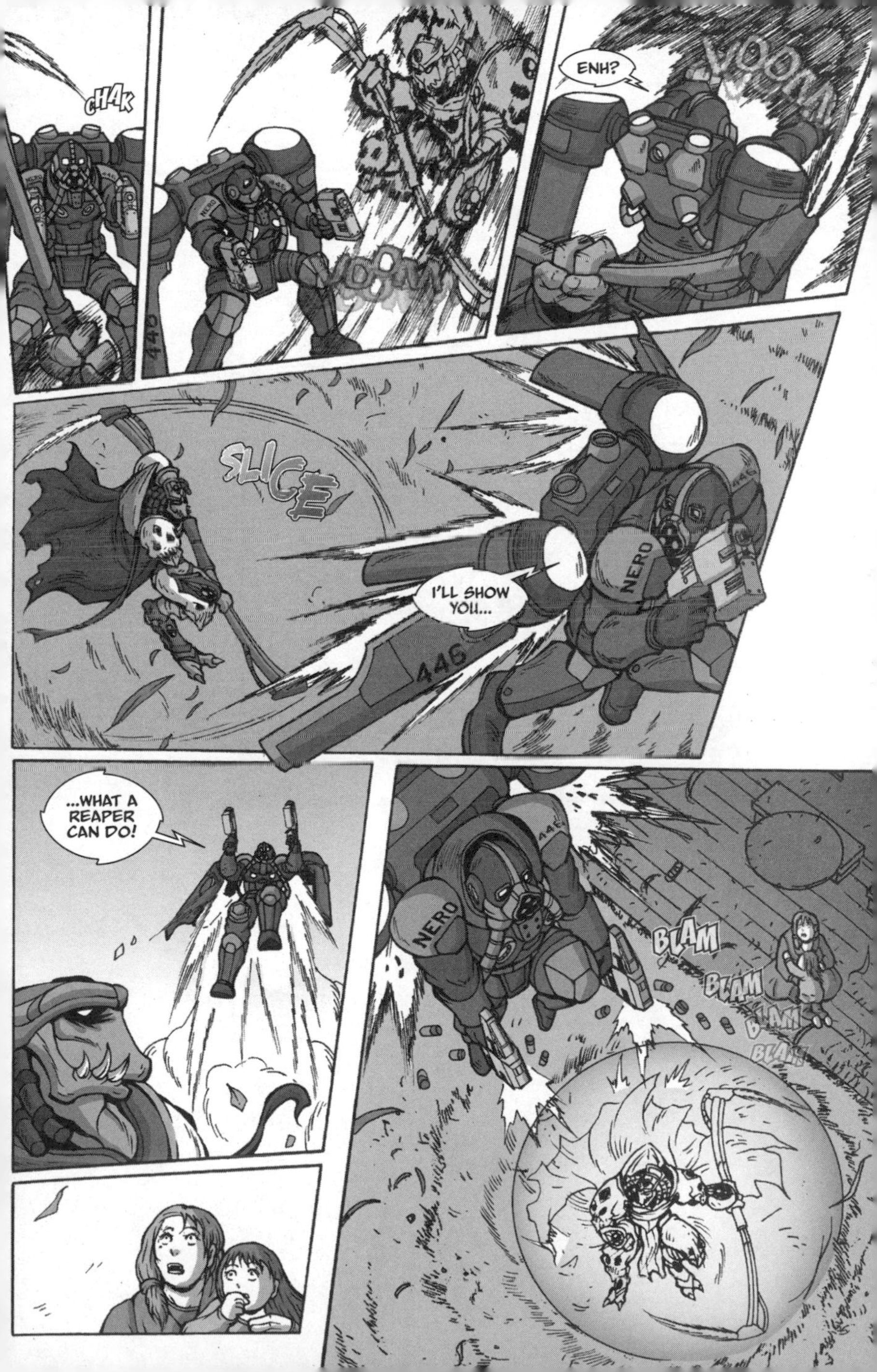

cHAK
ENH?
SLICE
I'LL SHOW YOU...
...WHAT A REAPER CAN DO!
BLAM
BLAM

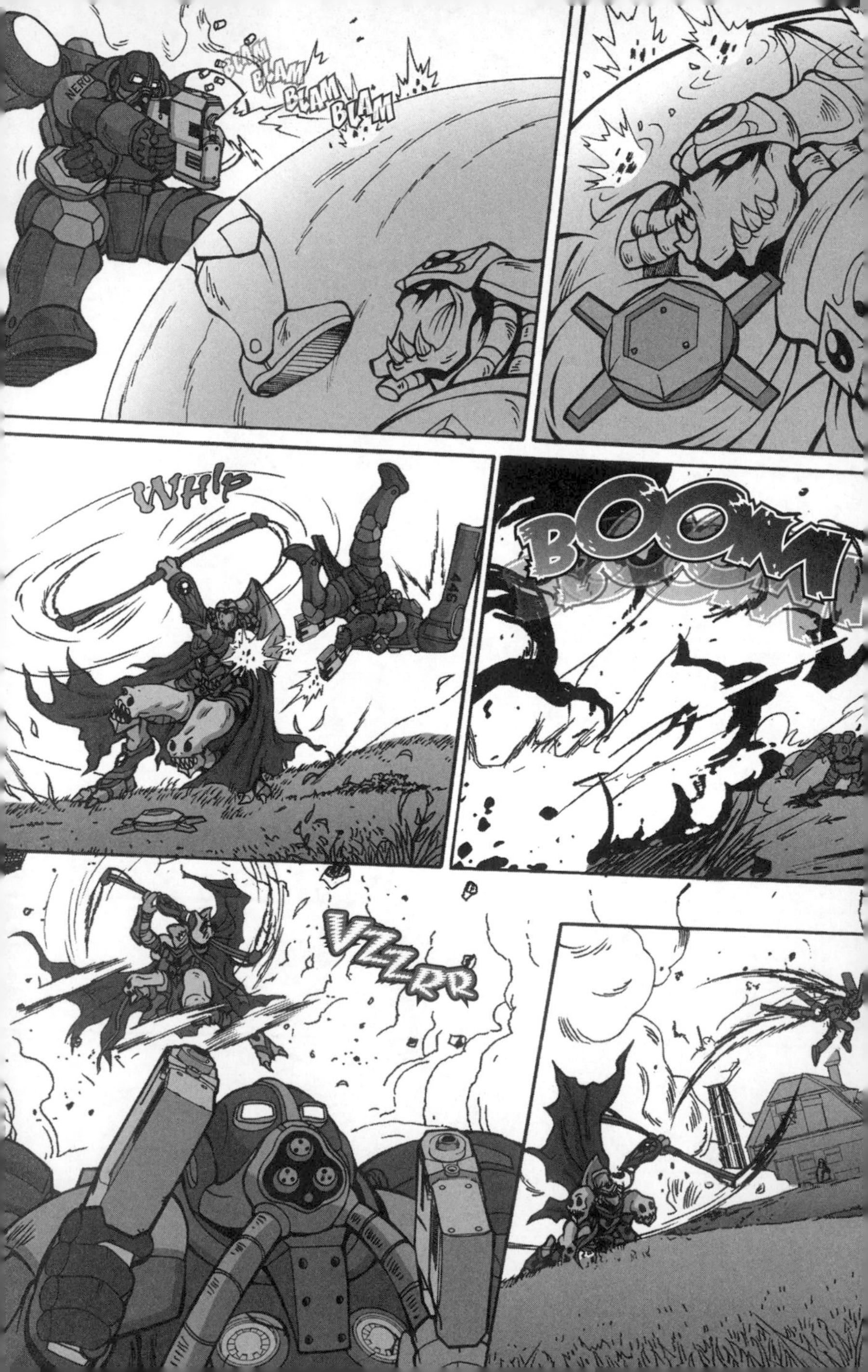
NERU
BLAM
BLAM
BLAM
BLAM
WHIP
446
BOOM
VZZRR

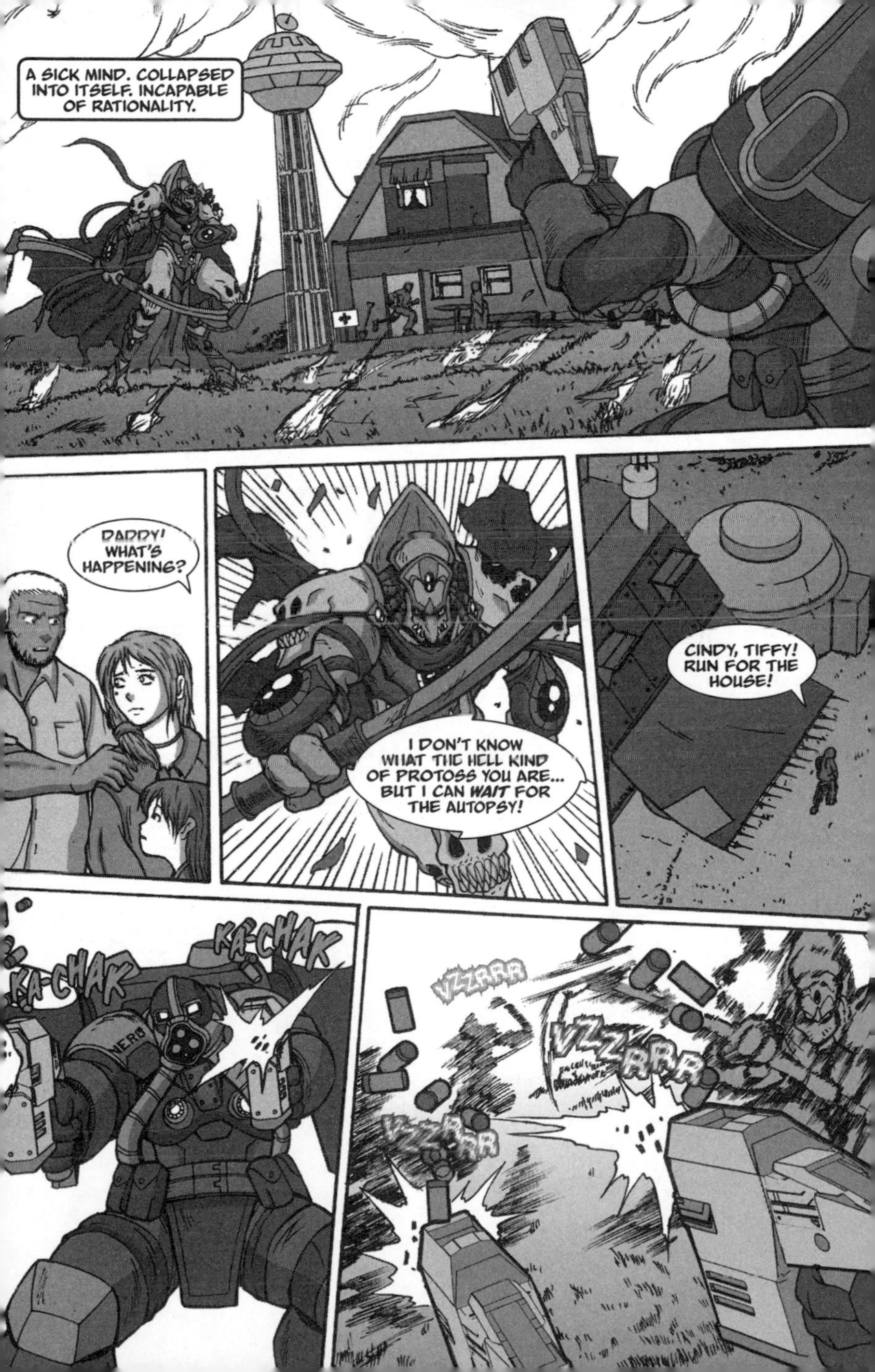
A SICK MIND. COLLAPSED INTO ITSELF. INCAPABLE OF RATIONALITY.
DADDY! WHAT'S HAPPENING?
I DON'T KNOW WHAT THE HELL KIND OF PROTOSS YOU ARE... BUT I CAN WAIT FOR THE AUTOPSY!
CINDY, TIFFY! RUN FOR THE HOUSE!
KA-CHAK
KA-CHAK
VZZRRR
VZZRRR
VZZRRR

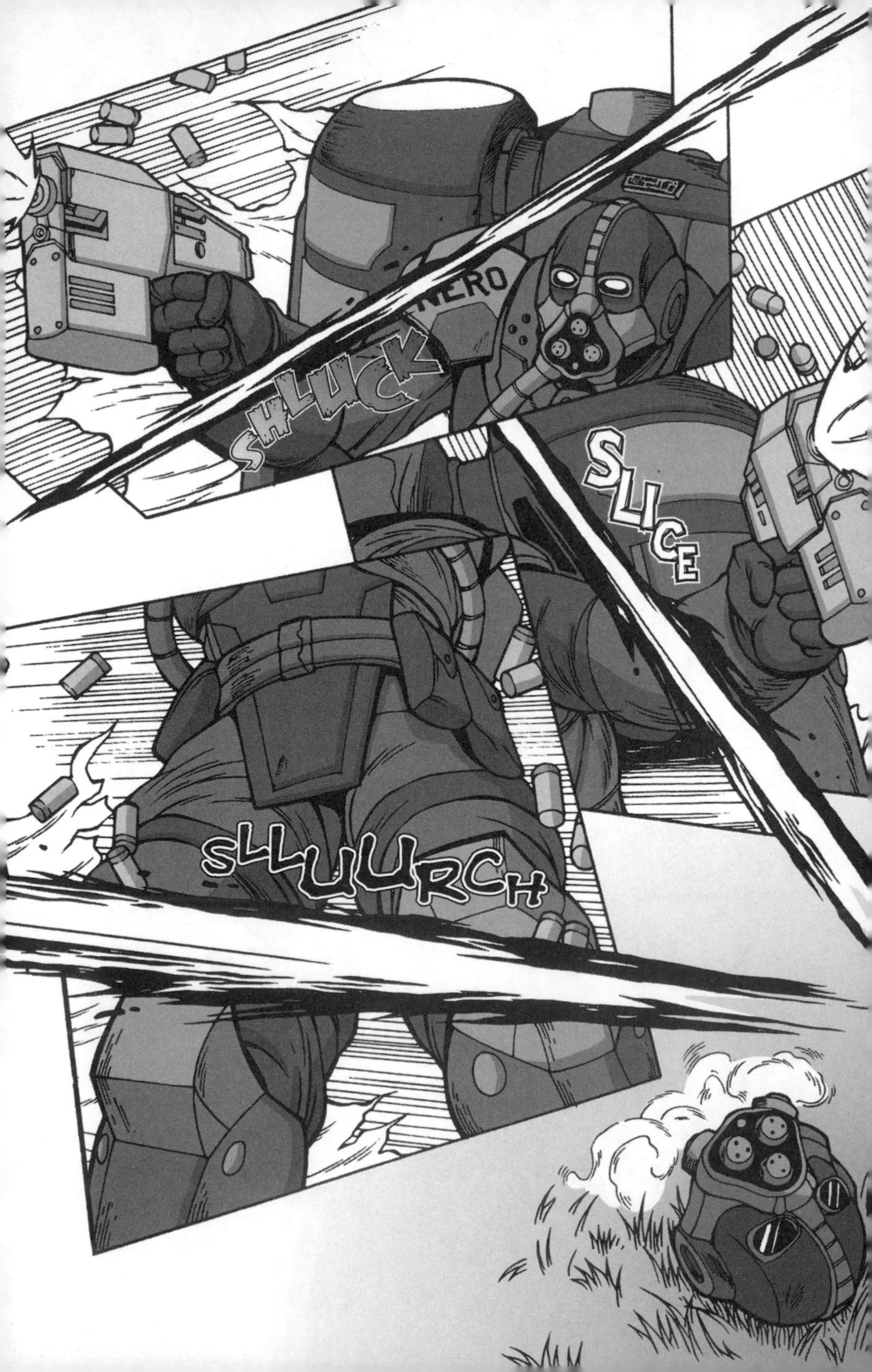
NERO
SHLUCK
SLICE
SLLUURCH

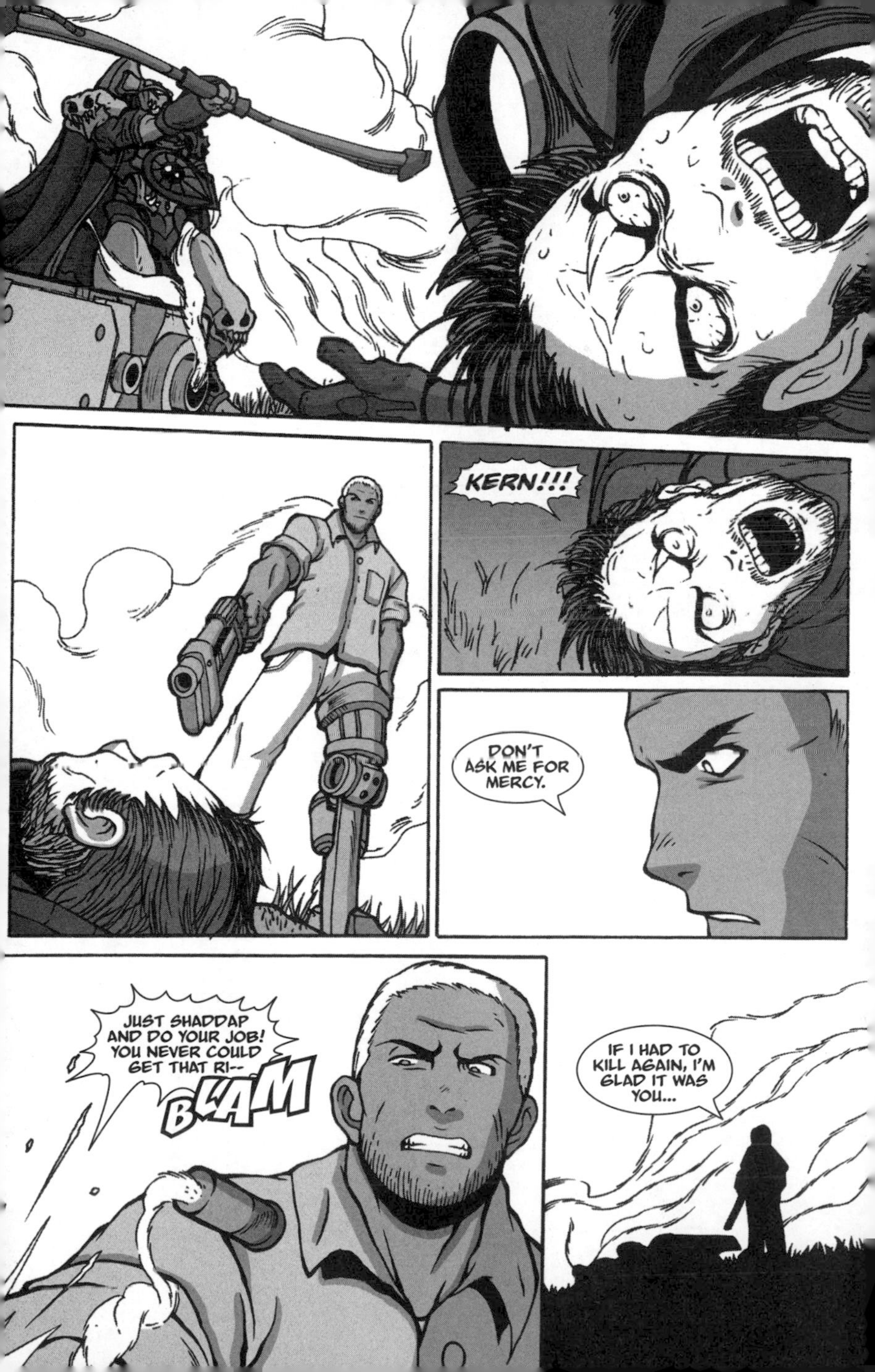
KERN!!!
DON'T ASK ME FOR MERCY.
JUST SHADDAP AND DO YOUR JOB! YOU NEVER COULD GET THAT RI--
BLAM
IF I HAD TO KILL AGAIN, I'M GLAD IT WAS YOU...

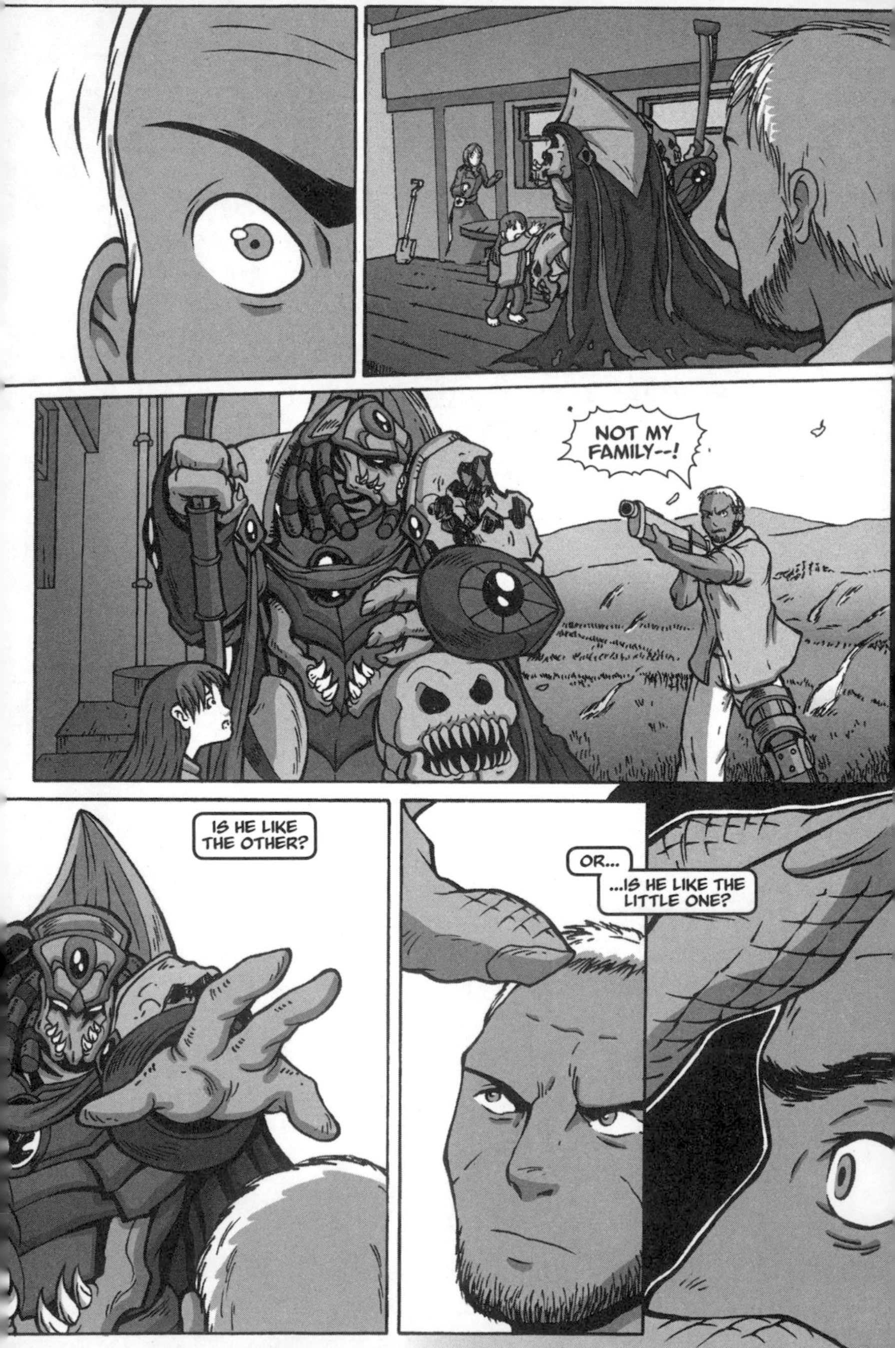

NOT MY FAMILY--!
IS HE LIKE THE OTHER?
OR...
...IS HE LIKE THE LITTLE ONE?

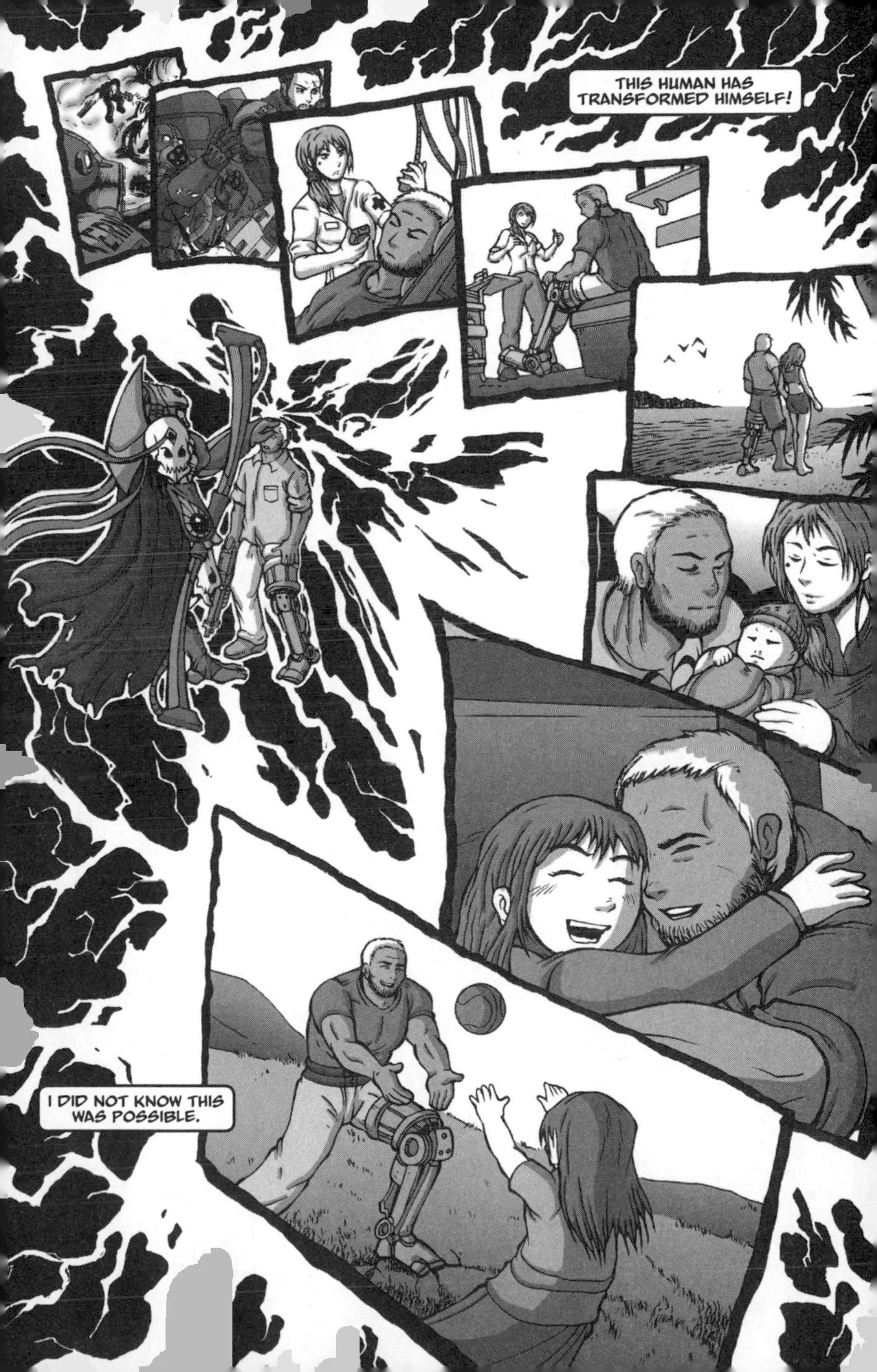
THIS HUMAN HAS
TRANSFORMED HIMSELF!
I DID NOT KNOW THIS
WAS POSSIBLE.

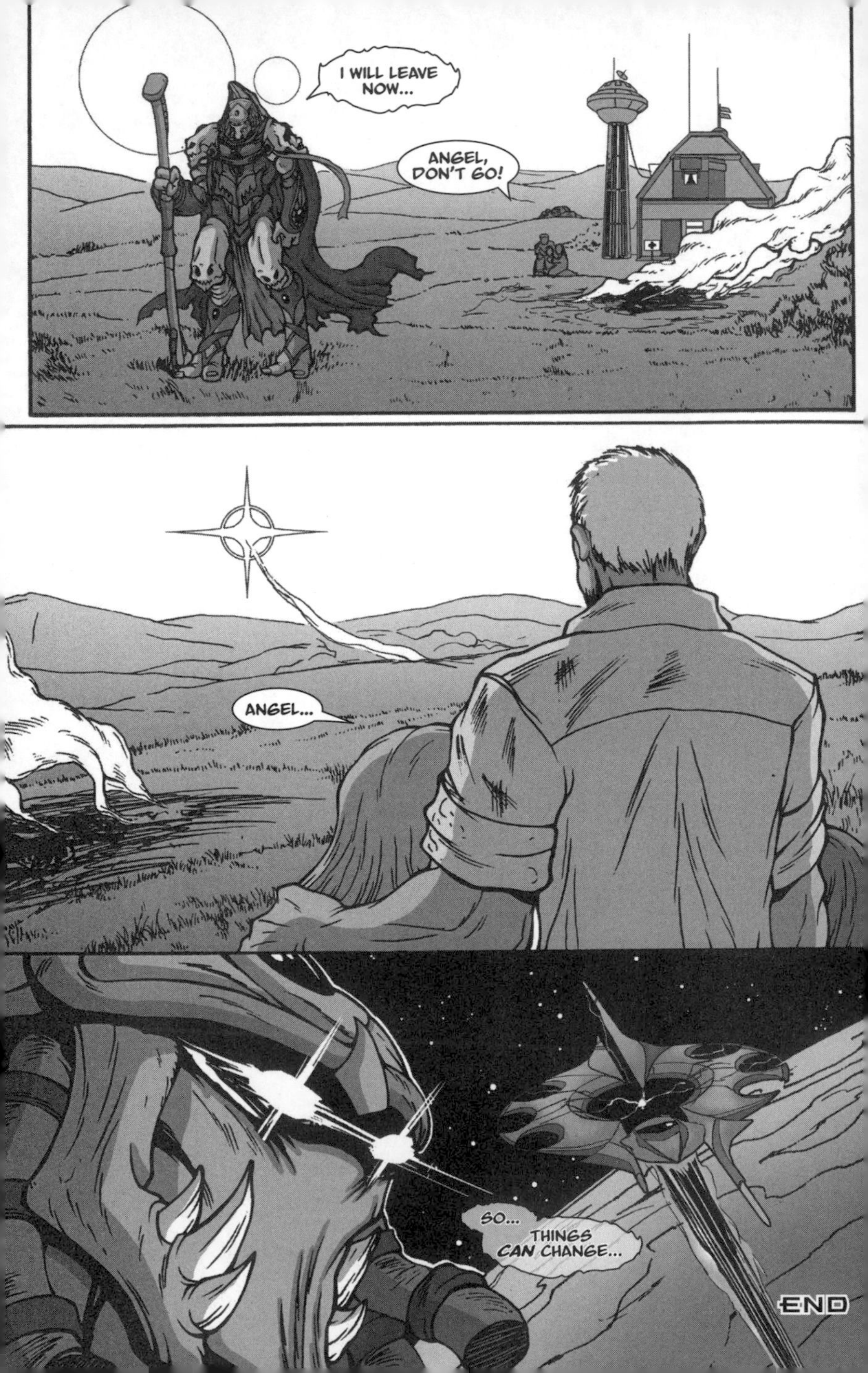
I WILL LEAVE NOW...
ANGEL, DON'T GO!
ANGEL...
SO... THINGS CAN CHANGE...
END

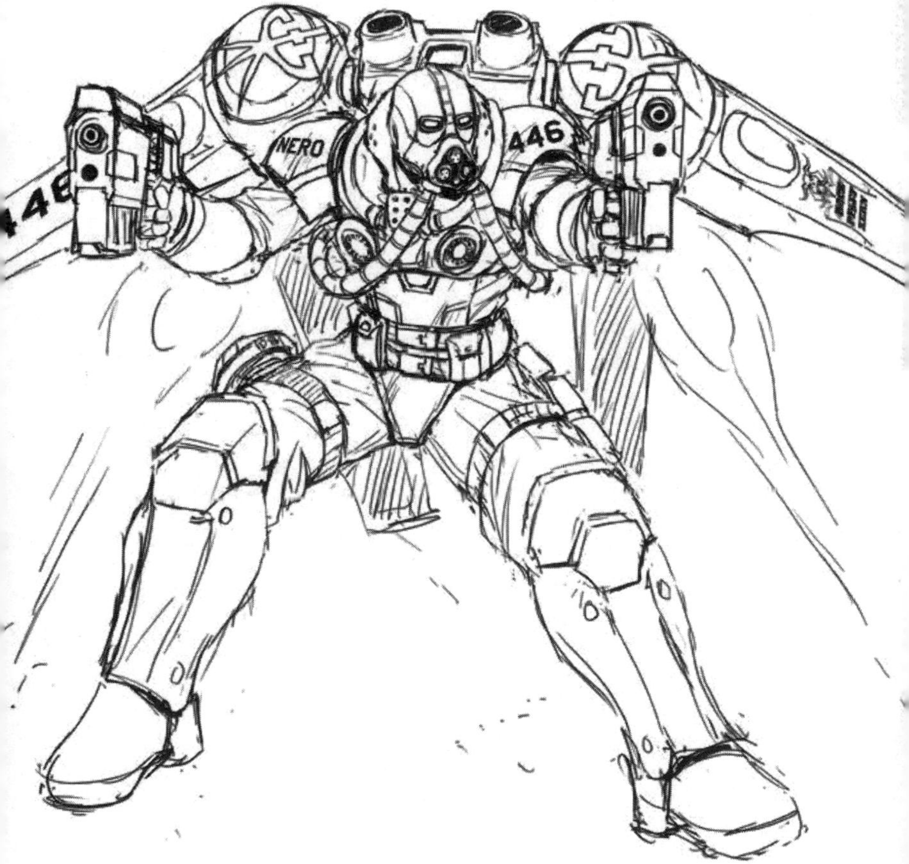
446
NERO
446

STARCRAFT

FRONTLINE
VOLUME 4

VOICE IN THE DARKNESS

Written by Josh Elder

Pencils by Ramanda Kamarga

Inks by Faisal, Junaidi and Ijur of Caravan Studio,
and Ryo Kawakami

Tones by Erfian Asafat of Caravan Studio, Beatusvir,
Lincy Chan, and Jake Myler

Letterer: Michael Paolilli

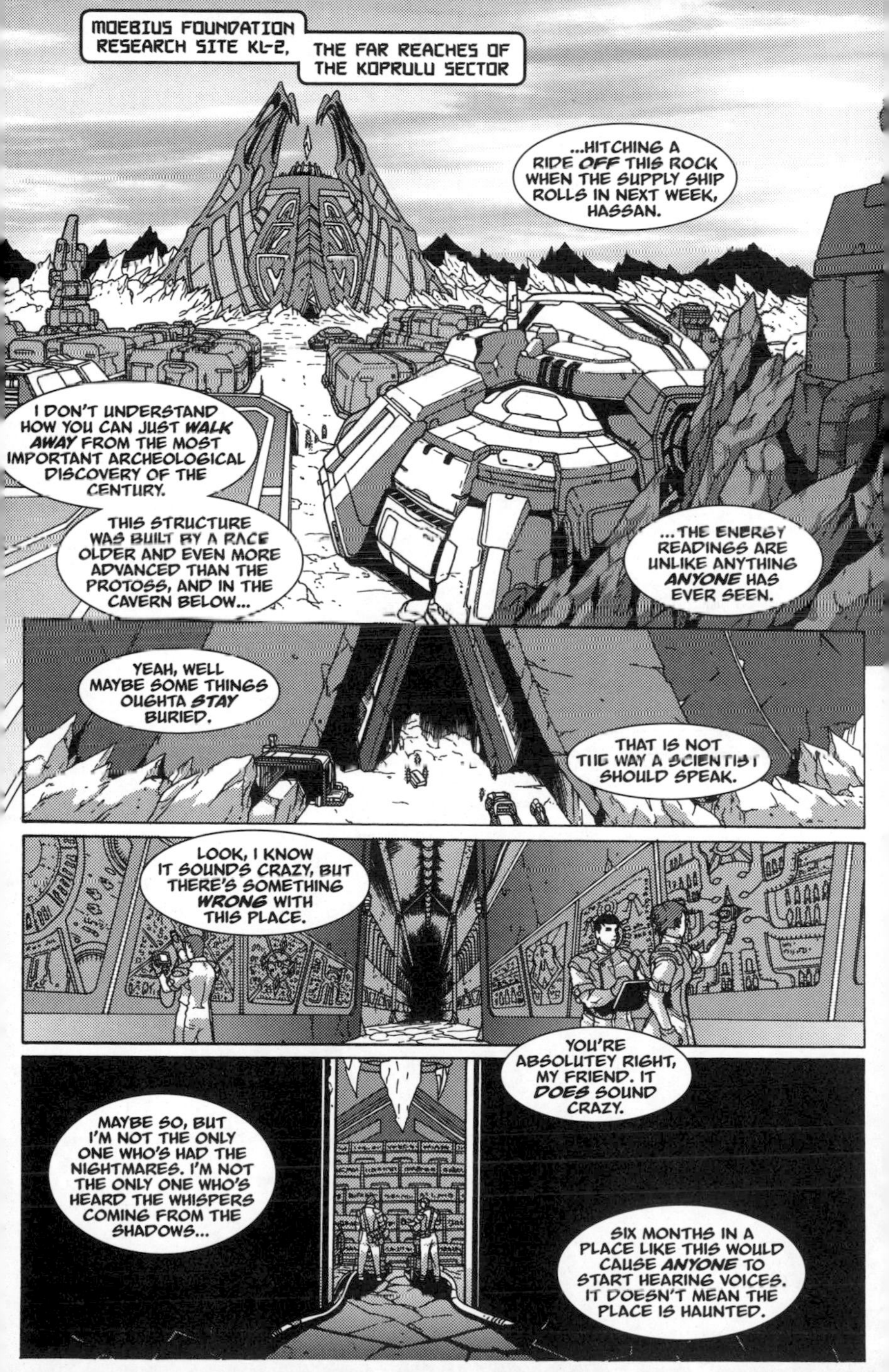
MOEBIUS FOUNDATION RESEARCH SITE KL-2,
THE FAR REACHES OF THE KOPRULU SECTOR
...HITCHING A RIDE OFF THIS ROCK WHEN THE SUPPLY SHIP ROLLS IN NEXT WEEK, HASSAN.
I DON'T UNDERSTAND HOW YOU CAN JUST WALK AWAY FROM THE MOST IMPORTANT ARCHEOLOGICAL DISCOVERY OF THE CENTURY.
THIS STRUCTURE WAS BUILT BY A RACE OLDER AND EVEN MORE ADVANCED THAN THE PROTOSS, AND IN THE CAVERN BELOW...
...THE ENERGY READINGS ARE UNLIKE ANYTHING ANYONE HAS EVER SEEN.
YEAH, WELL MAYBE SOME THINGS OUGHTA STAY BURIED.
THAT IS NOT THE WAY A SCIENTIST SHOULD SPEAK.
LOOK, I KNOW IT SOUNDS CRAZY, BUT THERE'S SOMETHING WRONG WITH THIS PLACE.
YOU'RE ABSOLUTEY RIGHT, MY FRIEND. IT DOES SOUND CRAZY.
MAYBE SO, BUT I'M NOT THE ONLY ONE WHO'S HAD THE NIGHTMARES. I'M NOT THE ONLY ONE WHO'S HEARD THE WHISPERS COMING FROM THE SHADOWS...
SIX MONTHS IN A PLACE LIKE THIS WOULD CAUSE ANYONE TO START HEARING VOICES. IT DOESN'T MEAN THE PLACE IS HAUNTED.

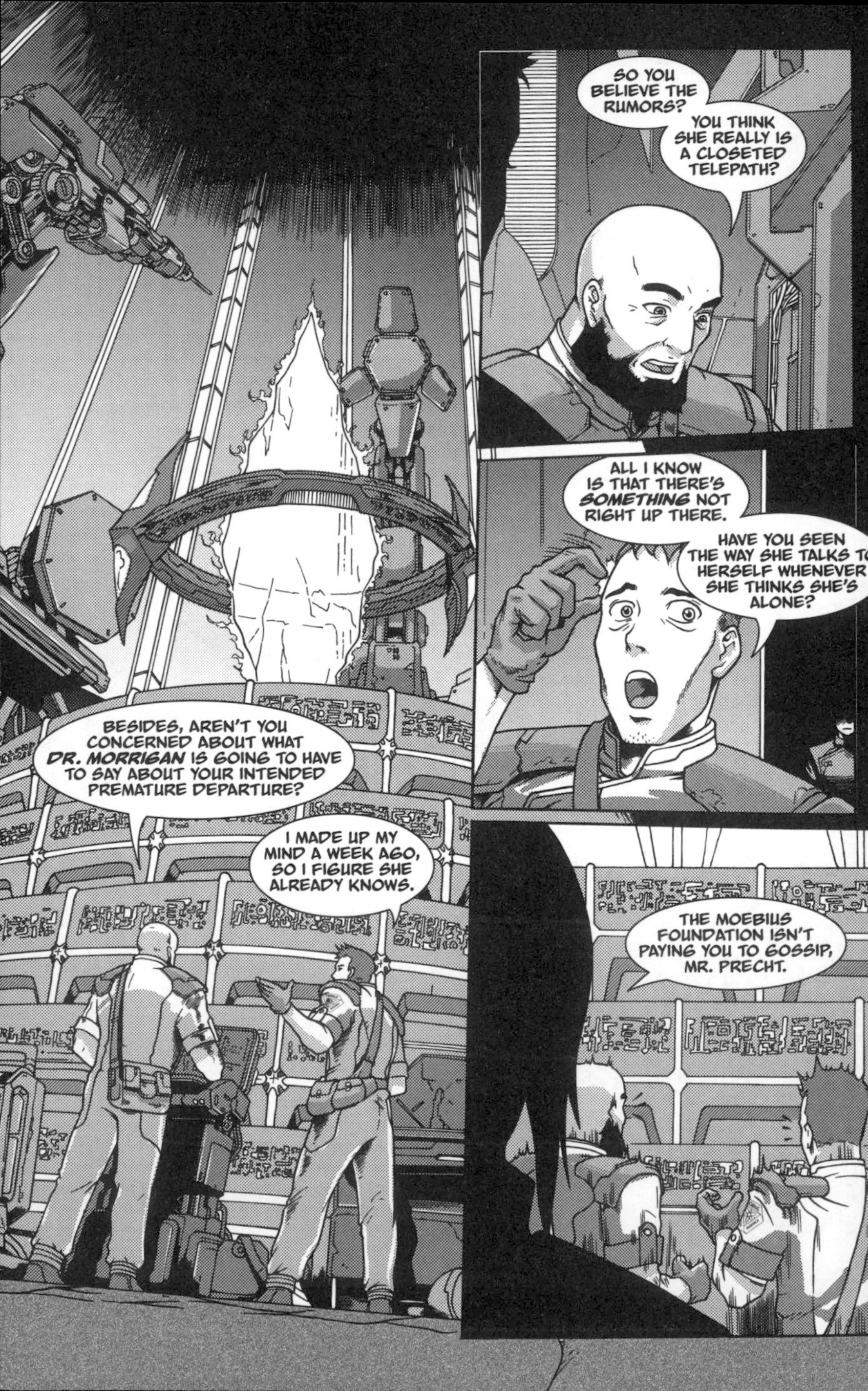
SO YOU BELIEVE THE RUMORS?
YOU THINK SHE REALLY IS A CLOSETED TELEPATH?
ALL I KNOW IS THAT THERE'S *SOMETHING* NOT RIGHT UP THERE.
HAVE YOU SEEN THE WAY SHE TALKS TO HERSELF WHENEVER SHE THINKS SHE'S ALONE?
BESIDES, AREN'T YOU CONCERNED ABOUT WHAT *DR. MORRIGAN* IS GOING TO HAVE TO SAY ABOUT YOUR INTENDED PREMATURE DEPARTURE?
I MADE UP MY MIND A WEEK AGO, SO I FIGURE SHE ALREADY KNOWS.
THE MOEBIUS FOUNDATION ISN'T PAYING YOU TO GOSSIP, MR. PRECHT.

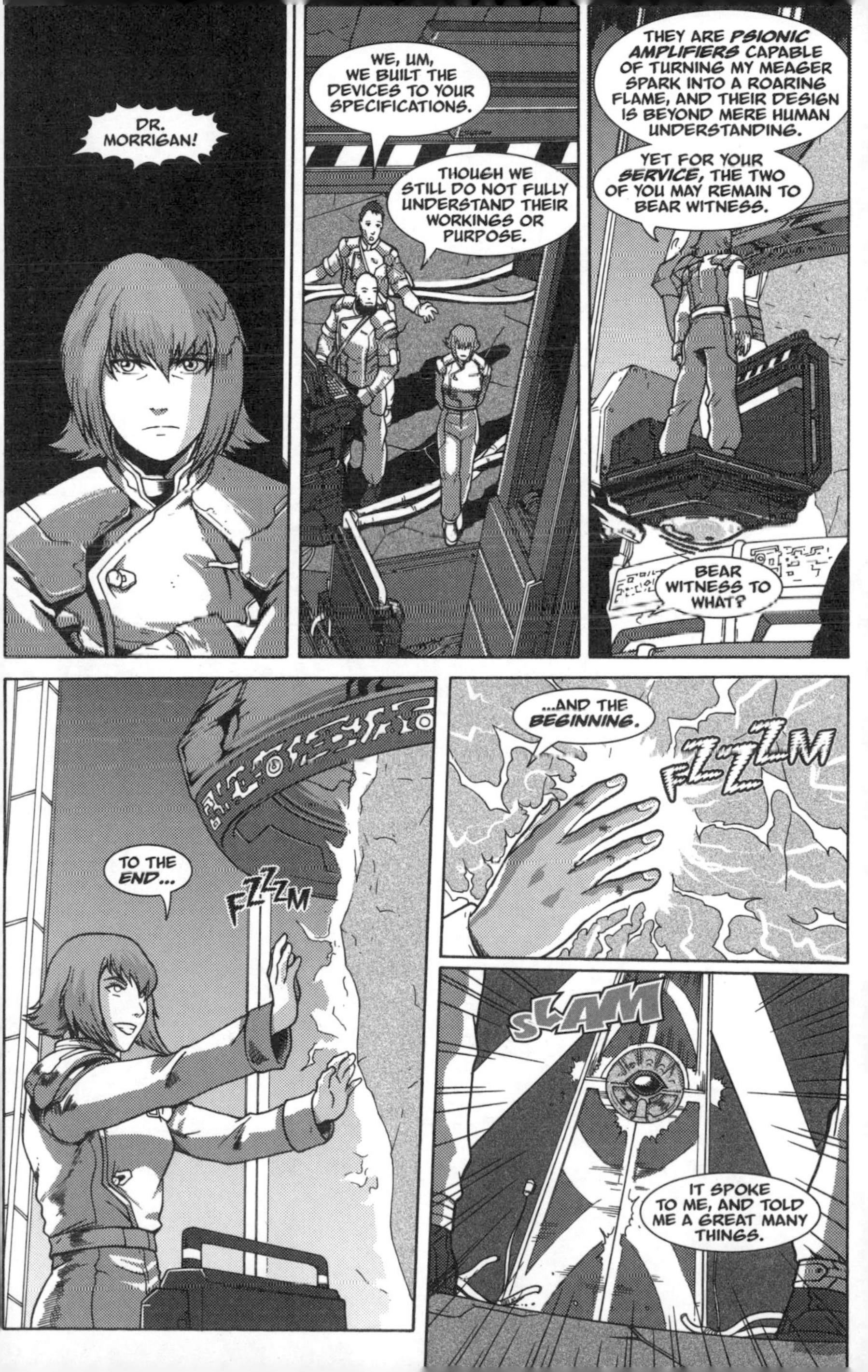
DR. MORRIGAN!
WE, UM, WE BUILT THE DEVICES TO YOUR SPECIFICATIONS.
THOUGH WE STILL DO NOT FULLY UNDERSTAND THEIR WORKINGS OR PURPOSE.
THEY ARE *PSIONIC AMPLIFIERS* CAPABLE OF TURNING MY MEAGER SPARK INTO A ROARING FLAME, AND THEIR DESIGN IS BEYOND MERE HUMAN UNDERSTANDING.
YET FOR YOUR *SERVICE*, THE TWO OF YOU MAY REMAIN TO BEAR WITNESS.
BEAR WITNESS TO WHAT?
TO THE *END*...
FZZZM
...AND THE *BEGINNING*.
FZZZM
SLAM
IT SPOKE TO ME, AND TOLD ME A GREAT MANY THINGS.

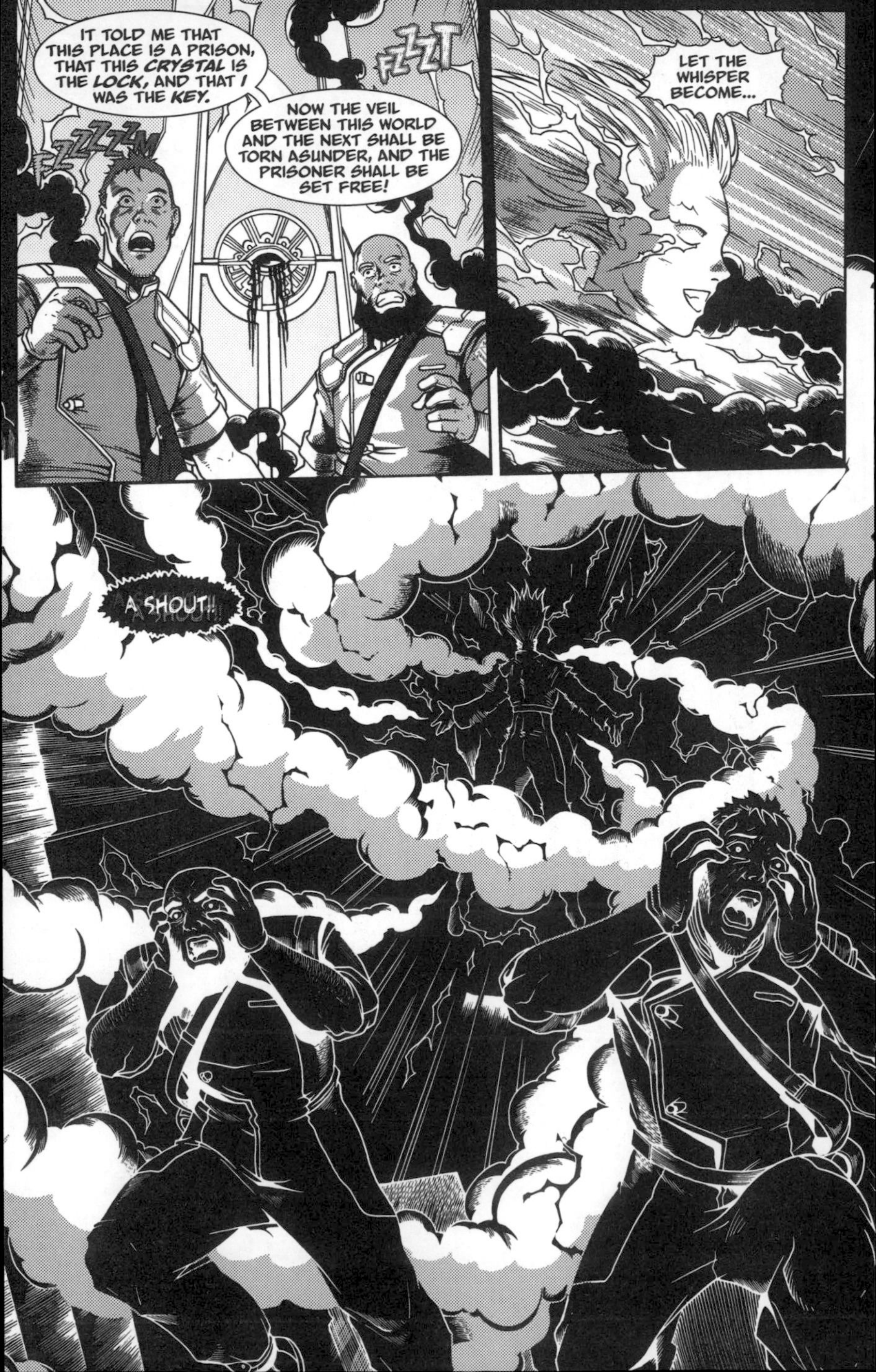
IT TOLD ME THAT THIS PLACE IS A PRISON, THAT THIS *CRYSTAL* IS THE *LOCK*, AND THAT *I* WAS THE *KEY*.
FZZZZZZM
FZZZT
NOW THE VEIL BETWEEN THIS WORLD AND THE NEXT SHALL BE TORN ASUNDER, AND THE PRISONER SHALL BE SET FREE!
LET THE WHISPER BECOME...
A SHOUT!!

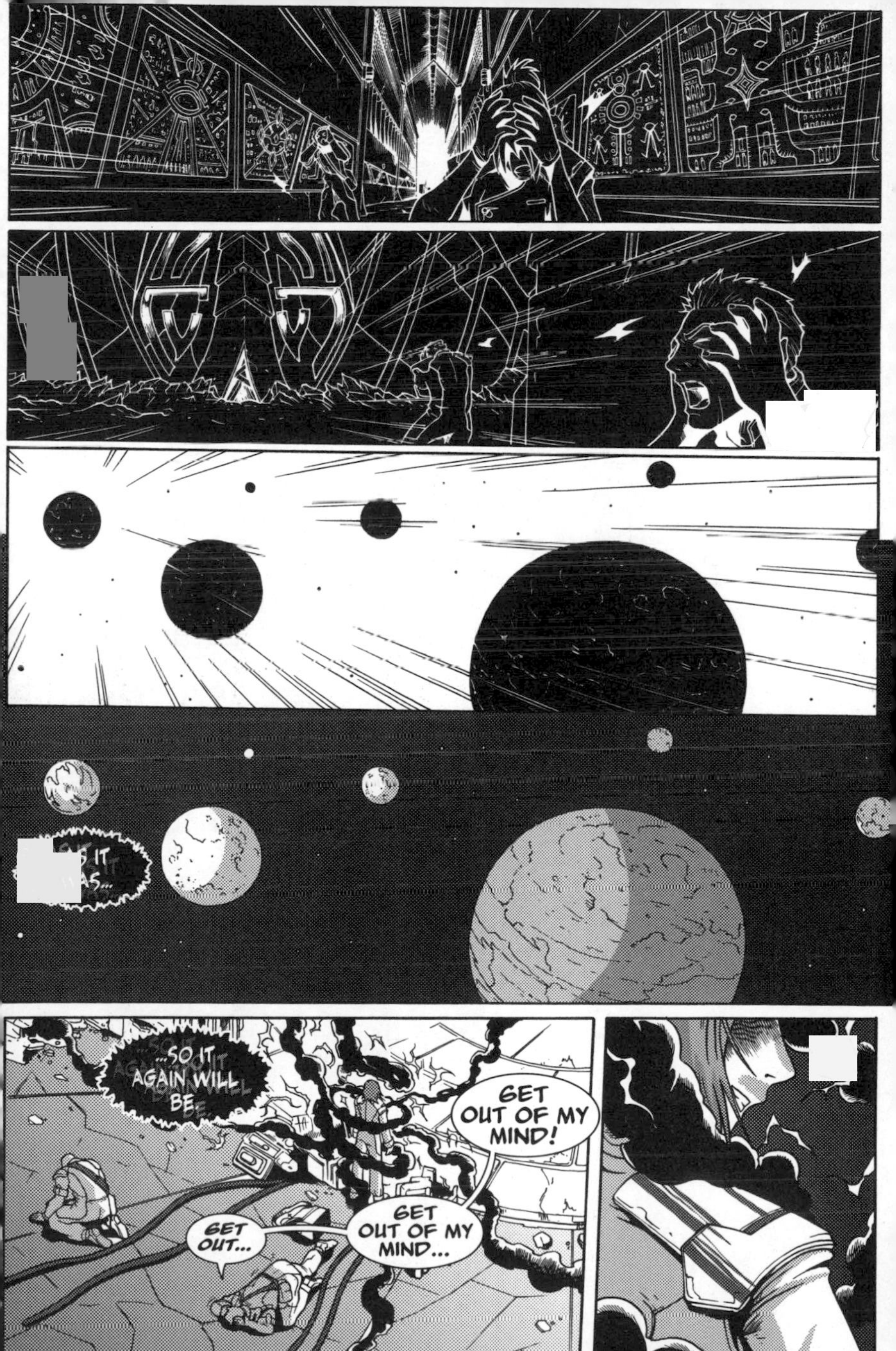
...SO IT AGAIN WILL BE
GET OUT...
GET OUT OF MY MIND...
GET OUT OF MY MIND!

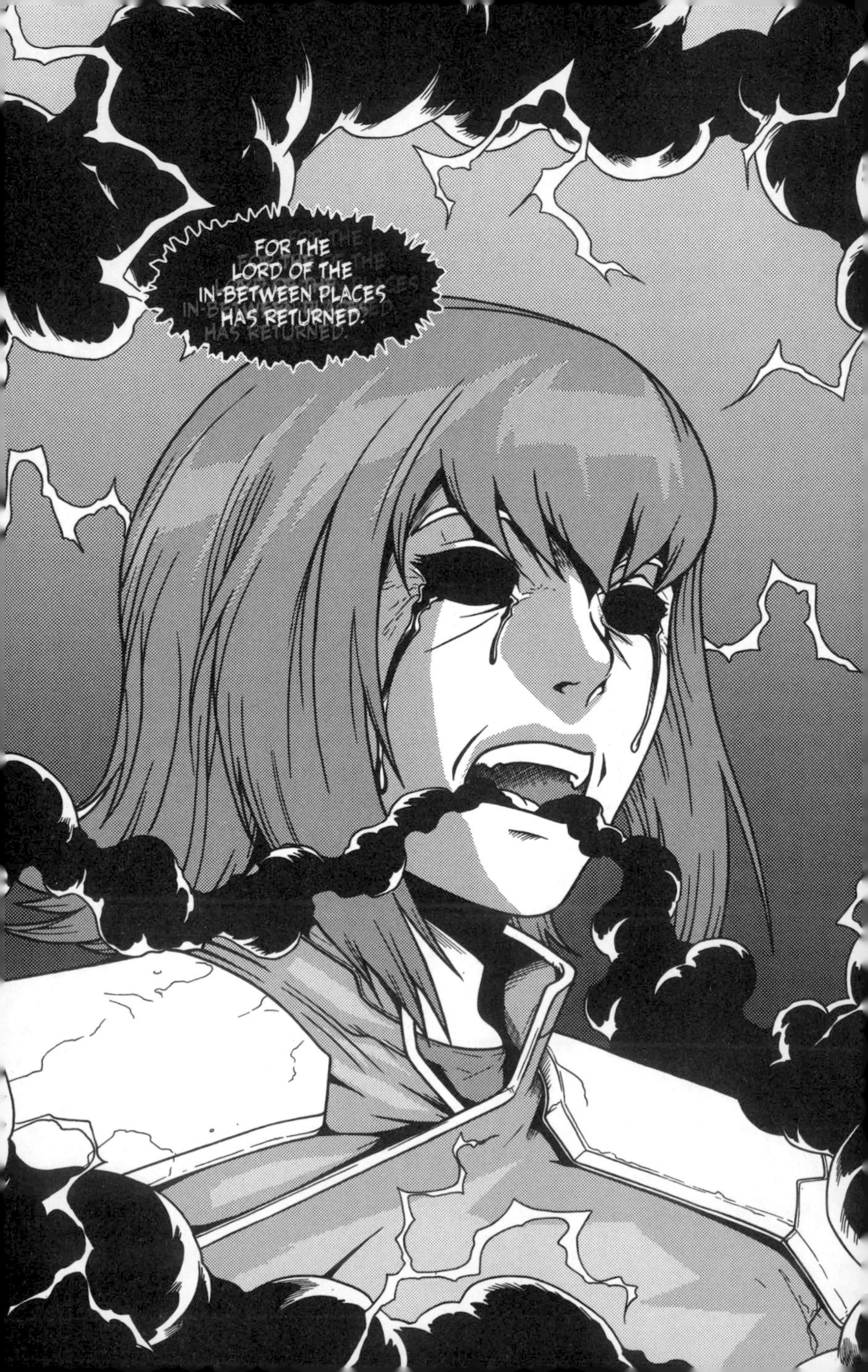
FOR THE
LORD OF THE
IN-BETWEEN PLACES
HAS RETURNED.

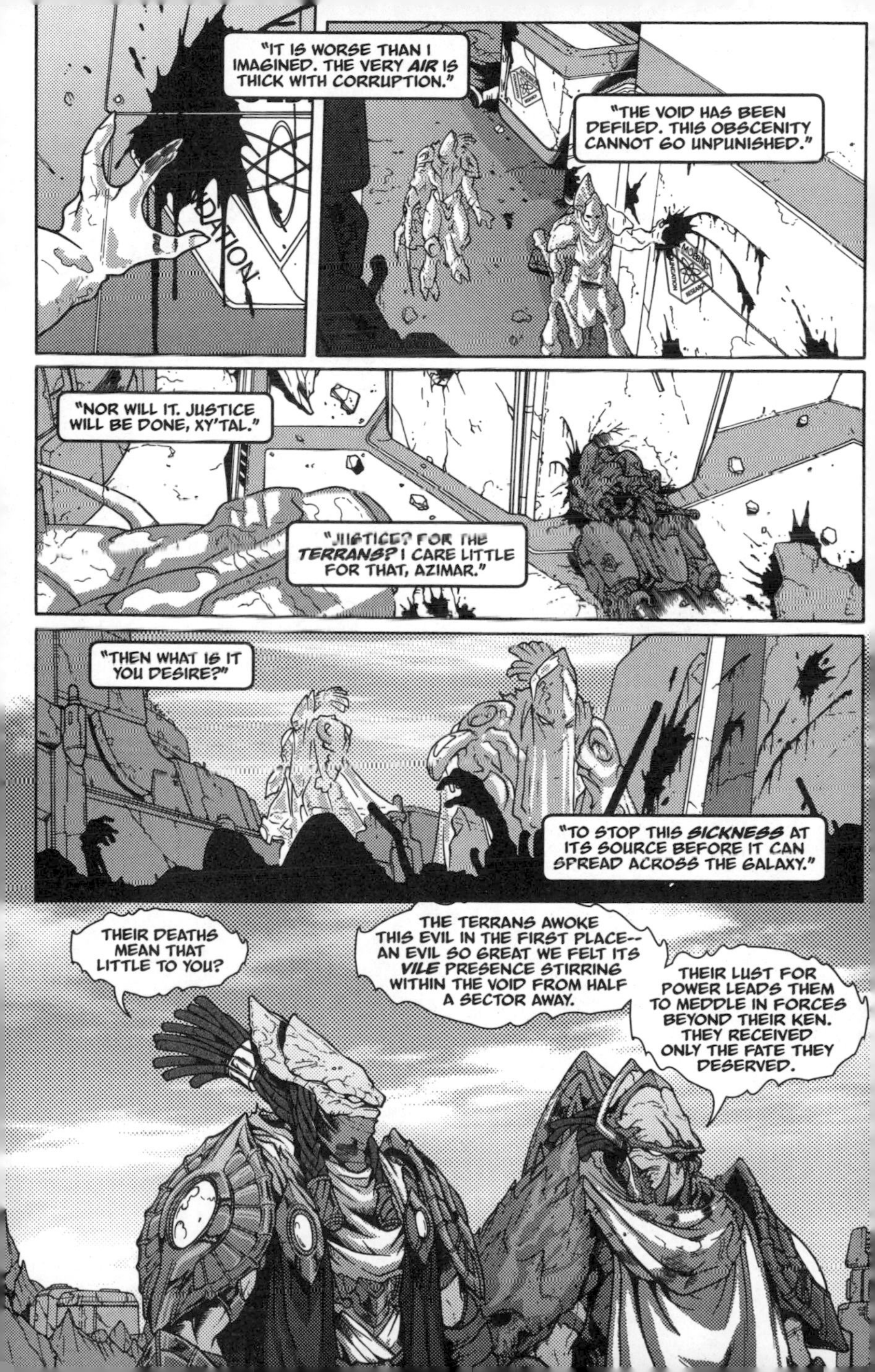
"IT IS WORSE THAN I IMAGINED. THE VERY AIR IS THICK WITH CORRUPTION."
"THE VOID HAS BEEN DEFILED. THIS OBSCENITY CANNOT GO UNPUNISHED."
"NOR WILL IT. JUSTICE WILL BE DONE, XY'TAL."
"JUSTICE? FOR THE TERRANS? I CARE LITTLE FOR THAT, AZIMAR."
"THEN WHAT IS IT YOU DESIRE?"
"TO STOP THIS SICKNESS AT ITS SOURCE BEFORE IT CAN SPREAD ACROSS THE GALAXY."
THEIR DEATHS MEAN THAT LITTLE TO YOU?
THE TERRANS AWOKE THIS EVIL IN THE FIRST PLACE-- AN EVIL SO GREAT WE FELT ITS VILE PRESENCE STIRRING WITHIN THE VOID FROM HALF A SECTOR AWAY.
THEIR LUST FOR POWER LEADS THEM TO MEDDLE IN FORCES BEYOND THEIR KEN. THEY RECEIVED ONLY THE FATE THEY DESERVED.

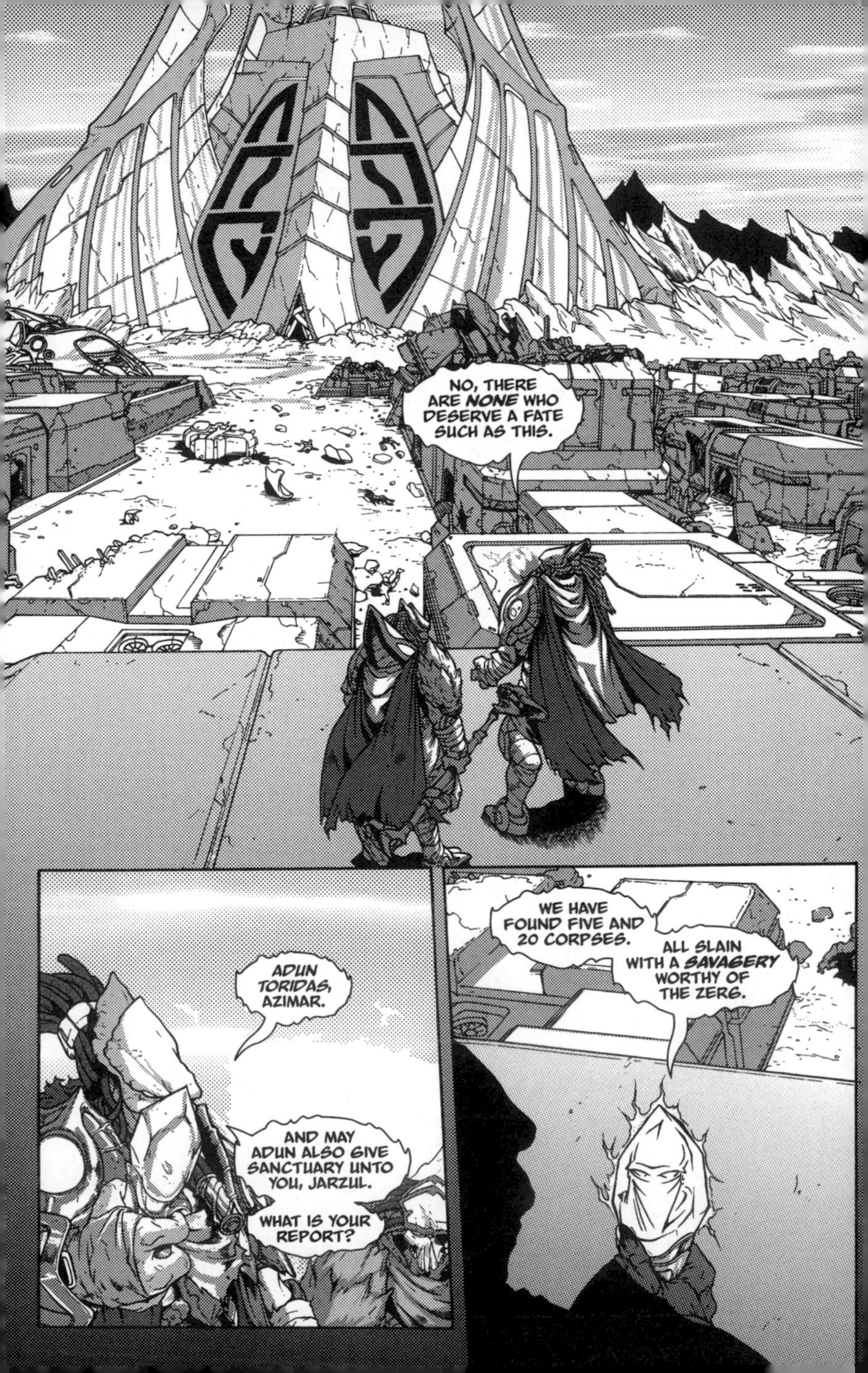
NO, THERE ARE NONE WHO DESERVE A FATE SUCH AS THIS.
ADUN TORIDAS, AZIMAR.
AND MAY ADUN ALSO GIVE SANCTUARY UNTO YOU, JARZUL.
WHAT IS YOUR REPORT?
WE HAVE FOUND FIVE AND 20 CORPSES.
ALL SLAIN WITH A SAVAGERY WORTHY OF THE ZERG.

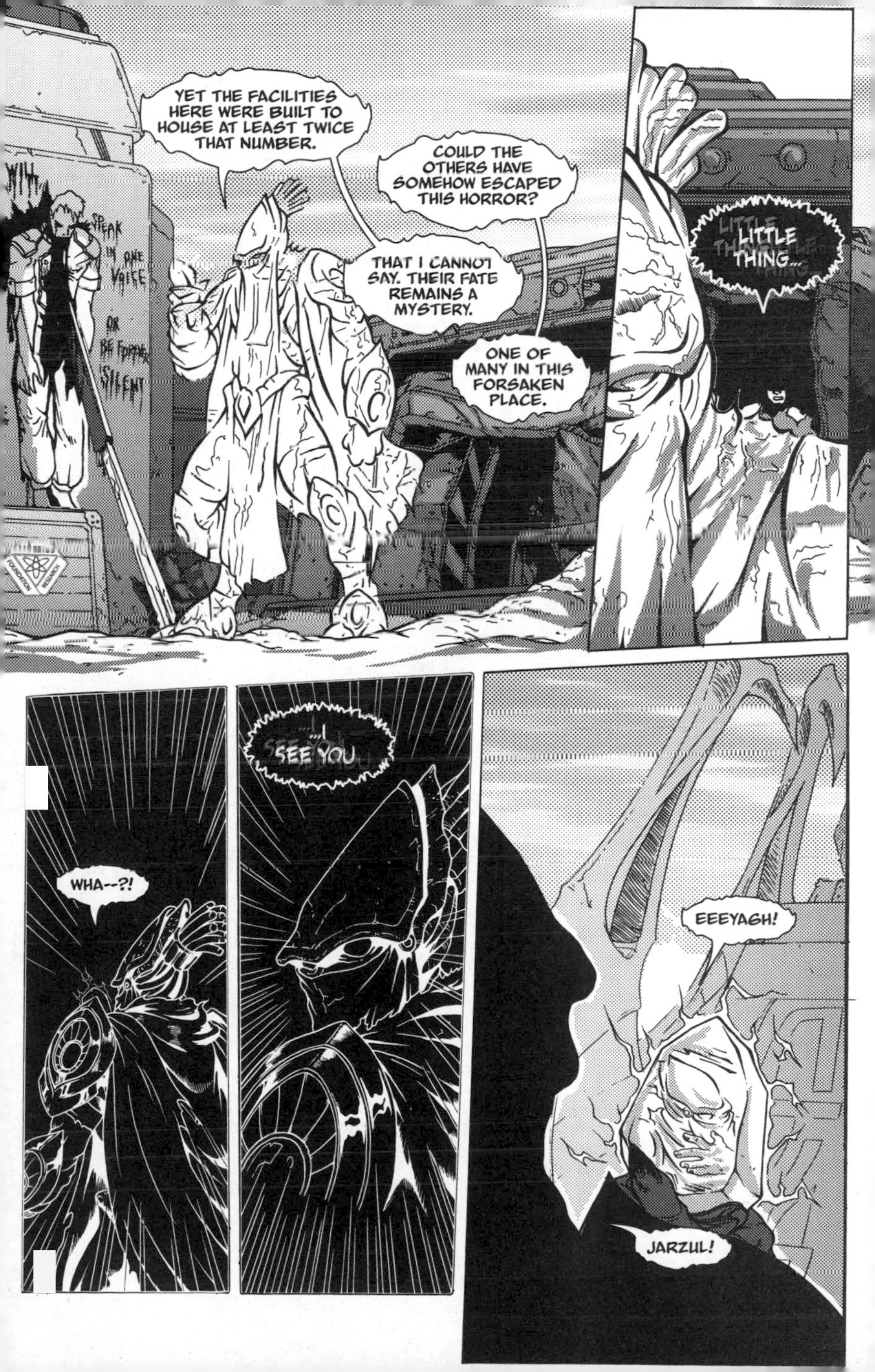
YET THE FACILITIES HERE WERE BUILT TO HOUSE AT LEAST TWICE THAT NUMBER.
COULD THE OTHERS HAVE SOMEHOW ESCAPED THIS HORROR?
THAT I CANNOT SAY. THEIR FATE REMAINS A MYSTERY.
ONE OF MANY IN THIS FORSAKEN PLACE.
LITTLE THING...
WHA--?!
...I SEE YOU
EEEYAGH!
JARZUL!

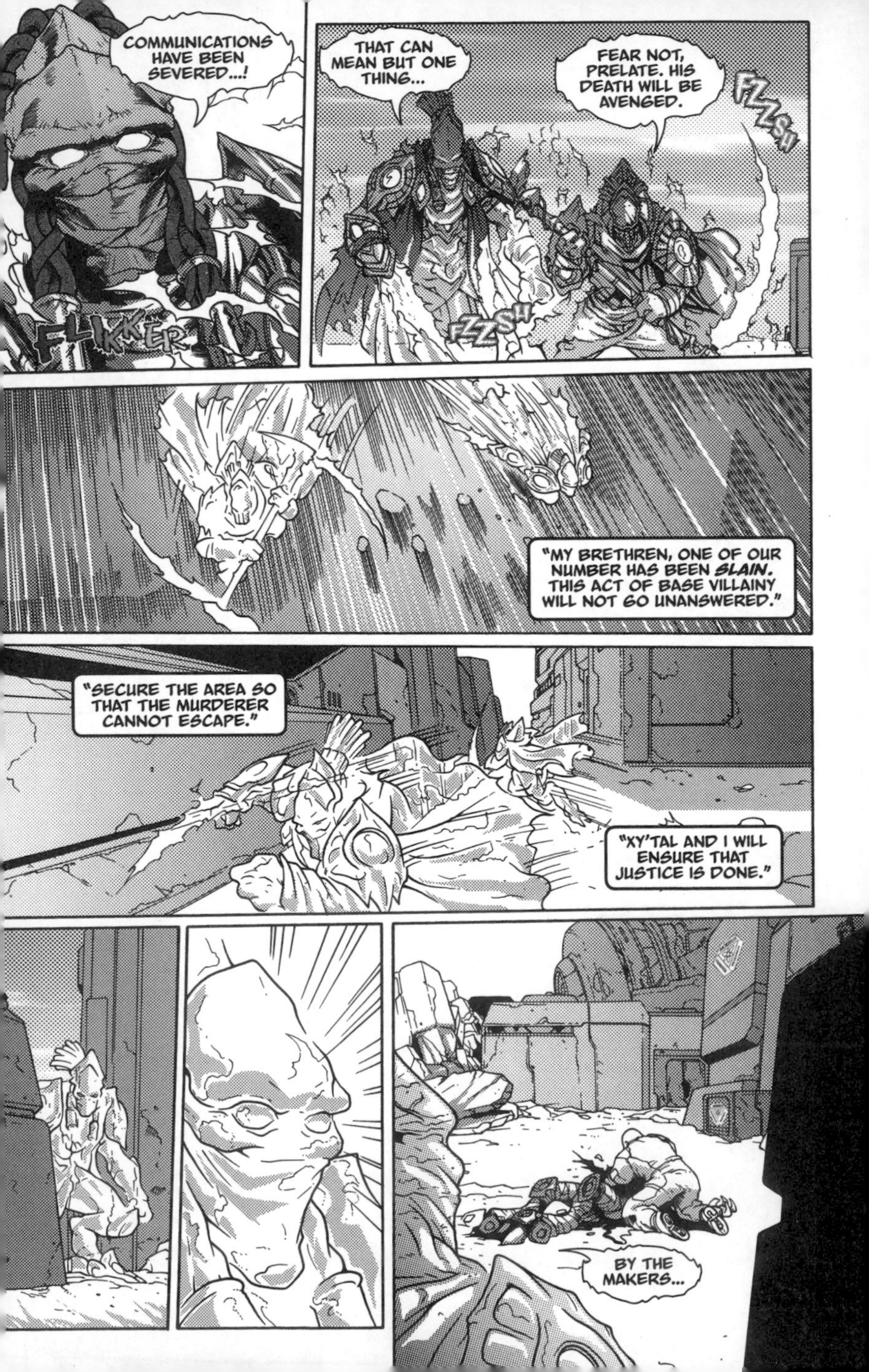
COMMUNICATIONS HAVE BEEN SEVERED...!
FLIKKER
THAT CAN MEAN BUT ONE THING...
FEAR NOT, PRELATE. HIS DEATH WILL BE AVENGED.
FZZSH
FZZSH
"MY BRETHREN, ONE OF OUR NUMBER HAS BEEN SLAIN. THIS ACT OF BASE VILLAINY WILL NOT GO UNANSWERED."
"SECURE THE AREA SO THAT THE MURDERER CANNOT ESCAPE."
"XY'TAL AND I WILL ENSURE THAT JUSTICE IS DONE."
BY THE MAKERS...

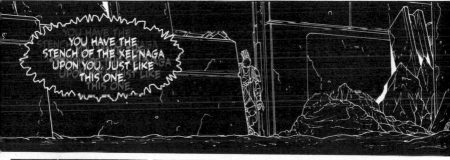

YOU HAVE THE STENCH OF THE XEL'NAGA UPON YOU, JUST LIKE THIS ONE.

I WONDER...

...WILL YOU DIE JUST AS EASILY?

AS FOR YOU, LITTLE THING...

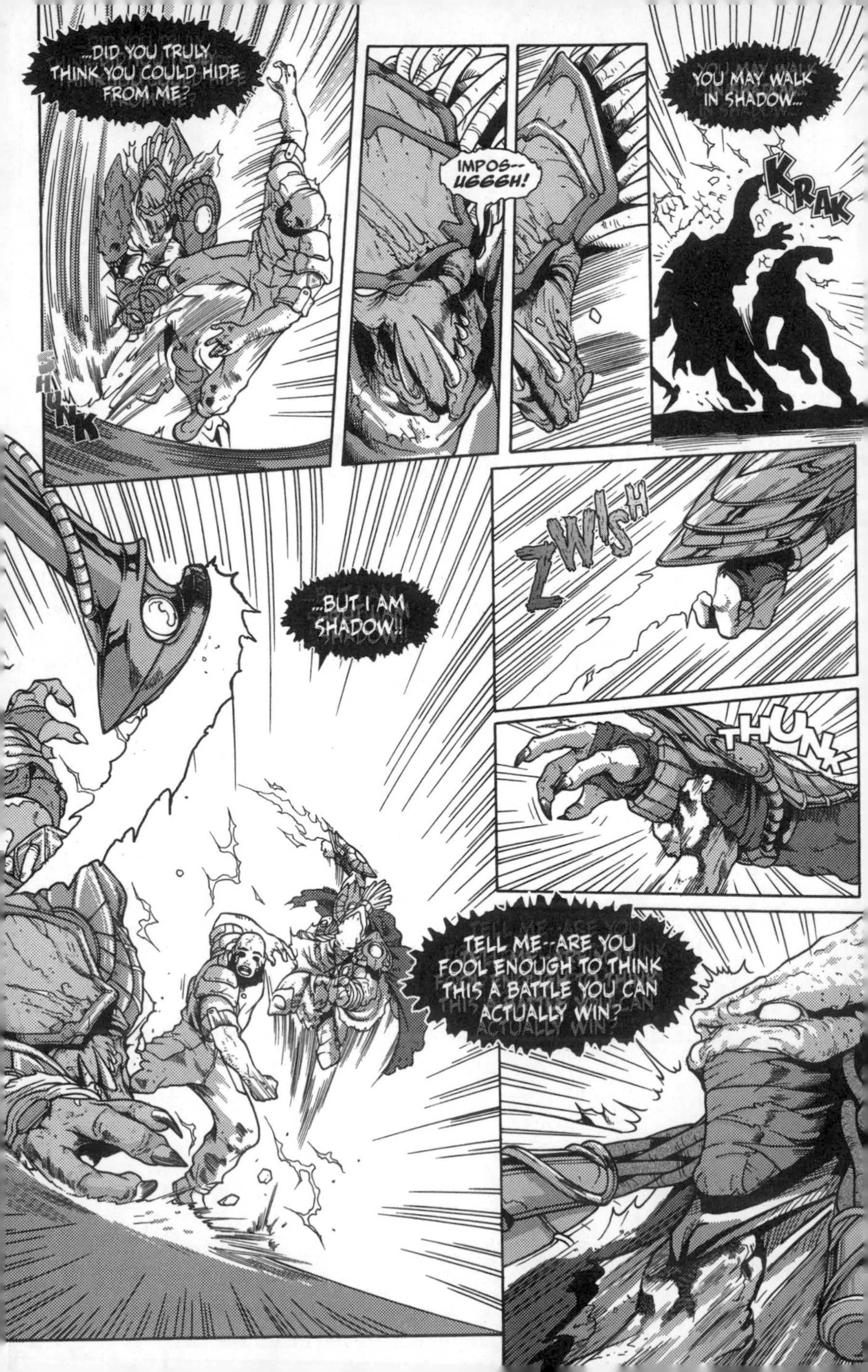
...DID YOU TRULY THINK YOU COULD HIDE FROM ME?
SHUNK
IMPOS-- UGGGH!
YOU MAY WALK IN SHADOW...
KRAK
...BUT I AM SHADOW!!
ZWISH
THUNK
TELL ME--ARE YOU FOOL ENOUGH TO THINK THIS A BATTLE YOU CAN ACTUALLY WIN?

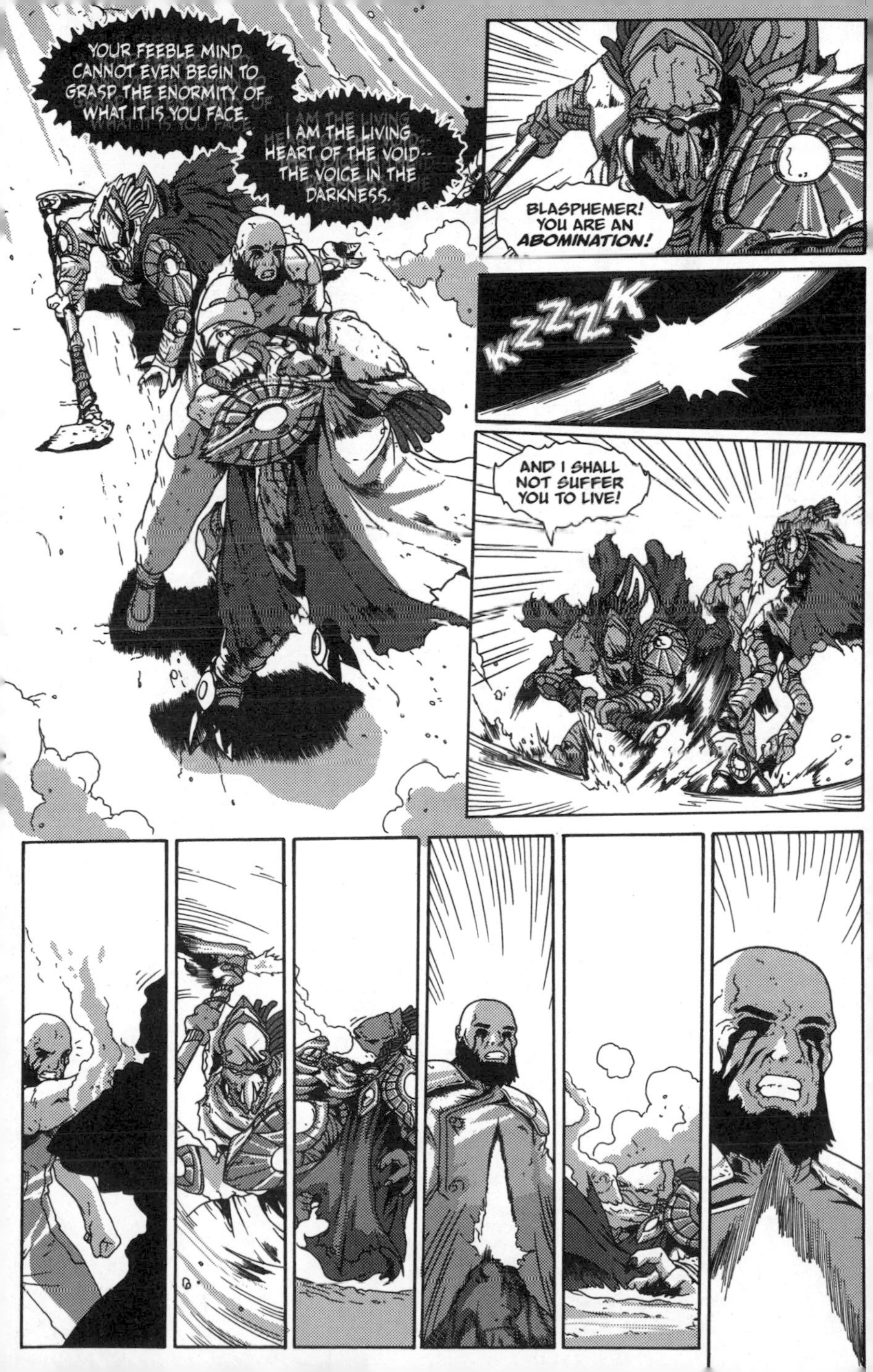
YOUR FEEBLE MIND CANNOT EVEN BEGIN TO GRASP THE ENORMITY OF WHAT IT IS YOU FACE.
I AM THE LIVING HEART OF THE VOID-- THE VOICE IN THE DARKNESS.
BLASPHEMER! YOU ARE AN ABOMINATION!
KZZZZK
AND I SHALL NOT SUFFER YOU TO LIVE!

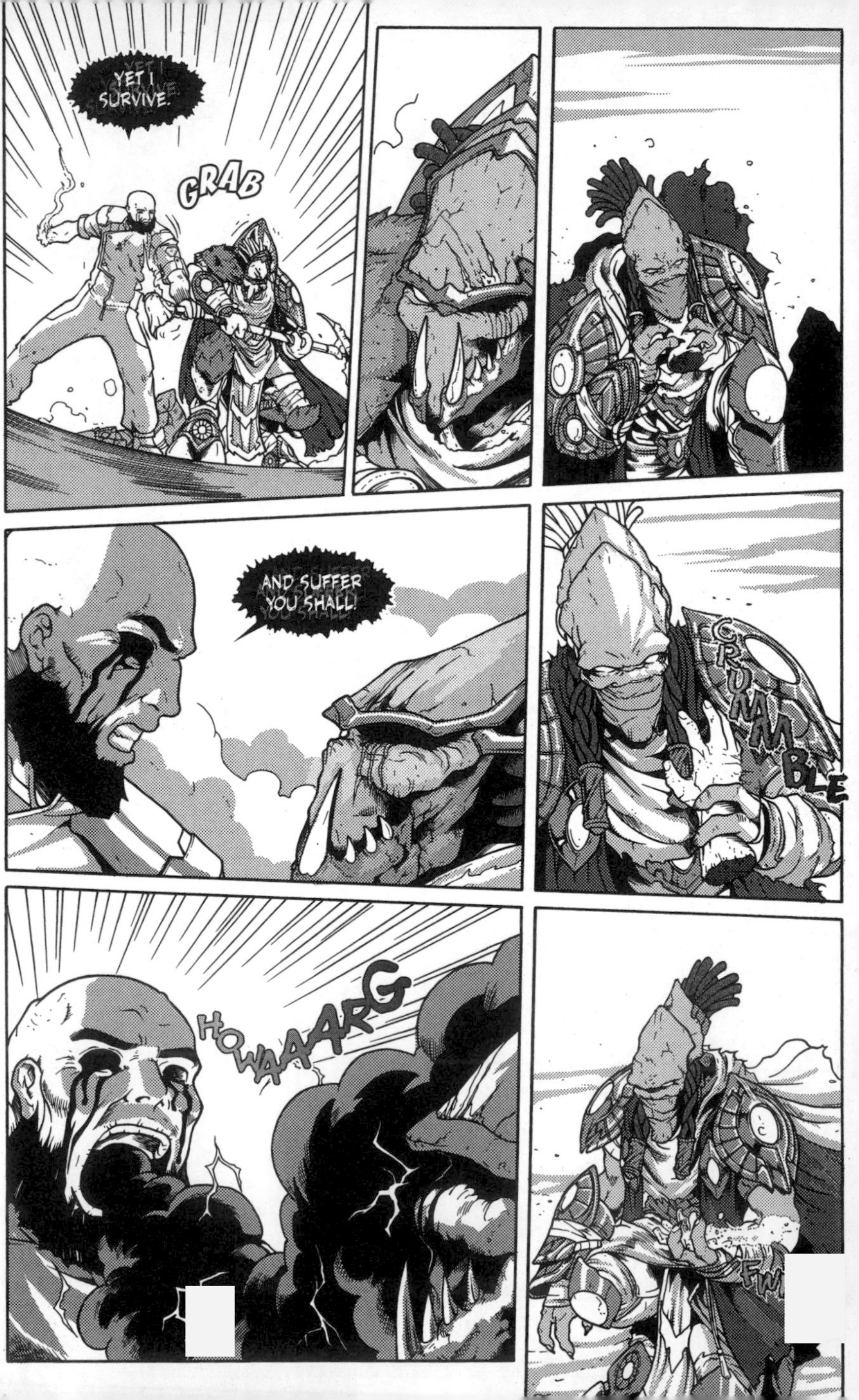
YET I SURVIVE.
GRAB
AND SUFFER YOU SHALL!
CRUMMBLE
HOWAAARG

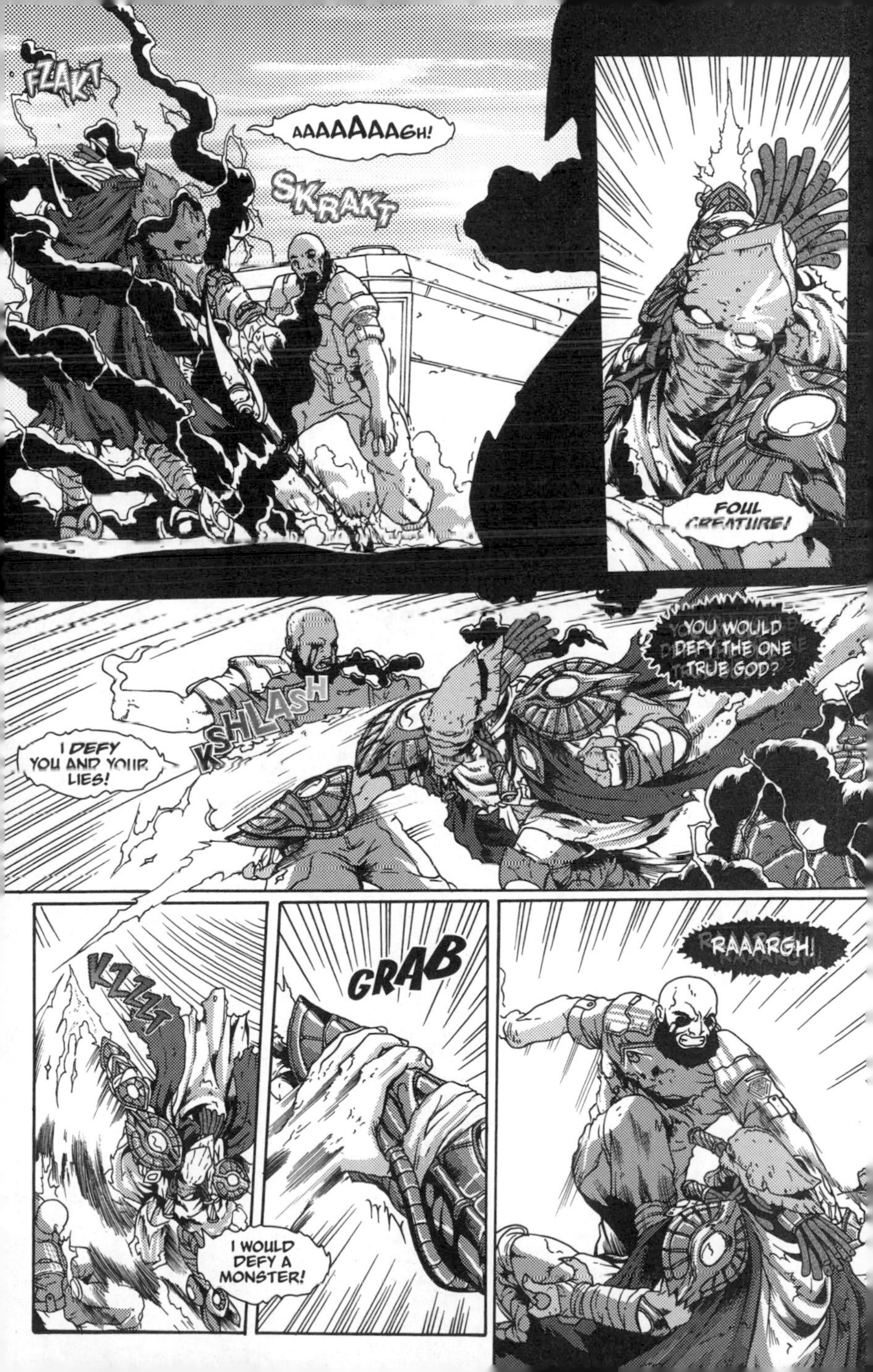

FZAKT
AAAAAAAGH!
SKRAKT
FOUL CREATURE!
YOU WOULD DEFY THE ONE TRUE GOD?
KSHLASH
I DEFY YOU AND YOUR LIES!
KZZZT
GRAB
I WOULD DEFY A MONSTER!
RAAARGH!

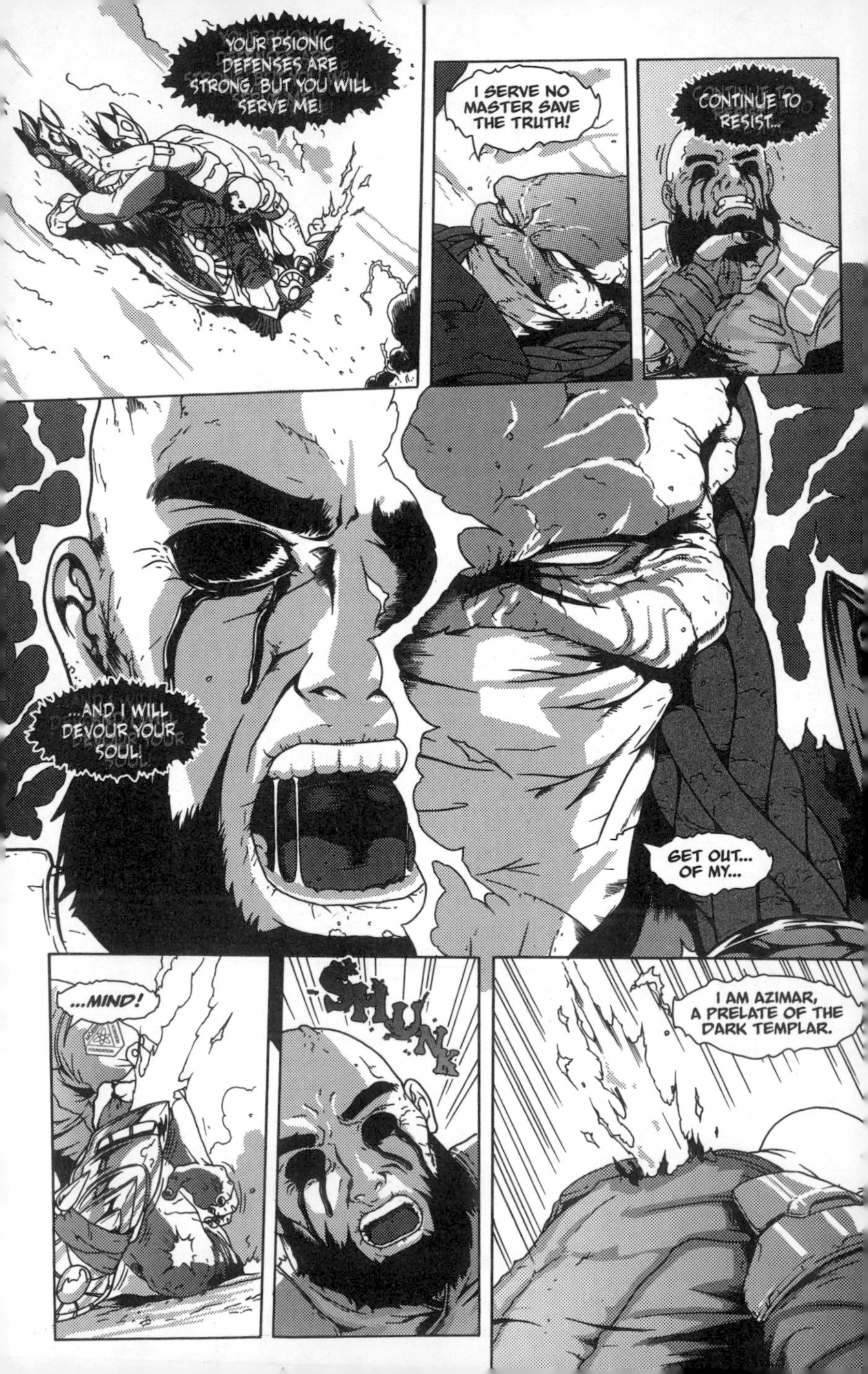
YOUR PSIONIC DEFENSES ARE STRONG, BUT YOU WILL SERVE ME!
I SERVE NO MASTER SAVE THE TRUTH!
CONTINUE TO RESIST...
...AND I WILL DEVOUR YOUR SOUL!
GET OUT... OF MY...
...MIND!
SHUNK
I AM AZIMAR, A PRELATE OF THE DARK TEMPLAR.

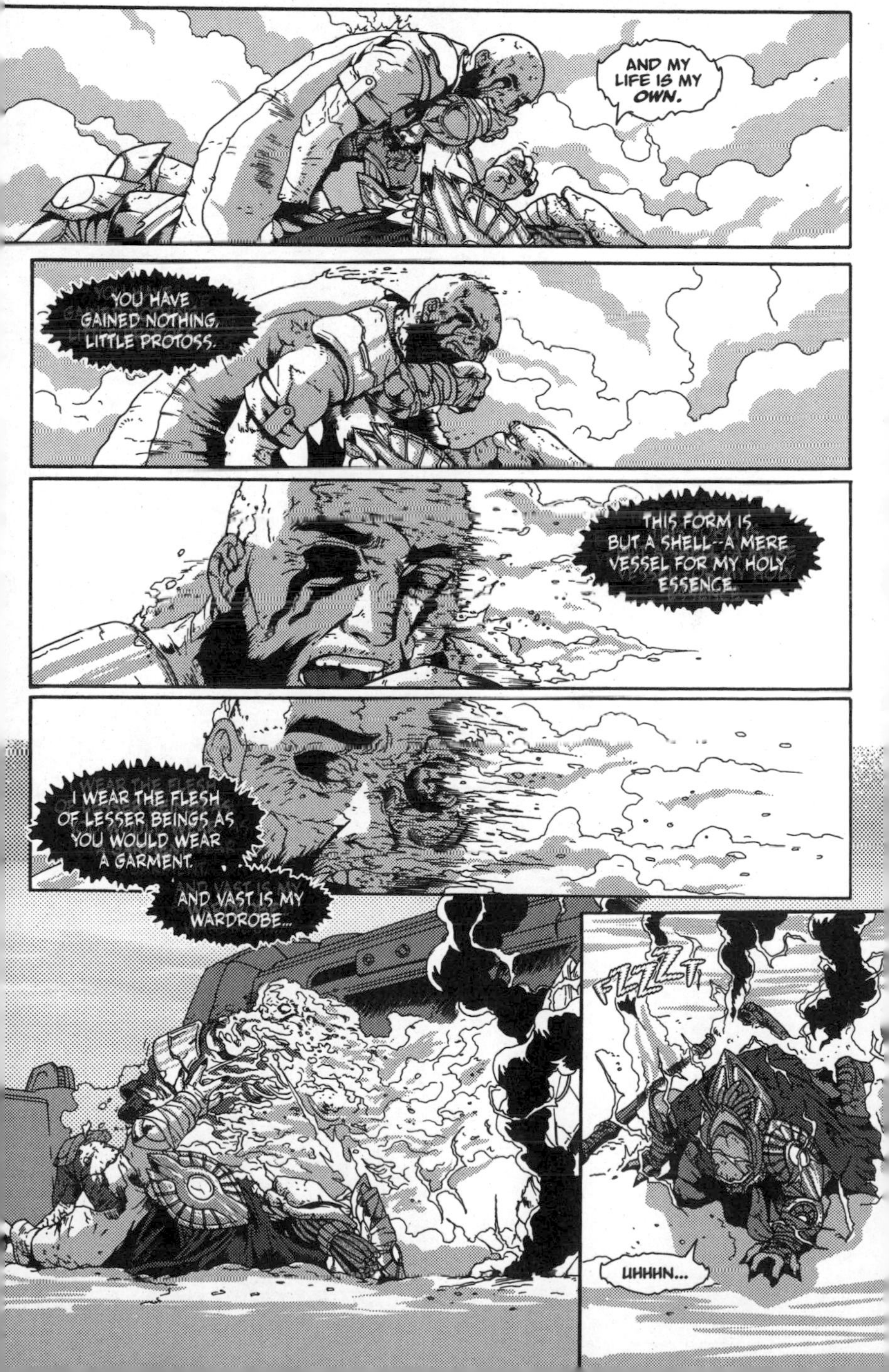
AND MY LIFE IS MY OWN.
YOU HAVE GAINED NOTHING, LITTLE PROTOSS.
THIS FORM IS BUT A SHELL--A MERE VESSEL FOR MY HOLY ESSENCE.
I WEAR THE FLESH OF LESSER BEINGS AS YOU WOULD WEAR A GARMENT.
AND VAST IS MY WARDROBE...
FZZZT
UHHHN...

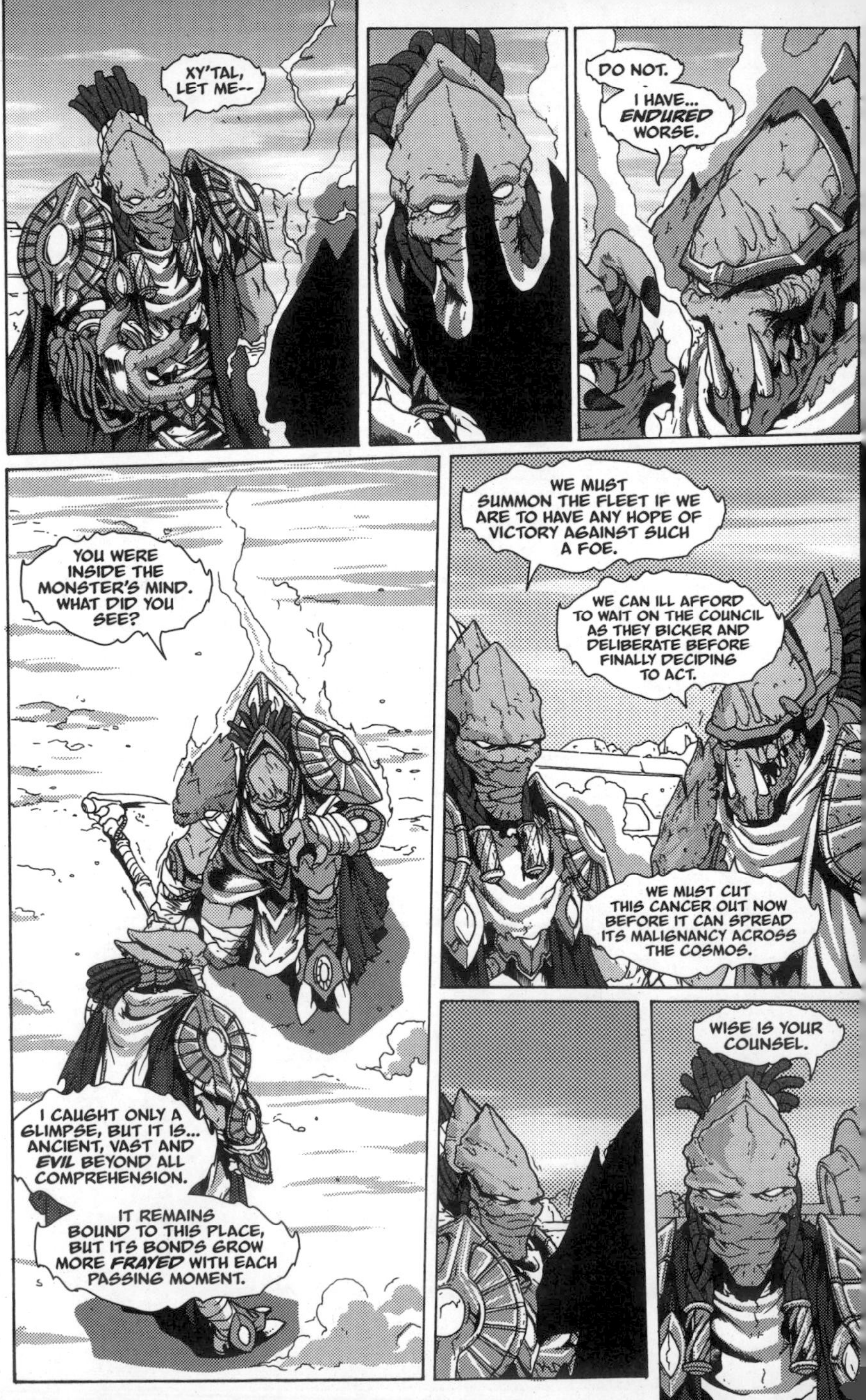
XY'TAL, LET ME--
DO NOT.
I HAVE... *ENDURED* WORSE.
YOU WERE INSIDE THE MONSTER'S MIND. WHAT DID YOU SEE?
I CAUGHT ONLY A GLIMPSE, BUT IT IS... ANCIENT, VAST AND *EVIL* BEYOND ALL COMPREHENSION.
IT REMAINS BOUND TO THIS PLACE, BUT ITS BONDS GROW MORE *FRAYED* WITH EACH PASSING MOMENT.
WE MUST SUMMON THE FLEET IF WE ARE TO HAVE ANY HOPE OF VICTORY AGAINST SUCH A FOE.
WE CAN ILL AFFORD TO WAIT ON THE COUNCIL AS THEY BICKER AND DELIBERATE BEFORE FINALLY DECIDING TO ACT.
WE MUST CUT THIS CANCER OUT NOW BEFORE IT CAN SPREAD ITS MALIGNANCY ACROSS THE COSMOS.
WISE IS YOUR COUNSEL.

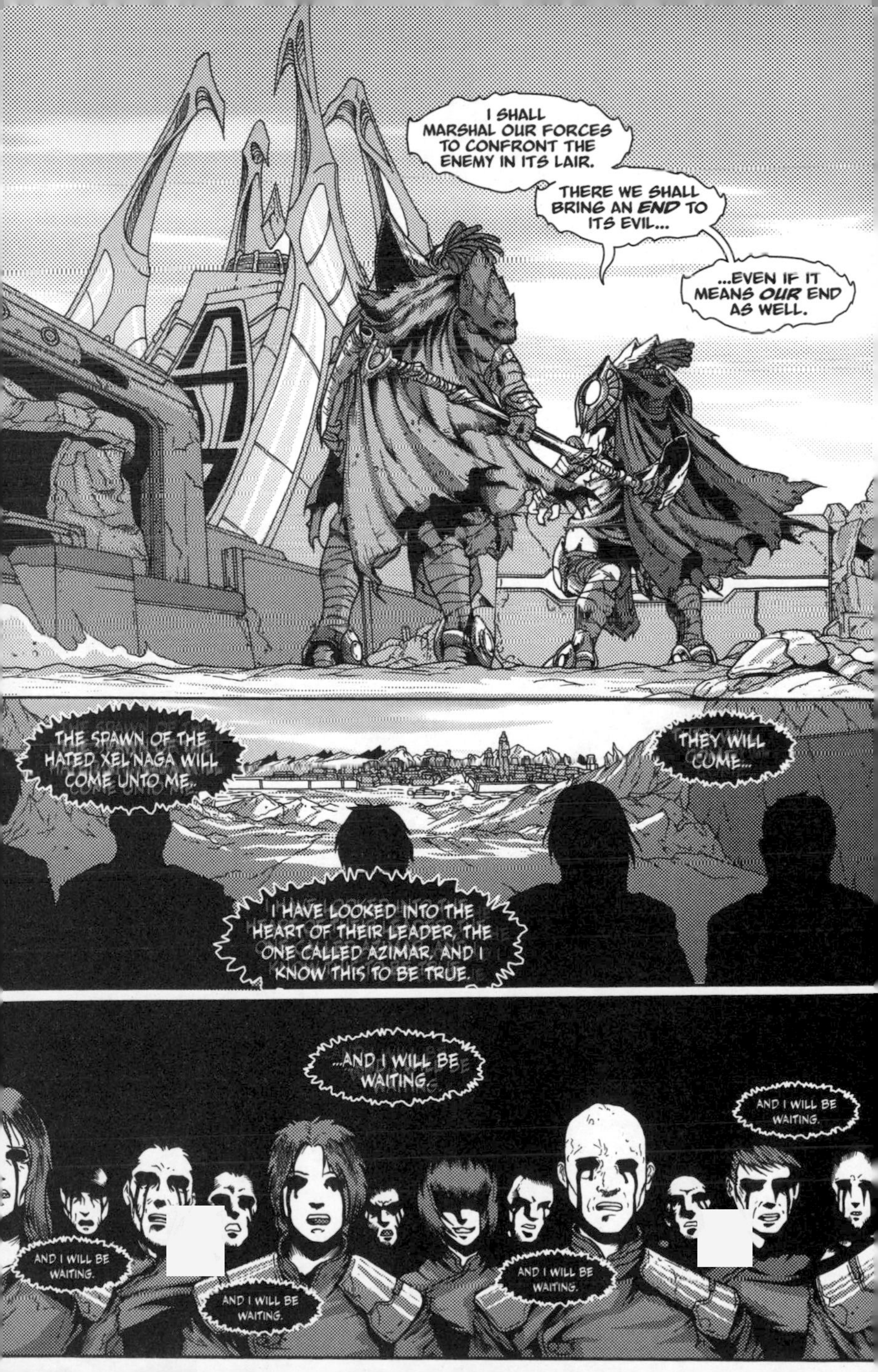
I SHALL MARSHAL OUR FORCES TO CONFRONT THE ENEMY IN ITS LAIR.
THERE WE SHALL BRING AN *END* TO ITS EVIL...
...EVEN IF IT MEANS *OUR* END AS WELL.
THE SPAWN OF THE HATED XEL'NAGA WILL COME UNTO ME.
THEY WILL COME...
I HAVE LOOKED INTO THE HEART OF THEIR LEADER, THE ONE CALLED AZIMAR, AND I KNOW THIS TO BE TRUE.
...AND I WILL BE WAITING.
AND I WILL BE WAITING.
AND I WILL BE WAITING.
AND I WILL BE WAITING.
AND I WILL BE WAITING.

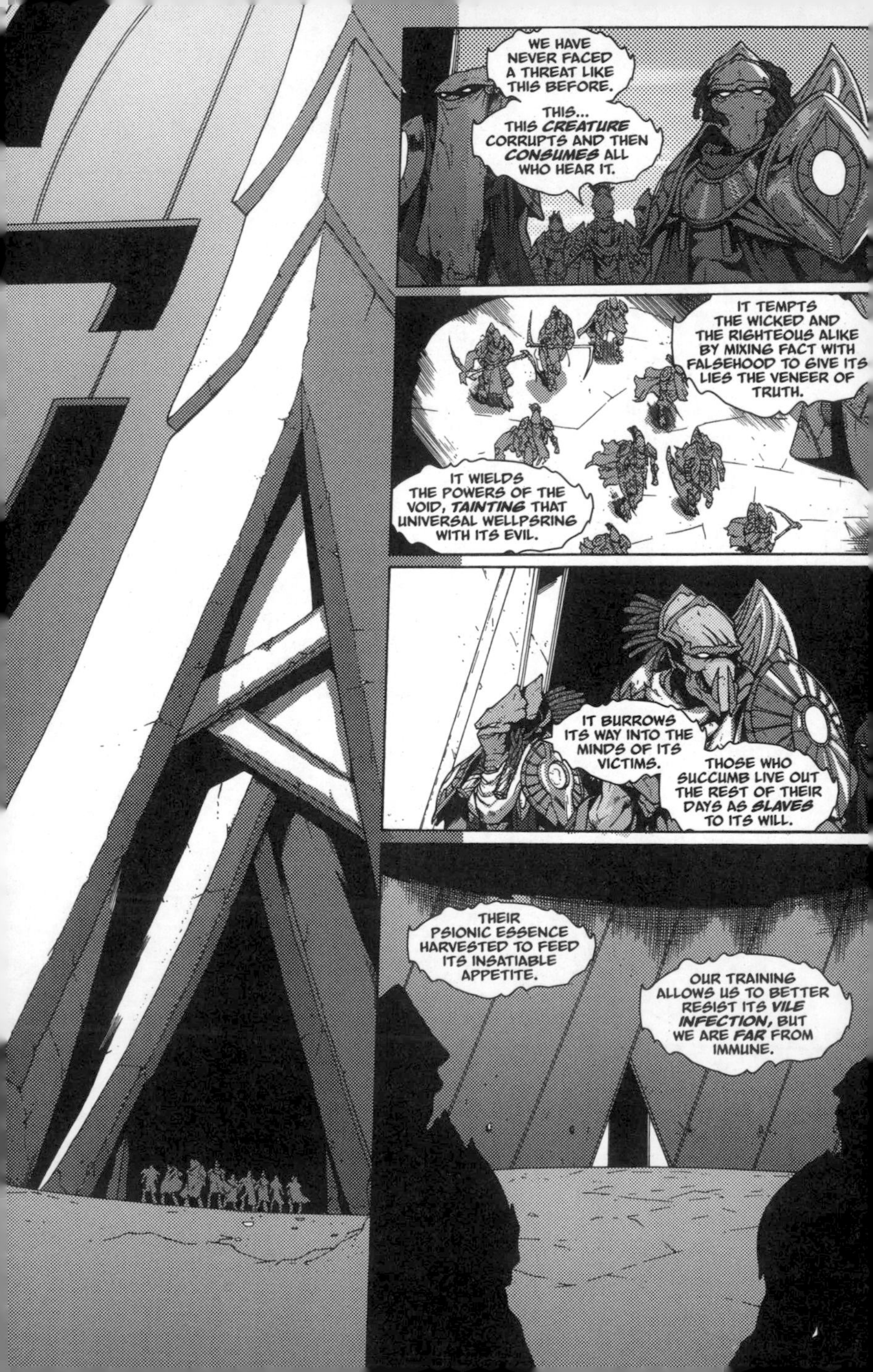
WE HAVE NEVER FACED A THREAT LIKE THIS BEFORE.
THIS... THIS CREATURE CORRUPTS AND THEN CONSUMES ALL WHO HEAR IT.
IT TEMPTS THE WICKED AND THE RIGHTEOUS ALIKE BY MIXING FACT WITH FALSEHOOD TO GIVE ITS LIES THE VENEER OF TRUTH.
IT WIELDS THE POWERS OF THE VOID, TAINTING THAT UNIVERSAL WELLPSRING WITH ITS EVIL.
IT BURROWS ITS WAY INTO THE MINDS OF ITS VICTIMS.
THOSE WHO SUCCUMB LIVE OUT THE REST OF THEIR DAYS AS SLAVES TO ITS WILL.
THEIR PSIONIC ESSENCE HARVESTED TO FEED ITS INSATIABLE APPETITE.
OUR TRAINING ALLOWS US TO BETTER RESIST ITS VILE INFECTION, BUT WE ARE FAR FROM IMMUNE.

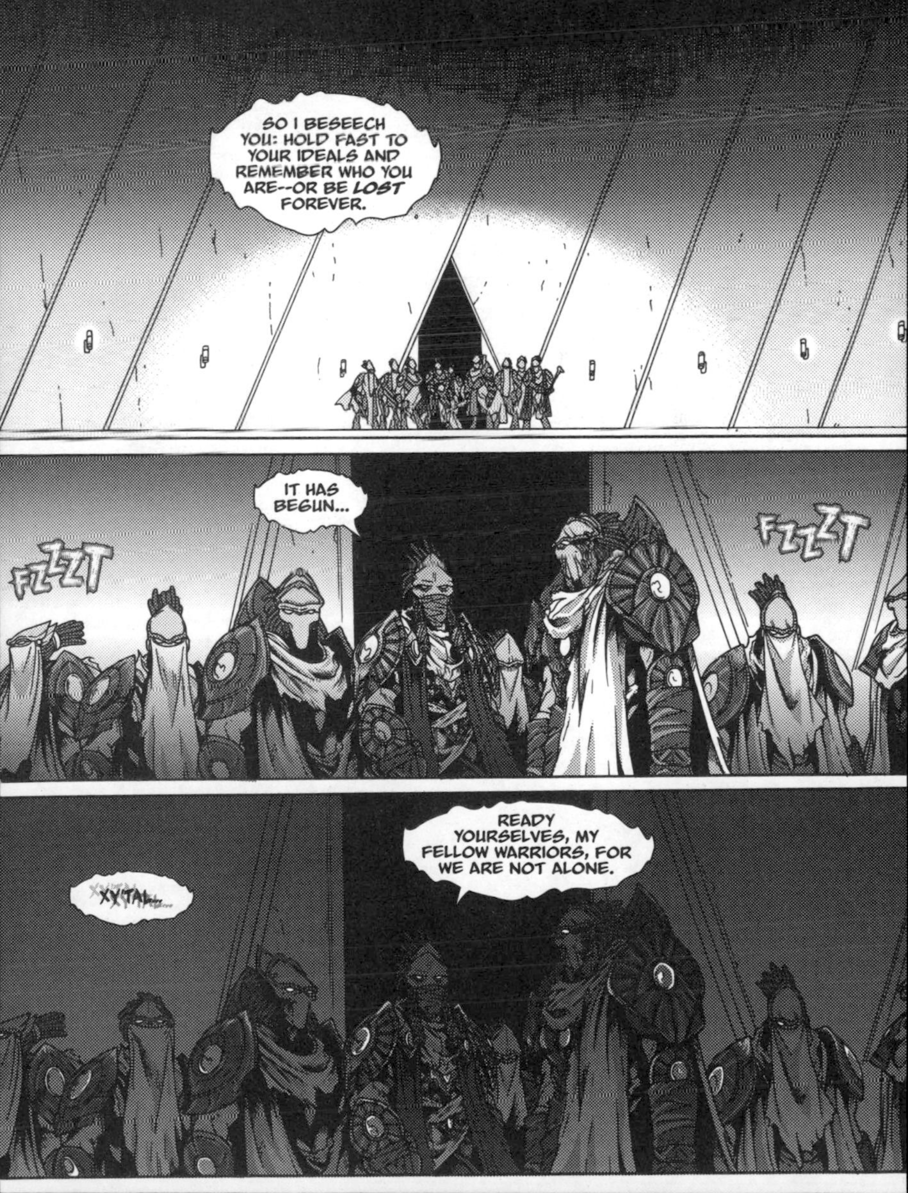
SO I BESEECH YOU: HOLD FAST TO YOUR IDEALS AND REMEMBER WHO YOU ARE--OR BE *LOST* FOREVER.
IT HAS BEGUN...
FZZZT
FZZZT
READY YOURSELVES, MY FELLOW WARRIORS, FOR WE ARE NOT ALONE.
XY'TAL...

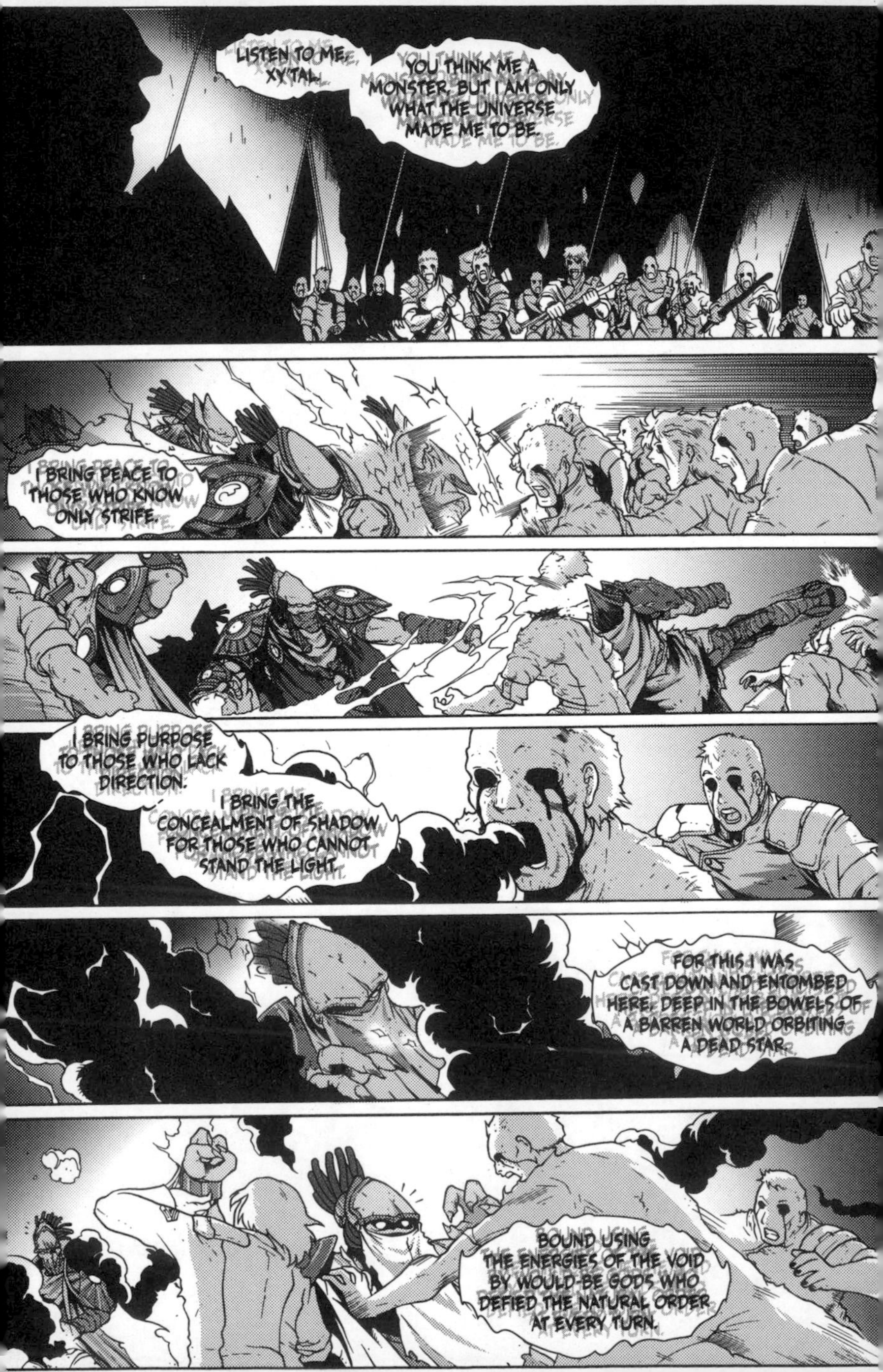
LISTEN TO ME, XY'TAL.
YOU THINK ME A MONSTER, BUT I AM ONLY WHAT THE UNIVERSE MADE ME TO BE.
I BRING PEACE TO THOSE WHO KNOW ONLY STRIFE.
I BRING PURPOSE TO THOSE WHO LACK DIRECTION.
I BRING THE CONCEALMENT OF SHADOW FOR THOSE WHO CANNOT STAND THE LIGHT.
FOR THIS I WAS CAST DOWN AND ENTOMBED HERE, DEEP IN THE BOWELS OF A BARREN WORLD ORBITING A DEAD STAR.
BOUND USING THE ENERGIES OF THE VOID BY WOULD-BE GODS WHO DEFIED THE NATURAL ORDER AT EVERY TURN.

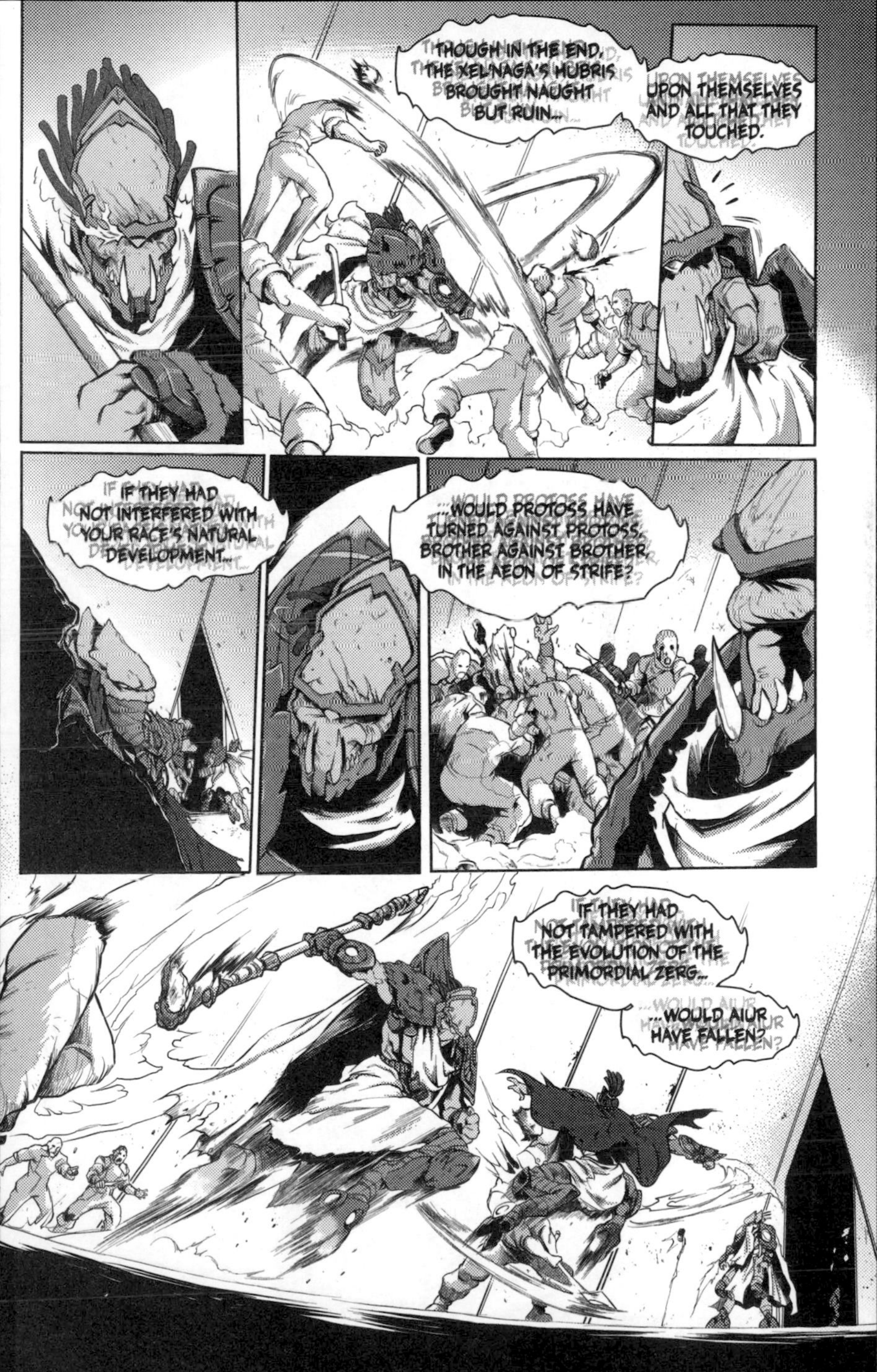
THOUGH IN THE END, THE XEL'NAGA'S HUBRIS BROUGHT NAUGHT BUT RUIN...
UPON THEMSELVES AND ALL THAT THEY TOUCHED.
IF THEY HAD NOT INTERFERED WITH YOUR RACE'S NATURAL DEVELOPMENT...
...WOULD PROTOSS HAVE TURNED AGAINST PROTOSS, BROTHER AGAINST BROTHER, IN THE AEON OF STRIFE?
IF THEY HAD NOT TAMPERED WITH THE EVOLUTION OF THE PRIMORDIAL ZERG...
...WOULD AIUR HAVE FALLEN?

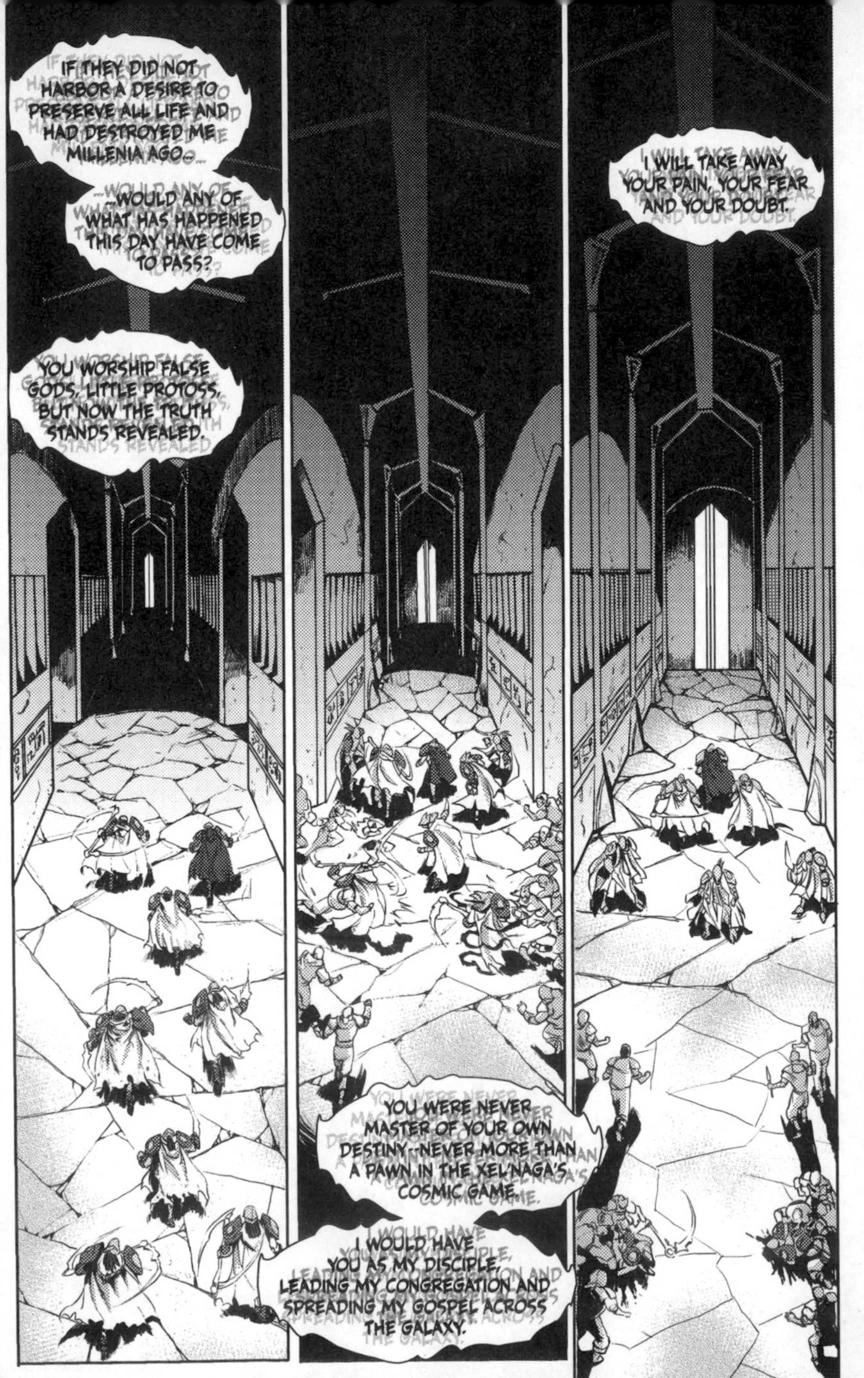

IF THEY DID NOT HARBOR A DESIRE TO PRESERVE ALL LIFE AND HAD DESTROYED ME MILLENIA AGO...
...WOULD ANY OF WHAT HAS HAPPENED THIS DAY HAVE COME TO PASS?
YOU WORSHIP FALSE GODS, LITTLE PROTOSS, BUT NOW THE TRUTH STANDS REVEALED.
YOU WERE NEVER MASTER OF YOUR OWN DESTINY--NEVER MORE THAN A PAWN IN THE XEL'NAGA'S COSMIC GAME.
I WOULD HAVE YOU AS MY DISCIPLE, LEADING MY CONGREGATION AND SPREADING MY GOSPEL ACROSS THE GALAXY.
I WILL TAKE AWAY YOUR PAIN, YOUR FEAR AND YOUR DOUBT.

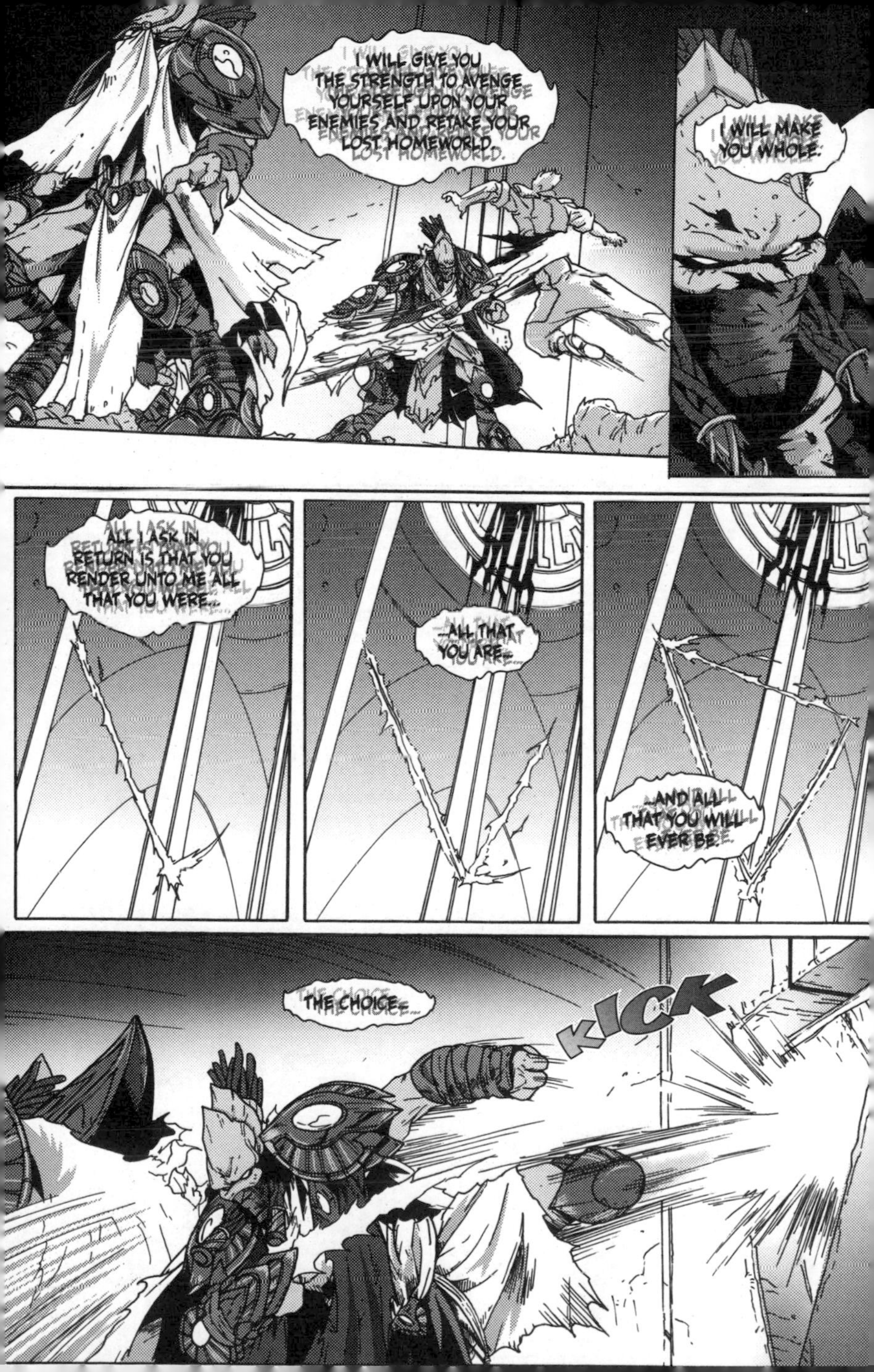
I WILL GIVE YOU THE STRENGTH TO AVENGE YOURSELF UPON YOUR ENEMIES AND RETAKE YOUR LOST HOMEWORLD.
I WILL MAKE YOU WHOLE.
ALL I ASK IN RETURN IS THAT YOU RENDER UNTO ME ALL THAT YOU WERE...
...ALL THAT YOU ARE...
...AND ALL THAT YOU WILL EVER BE.
THE CHOICE...
KICK

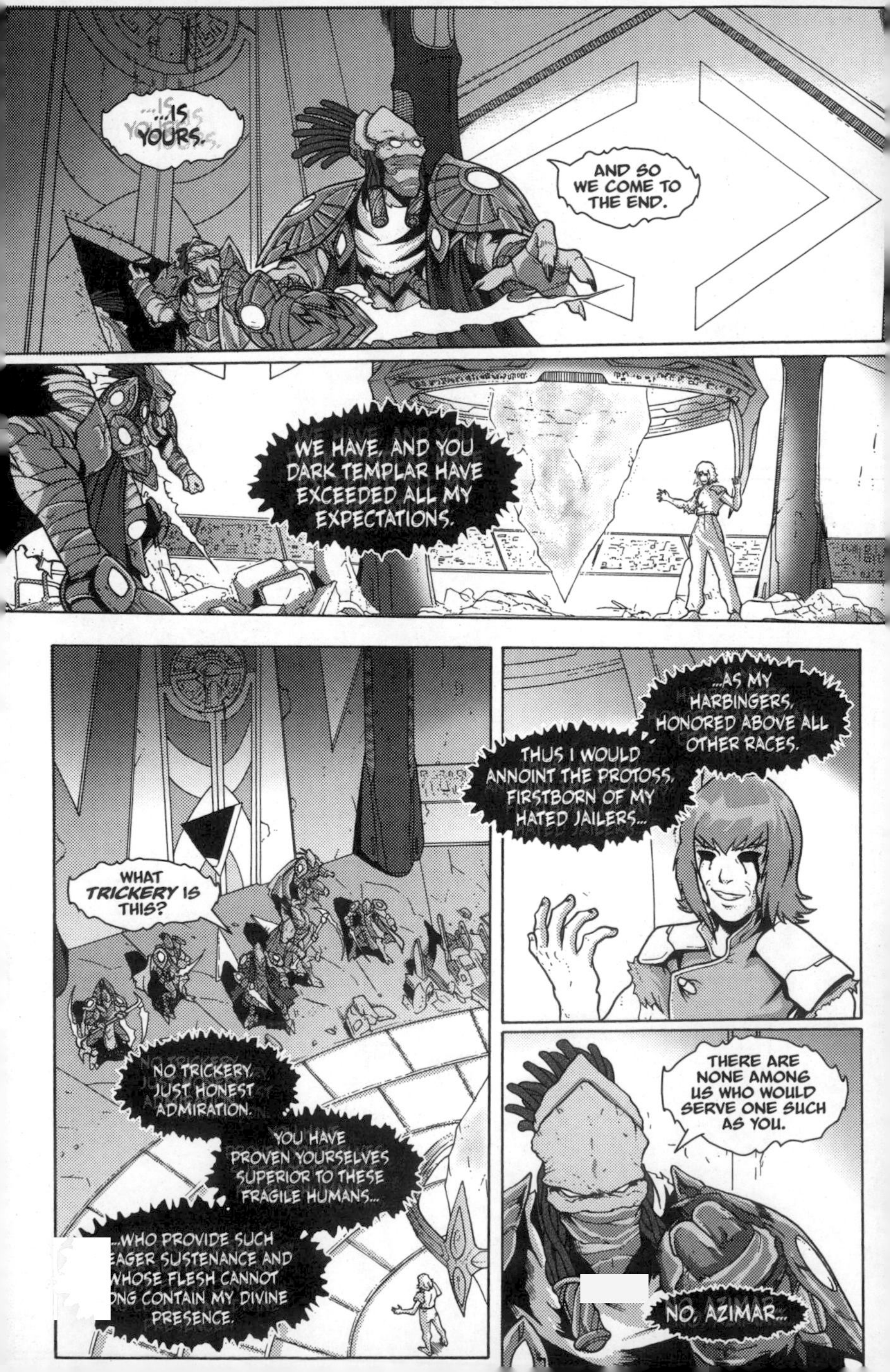
...IS YOURS.
AND SO WE COME TO THE END.
WE HAVE, AND YOU DARK TEMPLAR HAVE EXCEEDED ALL MY EXPECTATIONS.
WHAT TRICKERY IS THIS?
NO TRICKERY, JUST HONEST ADMIRATION.
YOU HAVE PROVEN YOURSELVES SUPERIOR TO THESE FRAGILE HUMANS...
...WHO PROVIDE SUCH EAGER SUSTENANCE AND WHOSE FLESH CANNOT ONG CONTAIN MY DIVINE PRESENCE.
THUS I WOULD ANNOINT THE PROTOSS, FIRSTBORN OF MY HATED JAILERS...
...AS MY HARBINGERS, HONORED ABOVE ALL OTHER RACES.
THERE ARE NONE AMONG US WHO WOULD SERVE ONE SUCH AS YOU.
NO, AZIMAR...

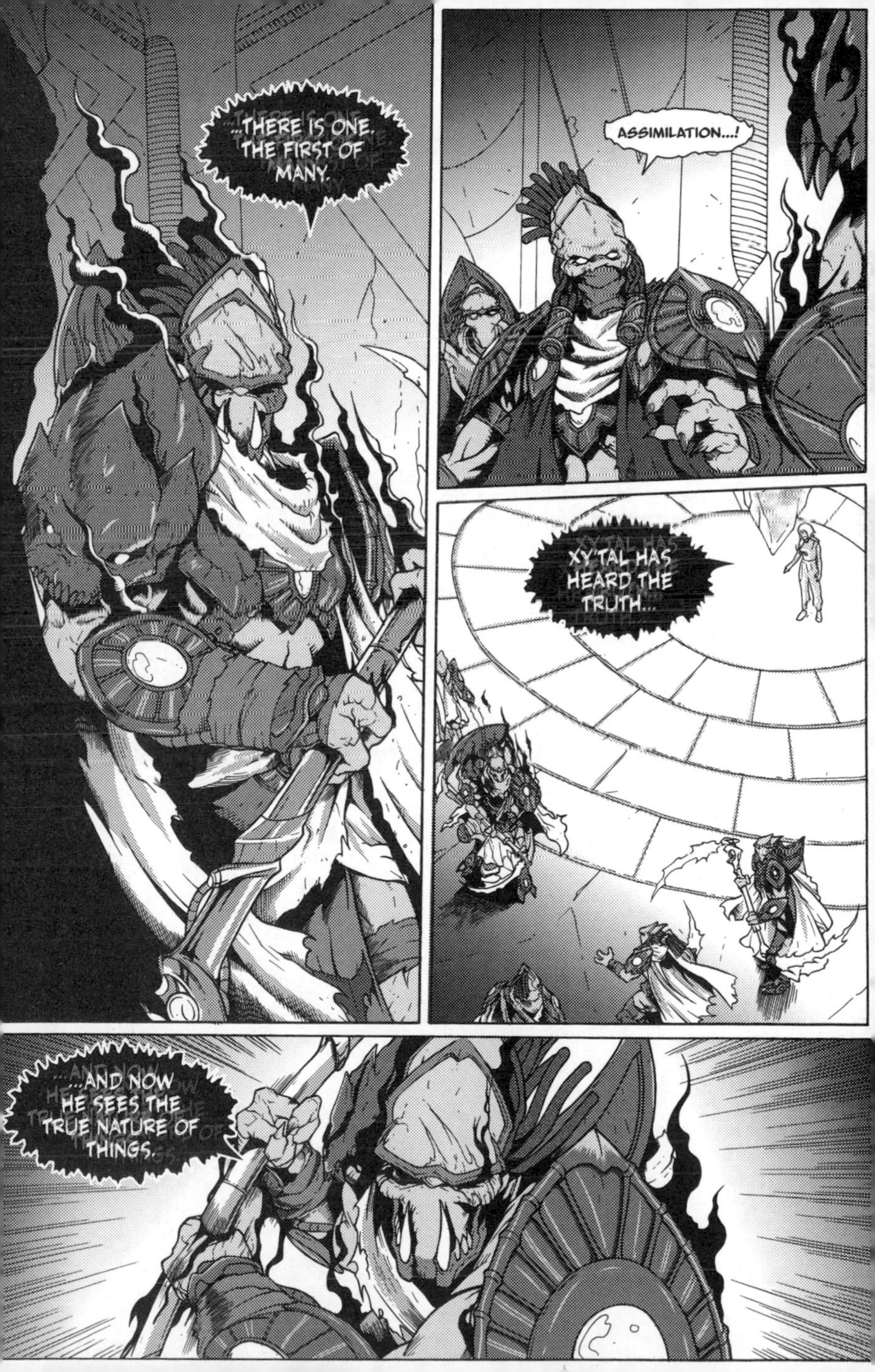
...THERE IS ONE. THE FIRST OF MANY.
ASSIMILATION...!
XY'TAL HAS HEARD THE TRUTH...
...AND NOW HE SEES THE TRUE NATURE OF THINGS.

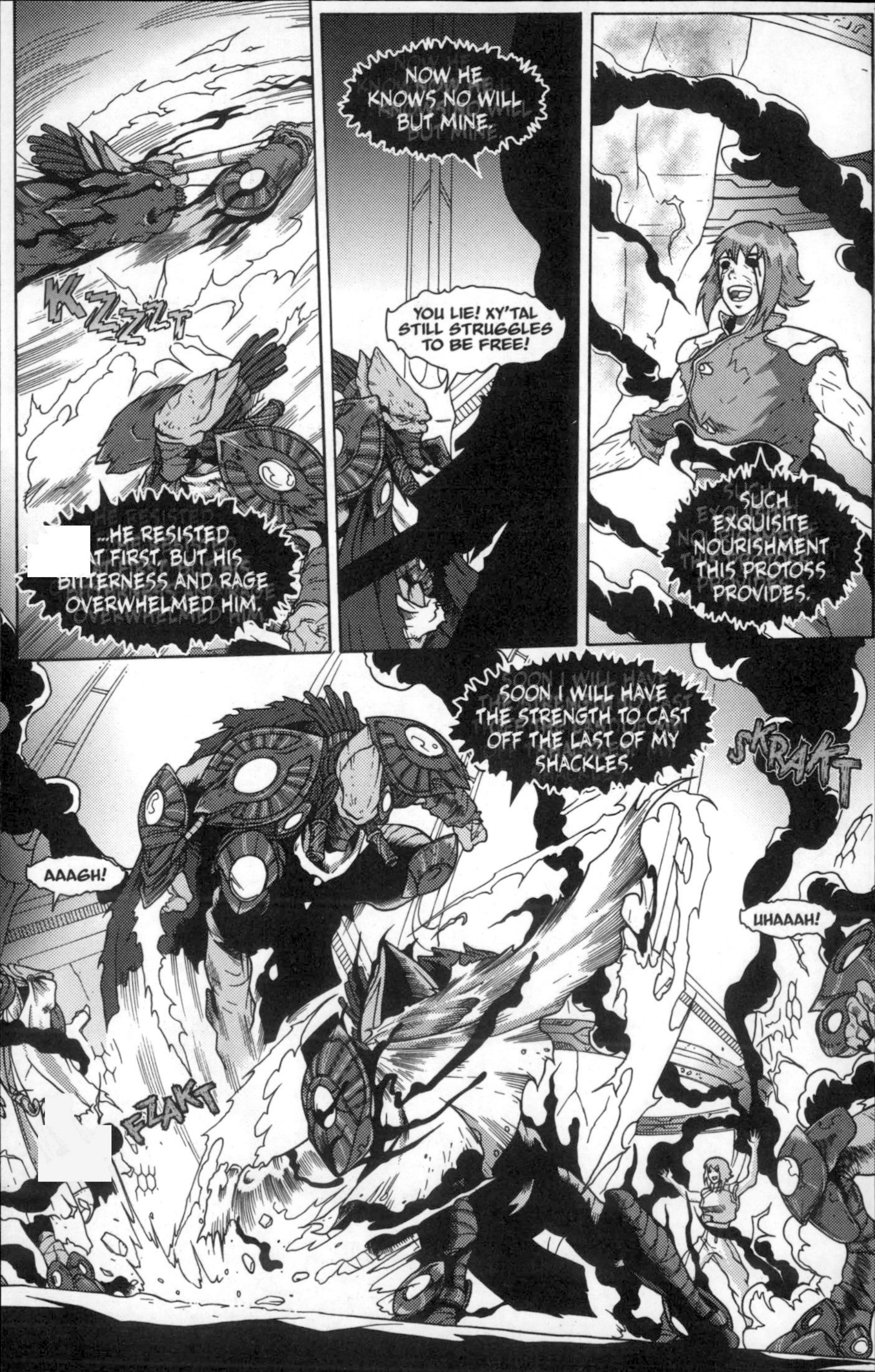
KZZZZT
...HE RESISTED AT FIRST, BUT HIS BITTERNESS AND RAGE OVERWHELMED HIM.
NOW HE KNOWS NO WILL BUT MINE.
YOU LIE! XY'TAL STILL STRUGGLES TO BE FREE!
SUCH EXQUISITE NOURISHMENT THIS PROTOSS PROVIDES.
SOON I WILL HAVE THE STRENGTH TO CAST OFF THE LAST OF MY SHACKLES.
SKRAKT
AAAGH!
UHAAAH!
FZAKT

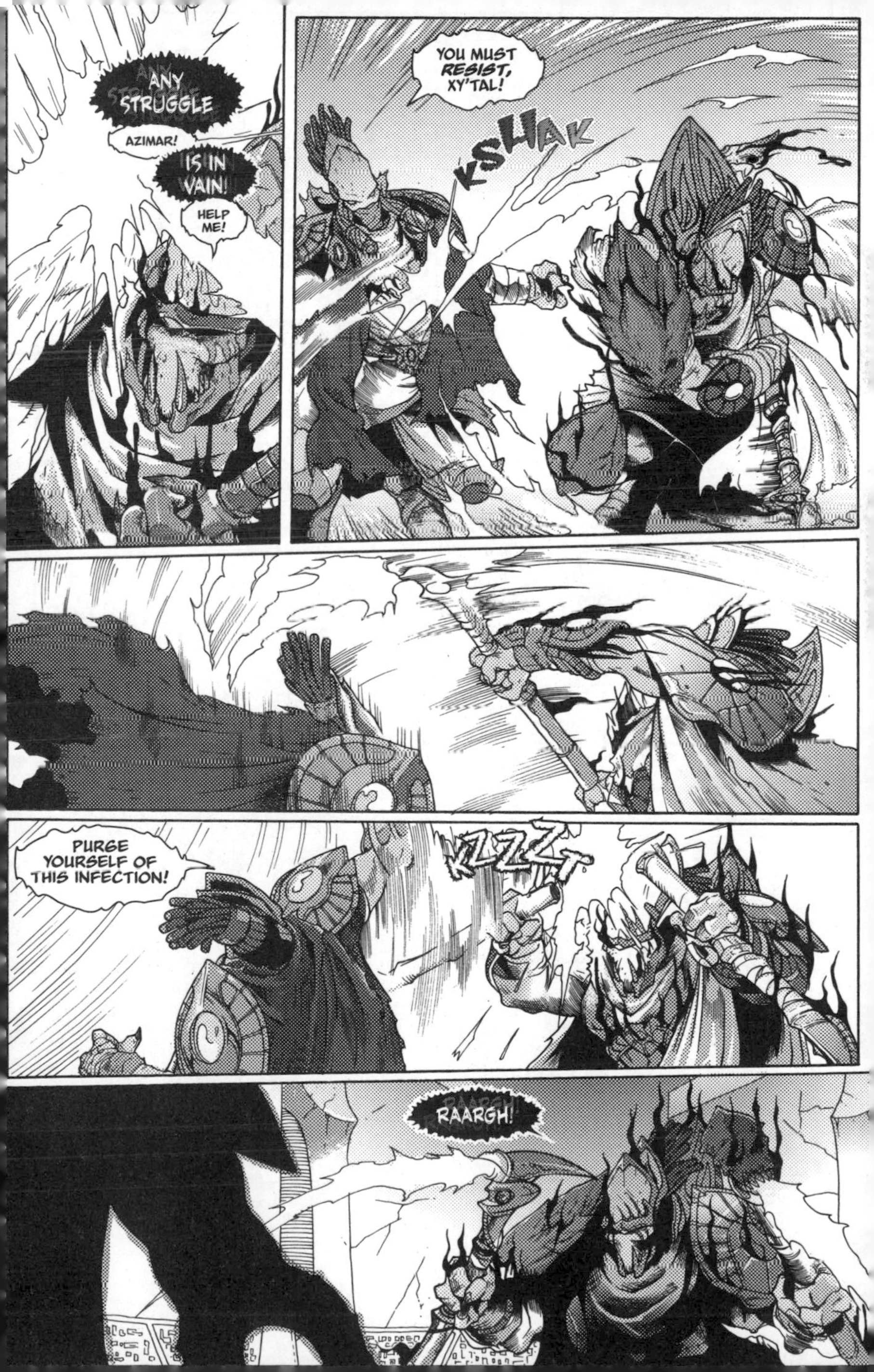
ANY STRUGGLE
AZIMAR!
IS IN VAIN!
HELP ME!
YOU MUST RESIST, XY'TAL!
KSHAK
PURGE YOURSELF OF THIS INFECTION!
KZZZT
RAARGH!

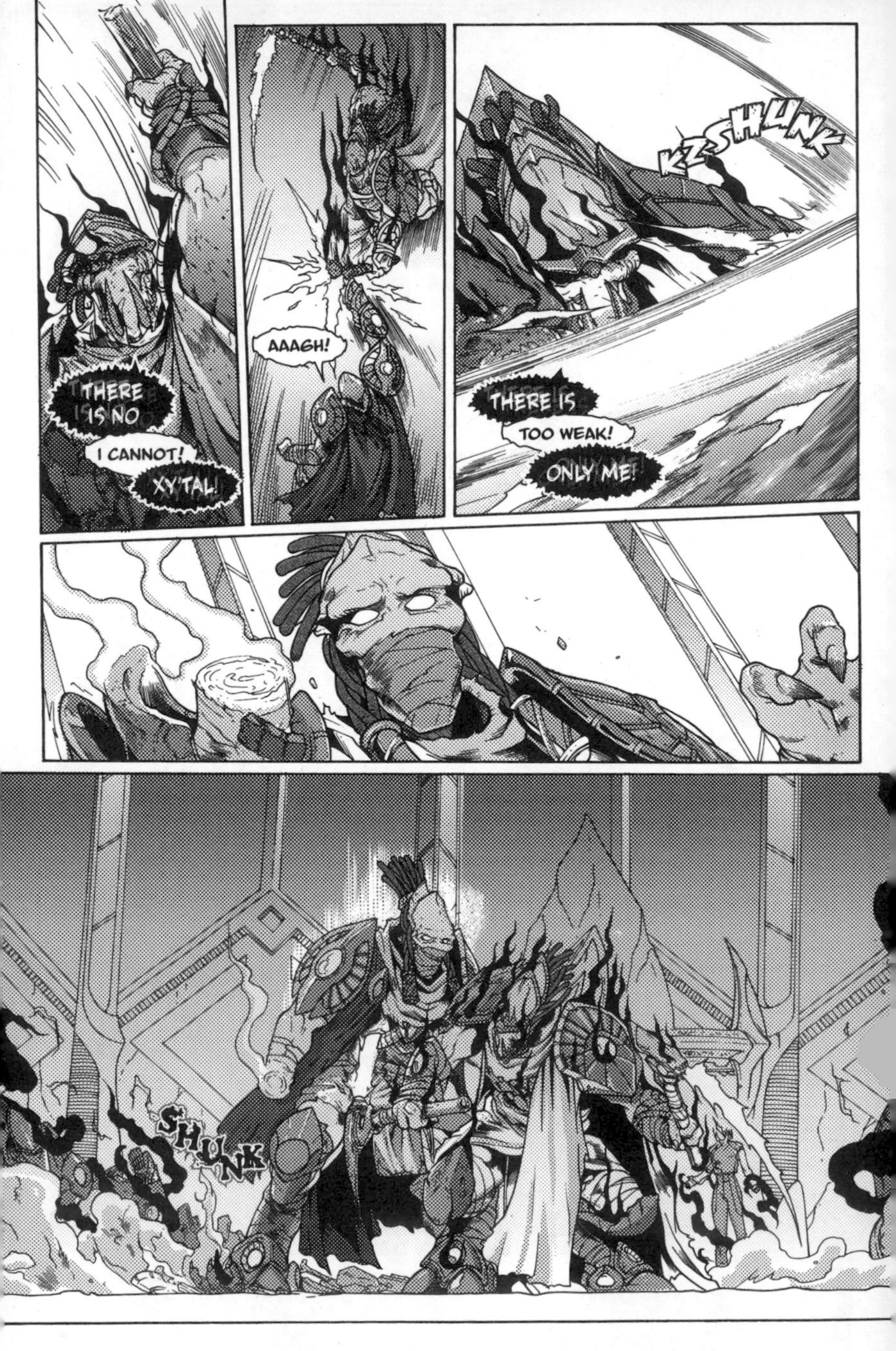
THERE IS NO
I CANNOT!
XY'TAL!
AAAGH!
KZSHUNK
THERE IS
TOO WEAK!
ONLY ME!
SHUNK

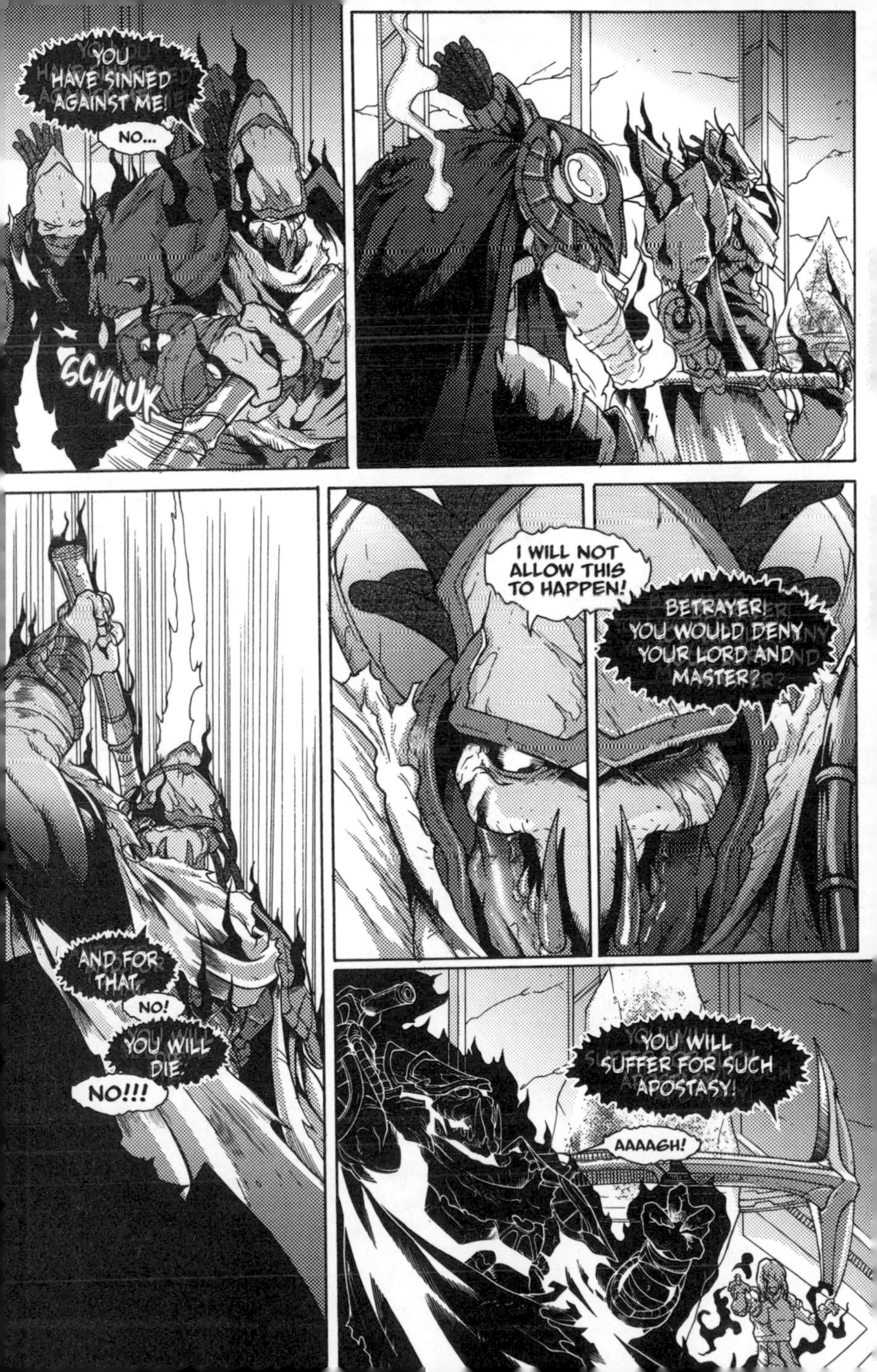
YOU HAVE SINNED AGAINST ME!
NO...
SCHLUK
I WILL NOT ALLOW THIS TO HAPPEN!
BETRAYER! YOU WOULD DENY YOUR LORD AND MASTER?
AND FOR THAT
NO!
YOU WILL DIE.
NO!!!
YOU WILL SUFFER FOR SUCH APOSTASY!
AAAAGH!

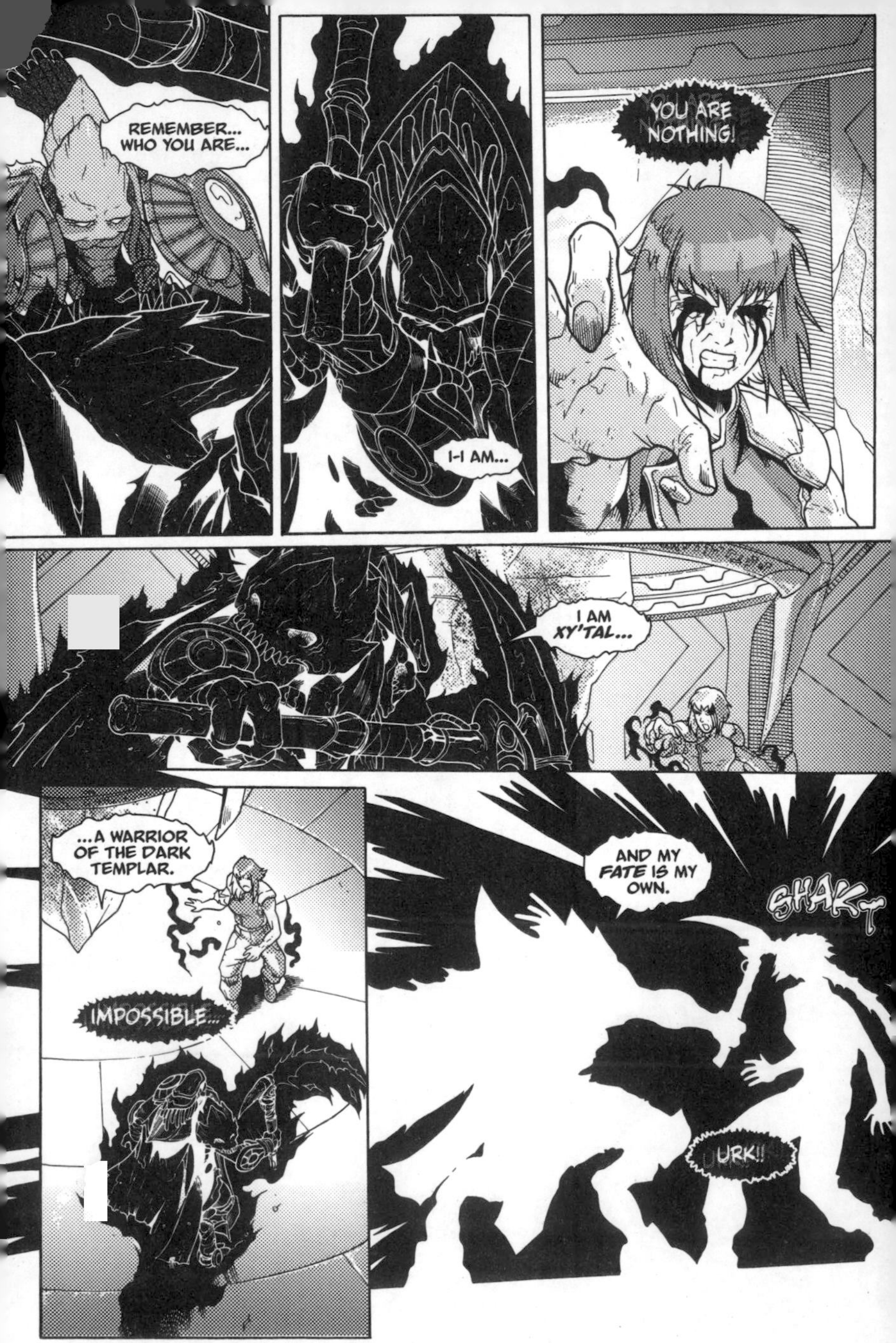
REMEMBER... WHO YOU ARE...
I-I AM...
YOU ARE NOTHING!
I AM XY'TAL...
...A WARRIOR OF THE DARK TEMPLAR.
IMPOSSIBLE...
AND MY FATE IS MY OWN.
SHAKT
URK!!

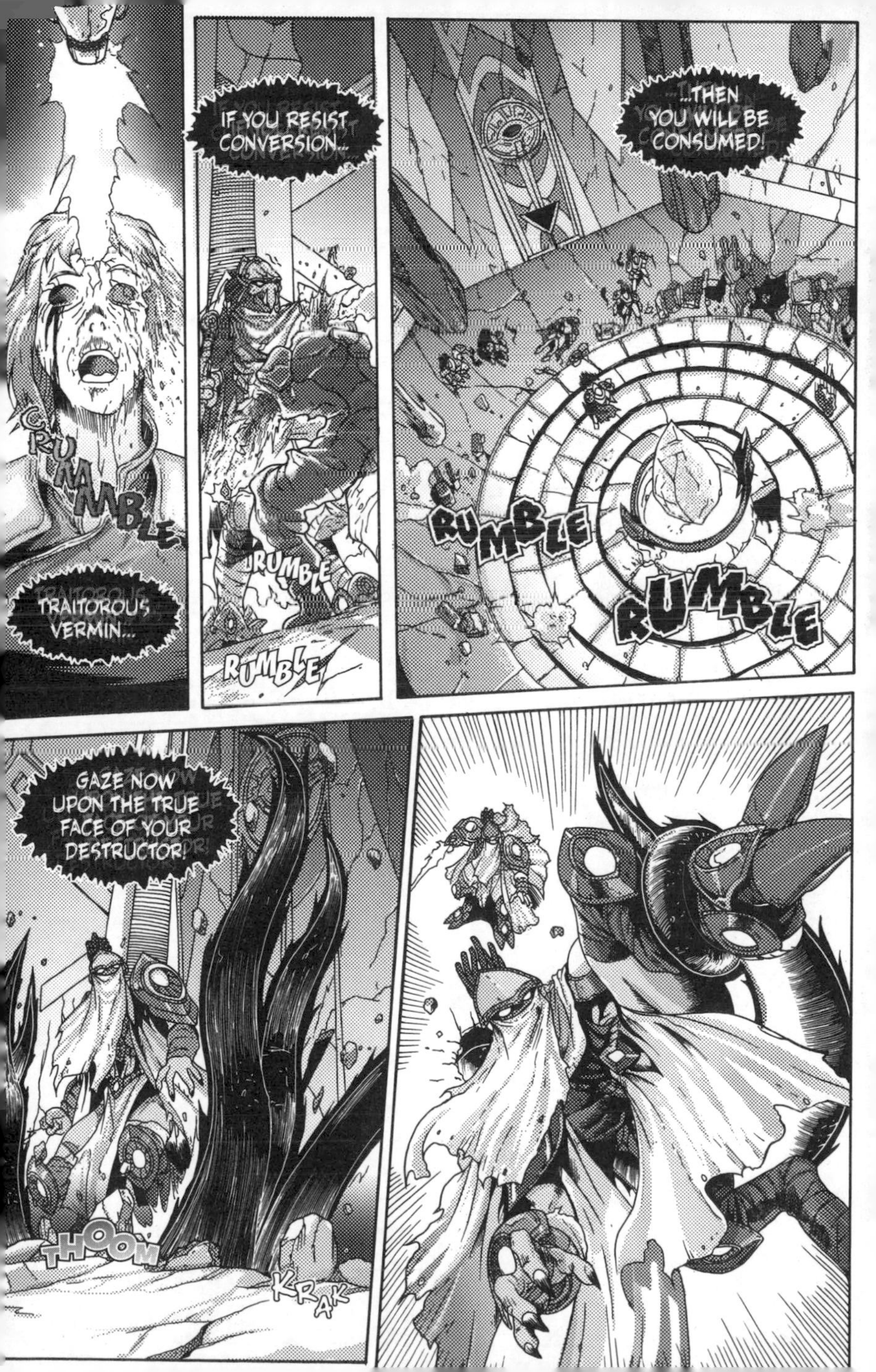
CRUMBLE
TRAITOROUS VERMIN...
IF YOU RESIST CONVERSION...
RUMBLE
RUMBLE
...THEN YOU WILL BE CONSUMED!
RUMBLE
RUMBLE
GAZE NOW UPON THE TRUE FACE OF YOUR DESTRUCTOR!
THOOM
KRAK

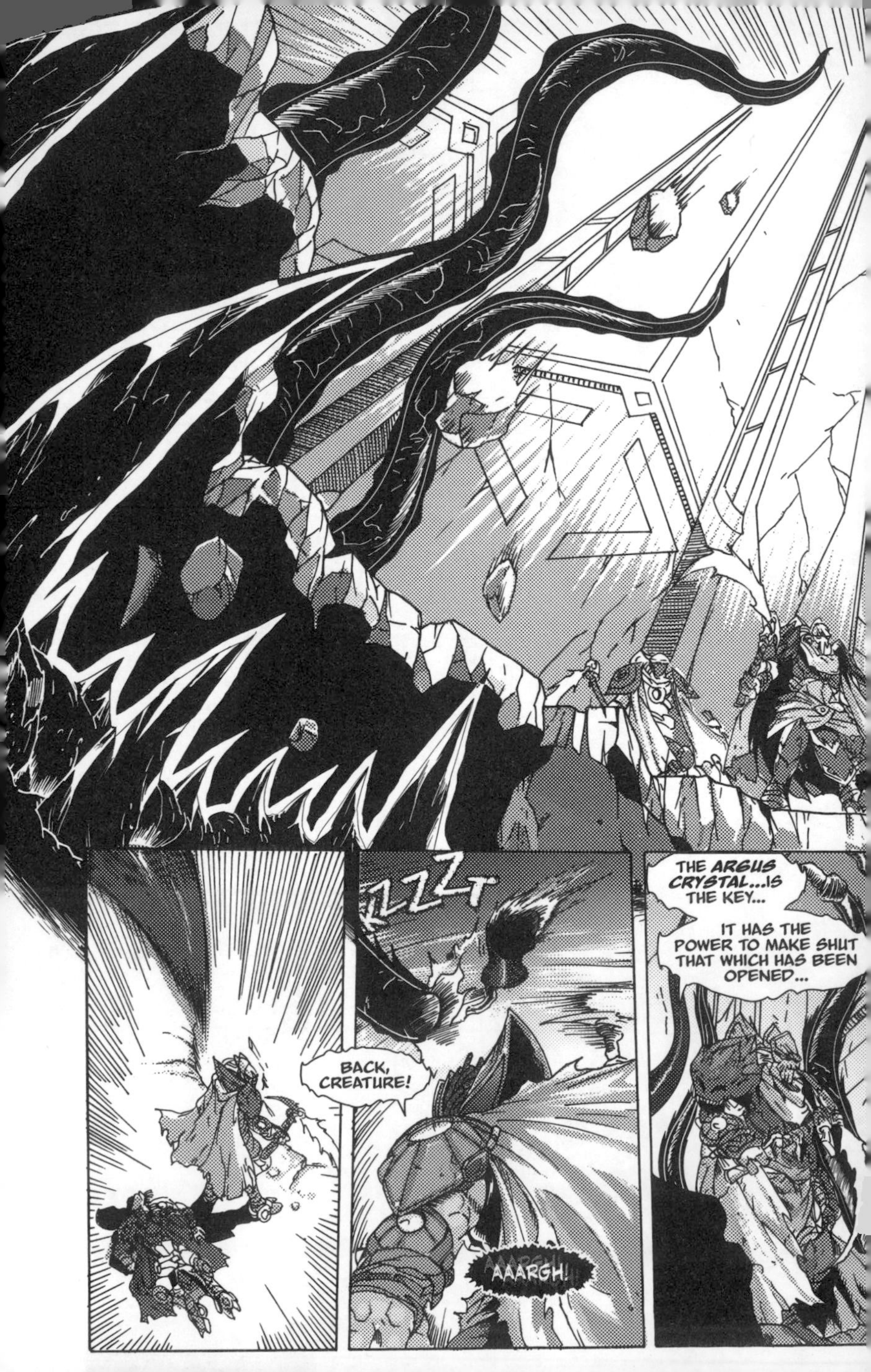
ZZZZT
BACK, CREATURE!
AAARGH!
THE ARGUS CRYSTAL...IS THE KEY...
IT HAS THE POWER TO MAKE SHUT THAT WHICH HAS BEEN OPENED...

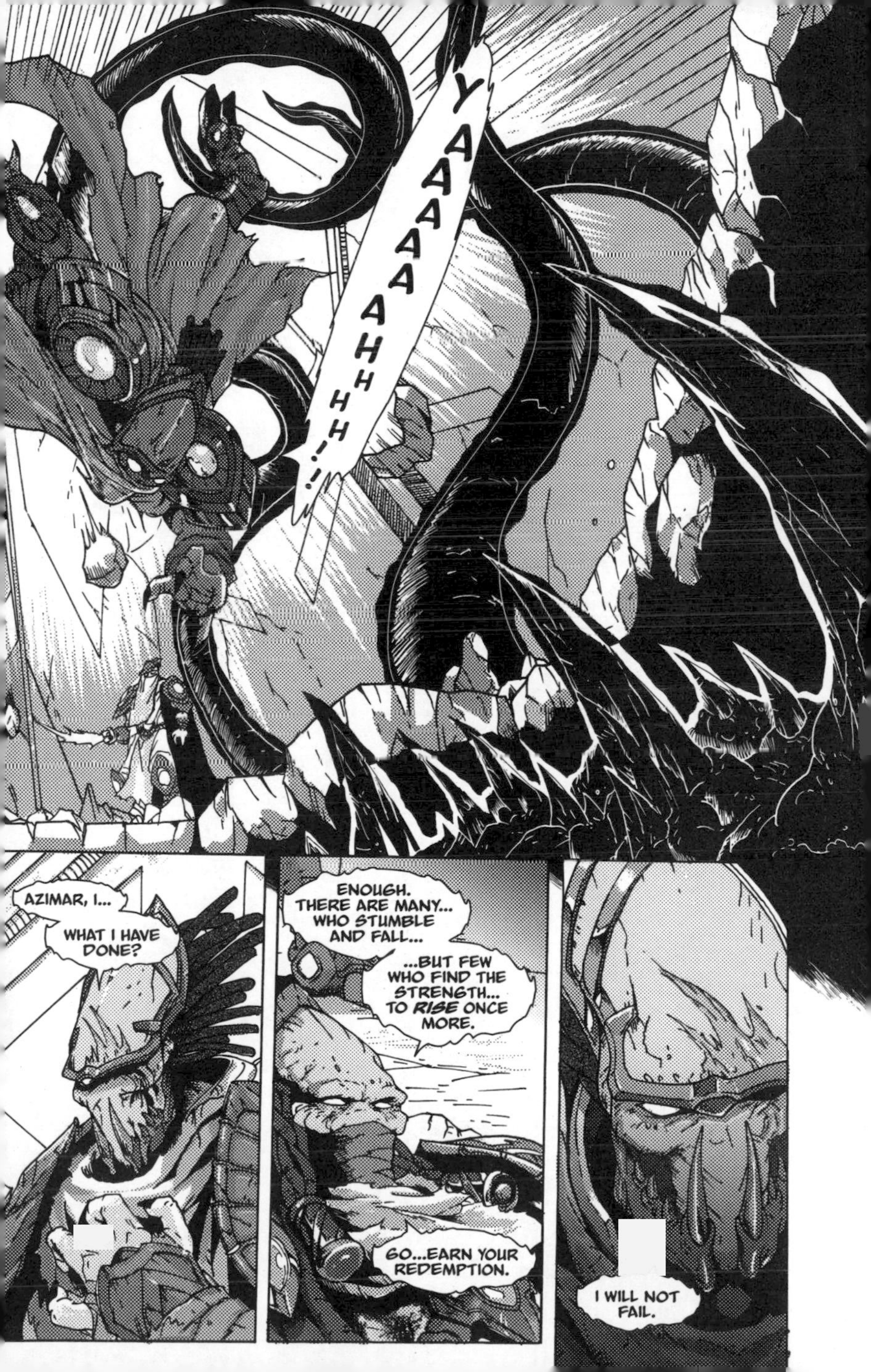
YAAAAAAAHHHH!!!
AZIMAR, I...
WHAT I HAVE DONE?
ENOUGH. THERE ARE MANY... WHO STUMBLE AND FALL...
...BUT FEW WHO FIND THE STRENGTH... TO *RISE* ONCE MORE.
GO...EARN YOUR REDEMPTION.
I WILL NOT FAIL.

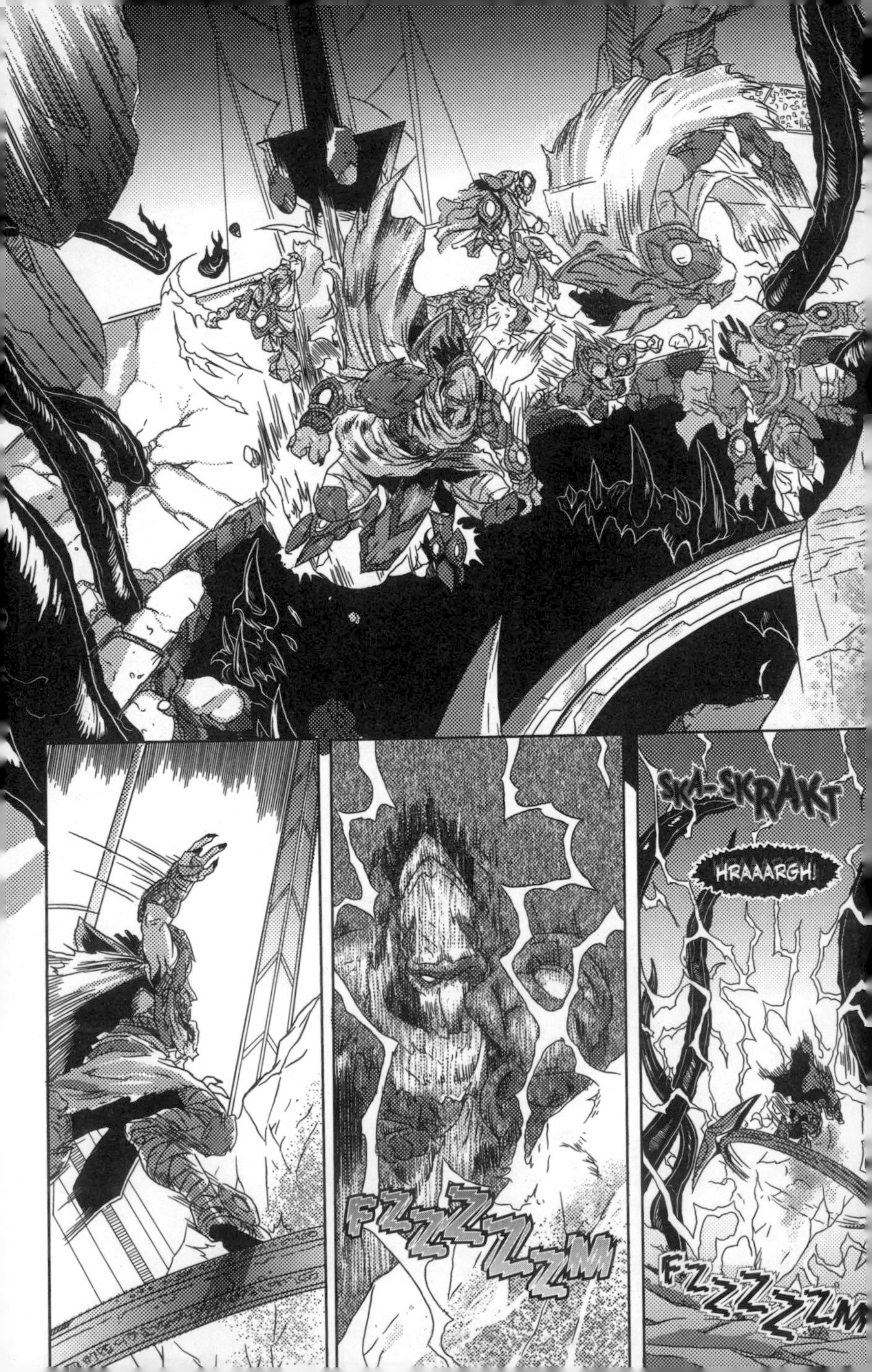

SKA-SKRAKT
HRAAARGH!
FZZZZZZM
FZZZZZZM

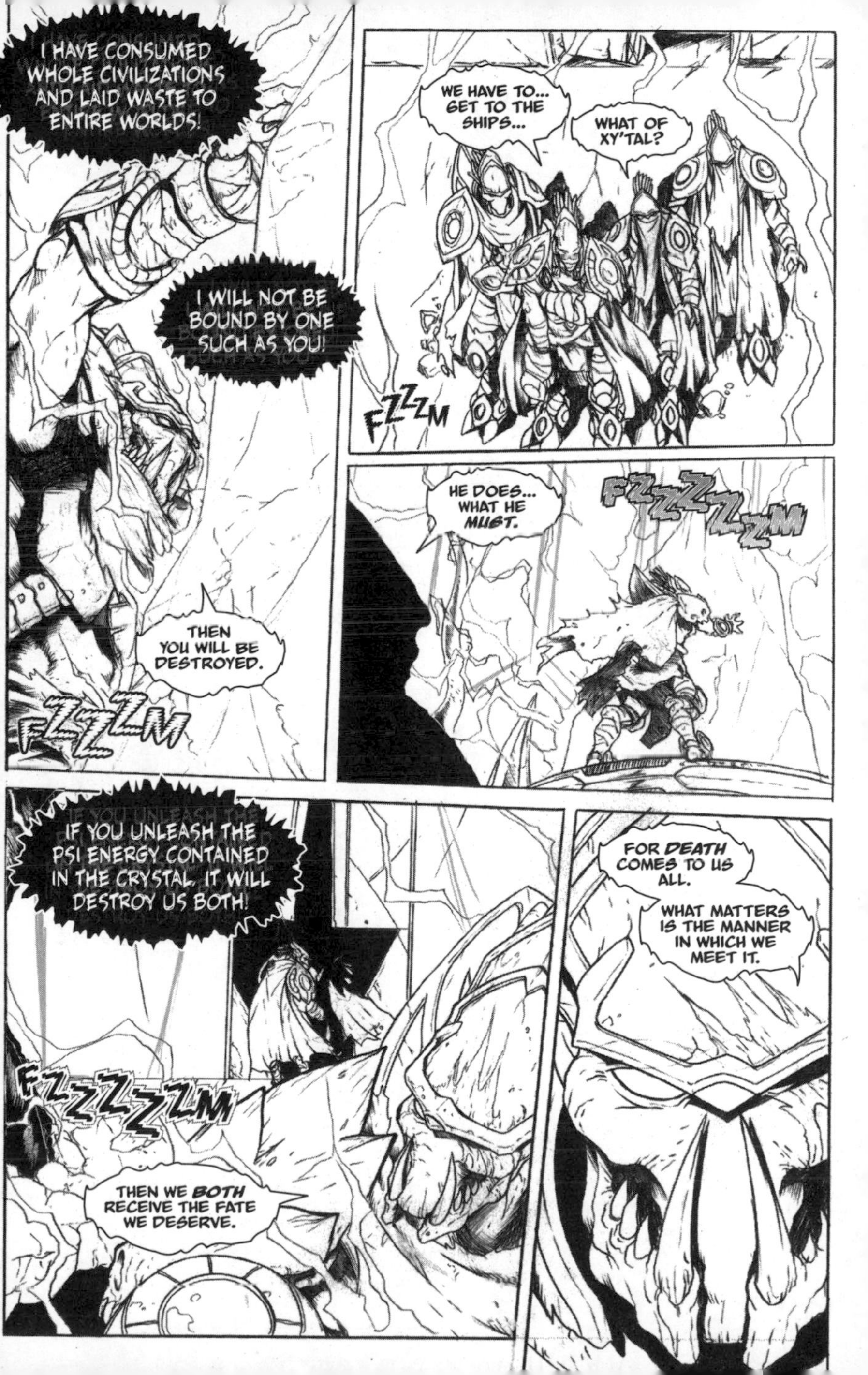
I HAVE CONSUMED WHOLE CIVILIZATIONS AND LAID WASTE TO ENTIRE WORLDS!
I WILL NOT BE BOUND BY ONE SUCH AS YOU!
THEN YOU WILL BE DESTROYED.
FZZZM
WE HAVE TO... GET TO THE SHIPS...
WHAT OF XY'TAL?
FZZZM
HE DOES... WHAT HE MUST.
FZZZZZZZM
IF YOU UNLEASH THE PSI ENERGY CONTAINED IN THE CRYSTAL, IT WILL DESTROY US BOTH!
FZZZZZZZM
THEN WE BOTH RECEIVE THE FATE WE DESERVE.
FOR DEATH COMES TO US ALL.
WHAT MATTERS IS THE MANNER IN WHICH WE MEET IT.

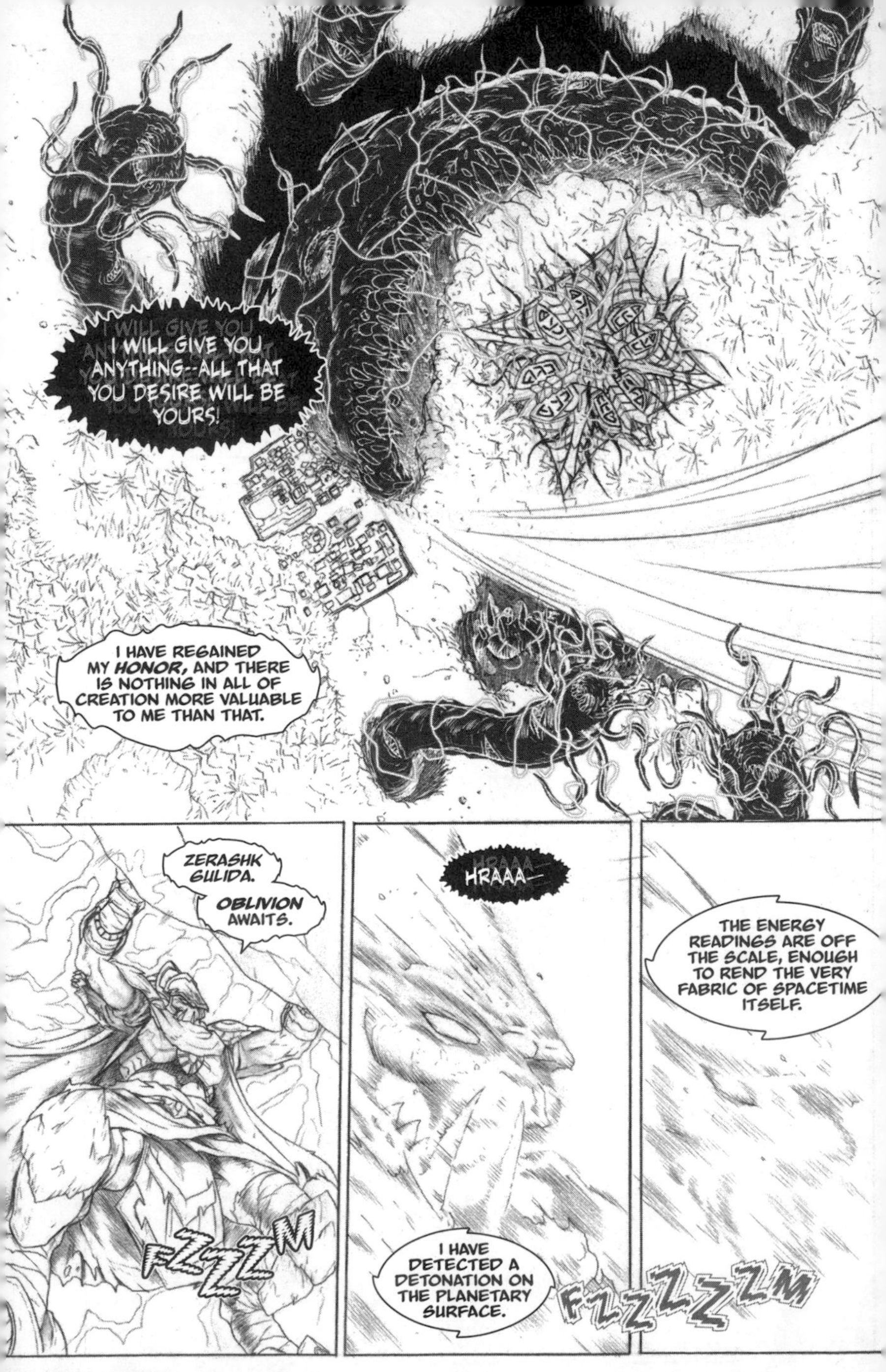
I WILL GIVE YOU ANYTHING--ALL THAT YOU DESIRE WILL BE YOURS!
I HAVE REGAINED MY HONOR, AND THERE IS NOTHING IN ALL OF CREATION MORE VALUABLE TO ME THAN THAT.
ZERASHK GULIDA.
OBLIVION AWAITS.
FZZZM
HRAAA—
I HAVE DETECTED A DETONATION ON THE PLANETARY SURFACE.
FZZZZZZM
THE ENERGY READINGS ARE OFF THE SCALE, ENOUGH TO REND THE VERY FABRIC OF SPACETIME ITSELF.

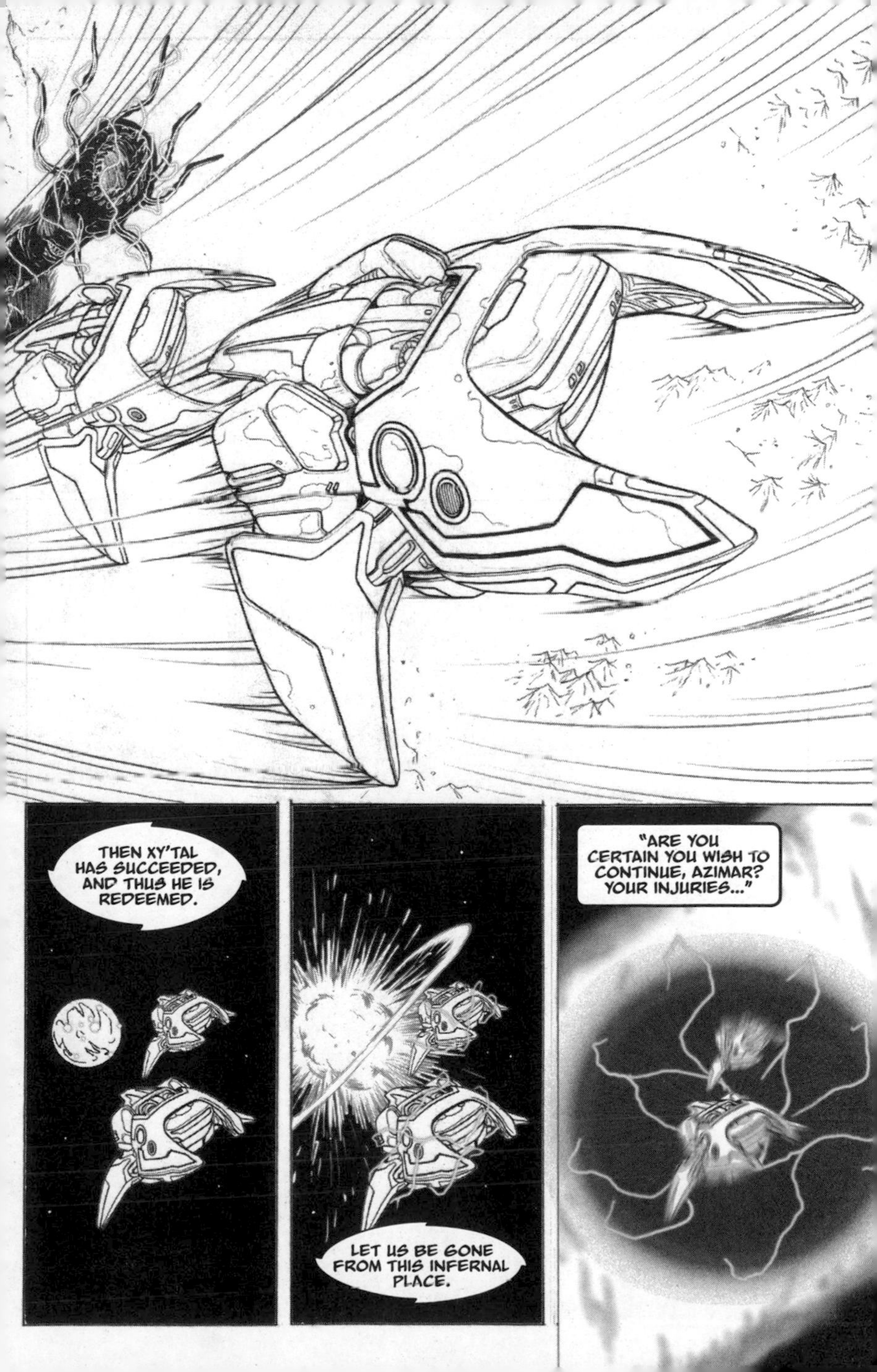
THEN XY'TAL HAS SUCCEEDED, AND THUS HE IS REDEEMED.
LET US BE GONE FROM THIS INFERNAL PLACE.
"ARE YOU CERTAIN YOU WISH TO CONTINUE, AZIMAR? YOUR INJURIES..."

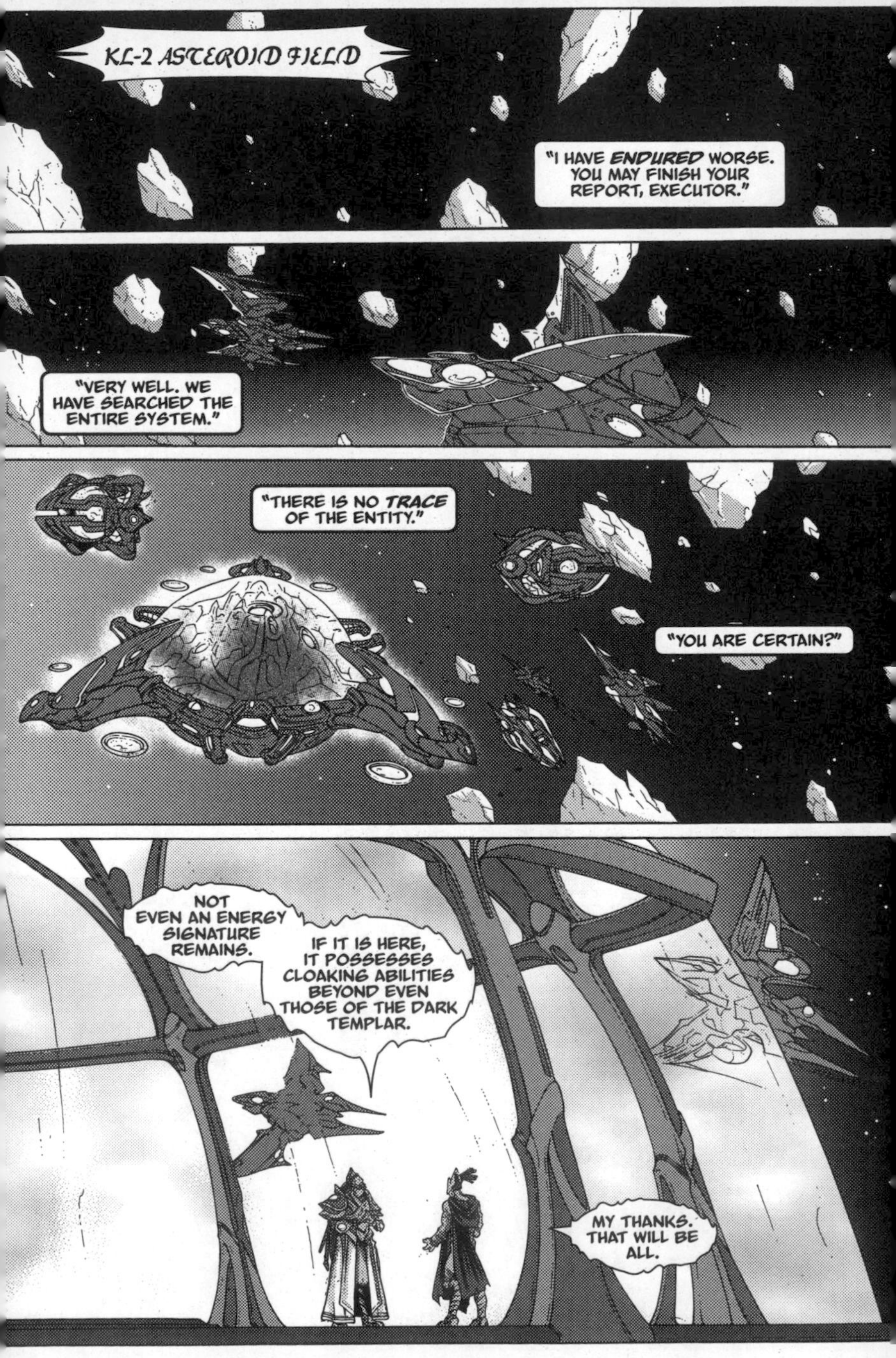
KL-2 ASTEROID FIELD
"I HAVE ENDURED WORSE. YOU MAY FINISH YOUR REPORT, EXECUTOR."
"VERY WELL. WE HAVE SEARCHED THE ENTIRE SYSTEM."
"THERE IS NO TRACE OF THE ENTITY."
"YOU ARE CERTAIN?"
NOT EVEN AN ENERGY SIGNATURE REMAINS.
IF IT IS HERE, IT POSSESSES CLOAKING ABILITIES BEYOND EVEN THOSE OF THE DARK TEMPLAR.
MY THANKS. THAT WILL BE ALL.

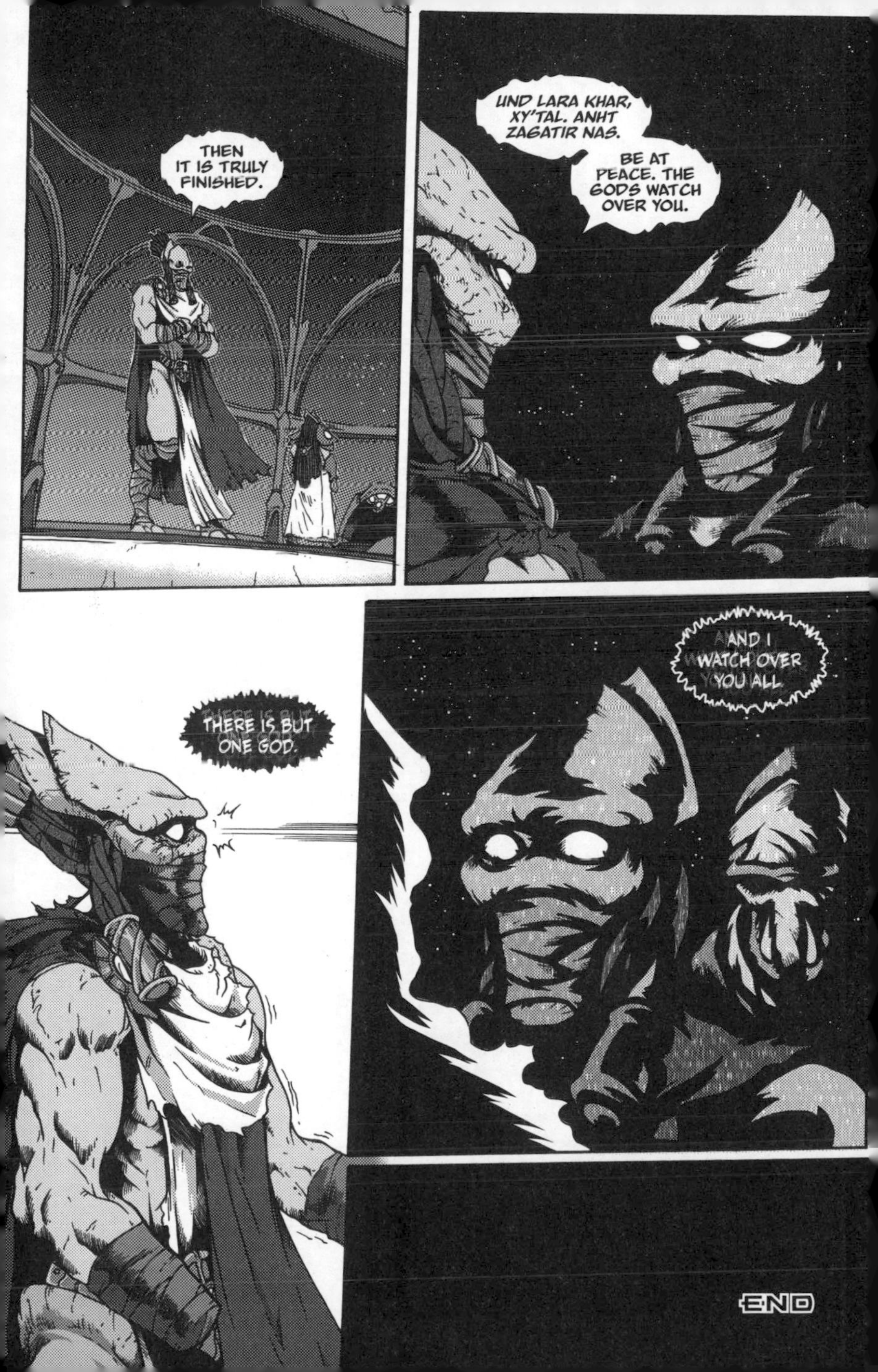
THEN IT IS TRULY FINISHED.
UND LARA KHAR, XY'TAL. ANHT ZAGATIR NAS.
BE AT PEACE. THE GODS WATCH OVER YOU.
THERE IS BUT ONE GOD.
AND I WATCH OVER YOU ALL.
END

STARCRAFT

FRONTLINE
VOLUME 4

ORIENTATION

Written by Paul Benjamin & Dave Shramek

Pencils by Mel joy San Juan

Inks by Noel Rodriguez, Jezreel Rojales, and Studio Sakka

Tones by Ryo Kawakami

Letterer: Michael Paolilli

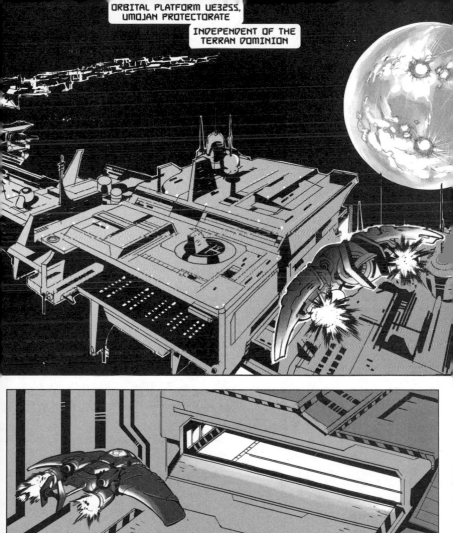

ORBITAL PLATFORM UE3255, UMOJAN PROTECTORATE

INDEPENDENT OF THE TERRAN DOMINION

RELAX, MR. PHASH.

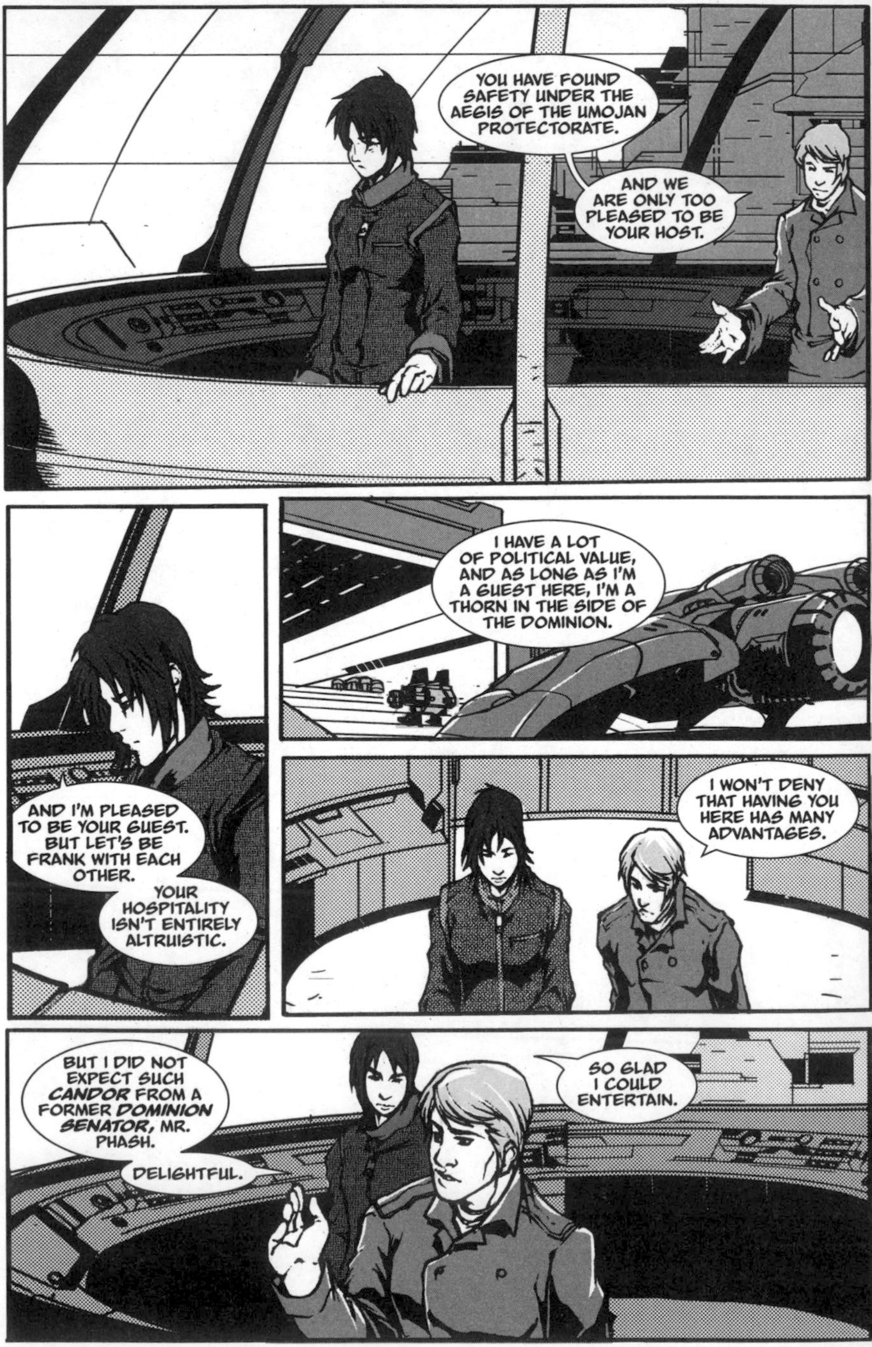
YOU HAVE FOUND SAFETY UNDER THE AEGIS OF THE UMOJAN PROTECTORATE.
AND WE ARE ONLY TOO PLEASED TO BE YOUR HOST.
AND I'M PLEASED TO BE YOUR GUEST. BUT LET'S BE FRANK WITH EACH OTHER.
YOUR HOSPITALITY ISN'T ENTIRELY ALTRUISTIC.
I HAVE A LOT OF POLITICAL VALUE, AND AS LONG AS I'M A GUEST HERE, I'M A THORN IN THE SIDE OF THE DOMINION.
I WON'T DENY THAT HAVING YOU HERE HAS MANY ADVANTAGES.
BUT I DID NOT EXPECT SUCH *CANDOR* FROM A FORMER *DOMINION SENATOR*, MR. PHASH.
DELIGHTFUL.
SO GLAD I COULD ENTERTAIN.

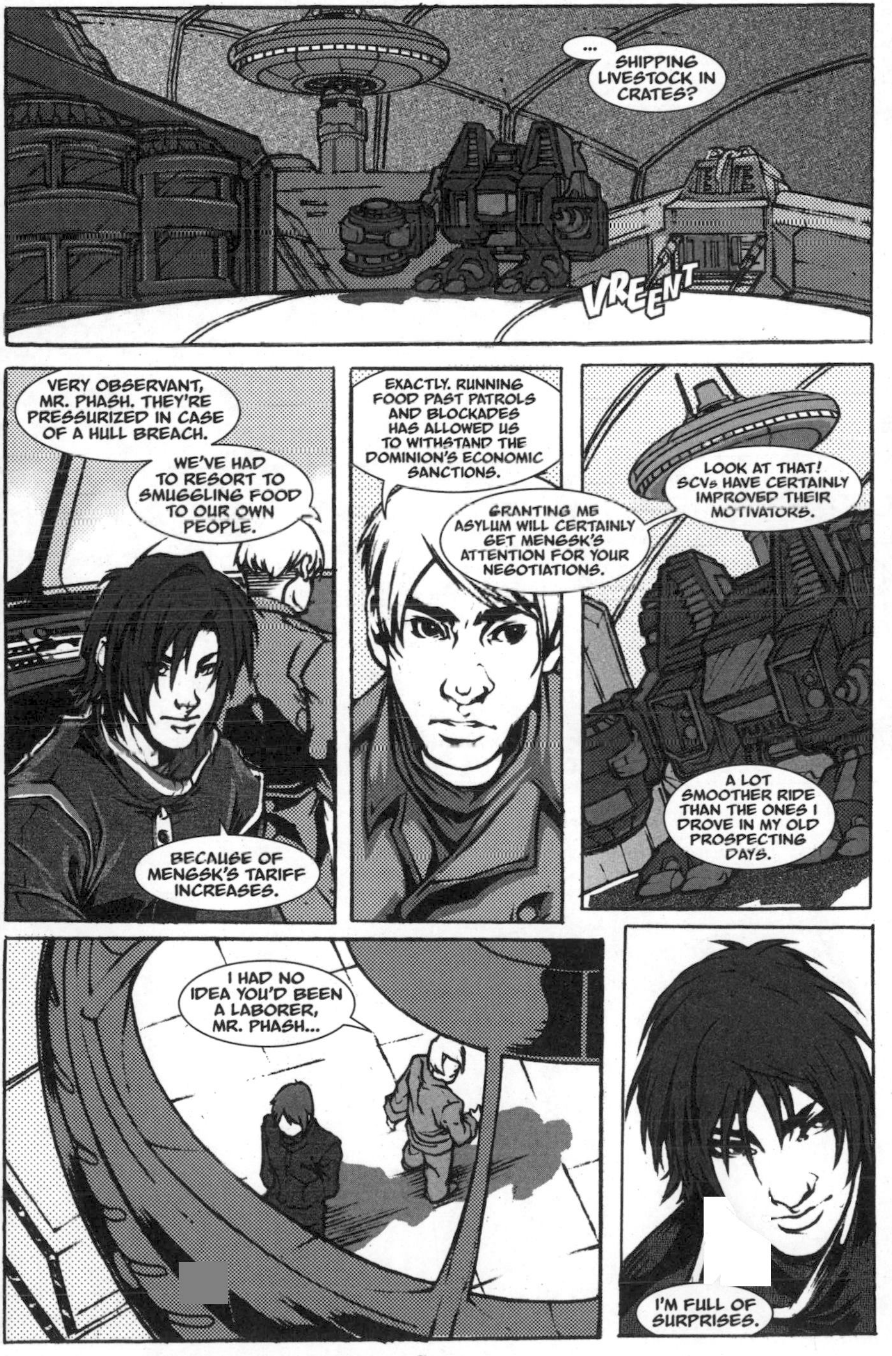
... SHIPPING LIVESTOCK IN CRATES?
VREEENT
VERY OBSERVANT, MR. PHASH. THEY'RE PRESSURIZED IN CASE OF A HULL BREACH.
WE'VE HAD TO RESORT TO SMUGGLING FOOD TO OUR OWN PEOPLE.
BECAUSE OF MENGSK'S TARIFF INCREASES.
EXACTLY. RUNNING FOOD PAST PATROLS AND BLOCKADES HAS ALLOWED US TO WITHSTAND THE DOMINION'S ECONOMIC SANCTIONS.
GRANTING ME ASYLUM WILL CERTAINLY GET MENGSK'S ATTENTION FOR YOUR NEGOTIATIONS.
LOOK AT THAT! SCVs HAVE CERTAINLY IMPROVED THEIR MOTIVATORS.
A LOT SMOOTHER RIDE THAN THE ONES I DROVE IN MY OLD PROSPECTING DAYS.
I HAD NO IDEA YOU'D BEEN A LABORER, MR. PHASH...
I'M FULL OF SURPRISES.

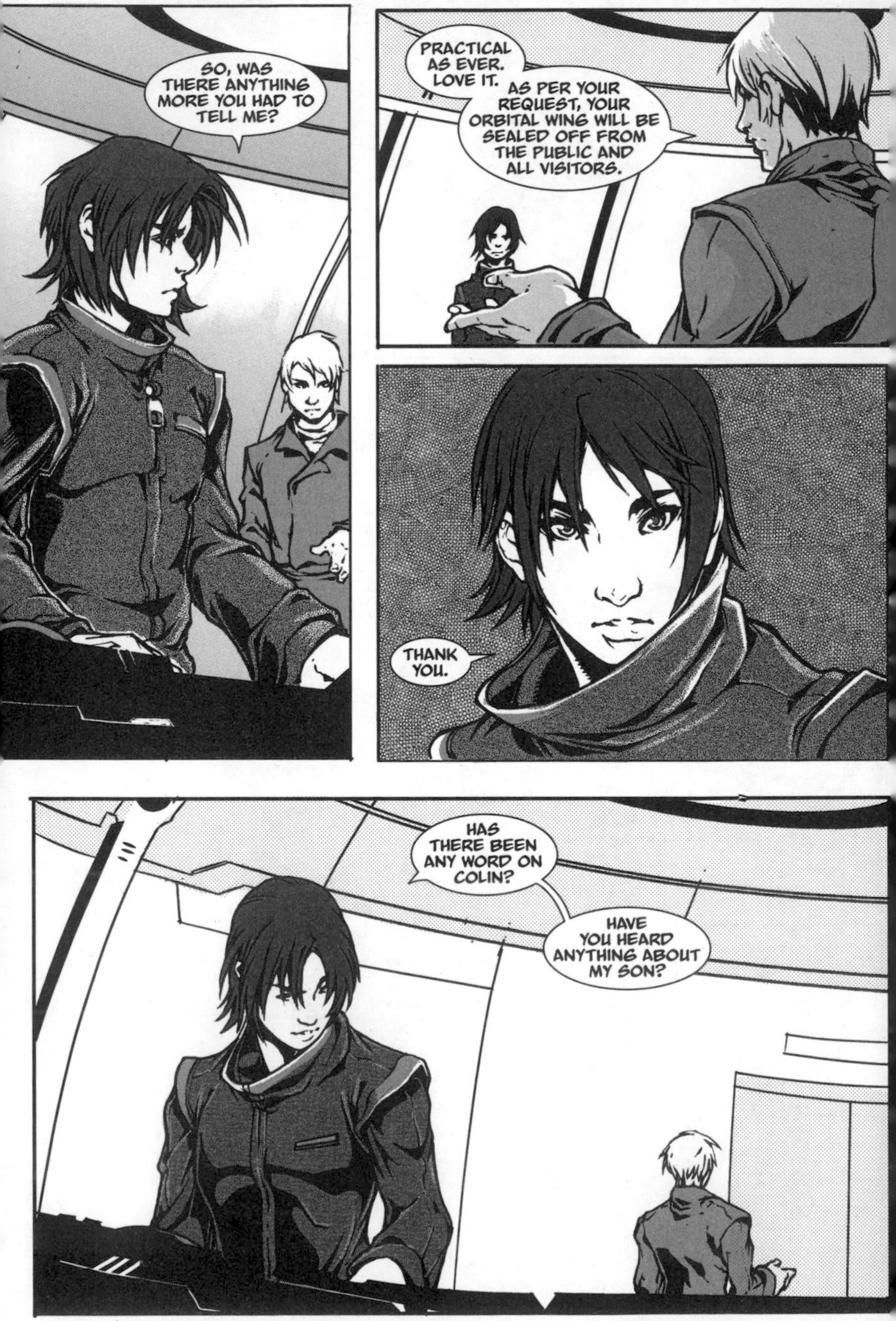
SO, WAS THERE ANYTHING MORE YOU HAD TO TELL ME?
PRACTICAL AS EVER. LOVE IT.
AS PER YOUR REQUEST, YOUR ORBITAL WING WILL BE SEALED OFF FROM THE PUBLIC AND ALL VISITORS.
THANK YOU.
HAS THERE BEEN ANY WORD ON COLIN?
HAVE YOU HEARD ANYTHING ABOUT MY SON?

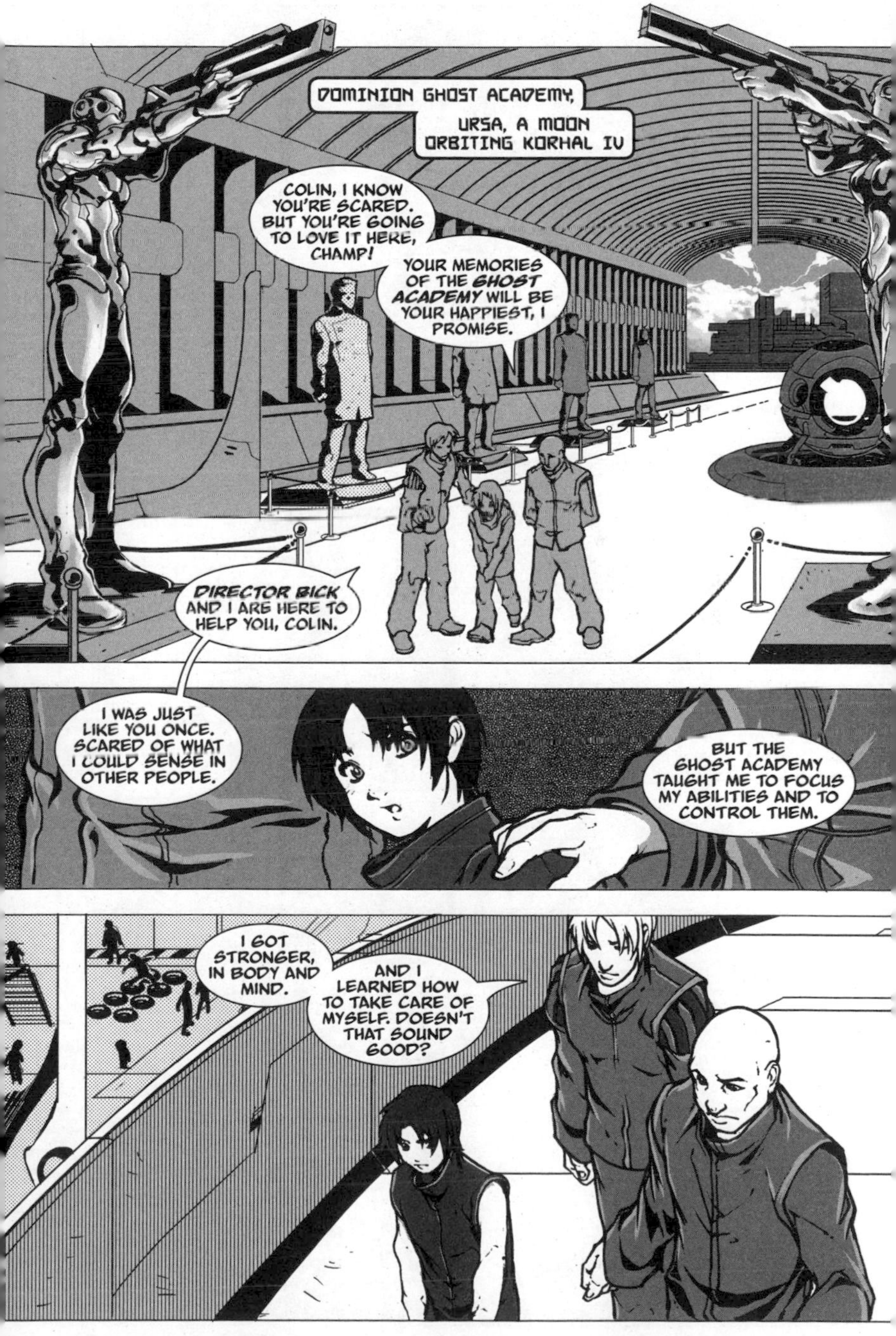
DOMINION GHOST ACADEMY,
URSA, A MOON ORBITING KORHAL IV
COLIN, I KNOW YOU'RE SCARED. BUT YOU'RE GOING TO LOVE IT HERE, CHAMP!
YOUR MEMORIES OF THE GHOST ACADEMY WILL BE YOUR HAPPIEST, I PROMISE.
DIRECTOR BICK AND I ARE HERE TO HELP YOU, COLIN.
I WAS JUST LIKE YOU ONCE. SCARED OF WHAT I COULD SENSE IN OTHER PEOPLE.
BUT THE GHOST ACADEMY TAUGHT ME TO FOCUS MY ABILITIES AND TO CONTROL THEM.
I GOT STRONGER, IN BODY AND MIND.
AND I LEARNED HOW TO TAKE CARE OF MYSELF. DOESN'T THAT SOUND GOOD?

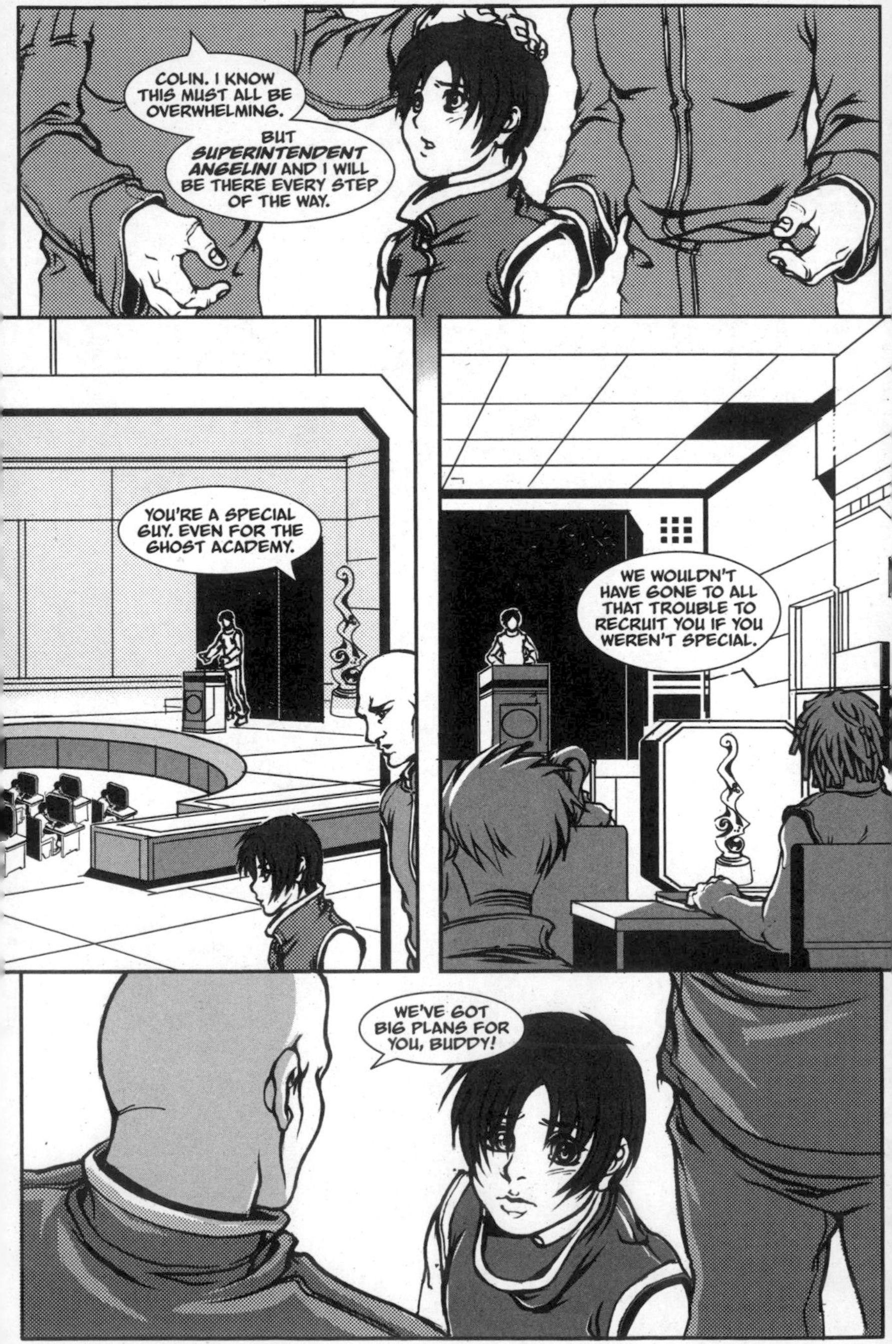
COLIN. I KNOW THIS MUST ALL BE OVERWHELMING.
BUT *SUPERINTENDENT ANGELINI* AND I WILL BE THERE EVERY STEP OF THE WAY.
YOU'RE A SPECIAL GUY. EVEN FOR THE GHOST ACADEMY.
WE WOULDN'T HAVE GONE TO ALL THAT TROUBLE TO RECRUIT YOU IF YOU WEREN'T SPECIAL.
WE'VE GOT BIG PLANS FOR YOU, BUDDY!

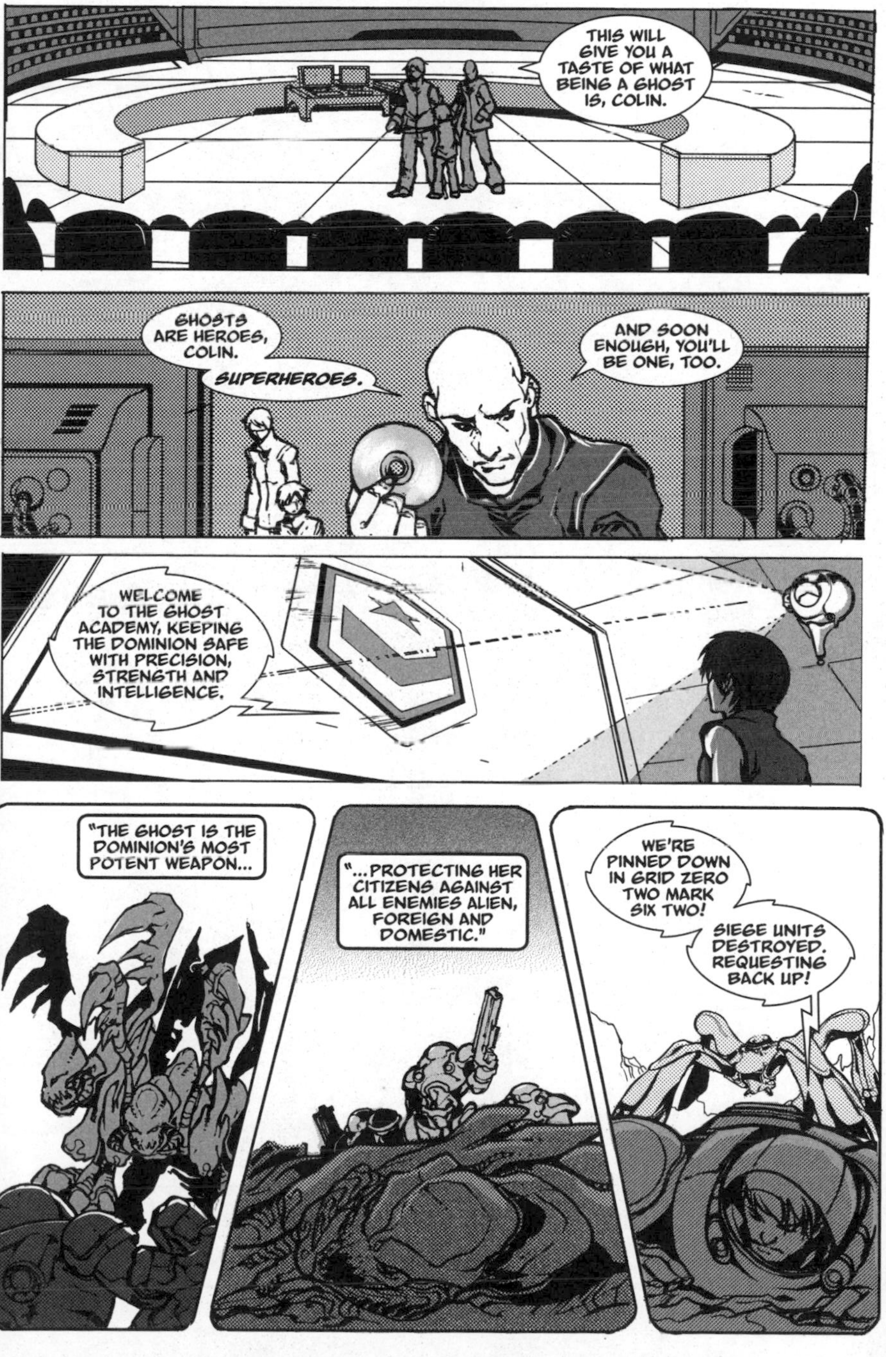
THIS WILL GIVE YOU A TASTE OF WHAT BEING A GHOST IS, COLIN.
GHOSTS ARE HEROES, COLIN.
SUPERHEROES.
AND SOON ENOUGH, YOU'LL BE ONE, TOO.
WELCOME TO THE GHOST ACADEMY, KEEPING THE DOMINION SAFE WITH PRECISION, STRENGTH AND INTELLIGENCE.
"THE GHOST IS THE DOMINION'S MOST POTENT WEAPON...
"...PROTECTING HER CITIZENS AGAINST ALL ENEMIES ALIEN, FOREIGN AND DOMESTIC."
WE'RE PINNED DOWN IN GRID ZERO TWO MARK SIX TWO!
SIEGE UNITS DESTROYED. REQUESTING BACK UP!

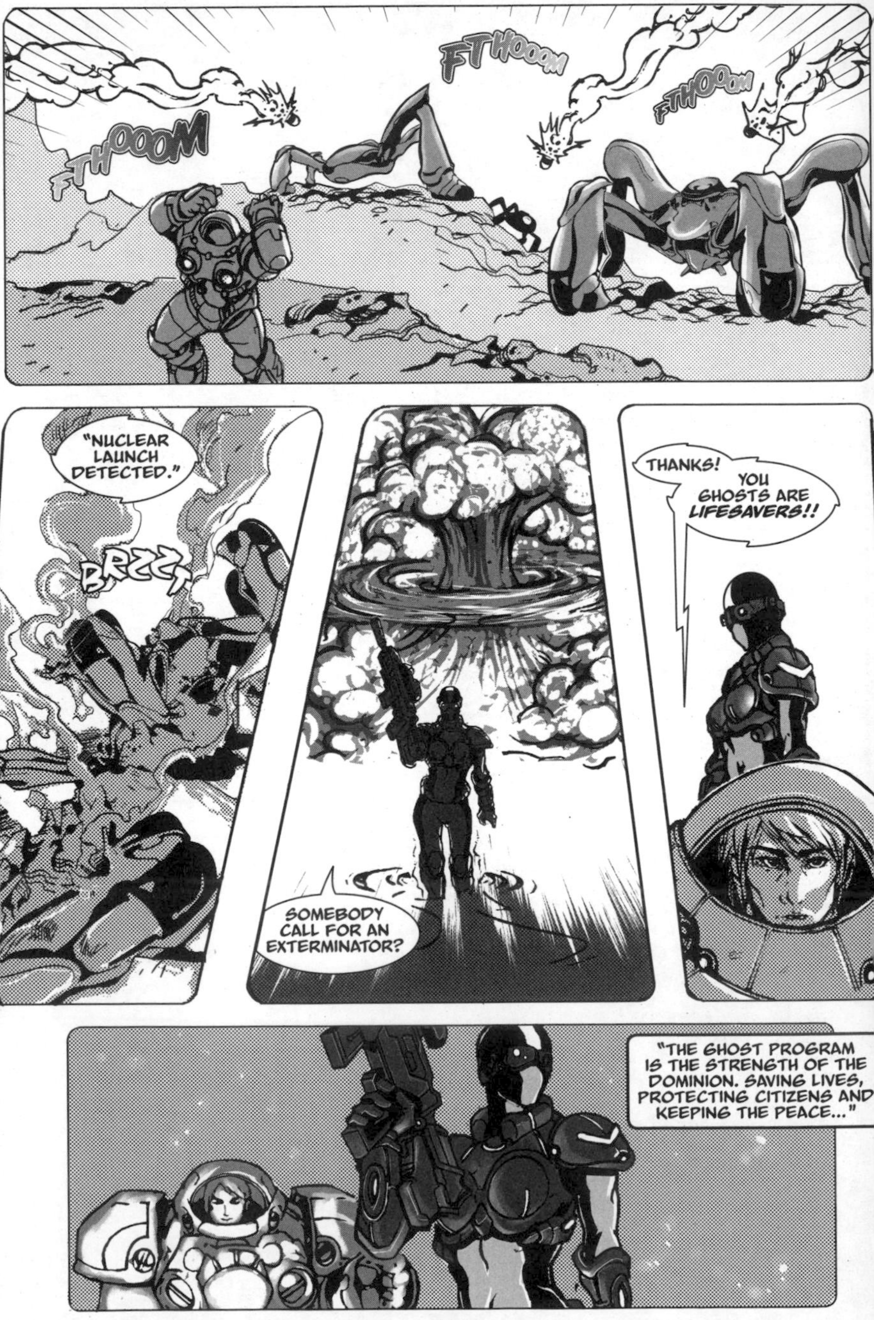
FTHOOOM
FTHOOOM
FTHOOOM
"NUCLEAR LAUNCH DETECTED."
BRZZT
SOMEBODY CALL FOR AN EXTERMINATOR?
THANKS!
YOU GHOSTS ARE *LIFESAVERS!!*
"THE GHOST PROGRAM IS THE STRENGTH OF THE DOMINION. SAVING LIVES, PROTECTING CITIZENS AND KEEPING THE PEACE..."

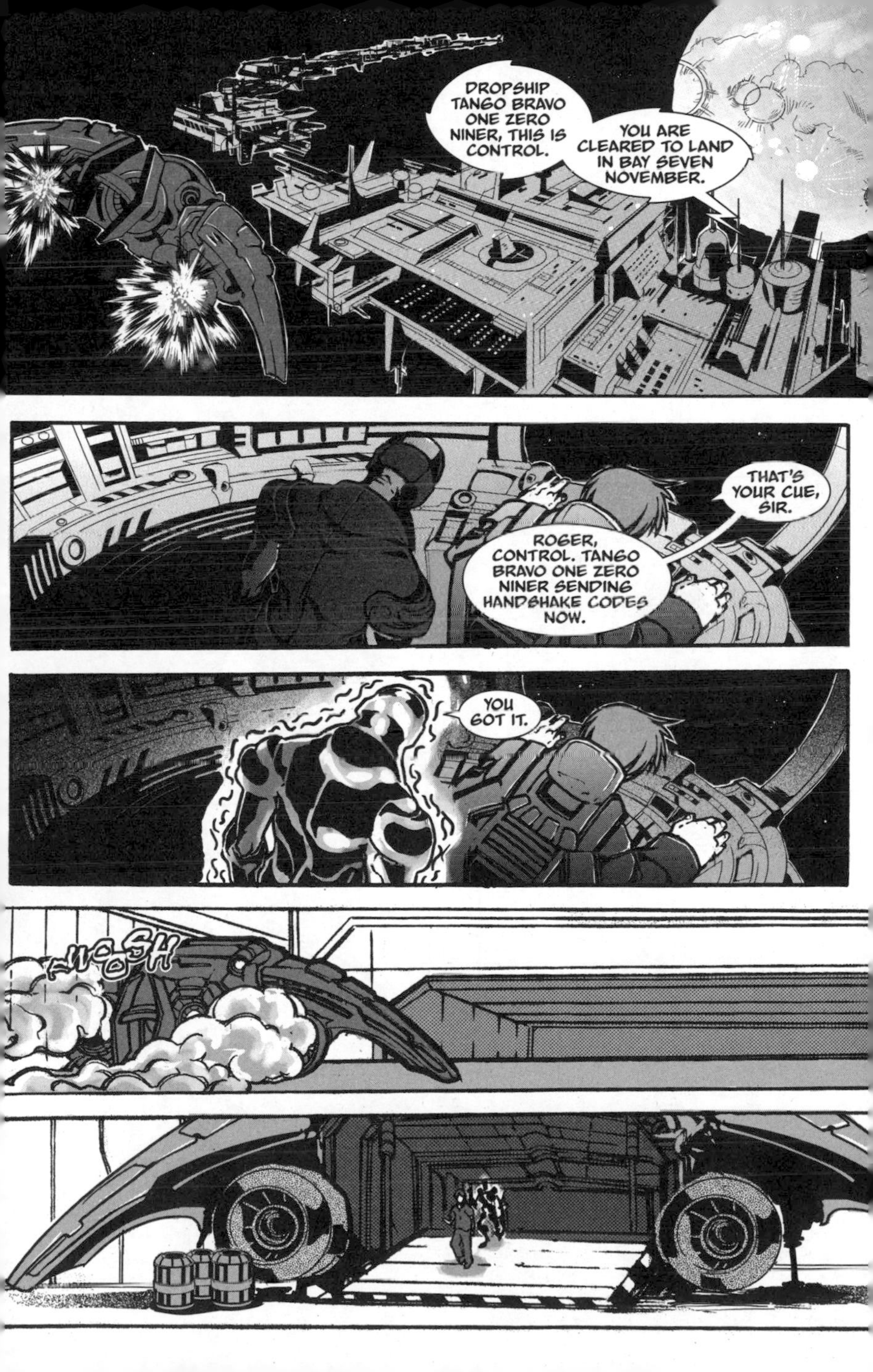
DROPSHIP TANGO BRAVO ONE ZERO NINER, THIS IS CONTROL.
YOU ARE CLEARED TO LAND IN BAY SEVEN NOVEMBER.
THAT'S YOUR CUE, SIR.
ROGER, CONTROL. TANGO BRAVO ONE ZERO NINER SENDING HANDSHAKE CODES NOW.
YOU GOT IT.
FWOOSH

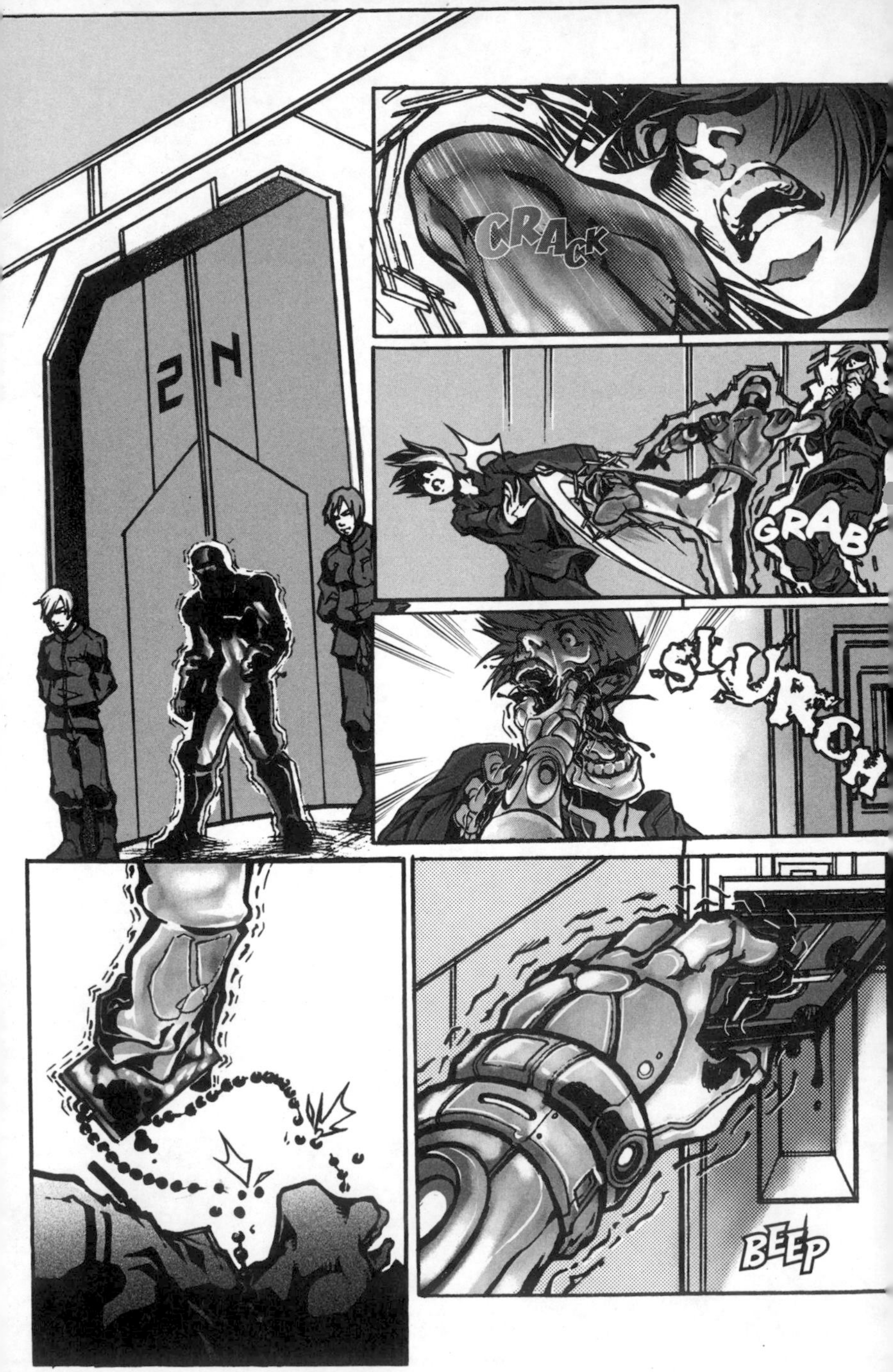
CRACK
GRAB
SLURCH
BEEP

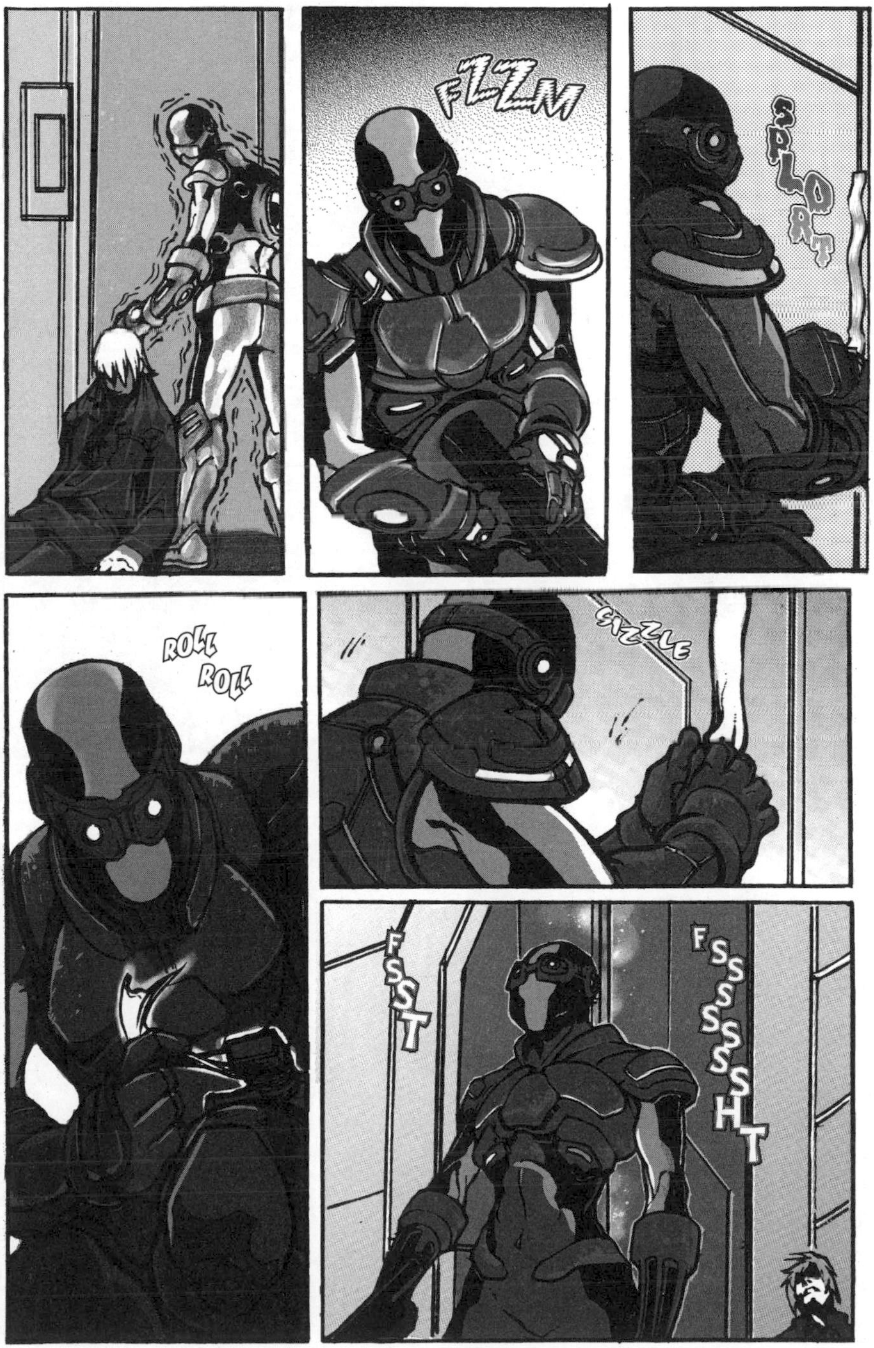
FZZM
SPLORT
ROLL
ROLL
SIZZLE
FSST
FSSSSSHT

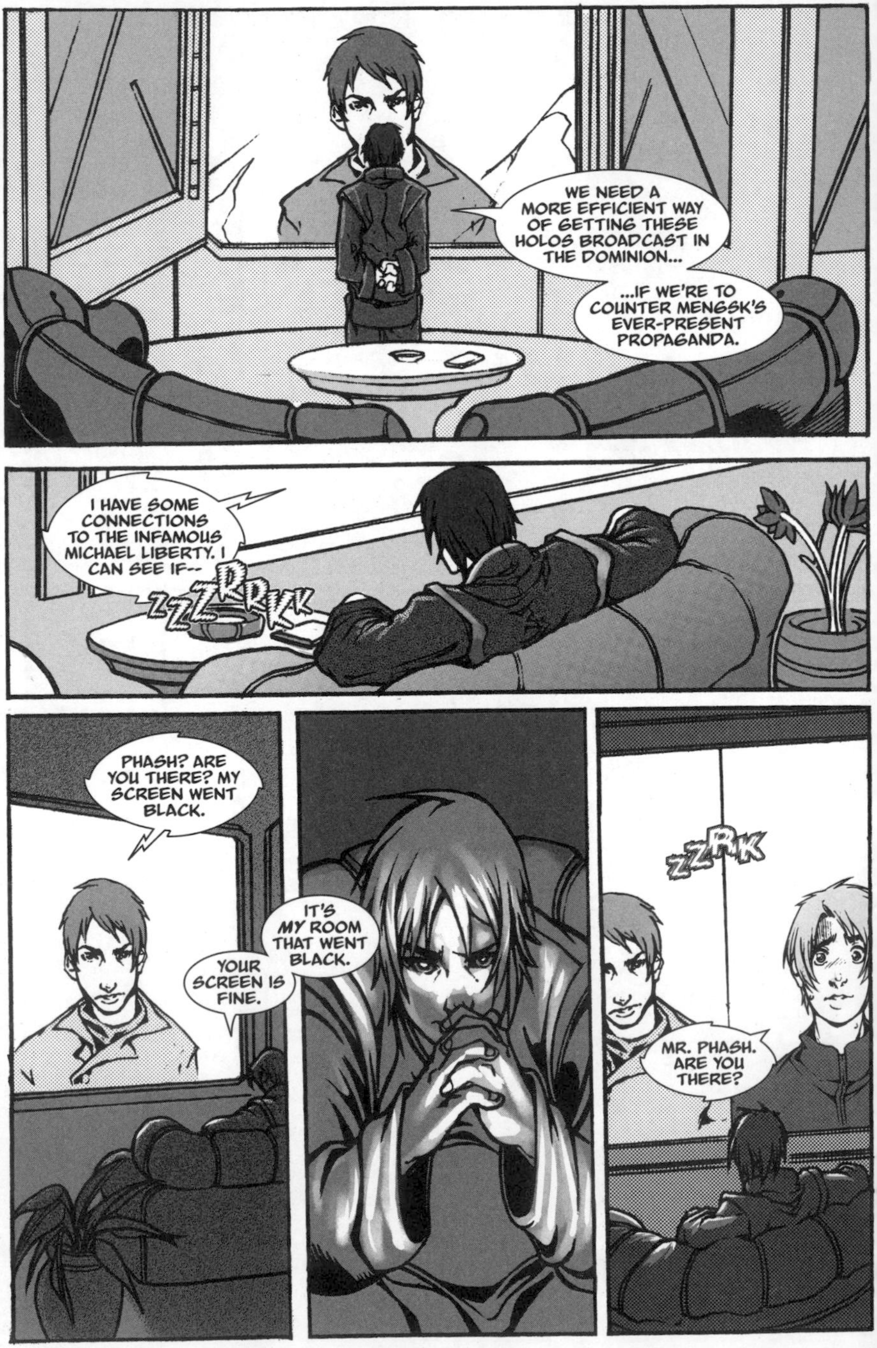

WE NEED A MORE EFFICIENT WAY OF GETTING THESE HOLOS BROADCAST IN THE DOMINION...
...IF WE'RE TO COUNTER MENGSK'S EVER-PRESENT PROPAGANDA.
I HAVE SOME CONNECTIONS TO THE INFAMOUS MICHAEL LIBERTY. I CAN SEE IF--
ZZZRRKK
PHASH? ARE YOU THERE? MY SCREEN WENT BLACK.
YOUR SCREEN IS FINE.
IT'S *MY* ROOM THAT WENT BLACK.
ZZRK
MR. PHASH. ARE YOU THERE?

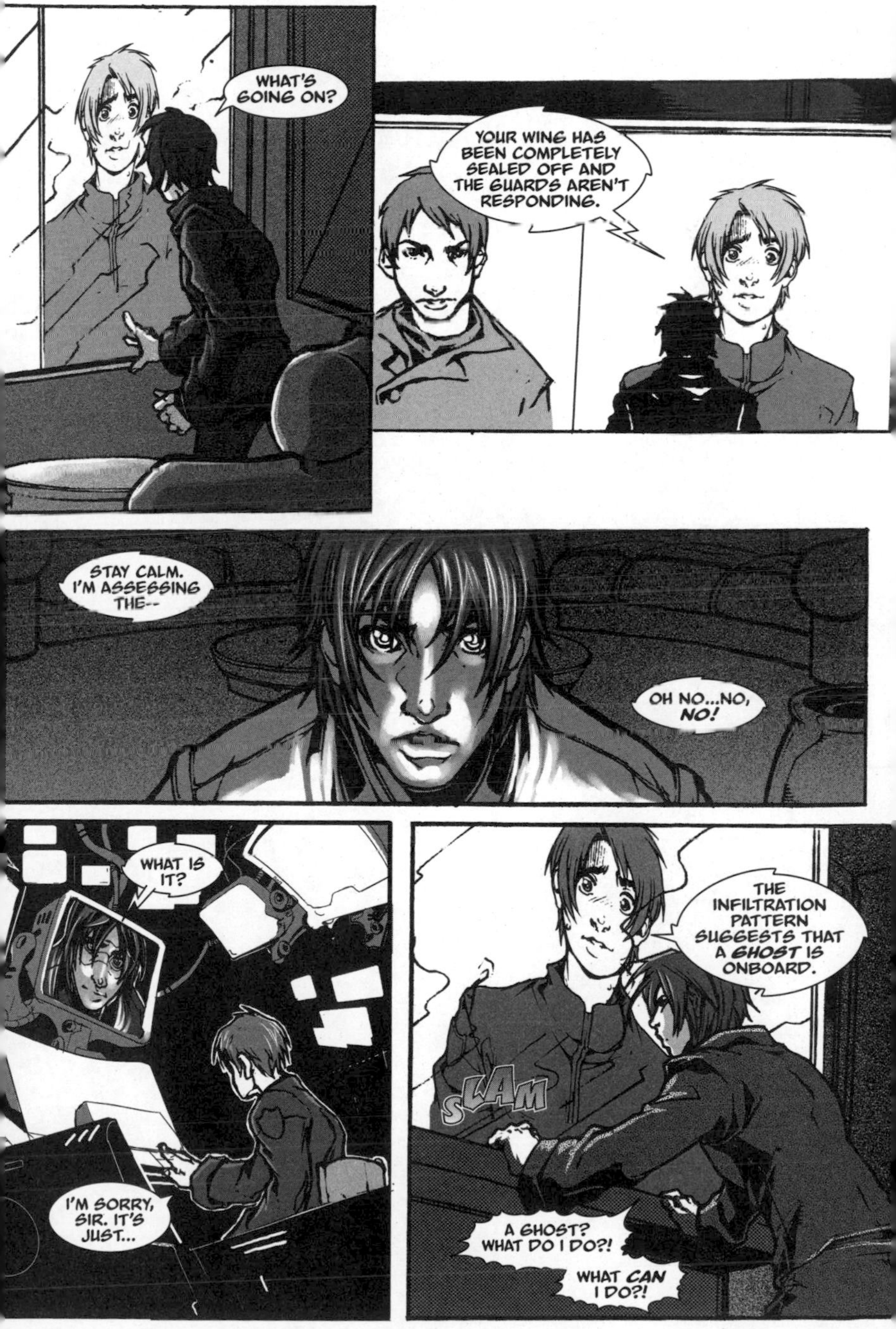
WHAT'S GOING ON?
YOUR WING HAS BEEN COMPLETELY SEALED OFF AND THE GUARDS AREN'T RESPONDING.
STAY CALM. I'M ASSESSING THE--
OH NO...NO, NO!
WHAT IS IT?
I'M SORRY, SIR. IT'S JUST...
THE INFILTRATION PATTERN SUGGESTS THAT A GHOST IS ONBOARD.
SLAM
A GHOST? WHAT DO I DO?!
WHAT CAN I DO?!

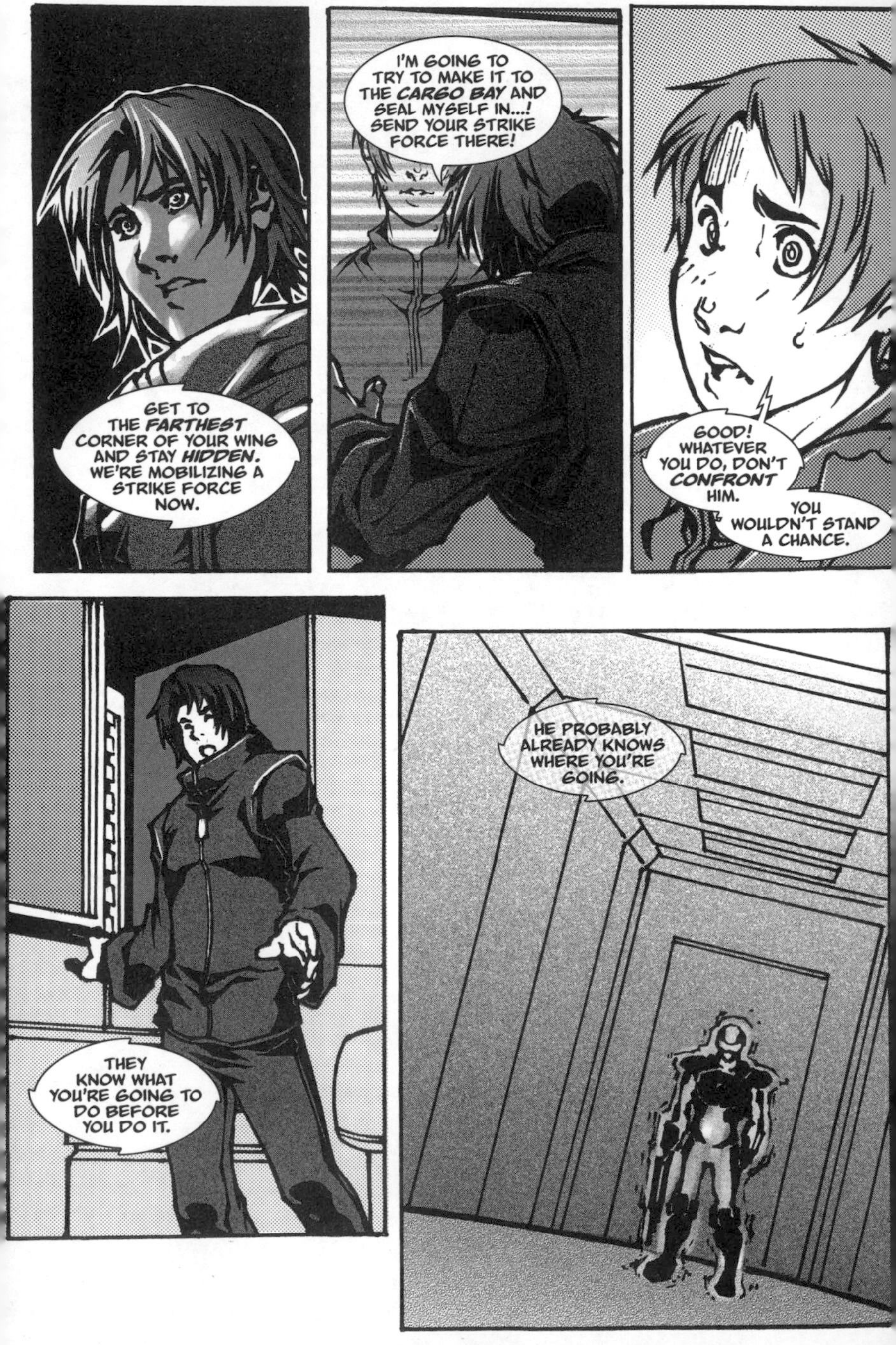
GET TO THE FARTHEST CORNER OF YOUR WING AND STAY HIDDEN. WE'RE MOBILIZING A STRIKE FORCE NOW.
I'M GOING TO TRY TO MAKE IT TO THE CARGO BAY AND SEAL MYSELF IN...! SEND YOUR STRIKE FORCE THERE!
GOOD! WHATEVER YOU DO, DON'T CONFRONT HIM.
YOU WOULDN'T STAND A CHANCE.
THEY KNOW WHAT YOU'RE GOING TO DO BEFORE YOU DO IT.
HE PROBABLY ALREADY KNOWS WHERE YOU'RE GOING.

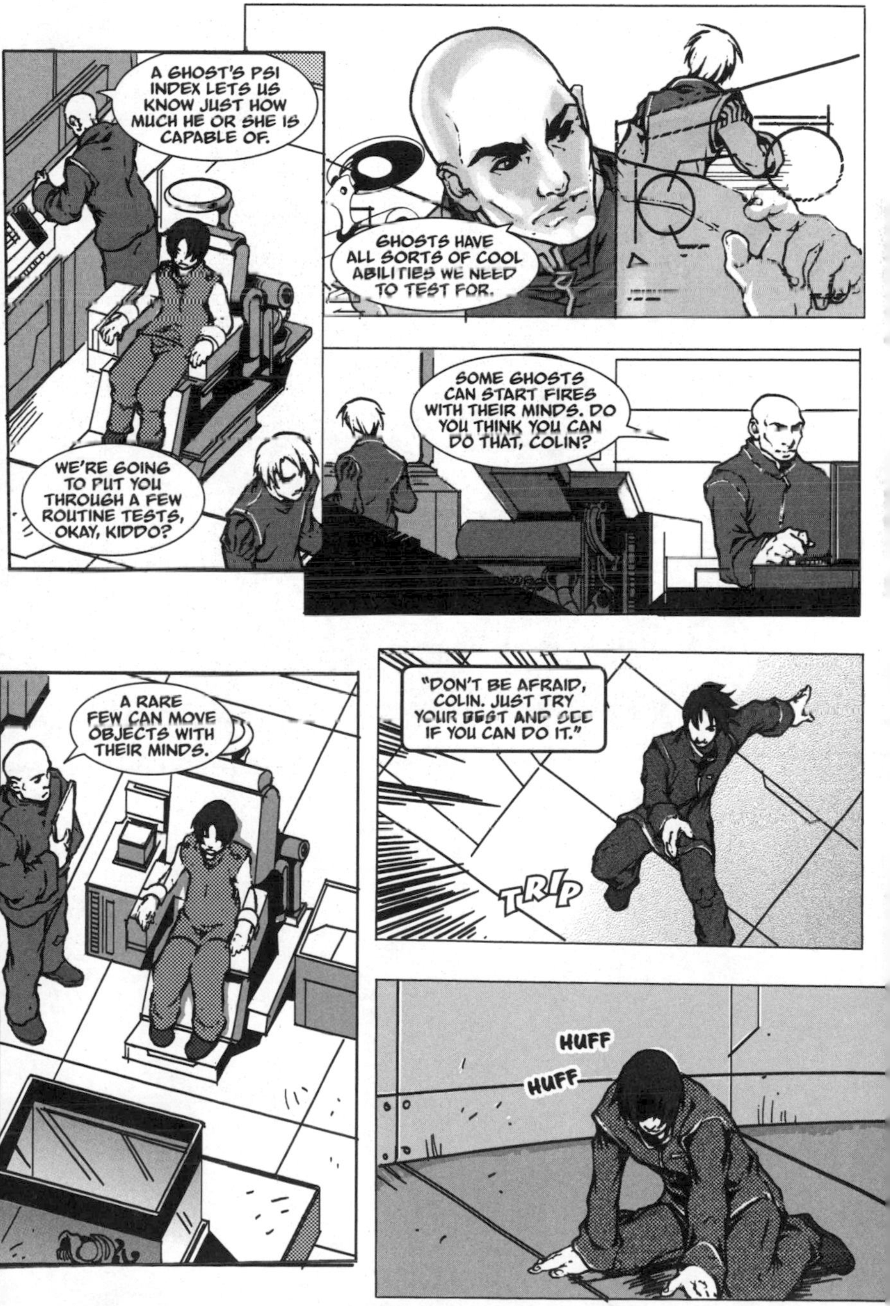
A GHOST'S PSI INDEX LETS US KNOW JUST HOW MUCH HE OR SHE IS CAPABLE OF.
GHOSTS HAVE ALL SORTS OF COOL ABILITIES WE NEED TO TEST FOR.
WE'RE GOING TO PUT YOU THROUGH A FEW ROUTINE TESTS, OKAY, KIDDO?
SOME GHOSTS CAN START FIRES WITH THEIR MINDS. DO YOU THINK YOU CAN DO THAT, COLIN?
A RARE FEW CAN MOVE OBJECTS WITH THEIR MINDS.
"DON'T BE AFRAID, COLIN. JUST TRY YOUR BEST AND SEE IF YOU CAN DO IT."
TRIP
HUFF
HUFF

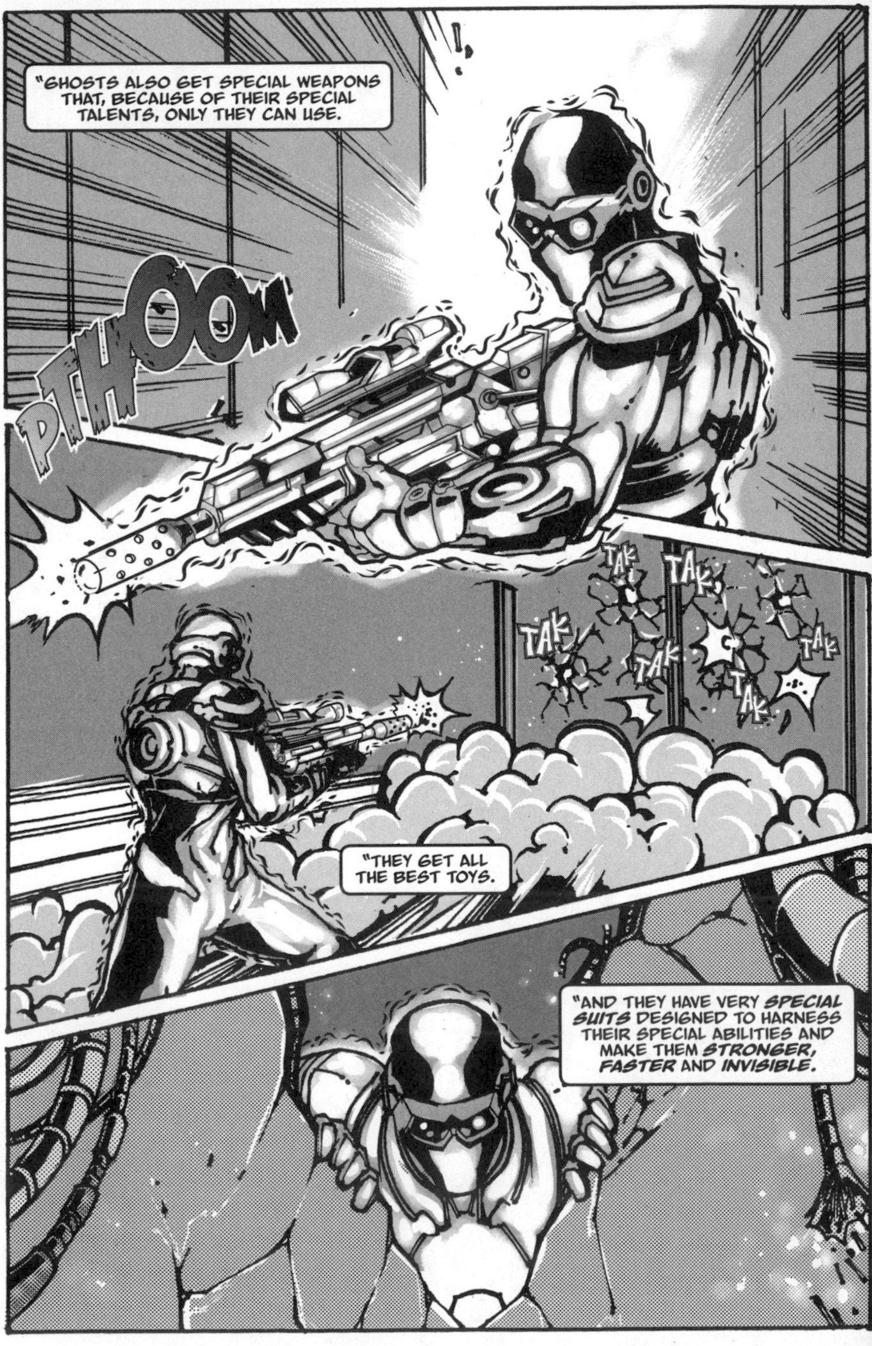
"GHOSTS ALSO GET SPECIAL WEAPONS THAT, BECAUSE OF THEIR SPECIAL TALENTS, ONLY THEY CAN USE.
PTHOOOM
TAK
TAK
TAK
TAK
TAK
TAK
TAK
"THEY GET ALL THE BEST TOYS.
"AND THEY HAVE VERY SPECIAL SUITS DESIGNED TO HARNESS THEIR SPECIAL ABILITIES AND MAKE THEM STRONGER, FASTER AND INVISIBLE.

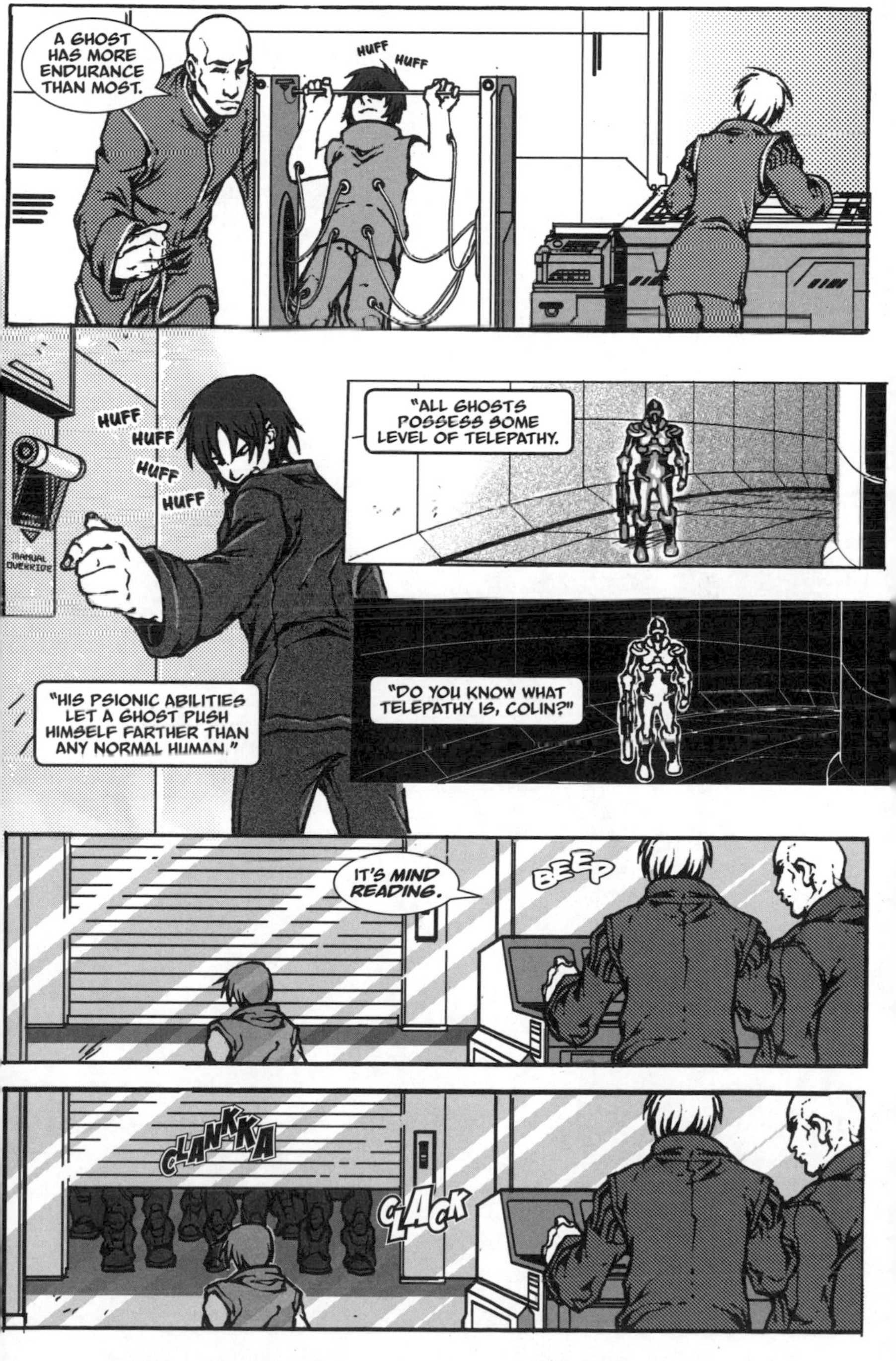
A GHOST HAS MORE ENDURANCE THAN MOST.
HUFF
HUFF
HUFF
HUFF
HUFF
HUFF
MANUAL OVERRIDE
"ALL GHOSTS POSSESS SOME LEVEL OF TELEPATHY.
"HIS PSIONIC ABILITIES LET A GHOST PUSH HIMSELF FARTHER THAN ANY NORMAL HUMAN."
"DO YOU KNOW WHAT TELEPATHY IS, COLIN?"
IT'S MIND READING.
BEEP
CLANKKA
CLACK

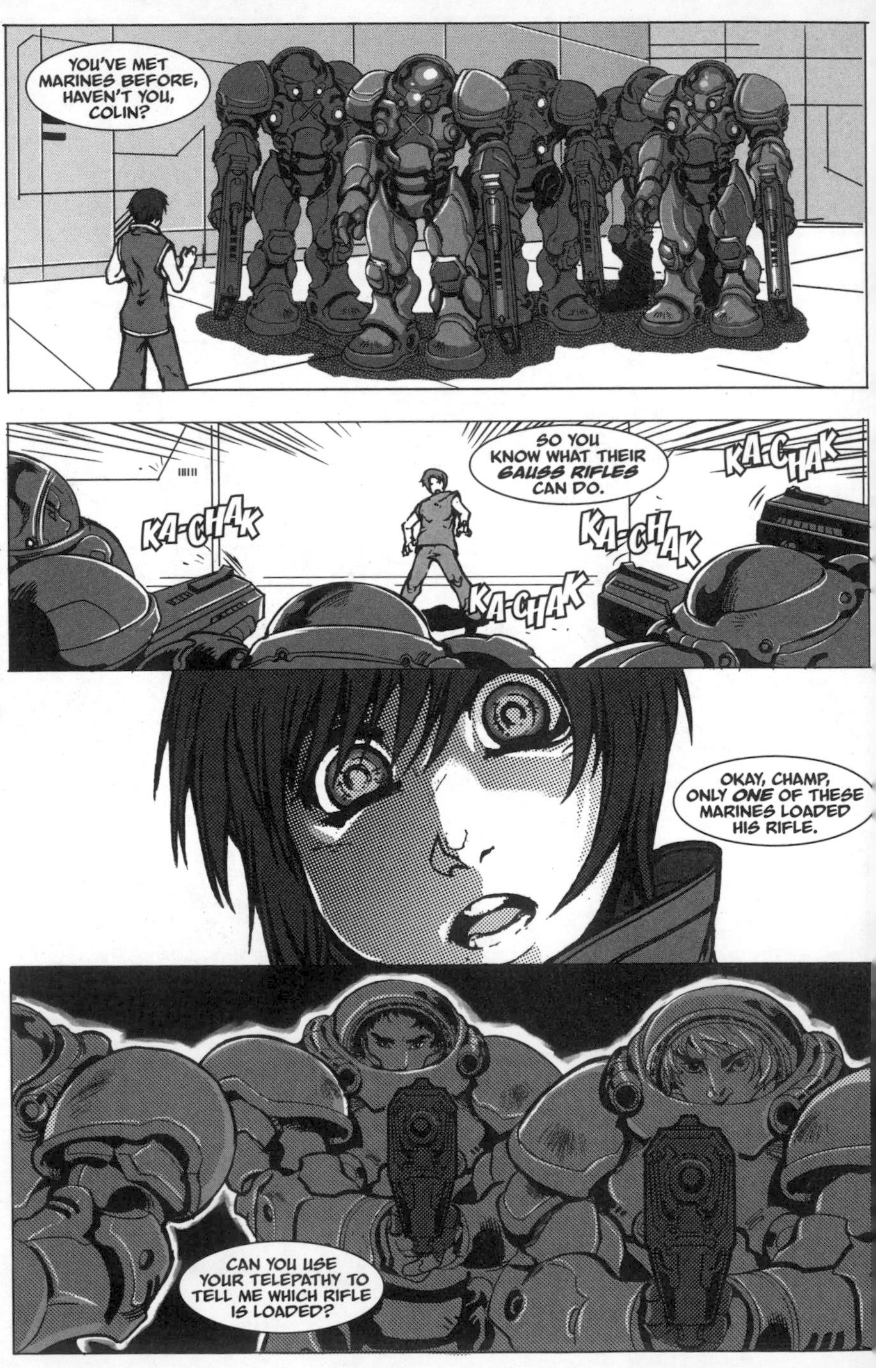
YOU'VE MET MARINES BEFORE, HAVEN'T YOU, COLIN?
SO YOU KNOW WHAT THEIR GAUSS RIFLES CAN DO.
KA-CHAK
KA-CHAK
KA-CHAK
KA-CHAK
OKAY, CHAMP, ONLY ONE OF THESE MARINES LOADED HIS RIFLE.
CAN YOU USE YOUR TELEPATHY TO TELL ME WHICH RIFLE IS LOADED?

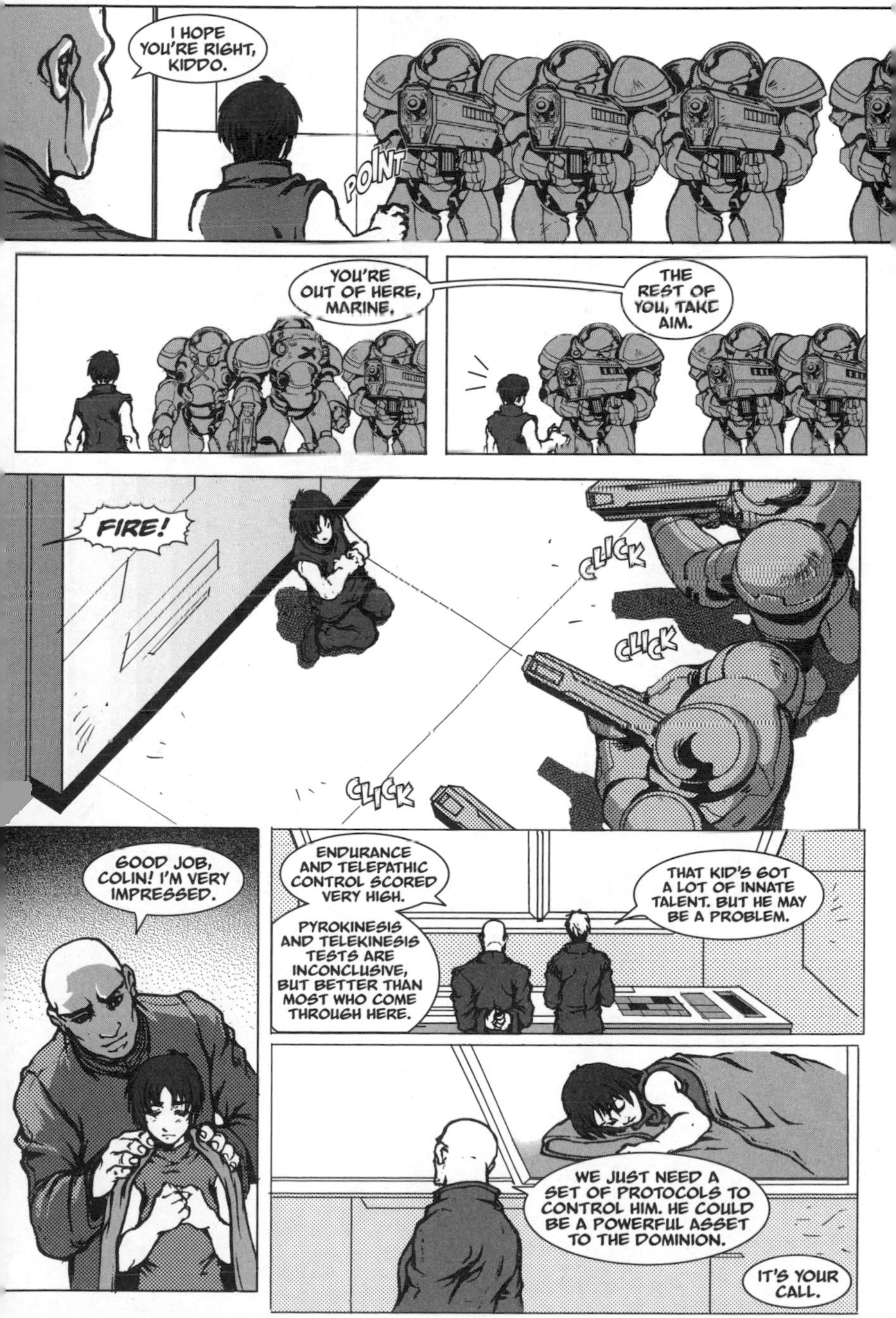
I HOPE YOU'RE RIGHT, KIDDO.
POINT
YOU'RE OUT OF HERE, MARINE.
THE REST OF YOU, TAKE AIM.
FIRE!
CLICK
CLICK
CLICK
GOOD JOB, COLIN! I'M VERY IMPRESSED.
ENDURANCE AND TELEPATHIC CONTROL SCORED VERY HIGH.
PYROKINESIS AND TELEKINESIS TESTS ARE INCONCLUSIVE, BUT BETTER THAN MOST WHO COME THROUGH HERE.
THAT KID'S GOT A LOT OF INNATE TALENT. BUT HE MAY BE A PROBLEM.
WE JUST NEED A SET OF PROTOCOLS TO CONTROL HIM. HE COULD BE A POWERFUL ASSET TO THE DOMINION.
IT'S YOUR CALL.

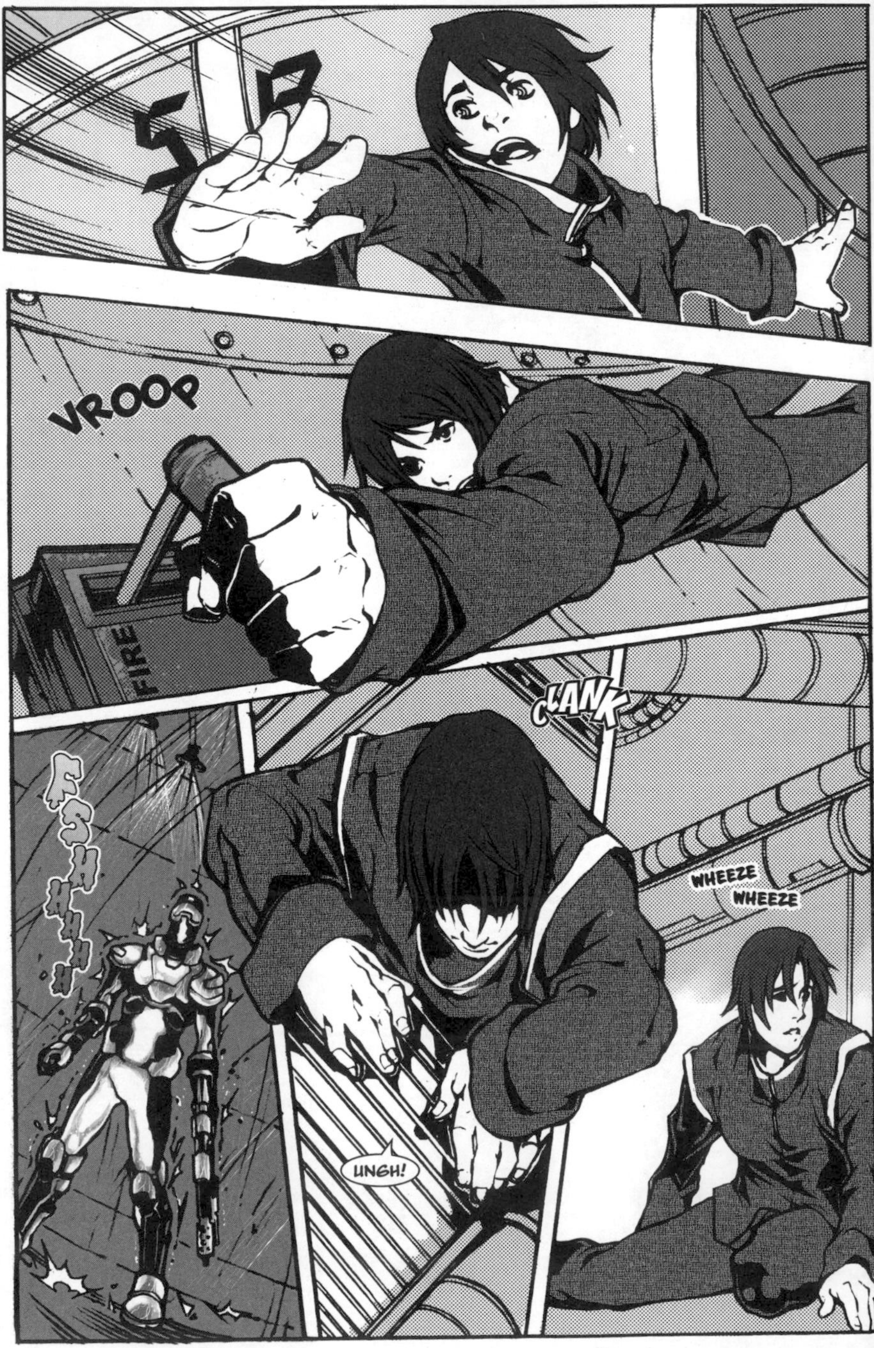
VROOP
FIRE
CLANK
FSHHHHH
WHEEZE
WHEEZE
UNGH!

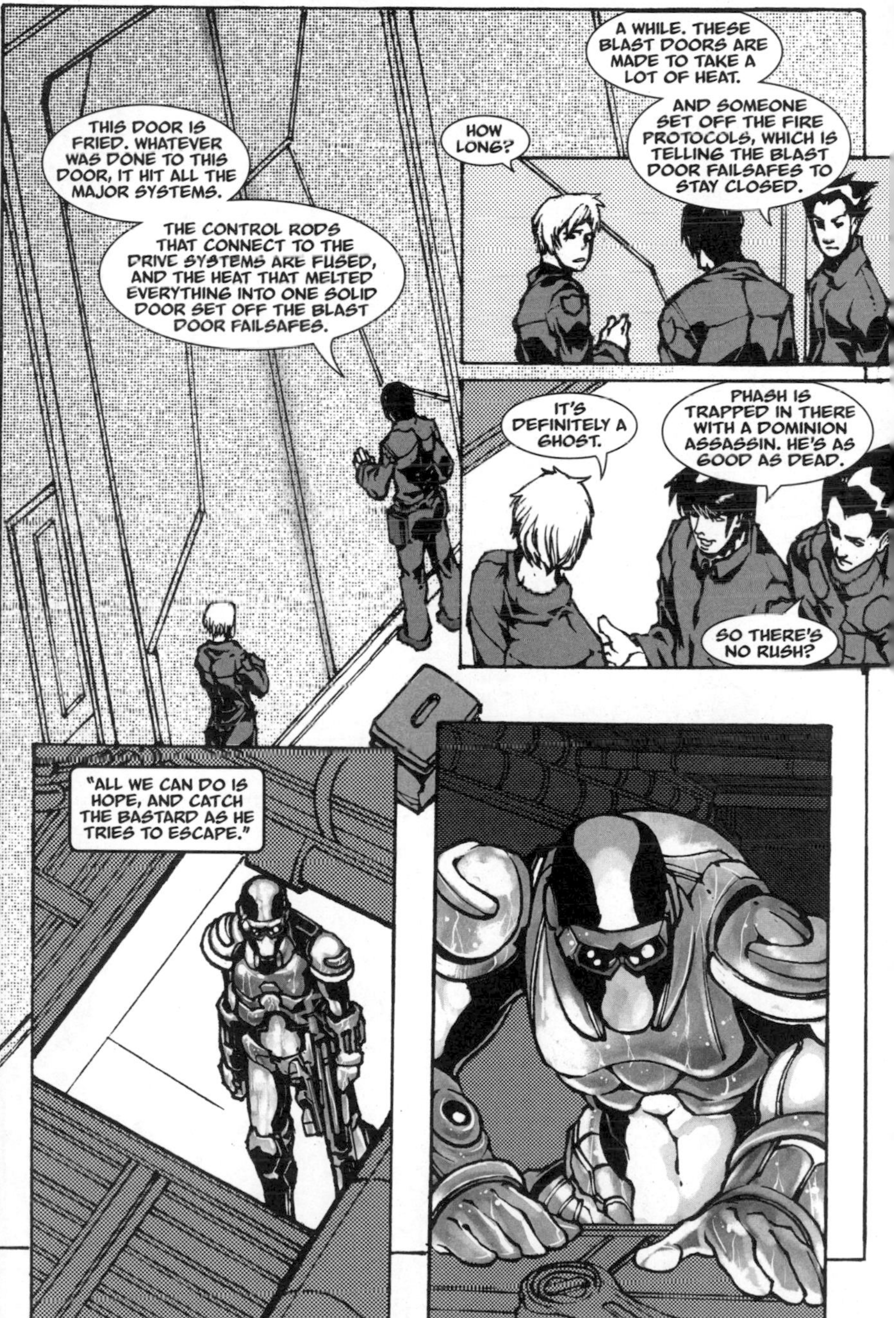
THIS DOOR IS FRIED. WHATEVER WAS DONE TO THIS DOOR, IT HIT ALL THE MAJOR SYSTEMS.
THE CONTROL RODS THAT CONNECT TO THE DRIVE SYSTEMS ARE FUSED, AND THE HEAT THAT MELTED EVERYTHING INTO ONE SOLID DOOR SET OFF THE BLAST DOOR FAILSAFES.
HOW LONG?
A WHILE. THESE BLAST DOORS ARE MADE TO TAKE A LOT OF HEAT.
AND SOMEONE SET OFF THE FIRE PROTOCOLS, WHICH IS TELLING THE BLAST DOOR FAILSAFES TO STAY CLOSED.
IT'S DEFINITELY A GHOST.
PHASH IS TRAPPED IN THERE WITH A DOMINION ASSASSIN. HE'S AS GOOD AS DEAD.
SO THERE'S NO RUSH?
"ALL WE CAN DO IS HOPE, AND CATCH THE BASTARD AS HE TRIES TO ESCAPE."

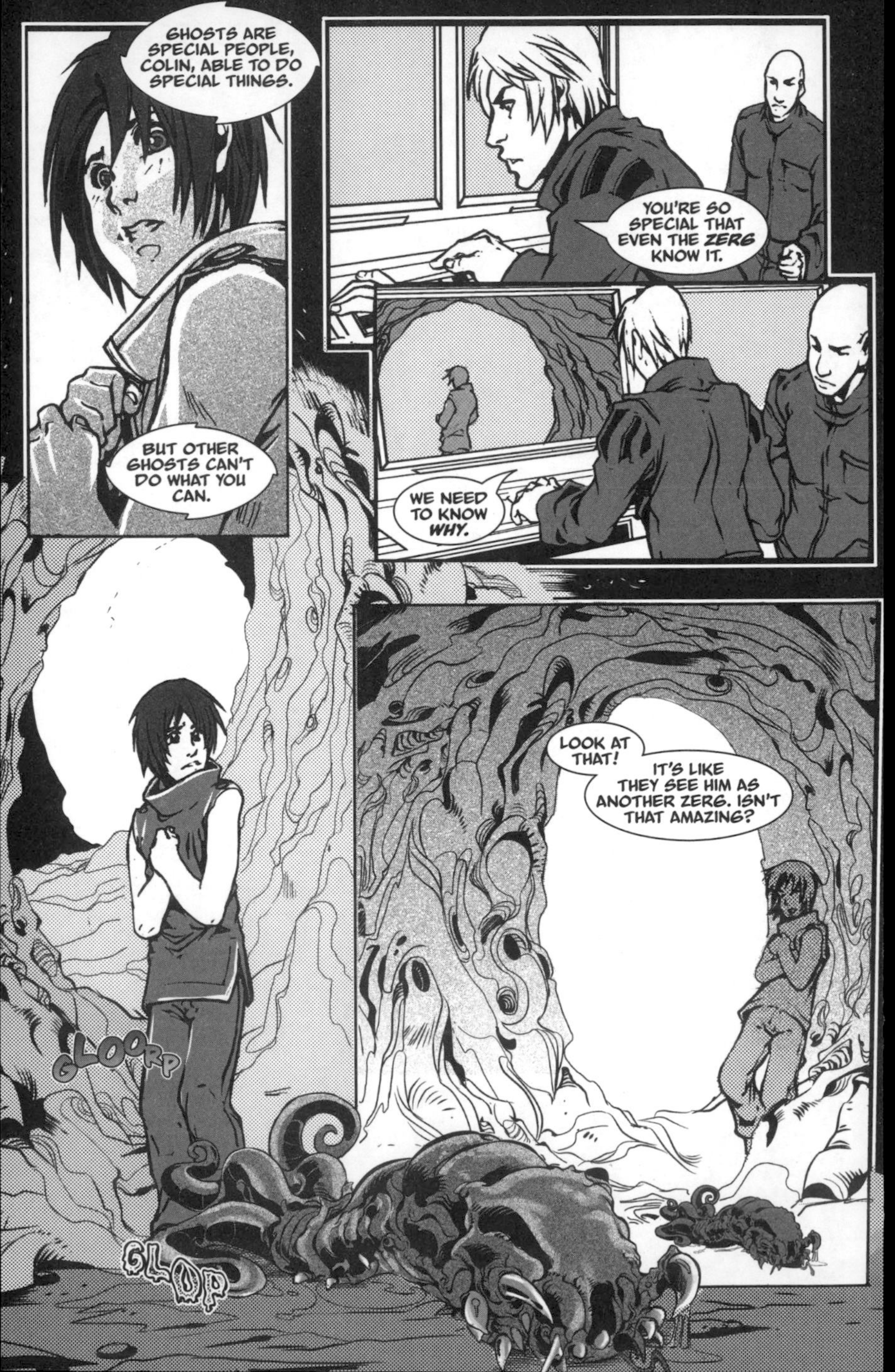
GHOSTS ARE SPECIAL PEOPLE, COLIN, ABLE TO DO SPECIAL THINGS.
BUT OTHER GHOSTS CAN'T DO WHAT YOU CAN.
YOU'RE SO SPECIAL THAT EVEN THE ZERG KNOW IT.
WE NEED TO KNOW WHY.
GLOORP
GLOP
LOOK AT THAT!
IT'S LIKE THEY SEE HIM AS ANOTHER ZERG. ISN'T THAT AMAZING?

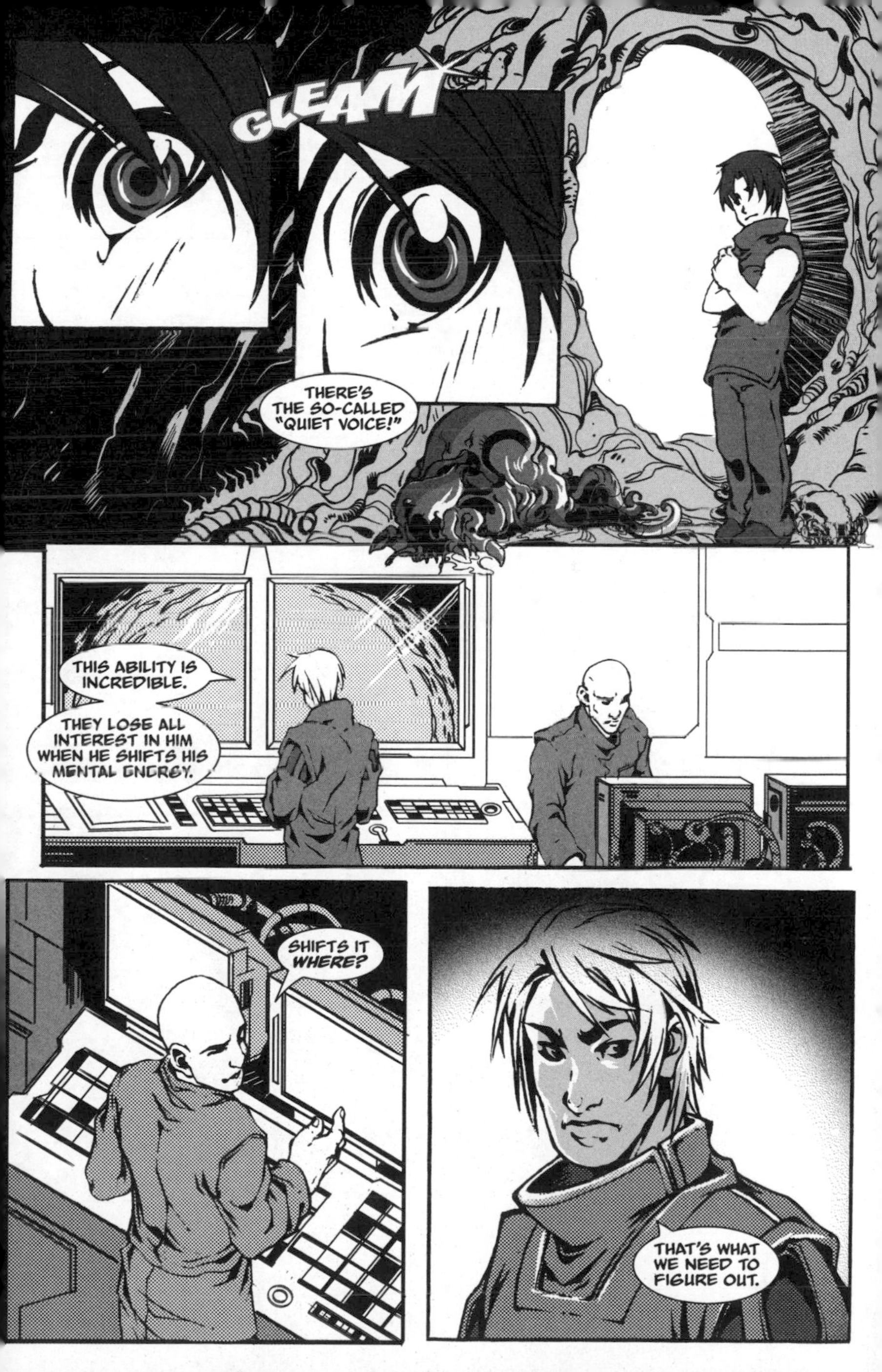
GLEAM
THERE'S THE SO-CALLED "QUIET VOICE!"
THIS ABILITY IS INCREDIBLE.
THEY LOSE ALL INTEREST IN HIM WHEN HE SHIFTS HIS MENTAL ENERGY.
SHIFTS IT WHERE?
THAT'S WHAT WE NEED TO FIGURE OUT.

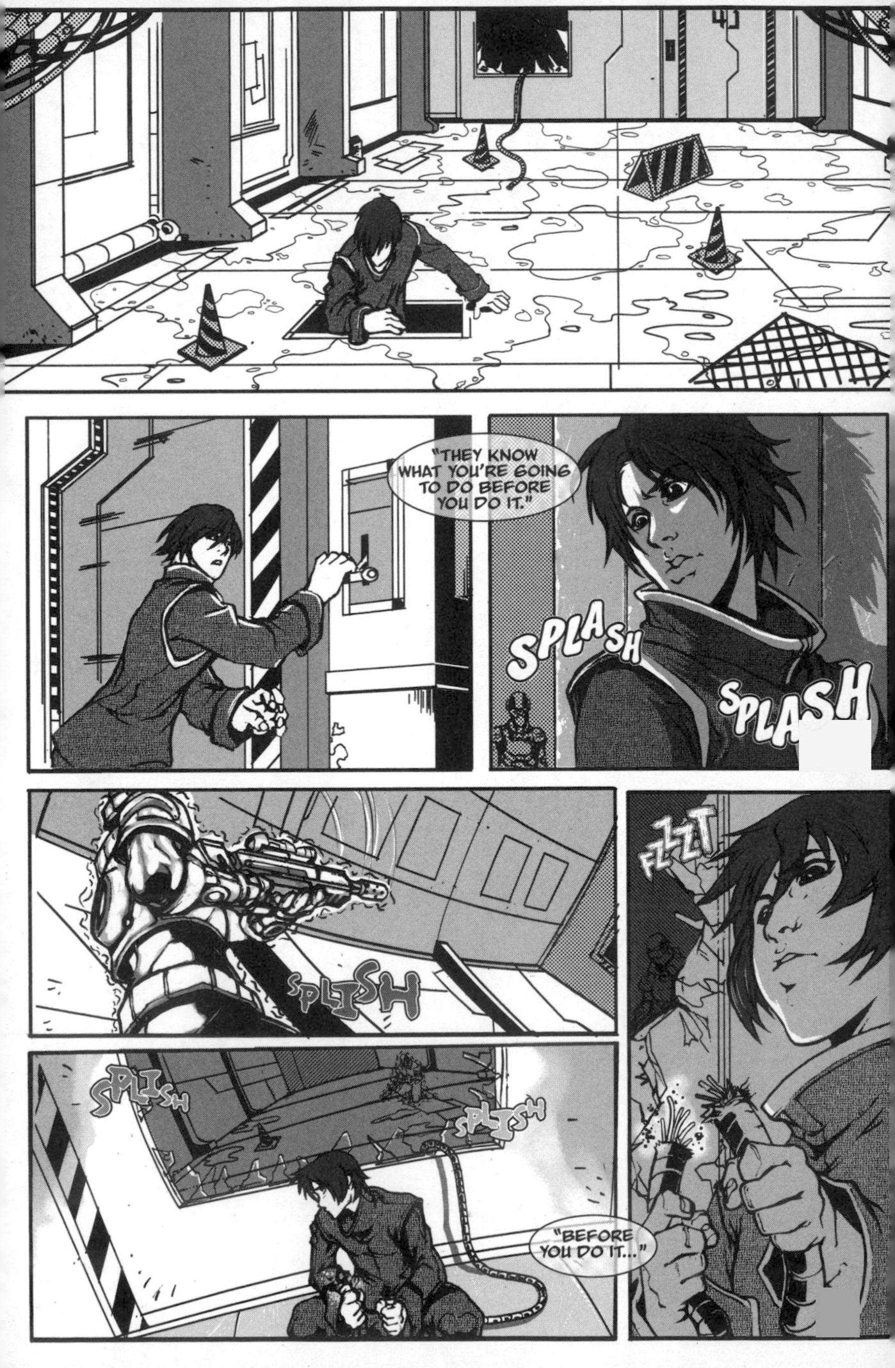
"THEY KNOW WHAT YOU'RE GOING TO DO BEFORE YOU DO IT."
SPLASH
SPLASH
FZZZT
SPLISH
SPLISH
SPLISH
"BEFORE YOU DO IT..."

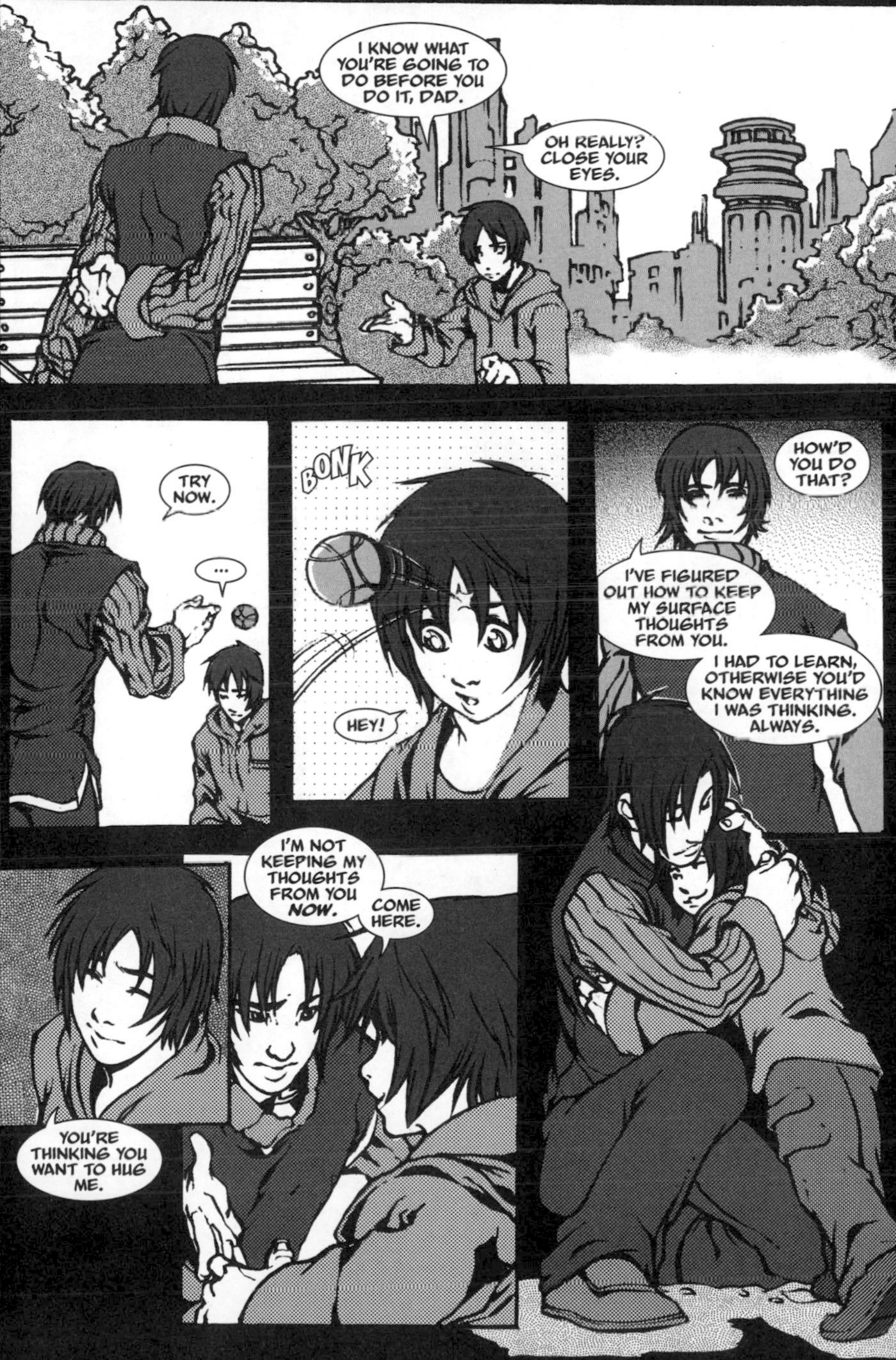

I KNOW WHAT YOU'RE GOING TO DO BEFORE YOU DO IT, DAD.
OH REALLY? CLOSE YOUR EYES.
TRY NOW.
...
BONK
HEY!
HOW'D YOU DO THAT?
I'VE FIGURED OUT HOW TO KEEP MY SURFACE THOUGHTS FROM YOU.
I HAD TO LEARN, OTHERWISE YOU'D KNOW EVERYTHING I WAS THINKING. ALWAYS.
YOU'RE THINKING YOU WANT TO HUG ME.
I'M NOT KEEPING MY THOUGHTS FROM YOU NOW.
COME HERE.

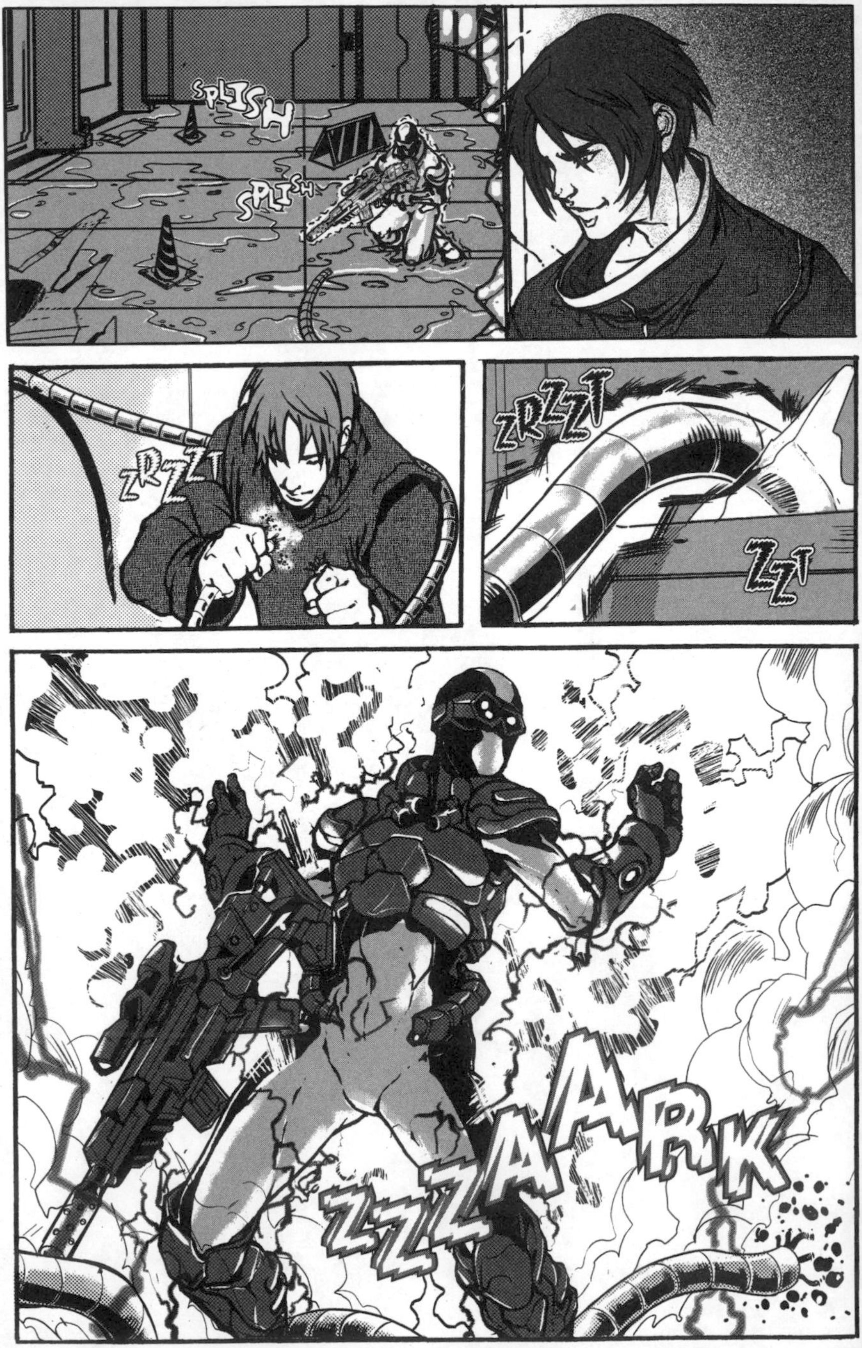
SPLISH
SPLISH
ZRZZT
ZRZZT
ZZT
ZZZAARK

POP
POP
CRAKL
CRACKL
KZZT

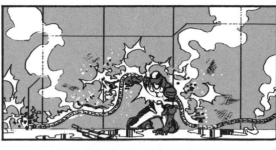

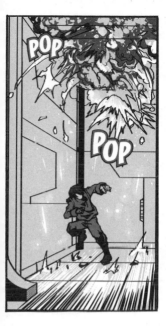

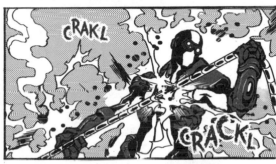

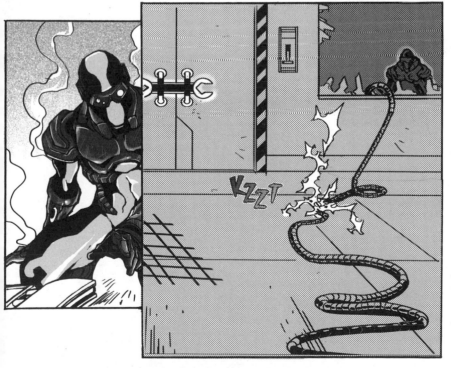

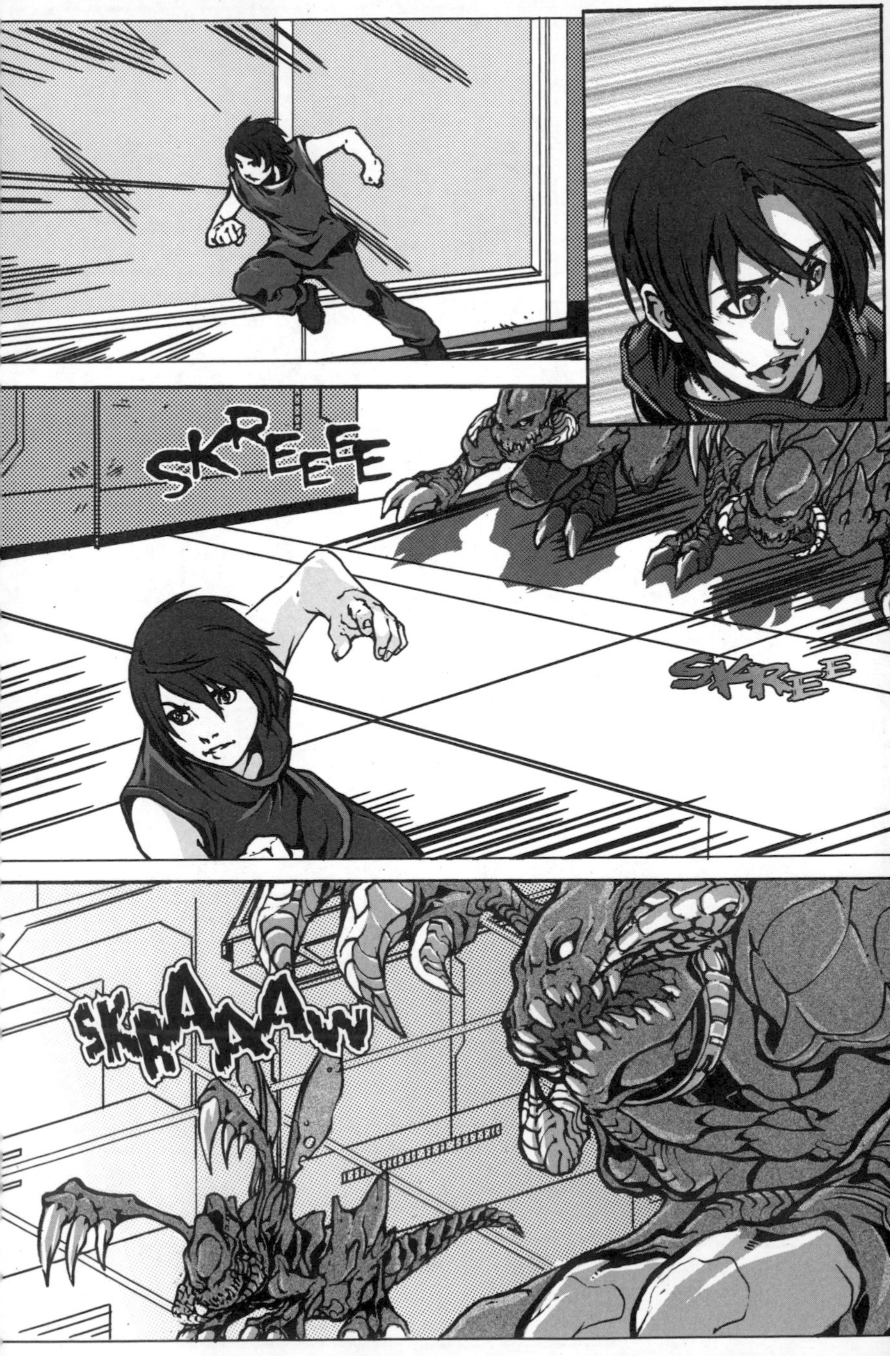
SKREEEE
SKREEE
SKRAAAW

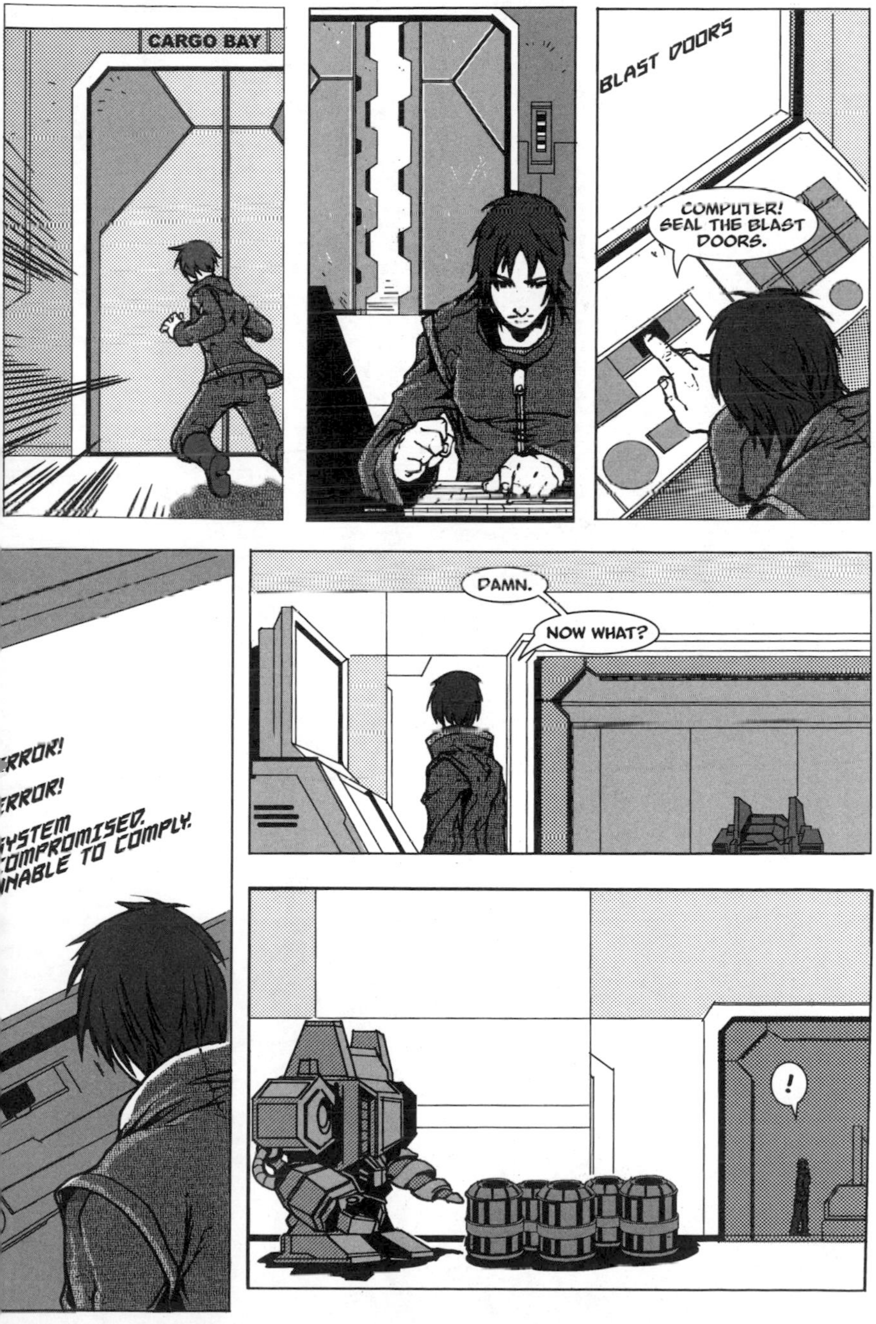
CARGO BAY
BLAST DOORS
COMPUTER! SEAL THE BLAST DOORS.
ERROR!
ERROR!
SYSTEM COMPROMISED. UNABLE TO COMPLY.
DAMN.
NOW WHAT?
!

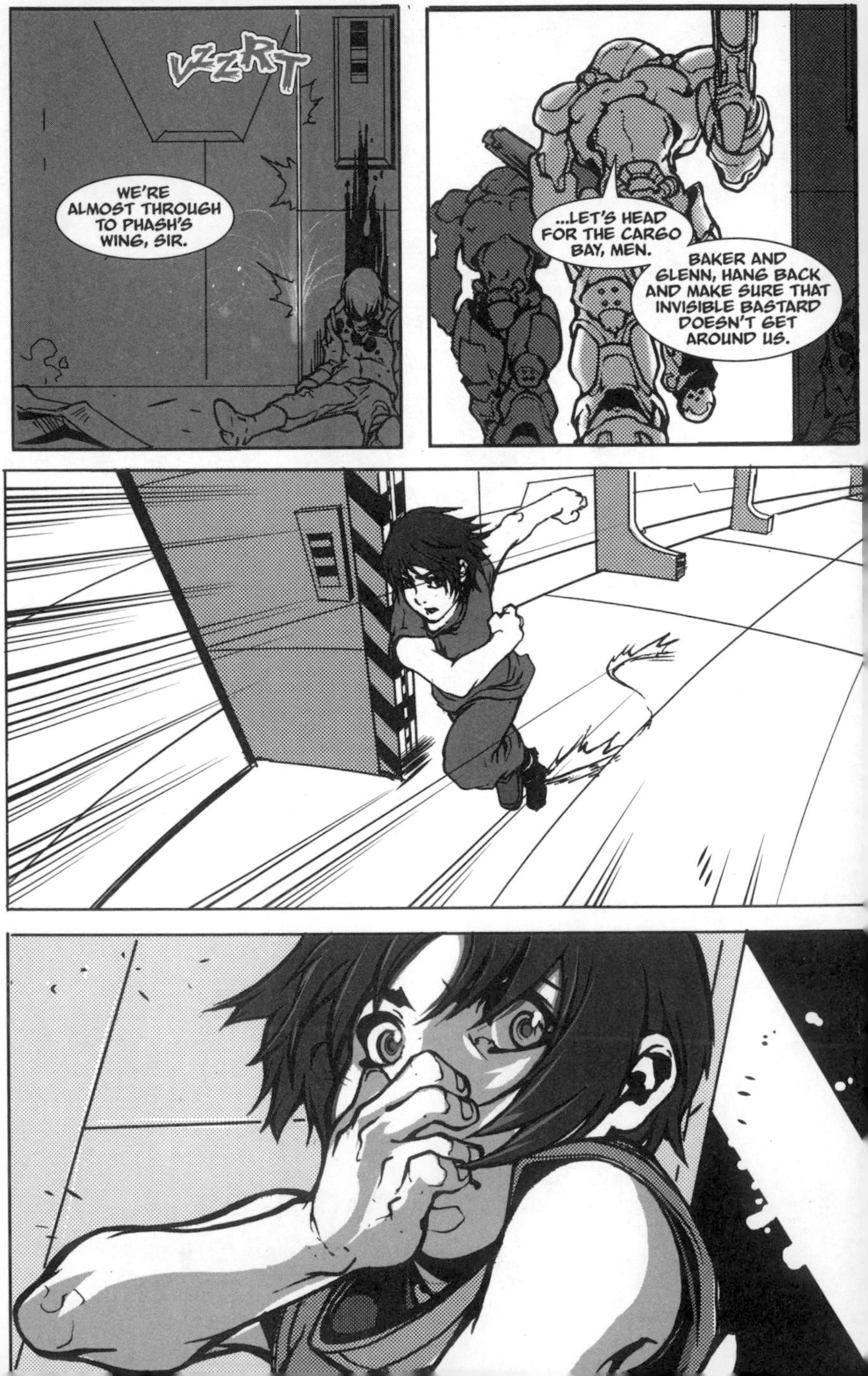
VZZRT
WE'RE ALMOST THROUGH TO PHASH'S WING, SIR.
...LET'S HEAD FOR THE CARGO BAY, MEN.
BAKER AND GLENN, HANG BACK AND MAKE SURE THAT INVISIBLE BASTARD DOESN'T GET AROUND US.

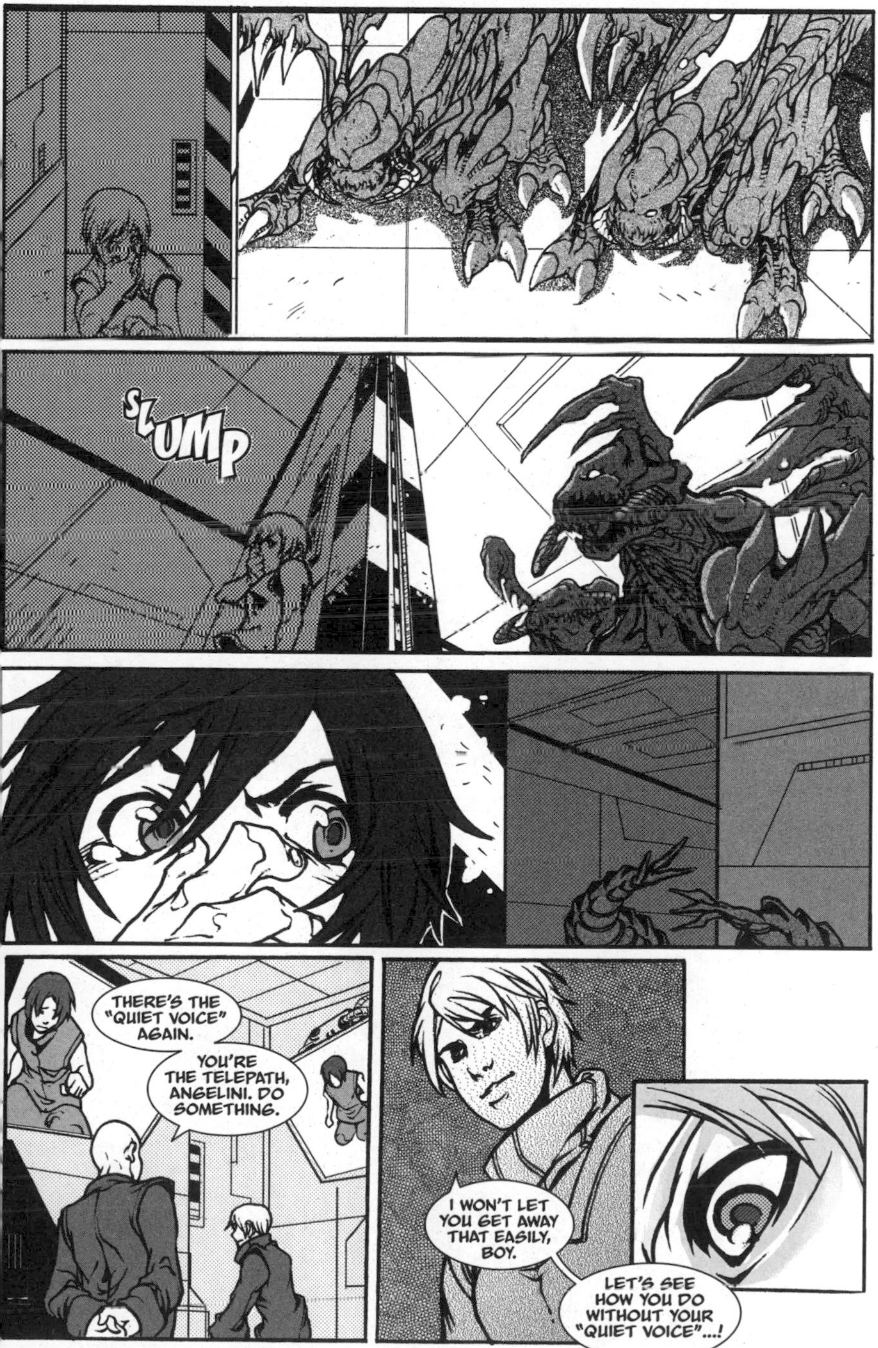
SLUMP
THERE'S THE "QUIET VOICE" AGAIN.
YOU'RE THE TELEPATH, ANGELINI. DO SOMETHING.
I WON'T LET YOU GET AWAY THAT EASILY, BOY.
LET'S SEE HOW YOU DO WITHOUT YOUR "QUIET VOICE"...!

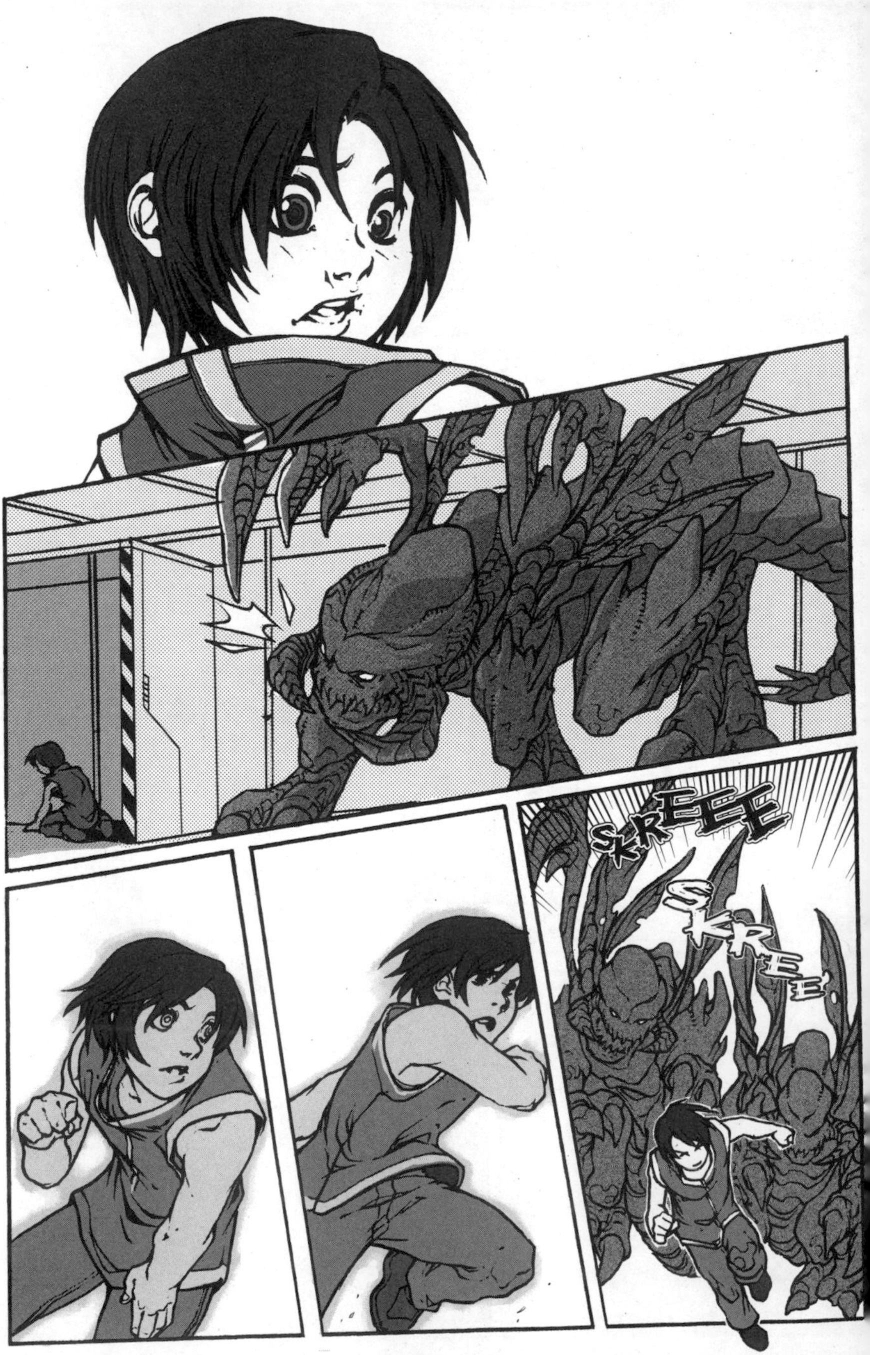
SKREEEE
SKREE

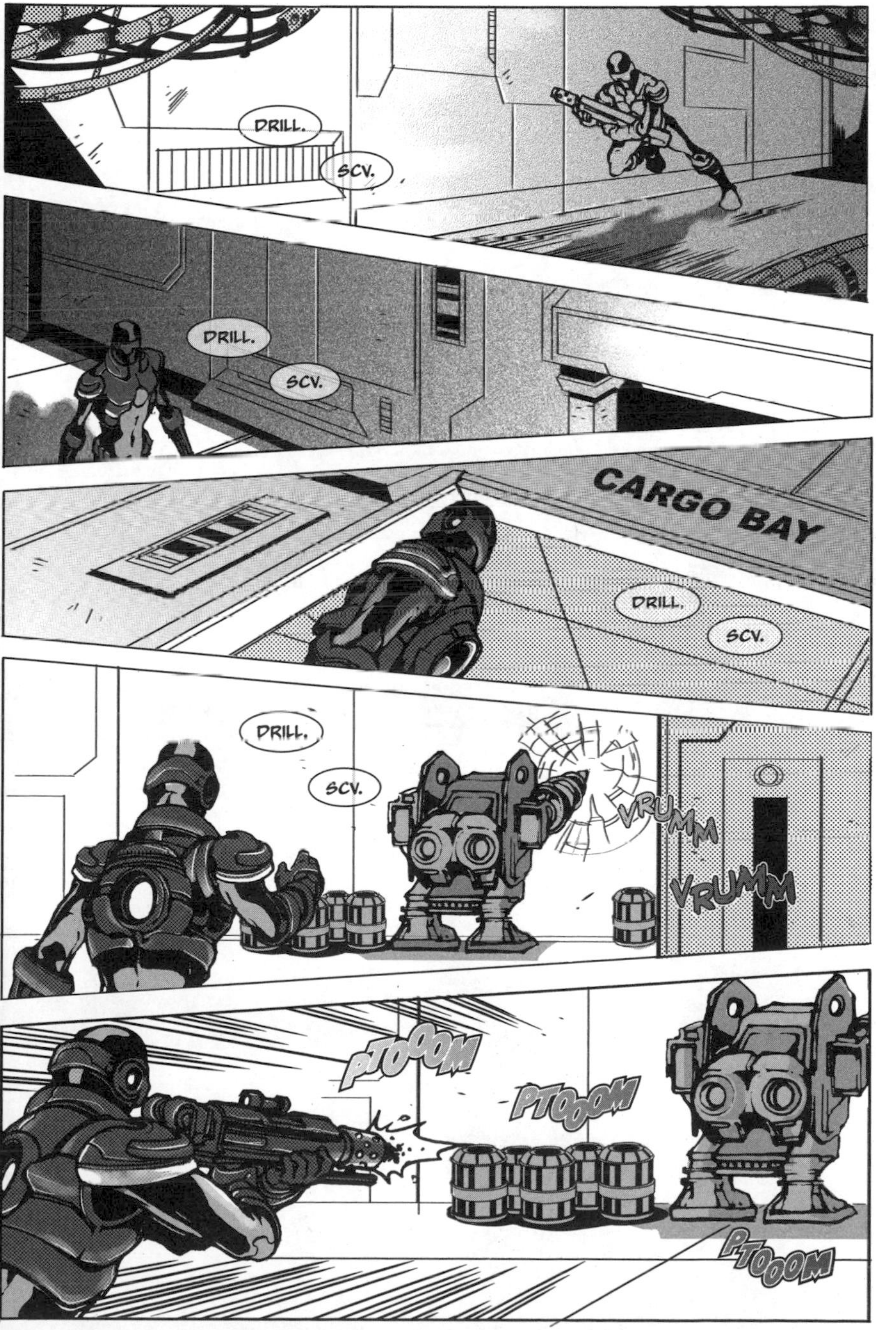

DRILL.
SCV.
DRILL.
SCV.
CARGO BAY
DRILL.
SCV.
DRILL.
SCV.
VRUMM
VRUMM
PTOOOM
PTOOOM
PTOOOM

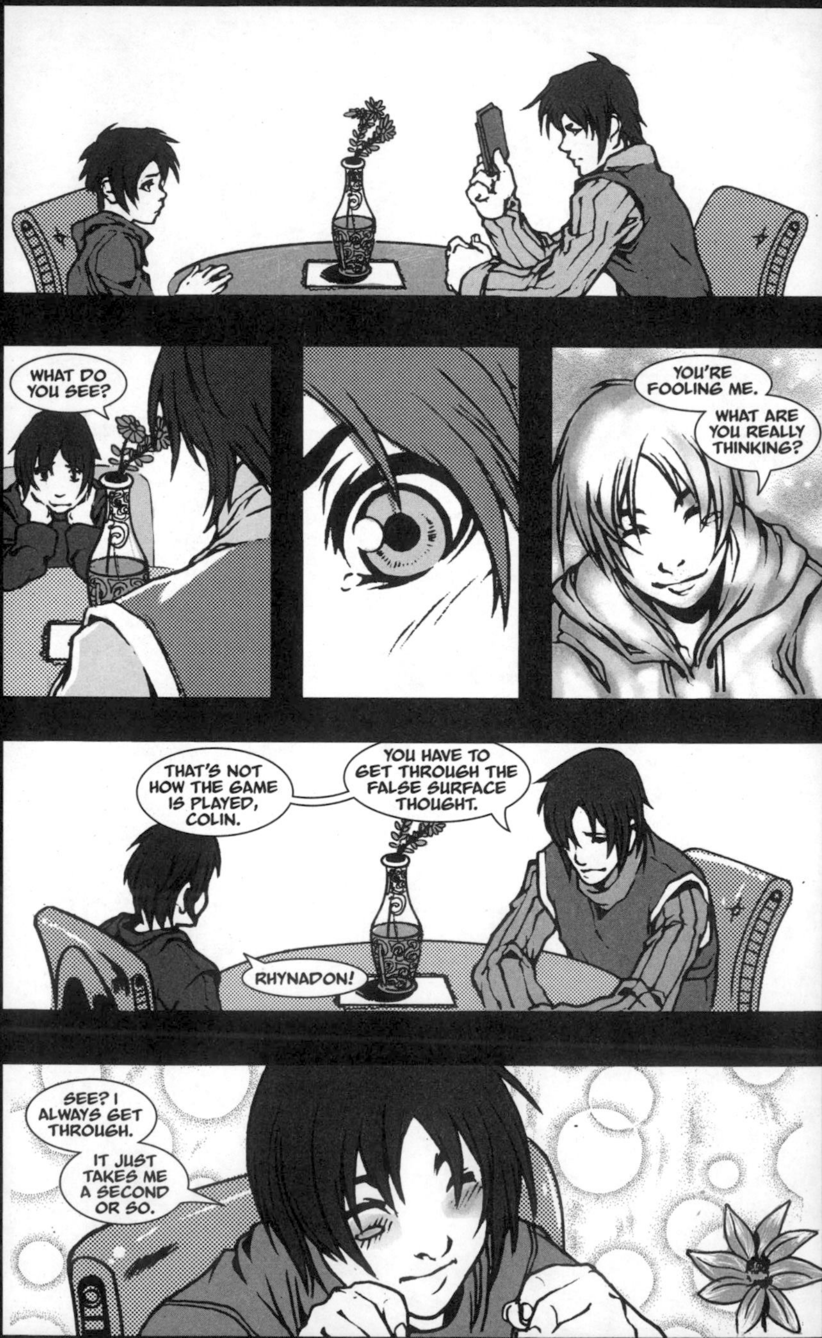
WHAT DO YOU SEE?
YOU'RE FOOLING ME.
WHAT ARE YOU REALLY THINKING?
THAT'S NOT HOW THE GAME IS PLAYED, COLIN.
YOU HAVE TO GET THROUGH THE FALSE SURFACE THOUGHT.
RHYNADON!
SEE? I ALWAYS GET THROUGH.
IT JUST TAKES ME A SECOND OR SO.

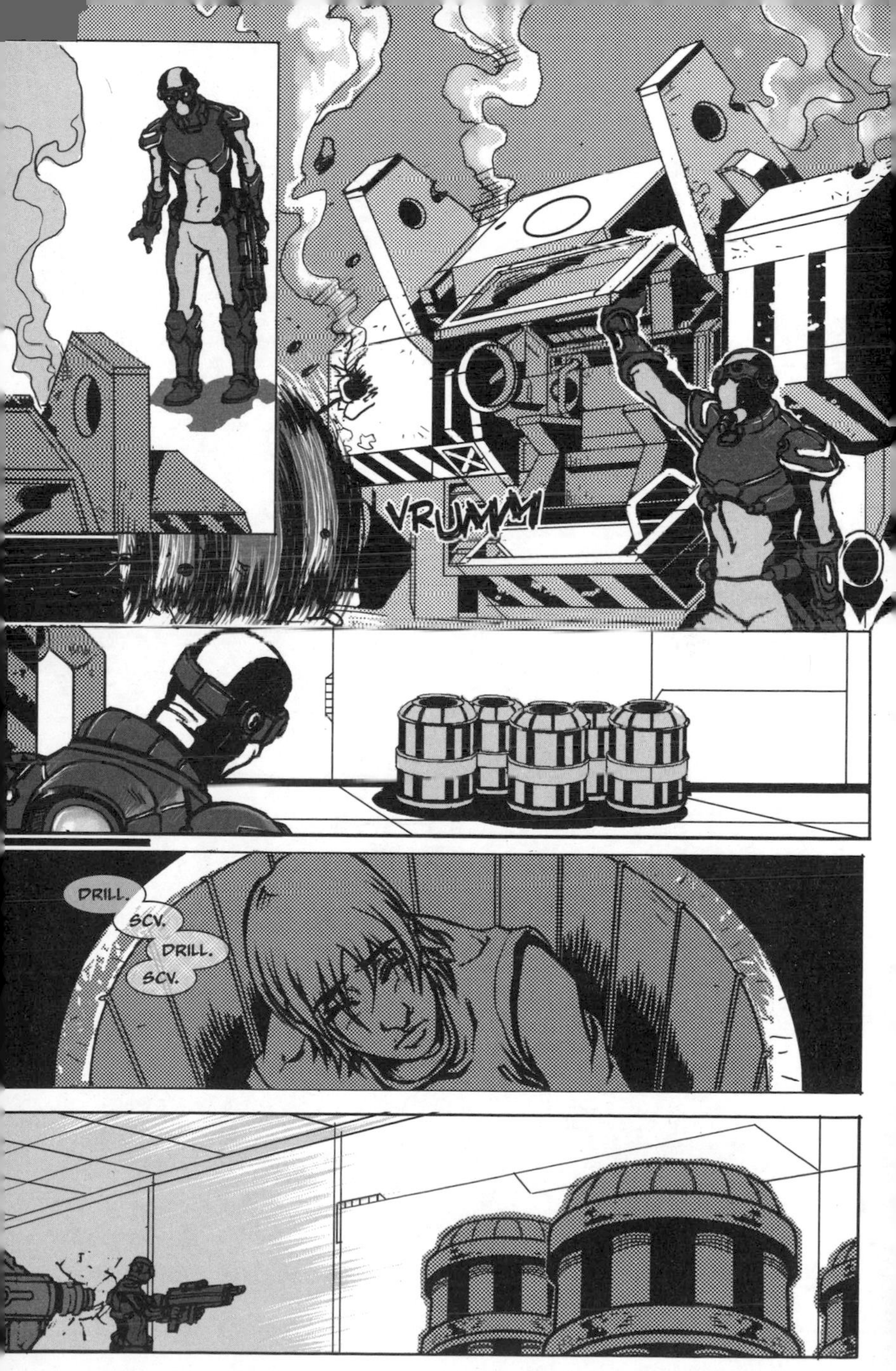
VRUMMM
DRILL.
SCV.
DRILL.
SCV.

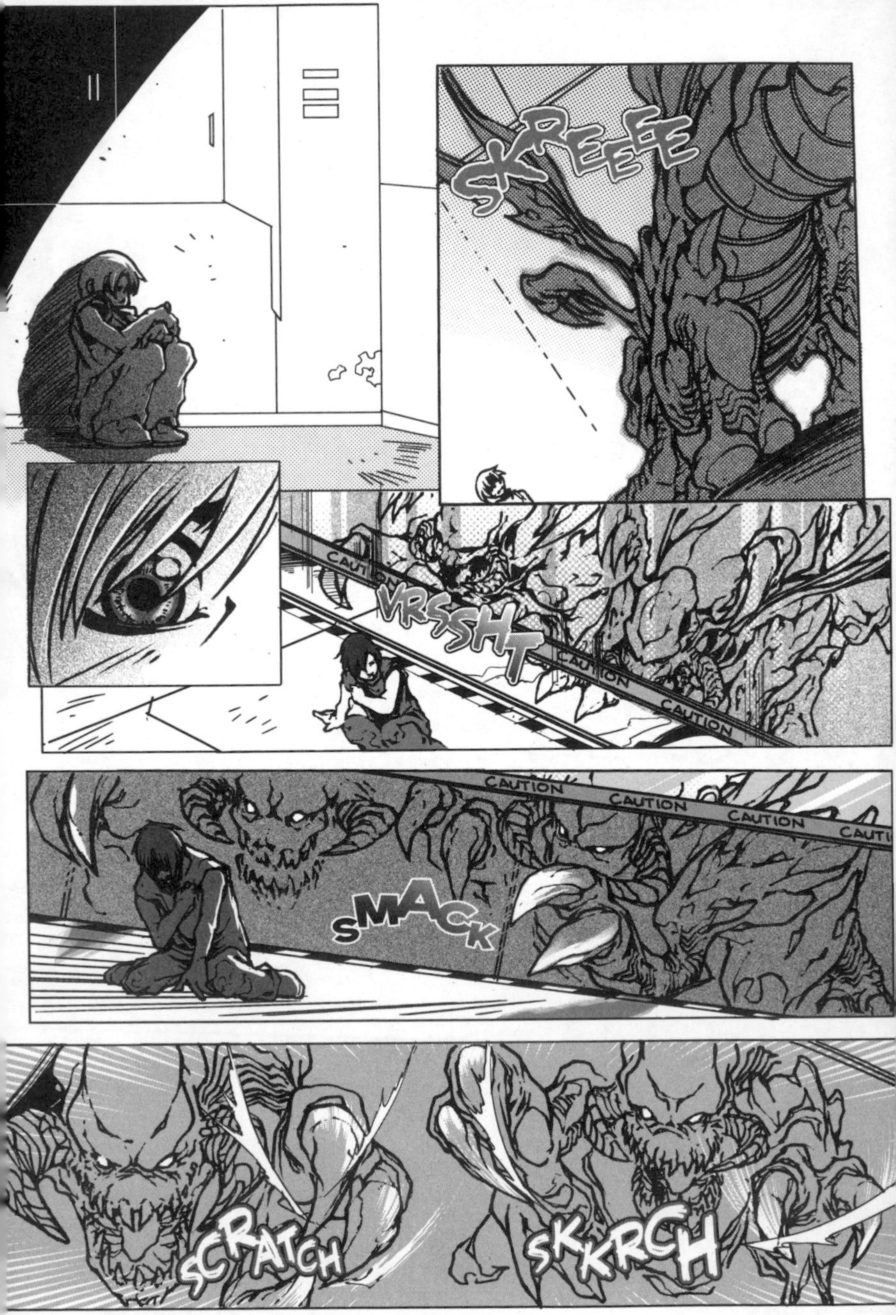
SKREEEE
VRSSHT
CAUTION
CAUTION
CAUTION
CAUTION
CAUTION
CAUTION
SMACK
SCRATCH
SKKRCH

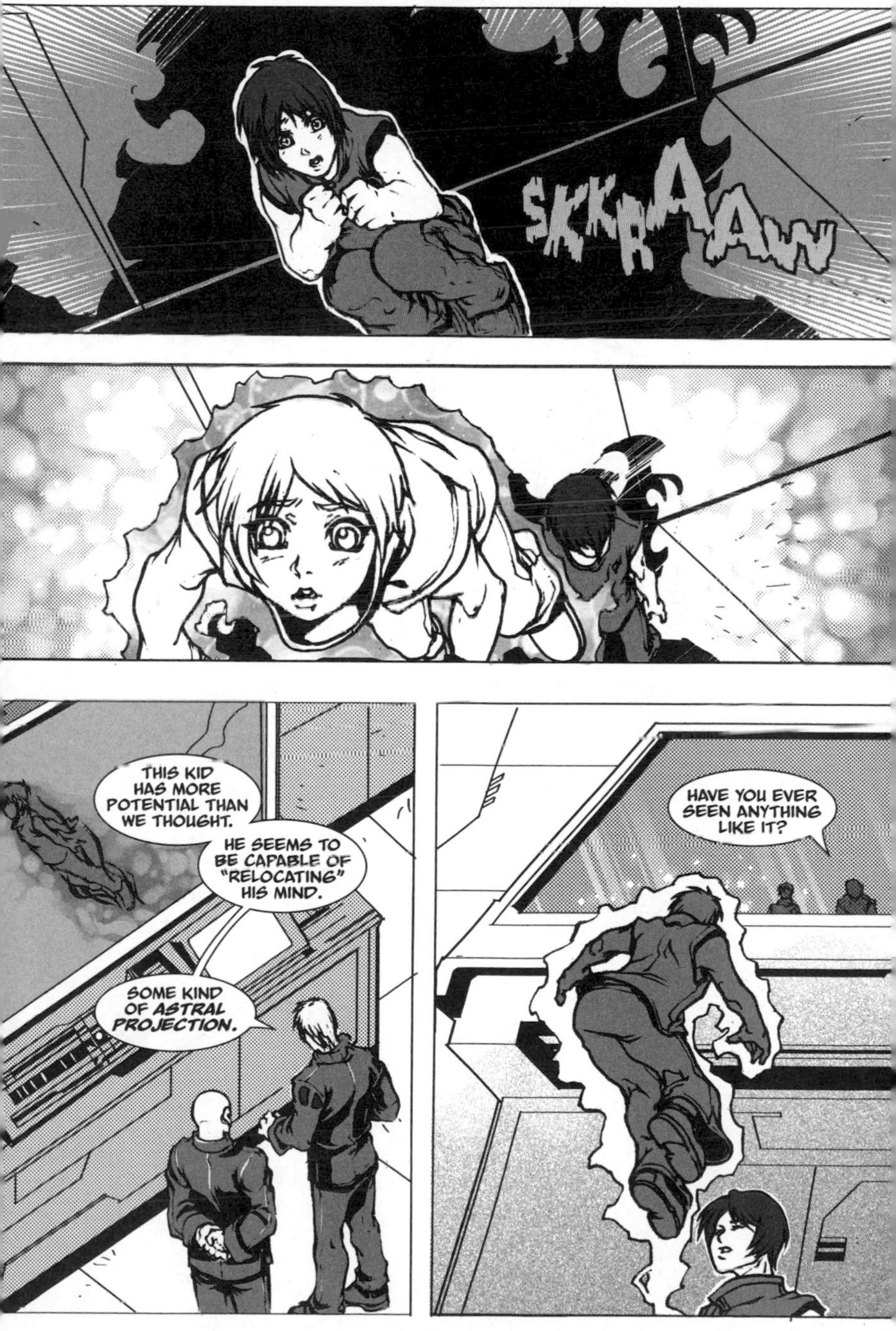
SKKRAAAW
THIS KID HAS MORE POTENTIAL THAN WE THOUGHT.
HE SEEMS TO BE CAPABLE OF "RELOCATING" HIS MIND.
SOME KIND OF ASTRAL PROJECTION.
HAVE YOU EVER SEEN ANYTHING LIKE IT?

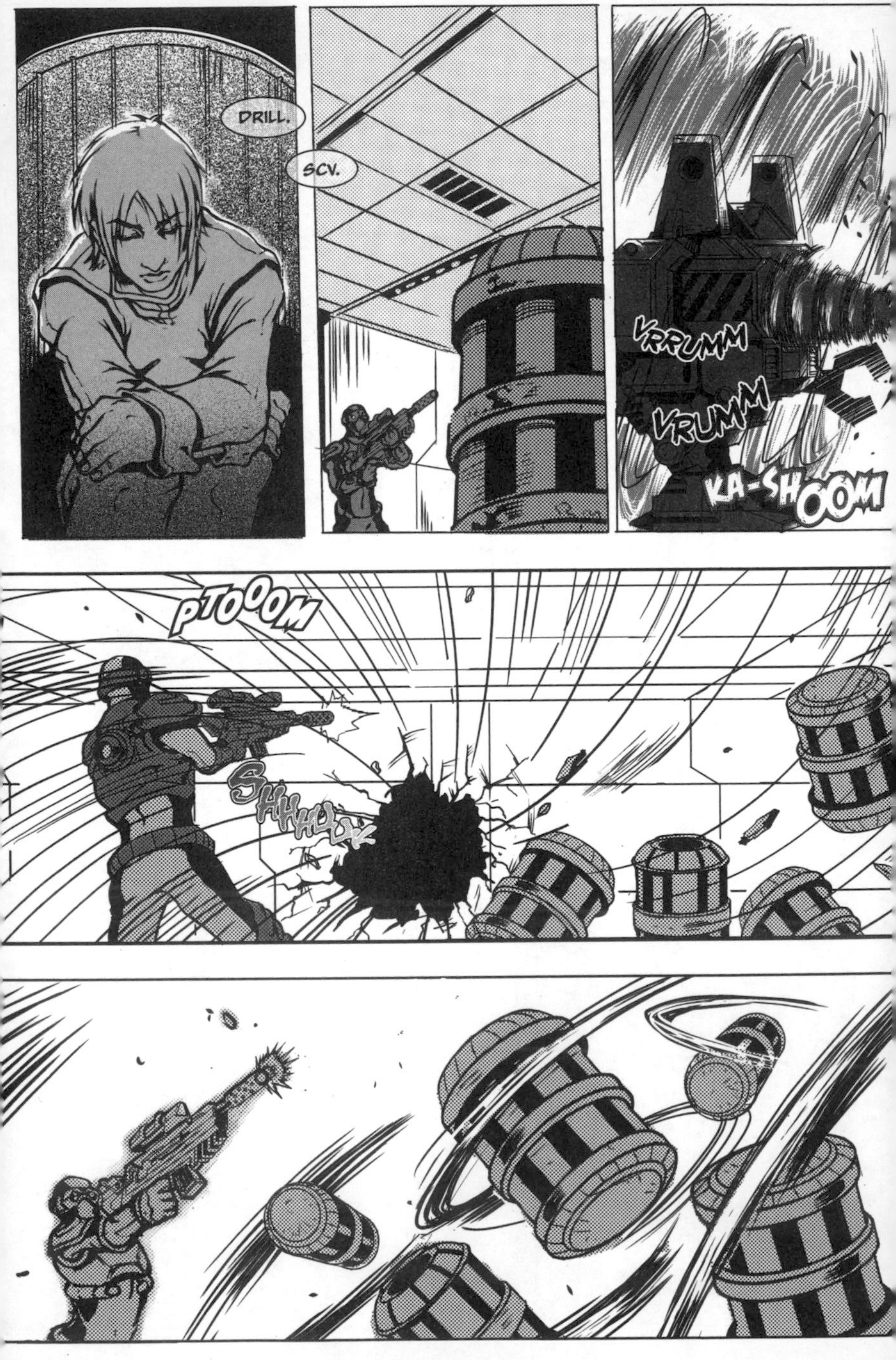
DRILL.
SCV.
VRRUMM
VRUMM
KA-SHOOM
PTOOOM
SHHHUK

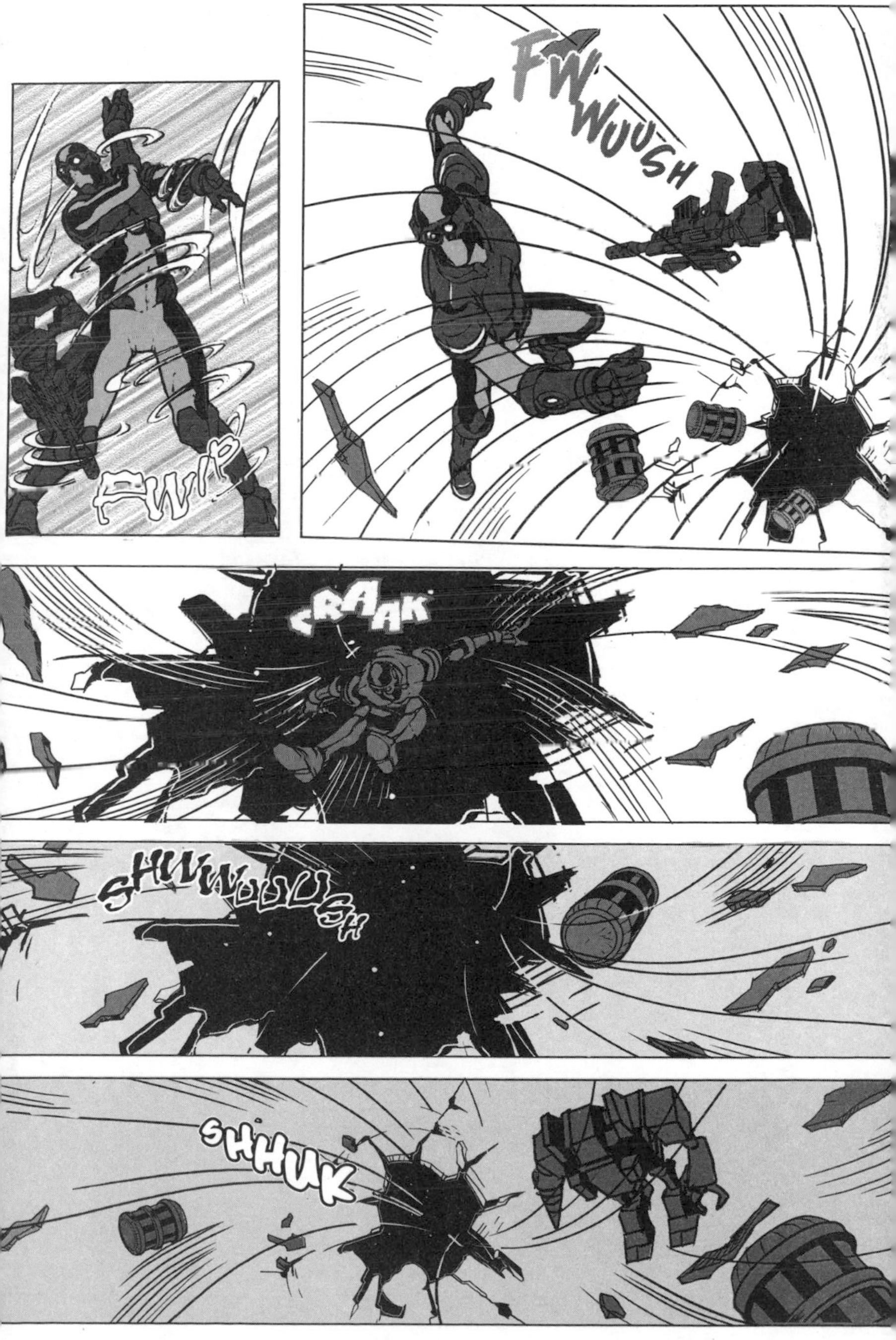

FWIP
FWUUSH
CRAAK
SHWWUUSH
SHHUK

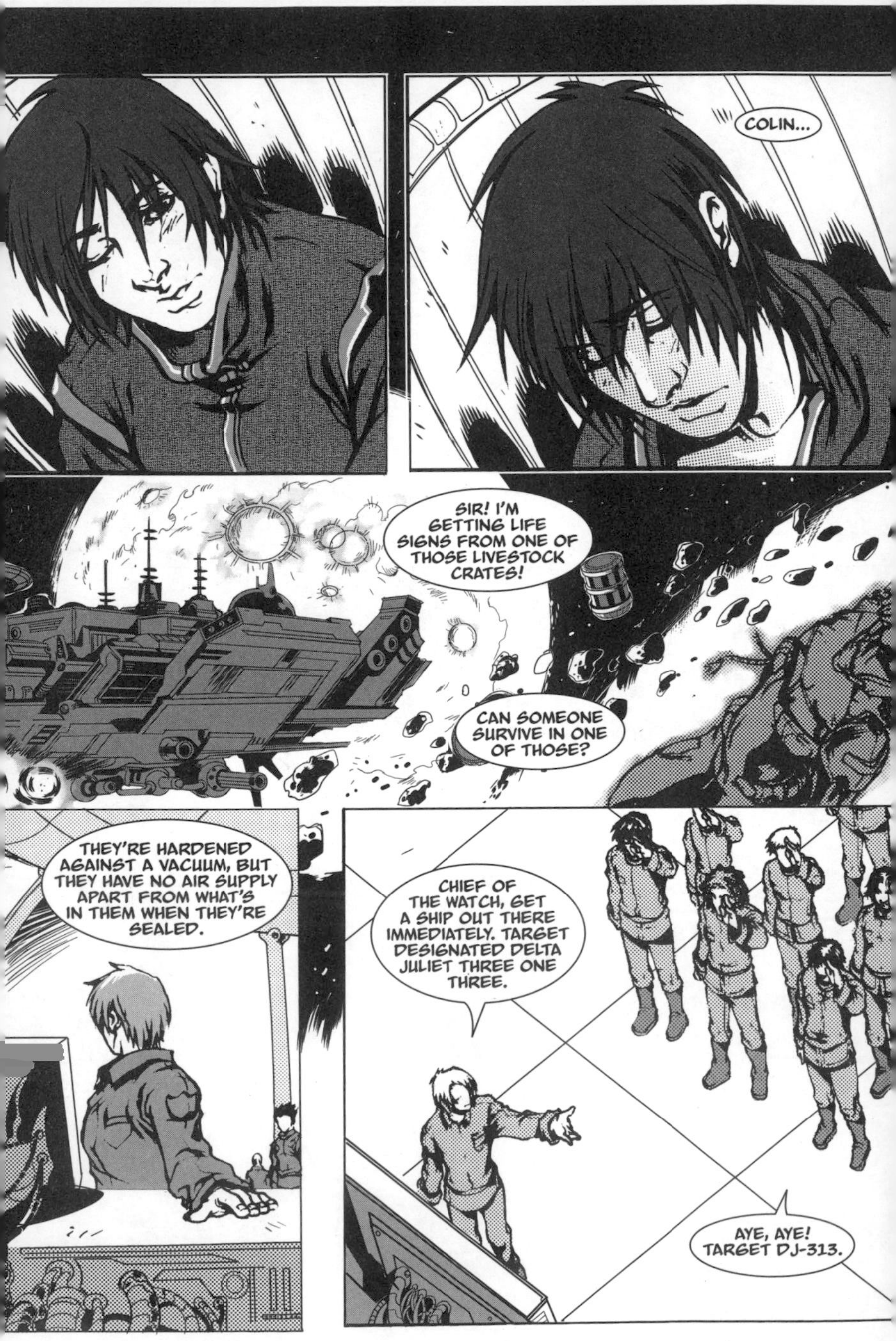
COLIN...
SIR! I'M GETTING LIFE SIGNS FROM ONE OF THOSE LIVESTOCK CRATES!
CAN SOMEONE SURVIVE IN ONE OF THOSE?
THEY'RE HARDENED AGAINST A VACUUM, BUT THEY HAVE NO AIR SUPPLY APART FROM WHAT'S IN THEM WHEN THEY'RE SEALED.
CHIEF OF THE WATCH, GET A SHIP OUT THERE IMMEDIATELY. TARGET DESIGNATED DELTA JULIET THREE ONE THREE.
AYE, AYE! TARGET DJ-313.

THAT ASTRAL PROJECTION COULD BE USEFUL...

...WE SHOULD SEE IF IT'S REPEATABLE.

I AGREE. MORE STUDY IS WARRANTED.

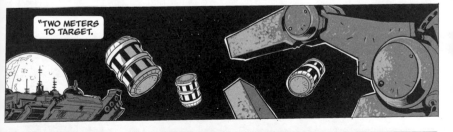

"TWO METERS TO TARGET.

"CONTROL, THIS IS UNIFORM OSCAR CHARLIE FIVE TWO. TARGET IS ACQUIRED."

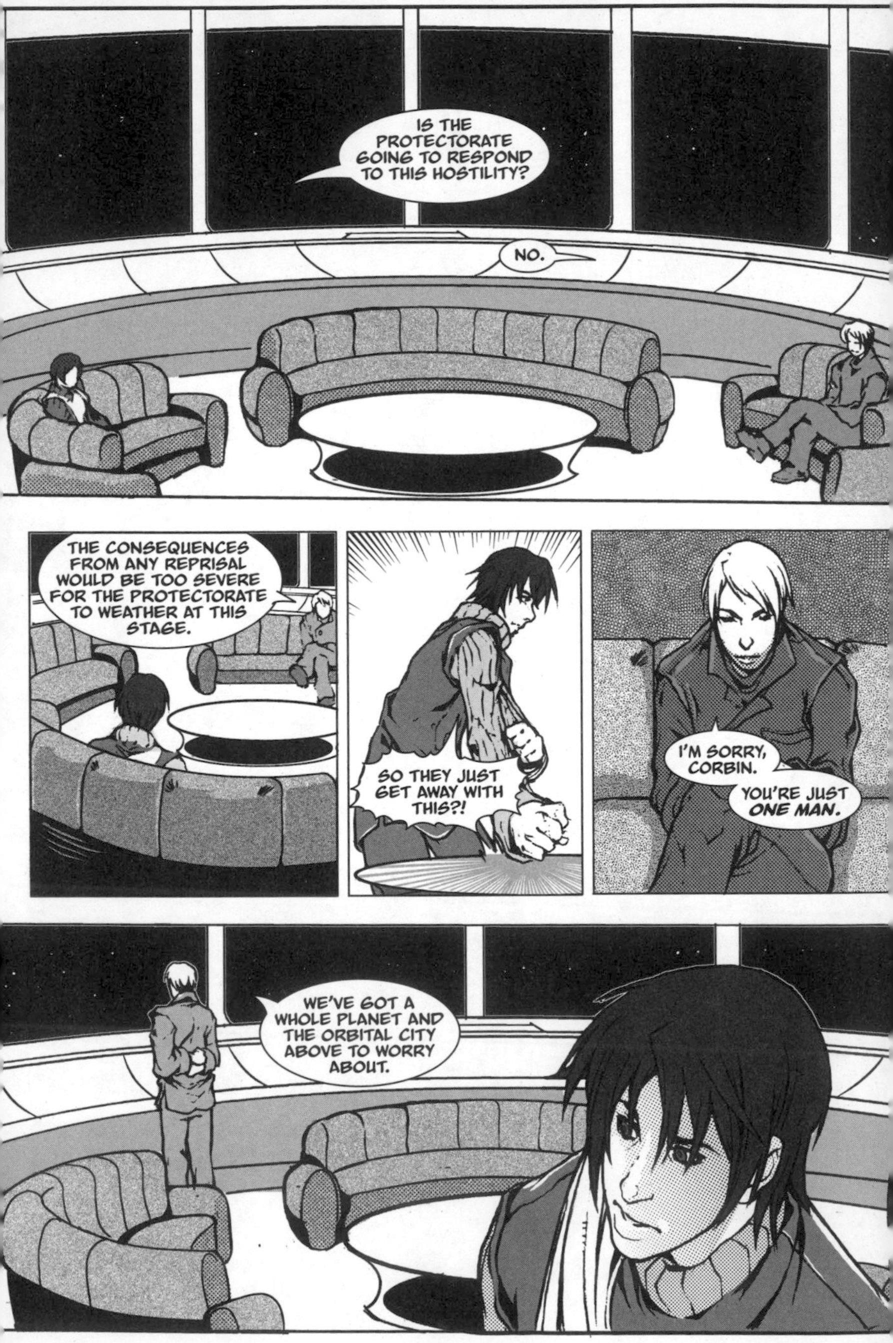
IS THE PROTECTORATE GOING TO RESPOND TO THIS HOSTILITY?
NO.
THE CONSEQUENCES FROM ANY REPRISAL WOULD BE TOO SEVERE FOR THE PROTECTORATE TO WEATHER AT THIS STAGE.
SO THEY JUST GET AWAY WITH THIS?!
I'M SORRY, CORBIN.
YOU'RE JUST ONE MAN.
WE'VE GOT A WHOLE PLANET AND THE ORBITAL CITY ABOVE TO WORRY ABOUT.

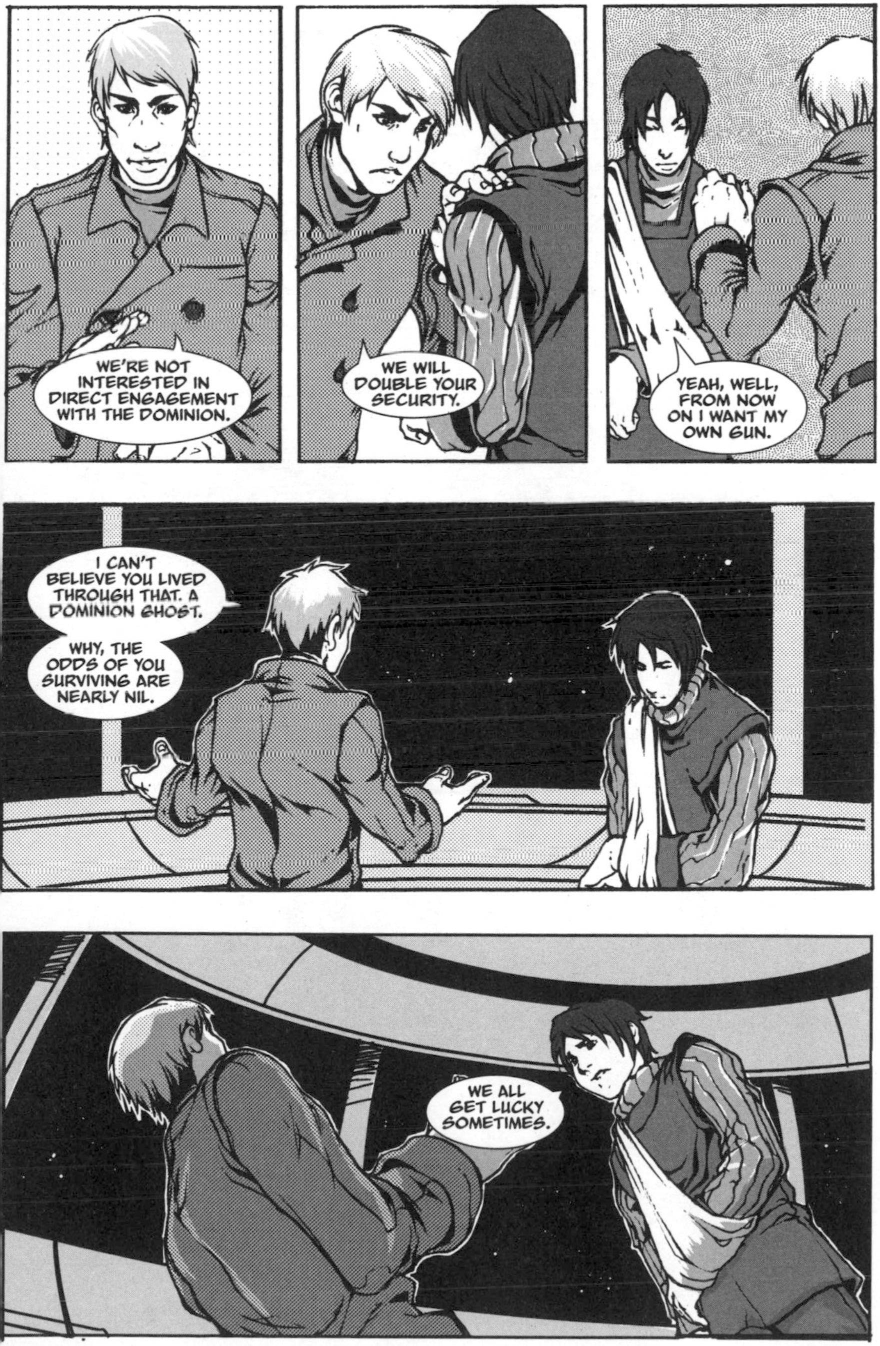
WE'RE NOT INTERESTED IN DIRECT ENGAGEMENT WITH THE DOMINION.
WE WILL DOUBLE YOUR SECURITY.
YEAH, WELL, FROM NOW ON I WANT MY OWN GUN.
I CAN'T BELIEVE YOU LIVED THROUGH THAT. A DOMINION GHOST.
WHY, THE ODDS OF YOU SURVIVING ARE NEARLY NIL.
WE ALL GET LUCKY SOMETIMES.

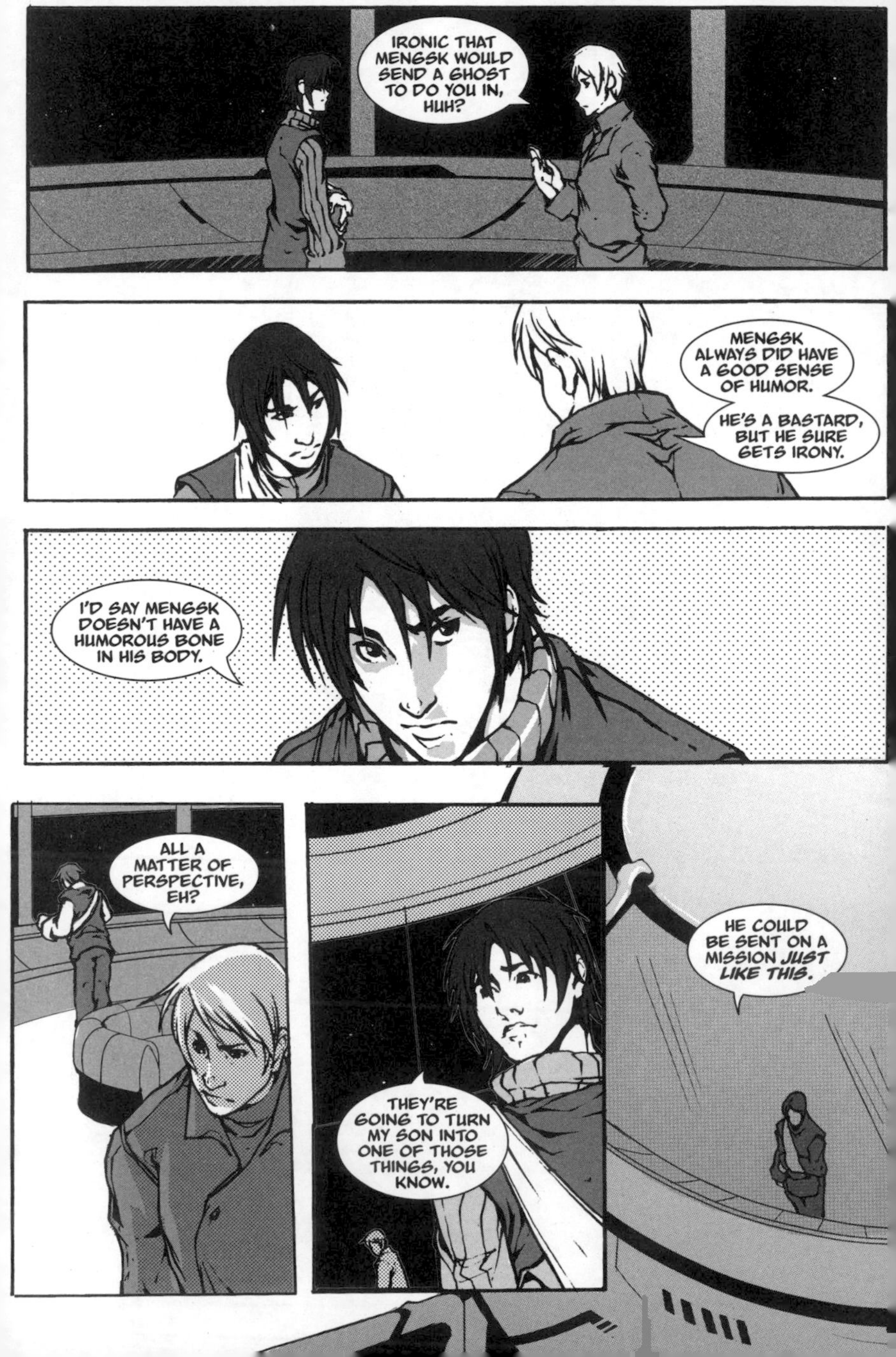
IRONIC THAT MENGSK WOULD SEND A GHOST TO DO YOU IN, HUH?
MENGSK ALWAYS DID HAVE A GOOD SENSE OF HUMOR.
HE'S A BASTARD, BUT HE SURE GETS IRONY.
I'D SAY MENGSK DOESN'T HAVE A HUMOROUS BONE IN HIS BODY.
ALL A MATTER OF PERSPECTIVE, EH?
THEY'RE GOING TO TURN MY SON INTO ONE OF THOSE THINGS, YOU KNOW.
HE COULD BE SENT ON A MISSION *JUST LIKE THIS.*

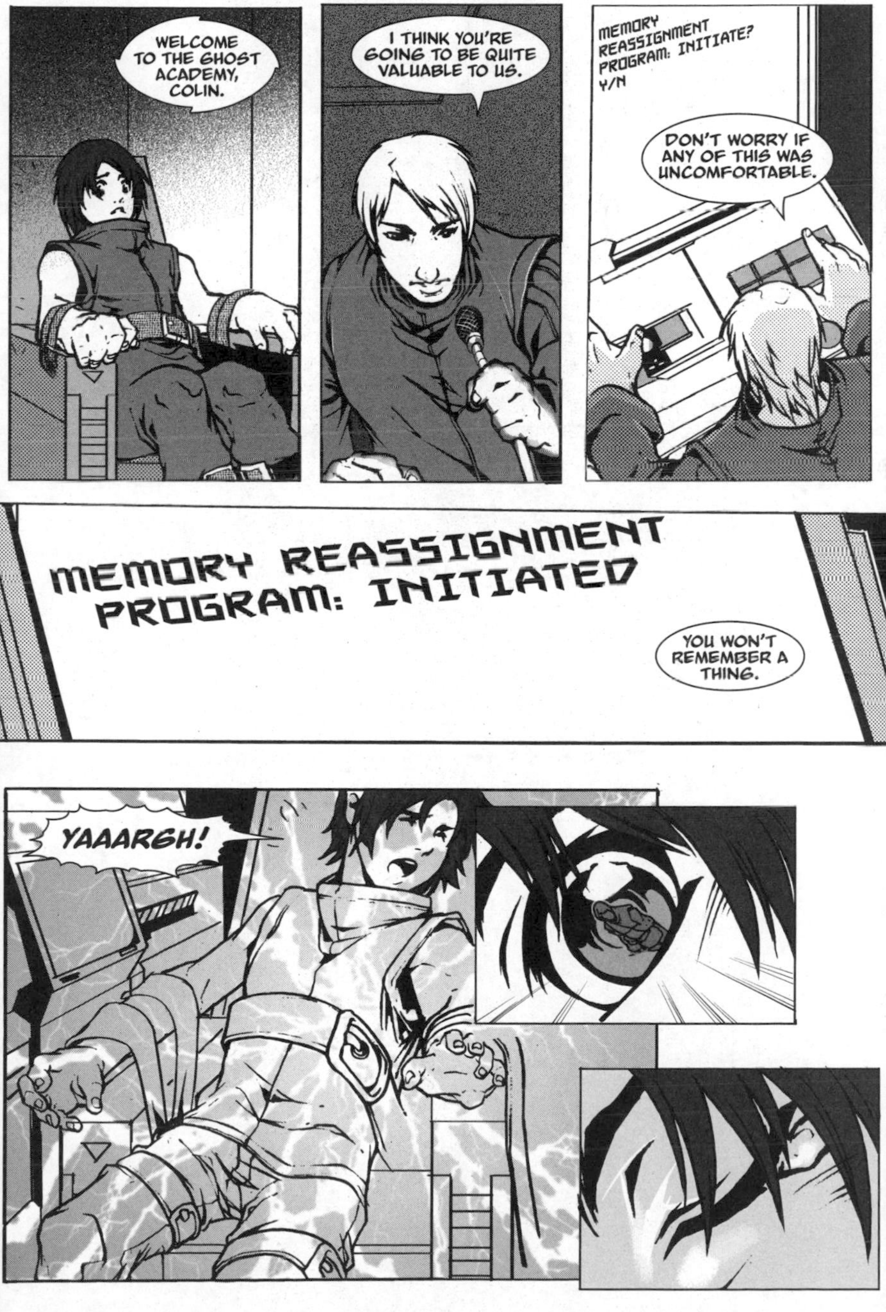
WELCOME TO THE GHOST ACADEMY, COLIN.
I THINK YOU'RE GOING TO BE QUITE VALUABLE TO US.
MEMORY REASSIGNMENT PROGRAM: INITIATE? Y/N
DON'T WORRY IF ANY OF THIS WAS UNCOMFORTABLE.
MEMORY REASSIGNMENT PROGRAM: INITIATED
YOU WON'T REMEMBER A THING.
YAAARGH!

WRITERS:

CHRIS METZEN

Some people write stories; **Chris Metzen** helps build worlds. As the former Vice President of Creative Development at Blizzard Entertainment, Metzen would oversee the creation of the memorable and immersive characters, places, events, and histories behind all of Blizzard's games. While the majority of his time was spent writing, Metzen also had a hand in game design, conceptual artwork, and voice direction of Blizzard Entertainment's titles. When he is not playing or working on building games, the Southern California native can be found reading comics, enjoying music, or reciting the dialogue from his favorite movies.

DAVID GERROLD

David Gerrold has been writing tales of wonder for more than forty years. His first script was "The Trouble With Tribbles" episode of **Star Trek**. He has written multiple episodes of **Twilight Zone, Land Of The Lost, Babylon 5, Tales From the Darkside,** and other hit TV series. His novels include **The Man Who Folded Himself, Jumping Off the Planet,** and **The War Against the Chtorr.** His autobiographical story of his son's adoption, **The Martian Child,** won the Hugo and the Nebula awards and was adapted into a movie starring John Cusack and Angela Peet.

JOSH ELDER

Josh Elder is the handsome and brilliant writer of **Mail Order Ninja**, which he's pretty sure has been acclaimed by some critic, somewhere. A graduate of Northwestern University with a degree in film, Joshua currently resides in the quaint, little midwestern town of Chicago, Illinois. A longtime **StarCraft** fanboy, Josh is still geek-gasming over the fact that he got to write for **Frontline**. But Josh also played football, so he isn't a total dork. But he also played *Dungeons & Dragons*. So yeah, he kind of is a total dork.

PAUL BENJAMIN

Paul Benjamin is a writer, editor, supermodel, and video game writer and producer based in Austin, Texas. His comic book and graphic novel work ranges from his original manga series **Pantheon High** to **Marvel Adventures: Hulk** and **Marvel Adventures: Spider-Man**. His stories have appeared in numerous other Marvel titles as well as **Star Trek: The Manga** and **StarCraft: Frontline** series. Paul's video game writing and producing credits include Sega's **The Incredible Hulk** and Activision's **Spider-Man: Web of Shadows** for the Nintendo DS as well as **X-Men Origins: Wolverine** for Wii and PlayStation 2 and Electronic Arts's **G.I. JOE: The Rise of COBRA** for many platforms.

DAVE SHRAMEK

Dave Shramek is a game designer and writer in Austin, Texas. As is so often the case, he settled there after graduating from the University of Texas with a degree in radio, television, and film. Much to the delight of his parents, he was able to turn this normally unemployable degree into an actual profession in the game development-rich environment of Austin. He resides there with his ambitions of global dominance and an unhealthy addiction to Tex-Mex.

ARTISTS:

HECTOR SEVILLA

Hector Sevilla hails from Chihuahua, Mexico. He is a huge fan of *StarCraft*, and never imagined he would help create a part of the *StarCraft* universe. He thanks Kathy Schilling, Paul Morrissey, and Blizzard Entertainment for the wonderful opportunity—and Hope Donovan for her great patience. In addition, Hector has created *Lullaby,* and worked on *Leviticus Cross* and Konami's *Lunar Knights.* He dedicates this manga to his parents for all the love and support they show each day to him.

RUBEN DE VELA

Ruben de Vela was born and raised in Manila, and graduated from the University of the Philippines. In school, he initially took up physics, but due to too much doodling, playing too many video games, and reading too many science-fiction and fantasy books, he shifted his field of study to fine arts. He has been trained in animation and worked as a background artist for Toei Animation, as well as dabbled in teaching and creating storyboards for ad agencies. Moving away from his usual role as a colorist, this book is his first major publication as a penciller.

RAMANDA KAMARGA

Like a superhero, **Ramanda Kamarga** holds a regular job during the day and draws comics at night. An avid gamer, he shares his free time with his wife and his PSP. Ramanda's previous works include *G.I. JOE: Sigma Six, Bristol Board Jungle, Psy*Comm* volumes 2 & 3, and of course *StarCraft: Frontline.*

MEL JOY SAN JUAN

Mel Joy San Juan began working for local Pinoy comics when she was sixteen and was published in several manga in her native country of the Philippines. She was discovered by Glass House Graphics's David Campiti while attending his comics creation seminar in Manila and began working for them a year later. After assisting on assorted jobs and co-illustrating *Dream Knight,* Mel Joy finally landed *StarCraft* as her very first solo pencilling assignment. She gives thanks to her friends and manager for helping her to finish this job.

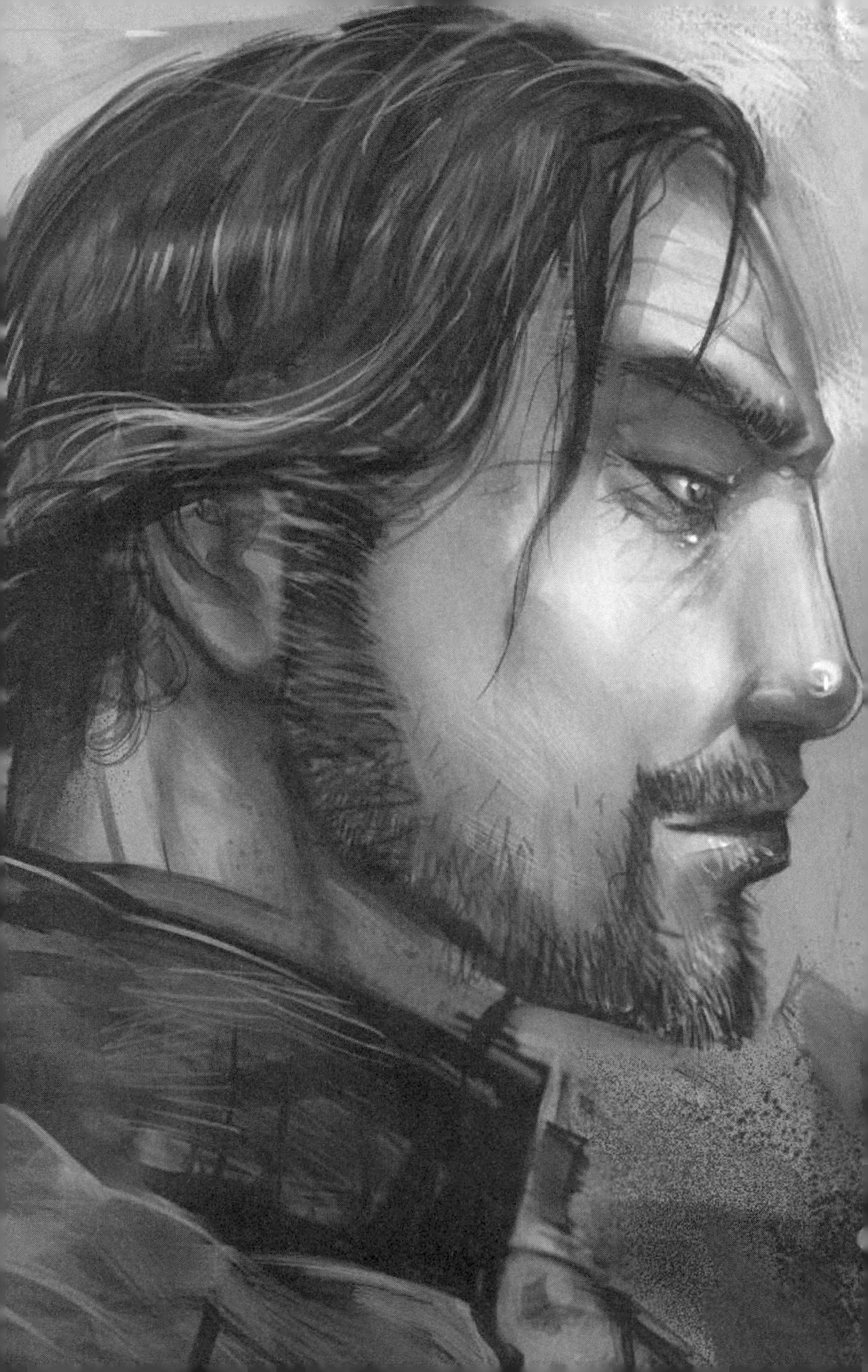

STARCRAFT

FRONTLINE

OWN THE SERIES!

You've just read four stories of ghosts, revenge, family, and horror . . . but still you look for further **StarCraft** adventures. Awaiting you are **StarCraft: Frontline** volumes 1-3 . . .

STARCRAFT: FRONTLINE VOLUMES 1-3 AVAILABLE NOW!

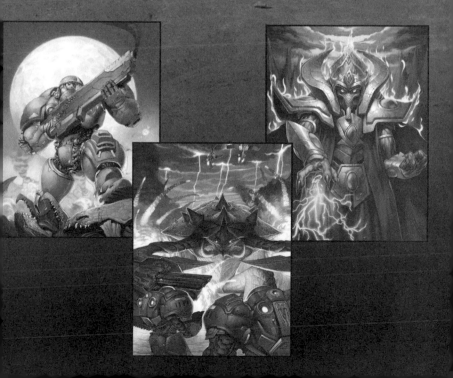

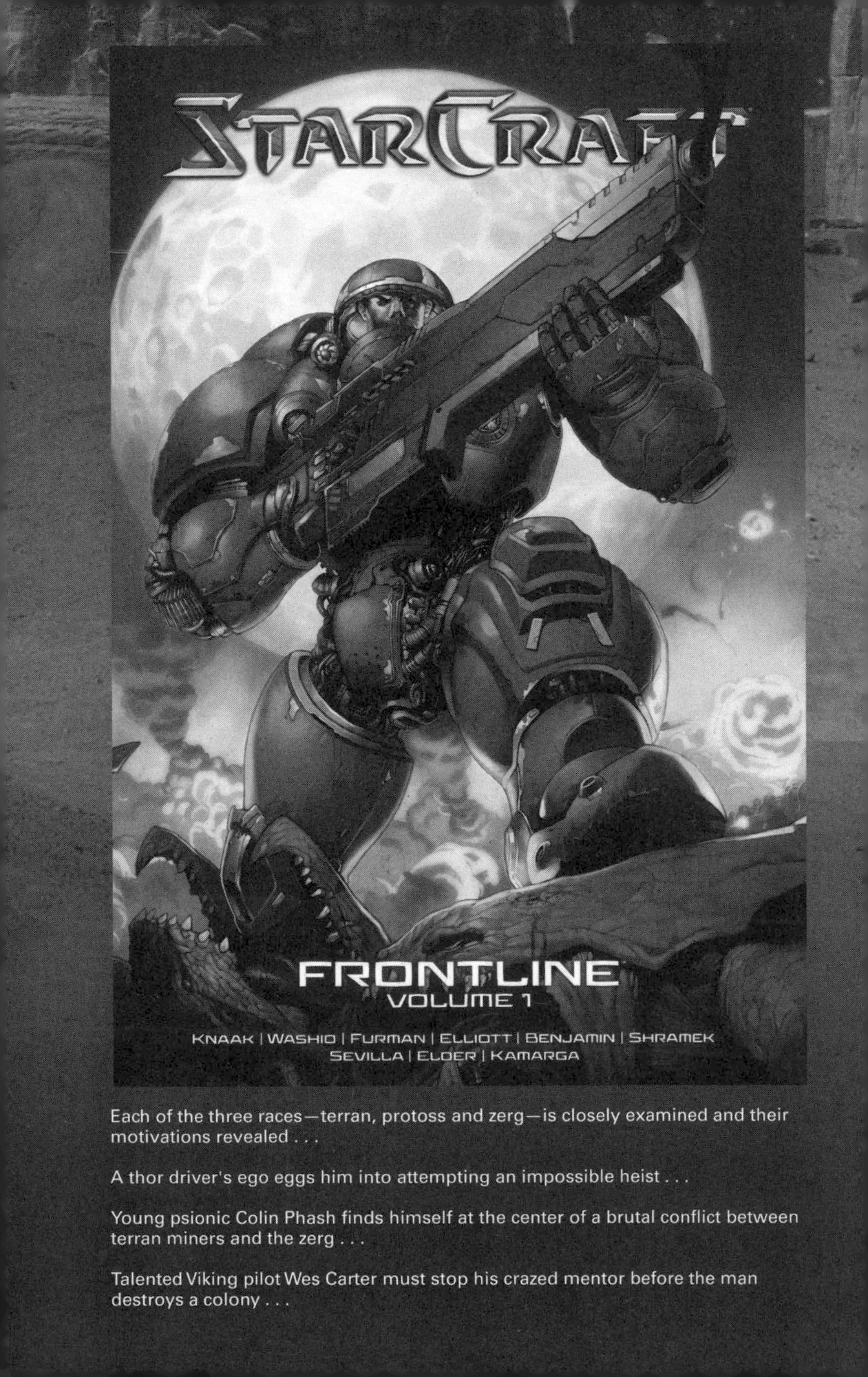
STARCRAFT
FRONTLINE
VOLUME 1
KNAAK | WASHIO | FURMAN | ELLIOTT | BENJAMIN | SHRAMEK
SEVILLA | ELDER | KAMARGA

Each of the three races—terran, protoss and zerg—is closely examined and their motivations revealed . . .

A thor driver's ego eggs him into attempting an impossible heist . . .

Young psionic Colin Phash finds himself at the center of a brutal conflict between terran miners and the zerg . . .

Talented Viking pilot Wes Carter must stop his crazed mentor before the man destroys a colony . . .

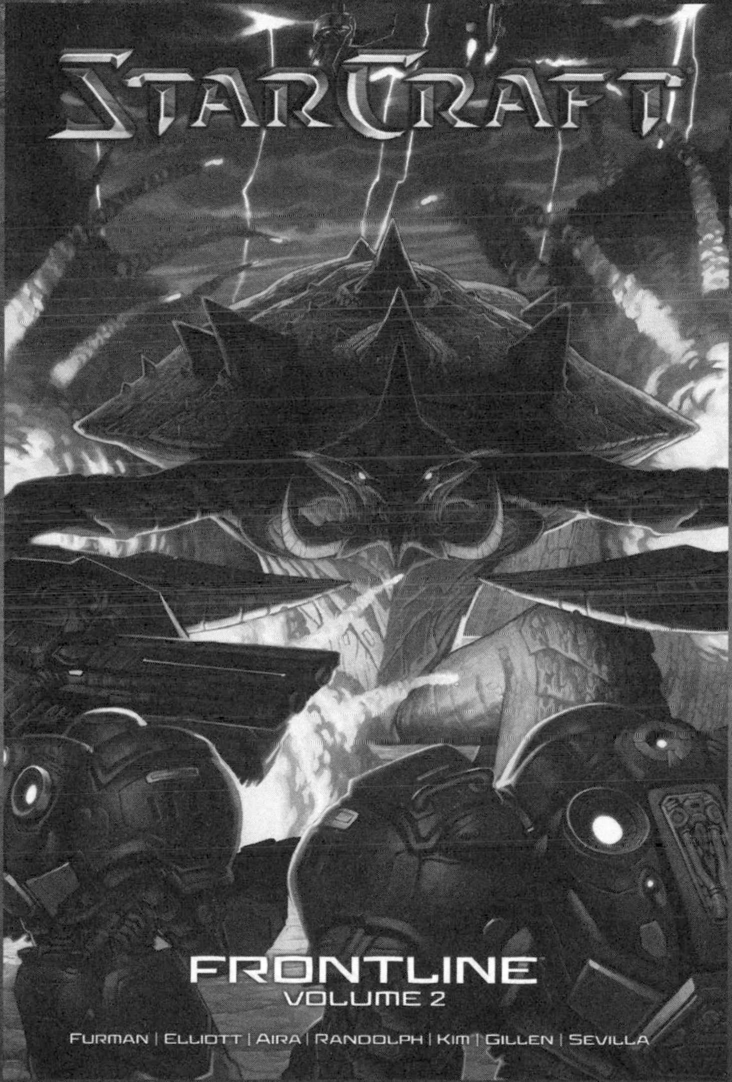
STARCRAFT
FRONTLINE
VOLUME 2
FURMAN | ELLIOTT | AIRA | RANDOLPH | KIM | GILLEN | SEVILLA

The haunting conclusion of Viking pilot Wes Carter's battle against the man who taught him everything about heavy armor . . .

Feared by all and understood by none, zerg creep comes under the knife in a protoss laboratory . . .

When a reporter comes face-to-face with atrocity, she must decide whether her loyalty to the truth outweighs her loyalty to the Dominion . . .

A Kel-Morian crew catches wind of a planet's huge bounty, but comes in contact with its dark secrets instead . . .

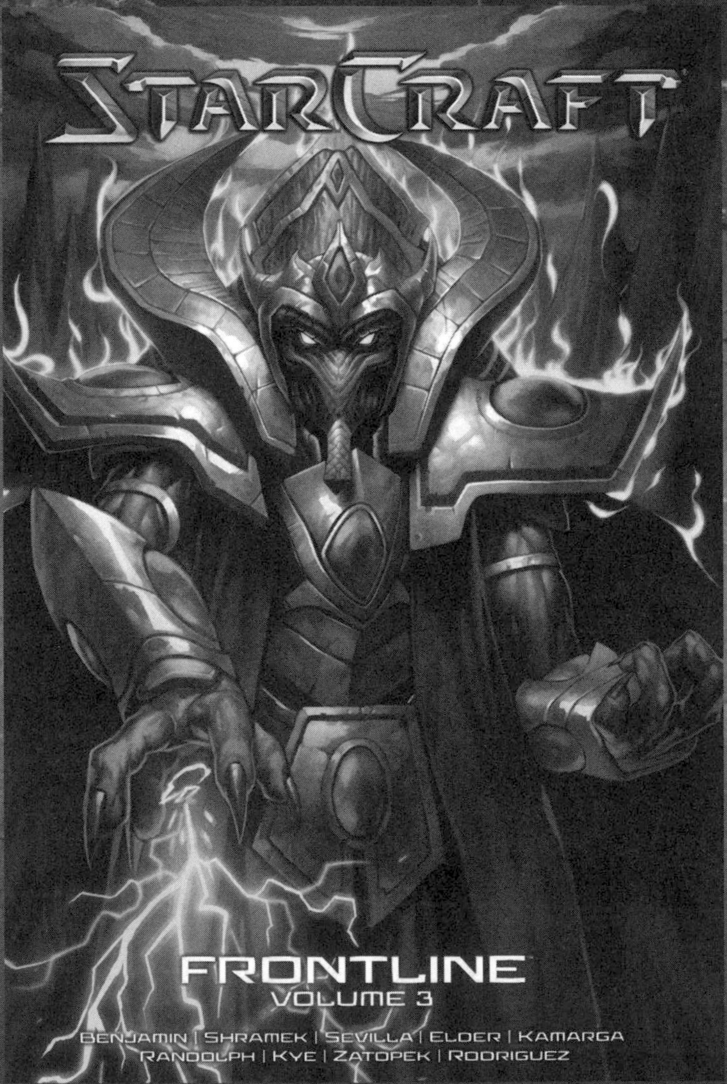
StarCraft
FRONTLINE
VOLUME 3
BENJAMIN | SHRAMEK | SEVILLA | ELDER | KAMARGA
RANDOLPH | KYE | ZATOPEK | RODRIGUEZ

With his psionic abilities exposed, Colin Phash hides out on a doomed refugee moon, where he's pursued by a fearsome wrangler . . .

A sadistic scientist captures a protoss high templar in order to perfect his horrifying protoss-terran soldiers . . .

A lounge singer becomes an unlikely diplomat between the Dominion and the Kel-Morians, but something else may be pulling the strings from behind the scenes . . .

A high templar loses her connection to the Khala and is willing to sacrifice even more to become whole again . . .

STARCRAFT: GHOST ACADEMY
SNEAK PEEK—CONCEPT ART

They're mysterious, elusive, and deadly. Psionically gifted terrans molded into lethal assassins: these are the highly trained ghosts of the *StarCraft* universe. Ghosts can infiltrate almost anywhere—including your mind. They can move with incredible swiftness, snipe targets from great distances, read thoughts, become invisible, and even call down nuclear strikes. All of these skills and more are learned and refined at the Ghost Academy.

At the Ghost Academy, powerful young students from disparate worlds confront terrifying training exercises, as well as each other, in a highly competitive environment. The following pages showcase several exciting works in progress, including cover sketches, character concepts, and penciled pages. Prepare to be taken on a journey into the secretive world of . . .

STARCRAFT
GHOST ACADEMY

At this school, failure is not an option.

When it was suggested that we create a sneak peek of the upcoming *StarCraft: Ghost Academy* manga, we jumped at the chance. We are really thrilled with the way this series is coming together, and we're excited to explore for the first time one of the most closely guarded secrets of the StarCraft universe: ghosts.

Although the academy is mentioned in the novel *StarCraft: Nova* and the novella *Uprising*, and *StarCraft* players can build ghost academies and create ghost operatives in the game, the *StarCraft: Ghost Academy* manga series is the closest examination ever of this vital (some would say vile) resource of the Terran Dominion.

We hope you enjoy the preview!

The Blizzard Publishing Team

Constructing a Cover

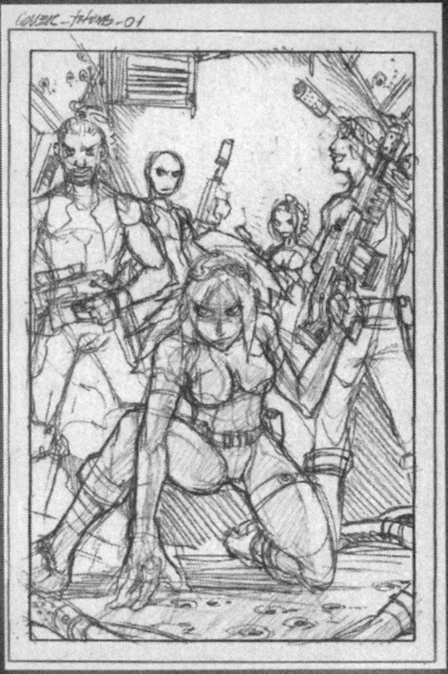
COVER_THUMB_01

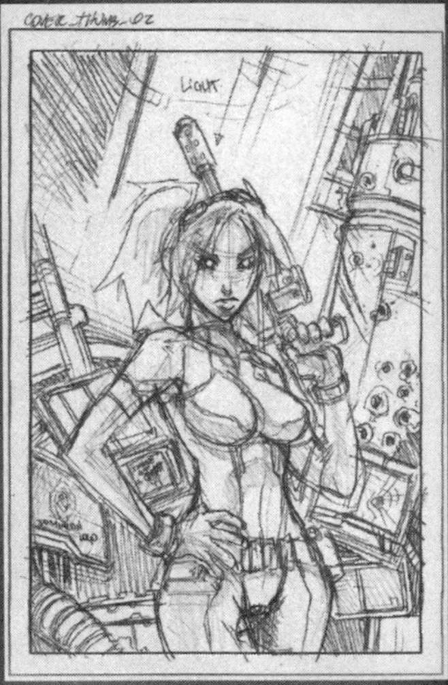
COVER_THUMB_02
LIGHT

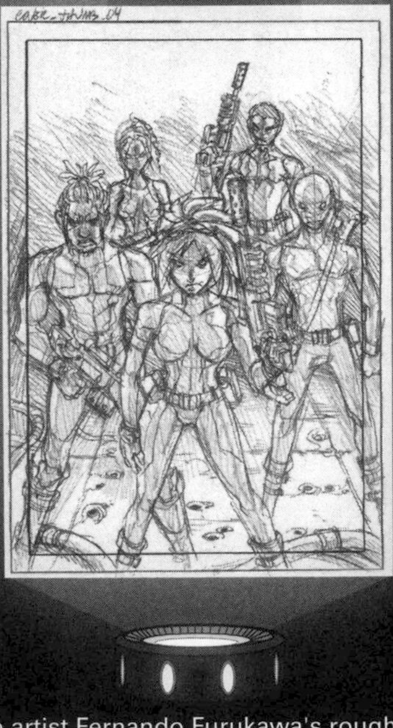

Here you can see artist Fernando Furukawa's rough cover concepts. From the beginning, Nova has been the focal character of ***Ghost Academy,*** so we went for cover designs that showcased her.

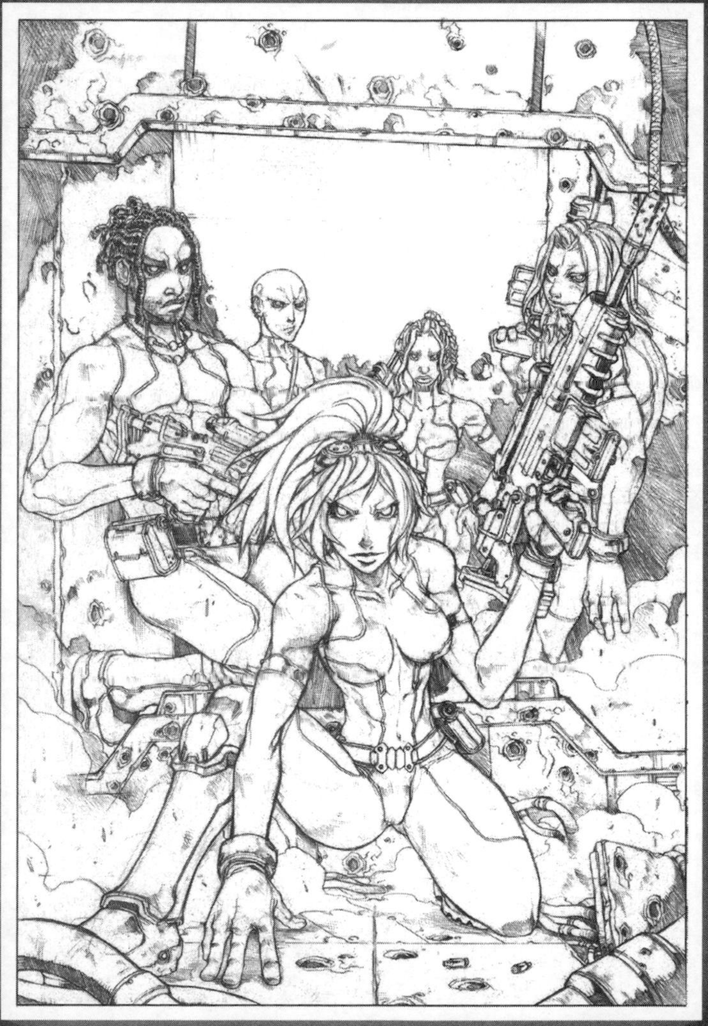

With the basic design picked, Fernando added detail with a pencil drawing . . .

. . . and added colors for a fantastic finish! So here we have Nova front and center, surrounded by her peers at the Ghost Academy.

CONSTRUCTING A CAST:
NOVA

An iconic ghost in the *StarCraft* universe, Nova was already
designed—as many gorgeous, detailed illustrations show. But for
Ghost Academy, Nova needed to be a little younger. We think
"high school" Nova is still pretty badass!

TOSH

You might say Tosh's time at the Ghost Academy is good preparation for
a wild ride. . . in *StarCraft II!* In the Academy, he's a little bit older than the
other students, and has already taken a leadership role as head of Team Blue.

Kath

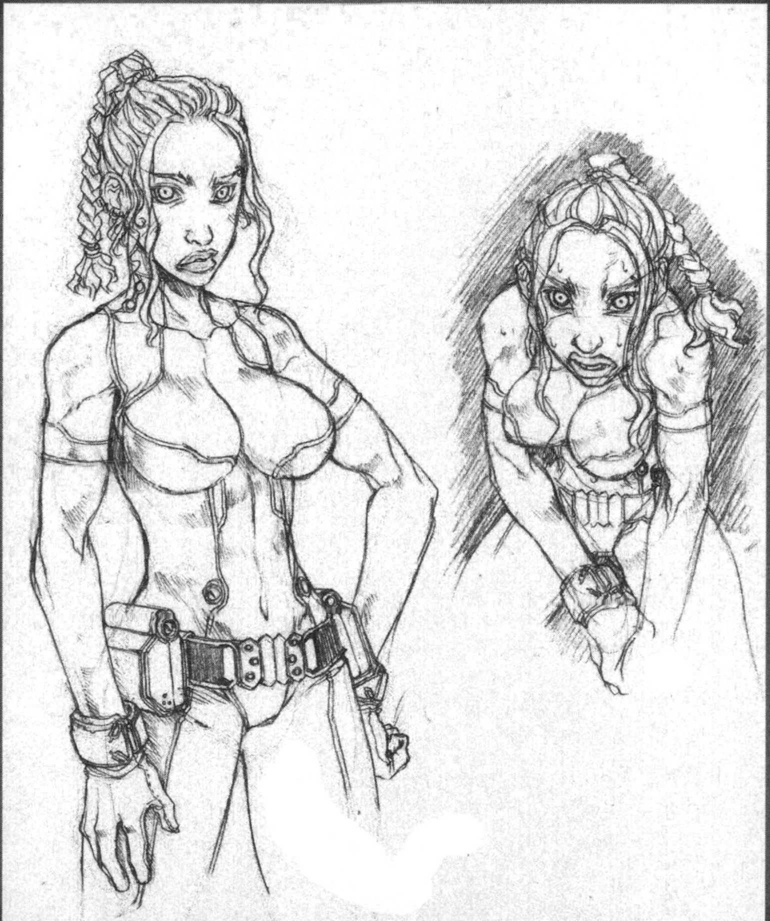

Kath's bright, tough, hot-headed, and says it like it is—which is not necessarily a good thing at the Ghost Academy.

Aal

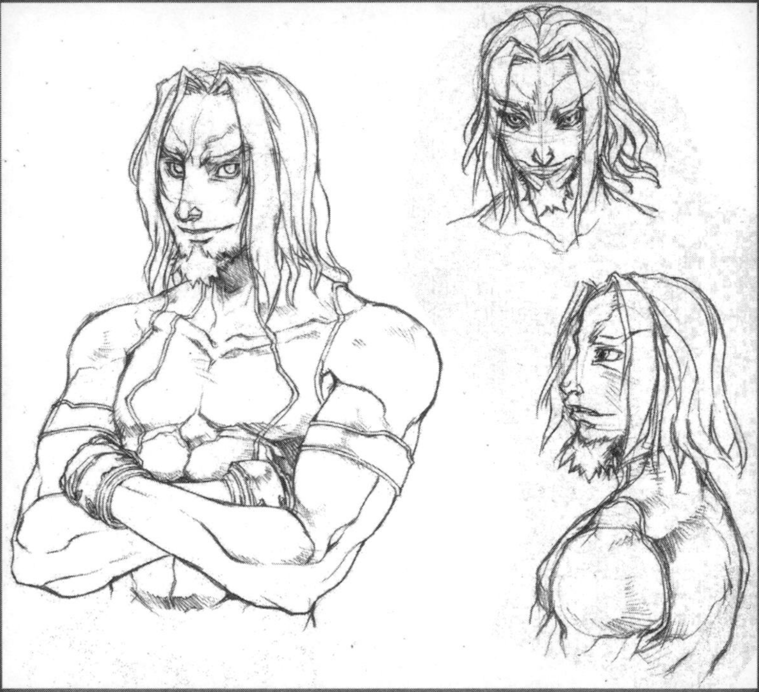

Not all [redacted]students at the Ghost Academy are exceptional [redacted]paths.
A low-[redacted] telepath, Aal's reasons for being at the Ghost [redacted]emy
have more to do with his dark past . . .

LIO

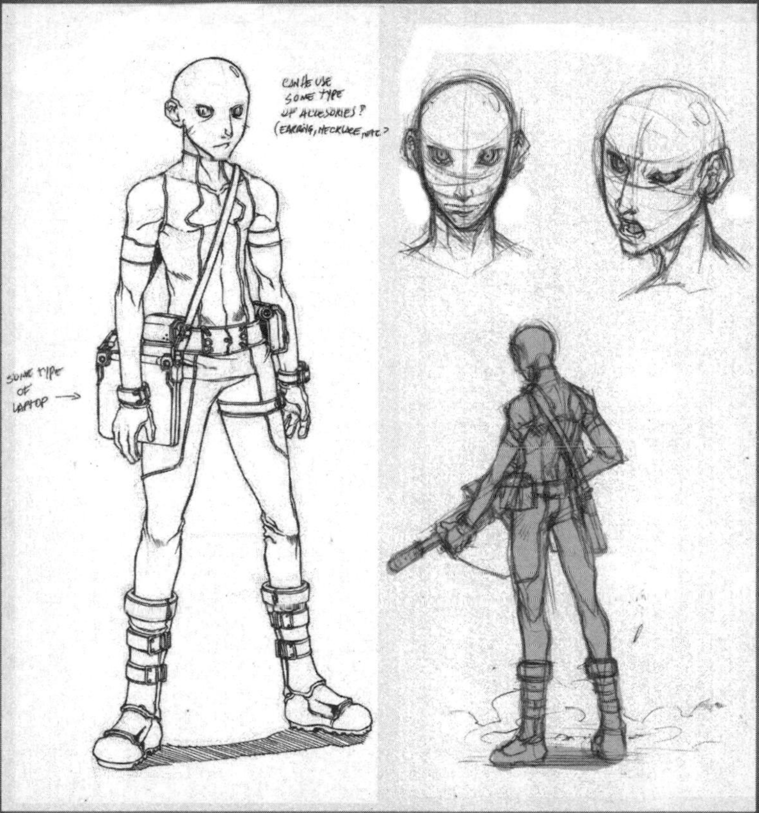
CAN HE USE SOME TYPE OF ACCESORIES? (EARRING, NECKLACE, ETC?
SOME TYPE OF LAPTOP →

Speaking of darkness, Lio is a technopath (which means he can mentally interface with certain machines in addition to organic minds). But, unknown to his teammates, he also has a secret addiction to the drug hab. Definitely not the best vice to have when you're enduring intense ghost training.

CONSTRUCTING PAGES

StarCraft: Ghost Academy is a view into a sinister and infamous institution—but at the same time, that view is through the eyes of its students. Just like at any school, socializing, learning, and growing are all part of the package. And Nova's got a lot of it to do!

The following is a sneak peek of early concept pages for ***Ghost Academy***. Though the art is not final, it's action-packed and we see Nova in high form!

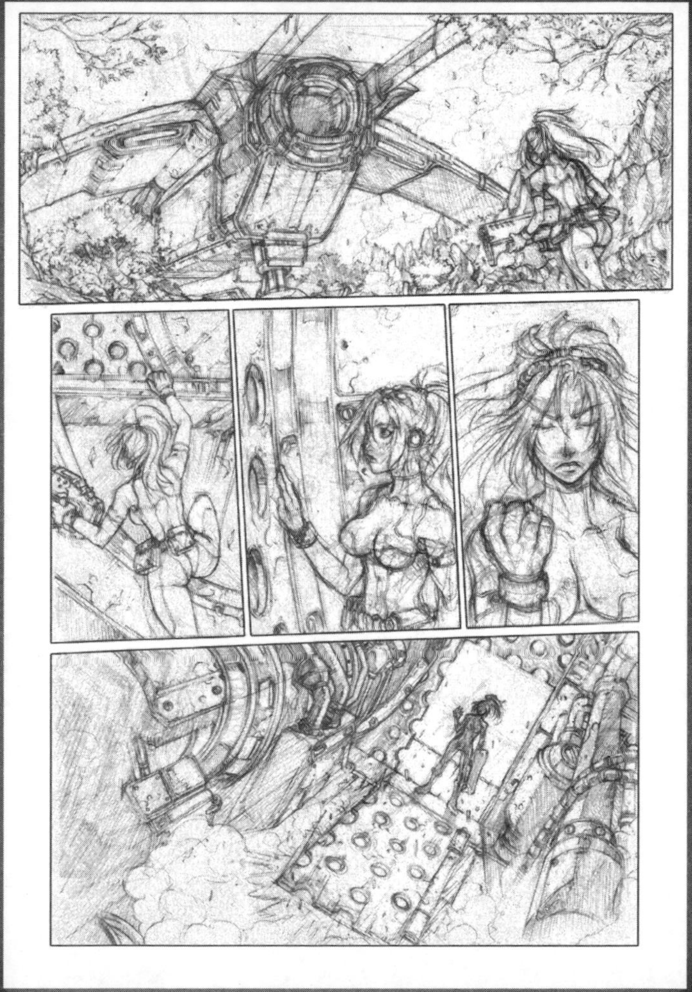

Hostages have been taken on a grounded planet hopper. Nova and her team must infiltrate the ship and rescue them.

Though she is an unusually gifted psionic . . .

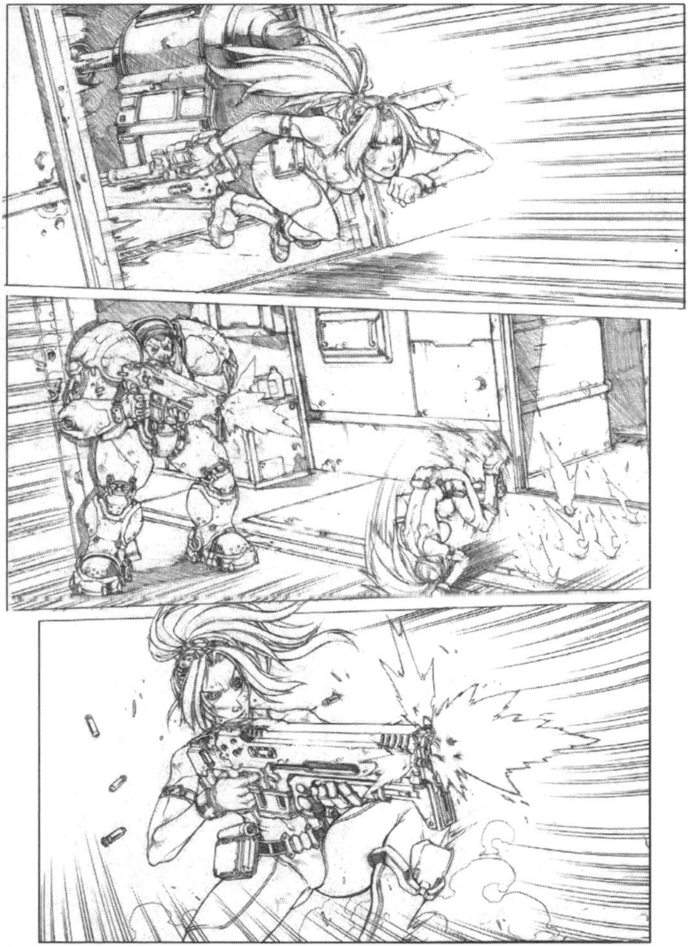

. . . this sort of mission requires a few of her other skills . . . mainly enhanced speed, agility, and dead-to-rights marksmanship.

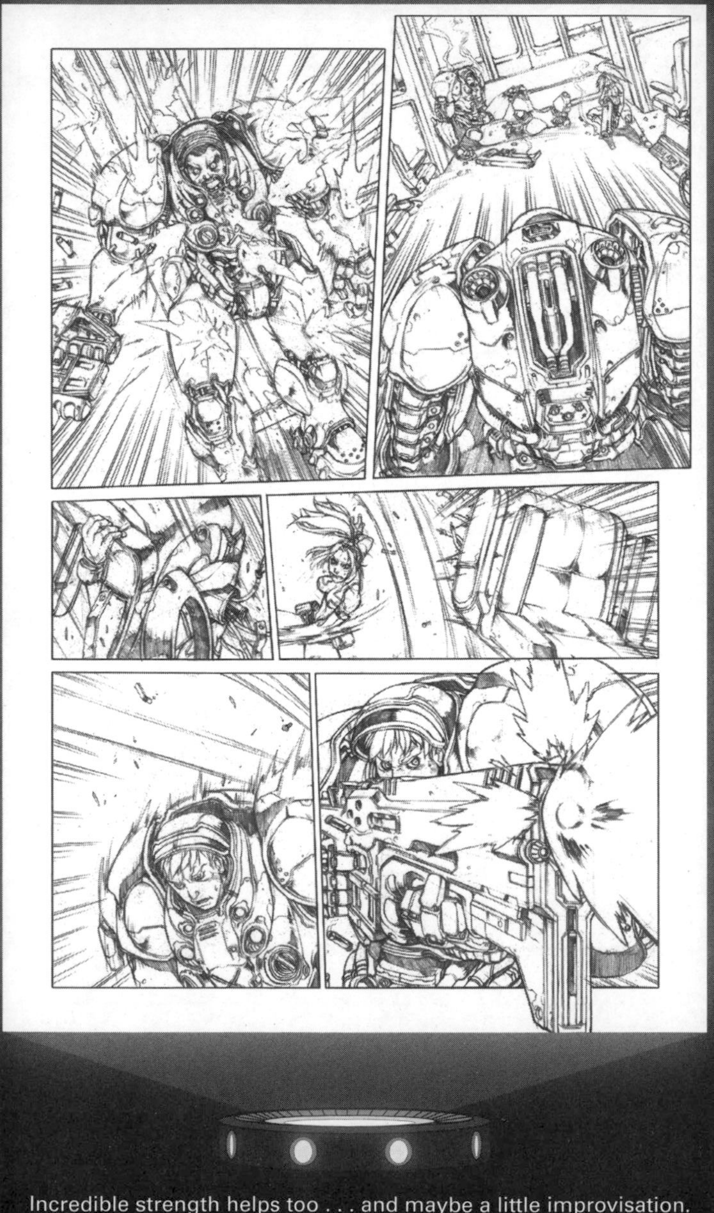

Incredible strength helps too . . . and maybe a little improvisation.

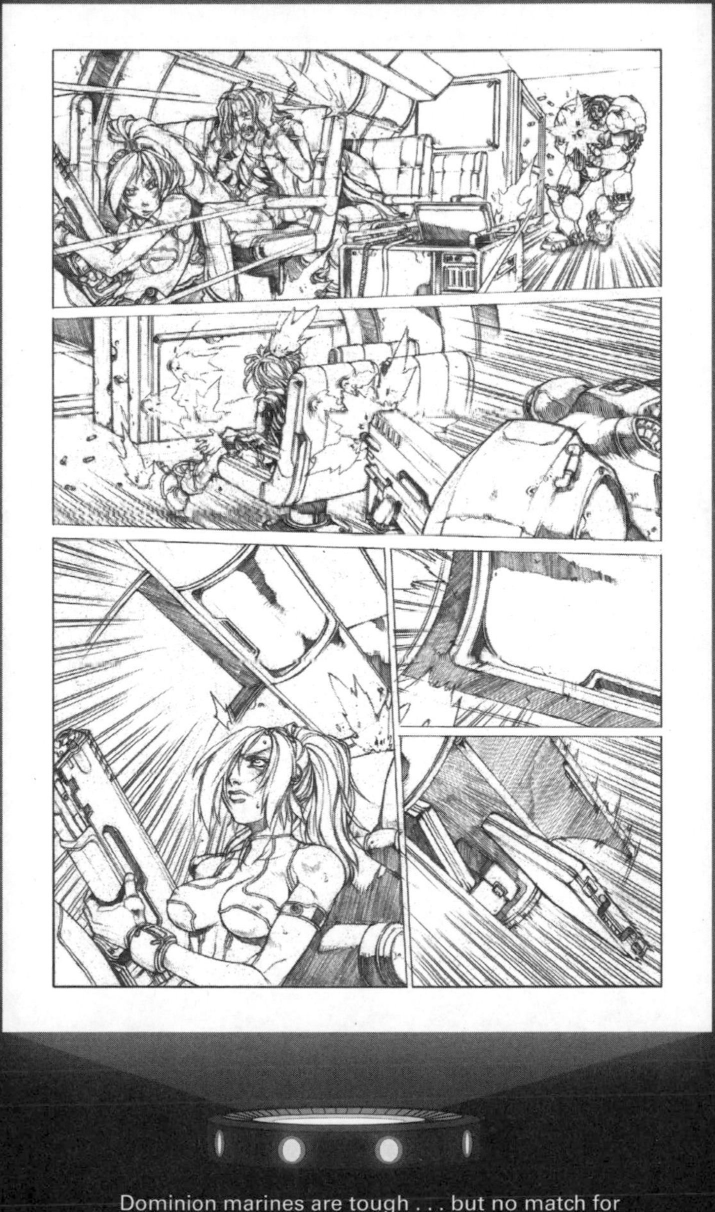

Dominion marines are tough . . . but no match for telepathy and telekinesis.

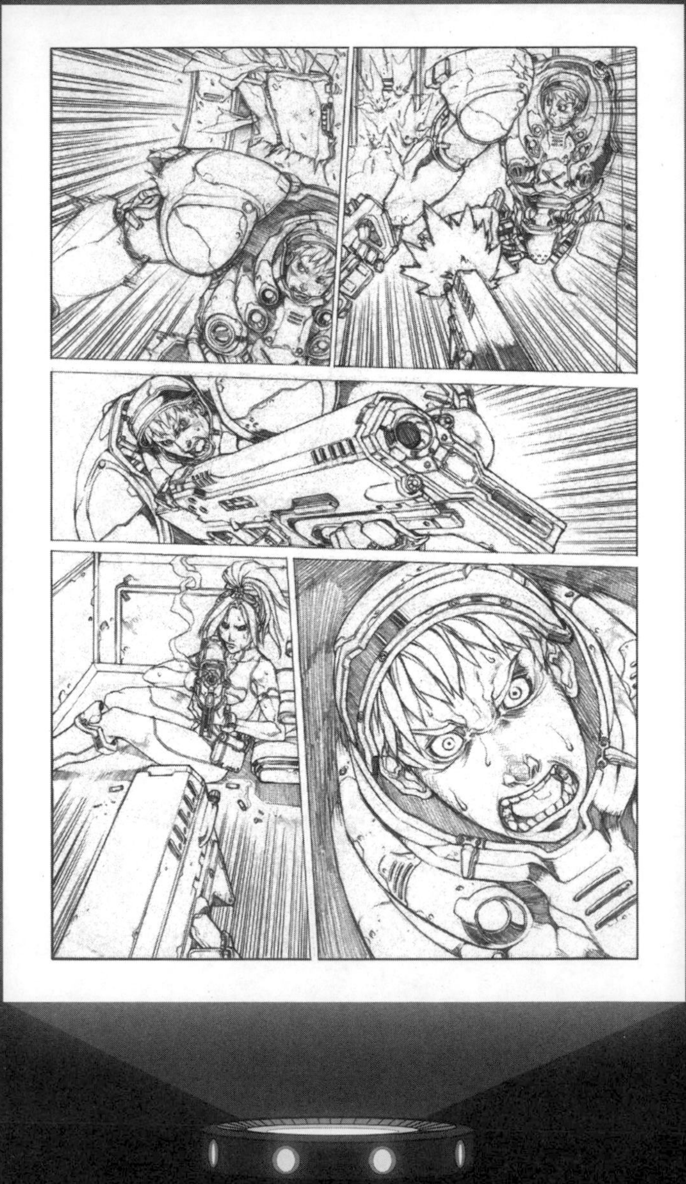

Ghosts are powerful weapons in Emperor Mengsk's arsenal . . .

. . . And he's training a lot of them.

We hope you enjoyed this glimpse into the Ghost Academy!